P9-CQR-034

# THE TURBULENT LIFE OF BILLY MARTIN

SIMON & SCHUSTER

NEW YORK LONDON TORONTO SYDNEY TOKYO SINGAPORE

# The Last Yankee

DAVID FALKNER

SIMON & SCHUSTER
Simon & Schuster Building
Rockefeller Center
1230 Avenue of the Americas
New York, New York 10020



Designed by Caroline Cunningham

Photo section designed by Pei Loi Koay

Manufactured in the United States of America

10 9 8 7 6 5 4 3 2 1

Library of Congress Cataloging in Publication Data

Falkner, David.
The last Yankee : the turbulent life of Billy Martin / David Falkner.
p. cm.
Includes index.
1. Martin, Billy, 1928–1990. 2. Baseball—United States—Managers—Biography. 3. New York Yankees (Baseball team)—History.
I. Title.
GV865.M35F35 1992
796.357'092—dc20
[B] 91–44457
CIP

ISBN: 0-671-72662-5

Permissions are gratefully acknowledged for the use of quoted material from the following: *Steinbrenner's Yankees* by Ed Linn, copyright © 1982 by Ed Linn, used by permission of Henry Holt and Company, Inc.; *Pinstripe Pandemonium* by Geoffrey Stokes, copyright © 1984 by Geoffrey Strokes, used by permission of HarperCollins Publishers; and *Number One* by Billy Martin and Peter Golenbock, copyright © 1980 by Billy Martin and Dynasty, Inc.; used by permission of Dell Books, a division of Bantam Doubleday Dell Publishing Group, Inc.

## PHOTO CREDITS

1, Collection of Joan Castillo; 2, Olla Podrida, 1946; 3,4,5, collection of Lewis Figone; 6,7,9,10,17,22, UPI/Bettmann; 8, Collection of Donald Honig; 11, Minnesota Twins; 12,13, Detroit Tigers; 14,15, Texas Rangers; 16,20,21, New York Yankees; 18,19, Oakland Athletics; 23,24,25, Collection of Bill Reedy; 26, AP/Wide World Photo; 27, Collection of Pat and Ken Irvine; The New York Yankees' photographs of Billy Martin were reproduced with the permission of the New York Yankees.

For Joni and Daniel

# ACKNOWLEDGMENTS

There are any number of people who were indispensable to the making of this book. Most obviously all of the Martin family members, wives, friends, teachers, officials, teammates, coaches, managers, umpires, executives, clubhouse people, and others whose voices appear in the narrative are owed a debt of obvious and undiminished gratitude. There simply would have been no book without the help of each individual involved. Because so many were involved—check the index—I will simply offer an apology here for not thanking each contributor once more separately and by name, though, most assuredly, my debt, while preferred collectively, remains unwaveringly individual. I owe additional thanks to family members and friends—duly credited—who supplied photos and graphics, often on impossibly short notice, for the production of the book.

There were still others whose names do not appear in the text whose help various and specific, was also indispensable. My brother, Dan, here as elsewhere, was as limitless in his generosity of spirit as he was in the practical and different ways he found to make sure the wheels turned and the motor kept running. My nephews Mike and Andrew, in their own ways, found time out of their own busy lives to keep the old guy alert, focused, on the page, and sometimes able to hit the right keys.

My daughter, Ellen, and my wife, Jenny, neither of them baseball fans, read and reread what I wrote. Their ideas, suggestions, hints, and queries were the resource of innings, seasons, leagues, and careers. To Ivan, who conducted interviews for me in Japan, and to Maggie, who listened endlessly and creatively to the litany of usual complaints, frustrations, and doubts that inevitably accompany projects of this sort—ditto.

My editor, Jeffrey Neuman, was exacting, demanding, patient and, above all, enormously insightful. I learned from him, and he was, throughout, a teacher as well as a colleague and a friend. My deep thanks, too, to my friend Jon Segal who took time and effort when his own plate was more than full.

Thanks to Esther Wanning, my friend of many years, who helped with interviewing, and who provided cheer and encouragement even when we went over the whys and wherefores of California earthquakes. Thanks to Joanne Curtis for transcribing and transcribing and transcribing. A standard biography invariably means, in this age of miniaturized electronic gadgets, shoeboxes full of tiny tapes. Thanks, too, to the media departments of the Twins, Tigers, Rangers, A's, and Yankees for photos.

The nature of this work inevitably called upon disciplines and specialties beyond dugouts and playing fields. In that regard I owe debts of gratitude to a number of people: to Jim Brown of the law firm of Bower and Gardner, and to the lawyers and investigators involved in the case surrounding the Port Crane accident. I owe special thanks to Fred Holquist of the Hazelden Clinic, to Marion Simpson, and to others in the helping professions who made me far more aware of and sensitive to an array of problems, myths, and realities surrounding drinking and alcohol.

Finally, I owe a particular and special debt to Andy Sears and to Dr. Bennett Marsh Derby, who took the time and had the patience to guide me through a maze of highly technical and often ambiguous material that otherwise might have remained wrapped in the special shrouds of legal and medical jargon and interested argument put forward at the trial of Bill Reedy. While Mr. Sears and Dr. Derby are in no way responsible for any of my conclusions and assertions, they did minister, at all times, to those impulses I had to tilt without thinking, to jump without looking. My debt to both men is, ultimately, not only to their expertise but, most of all, to their wisdom.

# PROLOGUE

No one remembers exactly how it happened—or even what it was that happened, other than that his sixty-year-old body was broken, bruised, and bloodied. It required forty stitches to sew back an ear that had nearly been torn off. It was always two A.M. in a charnel house bar when Billy Martin lost. The baseball world learned that long ago, and the rest of the tabloid-reading world tuned in regularly.

Of course there was a losing game this time. The Yankees came to Texas in first place with a 1988 record of 20–9. They lost one game; then, with the team's principal owner, George Steinbrenner, in the stands, they lost another, a tight one, 7–6. In the ninth inning of the 7–6 game, Don Mattingly protested a strike call by home plate umpire Tim Welke, and when he struck out, he continued the argument. Welke threw him out of the game—and pulled Billy into it, raging and screaming. Welke tossed him, too—instantly—saying Billy's profanities made ejection mandatory.

There were no profanities, Billy declared later. He'd take a lie-detector test to prove it, he said—would Welke?

After the ejection there was more than words. Billy kicked dirt all over the umpire and said that if he had a shovel he would have finished the job. Welke was not amused. And neither was Billy, who showered, dressed, and left the park early.

At the team hotel, he ran into his old pal, Mickey Mantle. He was surprised to see him, hadn't expected to until the following day—but things always happen at night in Texas.

The two sidekicks, as they had so many times in the past, began drinking. Several others, including Yankee coach Mike Ferraro, joined them in the hotel lounge. A waitress who served them said later that she could not bring the drinks fast enough. She was serving trays of Cutty Sark and water and even as she was setting the drinks down, the next round was automatically being ordered. Sometime after midnight, the drinking party broke up—or rather, a smaller party that included Billy and Mickey adjourned to a topless go-go bar named Lace, about a half mile away.

Contrary to some press accounts, Lace was no off-Broadway honkytonk. True, there was a history of trouble at Lace. Steve Howe, when he was with the Rangers, had apparently made one of his many drug connections in the place—and it had been off limits to Ranger players ever since. But Lace was Texas all the way. It was located in a suburban setting, not far from the Hilton and Six Flags. The women were gorgeous Texas-style, the money and the drinks flowed freely, the decor and furnishings were all J.R. Ewing upscale: there was a circular bar on top of which the women danced, and then a triangle of stages. A blackjack table was in one corner, and the walls were filled with music and sports videos. It was a place where even a self-respecting televangelist could sip a Virgin Mary without having to make explanations or beat a federal rap.

"We're in the Bible Belt here, so we run a real straight place," the night manager of the place said, sometime after Billy had been beaten senseless.

It was the beating that attracted all the attention.

A witness in the place, questioned by police, said that Billy, sometime in the course of his visit there, got into an exchange of words with a youngish-looking man, "someone around five foot eight with blond hair." Later, a man fitting this description was identified as one of two or three of Billy's possible assailants.

No one in the place remembers anything like a commotion or disturbance involving Billy beyond this brief exchange of words. No one remembers a quarrel involving any of the women, or any exchanges between Billy, his party, and the dancers.

Sometime later, Billy's friends, including Mantle and Mike Ferraro, left Lace. Billy, for some reason, remained.

It was near closing time, around two A.M., he said, when he went into the men's room to relieve himself. The movie here fades to black, and blood, and confusion.

Sometime during the next moments, the terrible work to Billy's body was done. This attack ended not in the men's room but in an alley adjoining the club. Internal police reports say that at about this time, a call was put out for an ambulance to go to Lace; this was later denied. Billy, with or without assistance, accompanied or unaccompanied, was placed in a taxicab and sent on his way back to the Hilton, where the Yankees were staying.

At the Hilton, a small fire in a sauna room on the first floor had set off the hotel fire alarm system and patrons, many of them in their nightclothes, were milling around downstairs when Billy arrived. Among the patrons was George Steinbrenner.

Billy was initially treated at the hotel by Yankee trainer Gene Monahan and later was taken to a local hospital where stitches secured the ear that had nearly been severed. At the same time police, by now having heard about the incident—but summoned neither by Billy nor by anyone else—arrived on the scene to take a statement.

Billy told them what he later told everyone else: that three men jumped him in the men's room at Lace. One of them held him while another struck him in the head with a blunt instrument. He was then further pummeled and thrown into an alley and left there. He somehow got back to the hotel on his own.

The following day, Billy, summoning his last reserves of strength, turned up in the dugout to lead his team to their third consecutive defeat. Afterward, barely able to stand up, he joined his mates for the long flight back to New York.

At LaGuardia Airport, Billy's personal chauffeur, Tex Gernand, was waiting for him. He had been alerted to his boss's condition and had prepared the long gold limousine to make the trip home from the airport as comfortable as possible. A drink was set out on the bar—Billy's favorite, Chivas and soda; a John Wayne movie was in place in the VCR.

Billy looked half dead, Tex said later; in all the years he'd been with him he had never seen him so badly chewed up. "We were on the road for about ten minutes," he said, "and he just passed out there in the back—he didn't come to the whole trip."

This was hardly the end of it. In Texas, police pursued an investigation. A restroom attendant, thought to be present when the fracas began, who may himself have been involved, said that he overheard

Billy and someone else—a blond man—arguing, that Billy referred to this person as a "faggot," that this other person then said something like, "I love to hear you talk like that," and that then a punch was thrown—by Billy. The attendant and someone else from the club broke up the fight before any damage was done, and escorted Billy to a side entrance where they left him. It was their belief that whatever wounds Billy sustained occurred when he lost his footing and hit a stucco wall.

The police treated this version as skeptically as they did Billy's and other purported eyewitness accounts. A detective with some investigative years on him said—for the record—"I'm noticing a lot of discrepancies in these accounts. In cases like this rarely do you find out the truth."

In the absence of truth, speculation disguised as truth always becomes a kind of commodity, offered and purchased by self-interested parties. In this case, there was only one such purchase agreement that mattered.

The principal owner of the New York Yankees, the man who held what everyone assumed was Billy Martin's last managing job in his hands, said that he believed his man was a victim in the incident, that he was his manager, and that the case was closed.

Billy, better than anyone, understood the meaning of those words: His days were numbered. His career, everything he lived, dreamed, and fought for over a lifetime, was about to come to an end.

# CHAPTER 1

The Great San Francisco Earthquake of 1904 was the first significant event in shaping Billy Martin's life. True, it occurred a quarter of a century before he was born, but its shock waves reached across the bay and across decades, uniting two families that in all probability would never have crossed paths otherwise. Before a pitch was thrown, there was this matter of the families.

The Salvinis, Billy's maternal family, never intended to settle in Berkeley, where Billy was born in 1928. They were part of the great wave of immigration that followed the gold rush and the completion of the railroad system linking the ends of the continent during the ninteenth century. California was their destination and San Francisco the place where they settled and intended to stay. The beautiful hilly regions around the North Bay, so perfect for farming, fruit growing, and wine making, were very much like home, the Abruzzi whence they came sometime in the last decades of the century.

The Martins' arrival in the Berkeley area also has a measure of accident to it. Their migration from Portugal, also in the latter decades of the last century, was not to California but to Hawaii—to the island of Kauai, perfect for fishing, like the Iberian coast. A part of the family moved on to the Bay Area—to Oakland rather than San Francisco—looking for better work opportunities sometime after the great and unnerving quake.

Chance turned up once again in the marital unions within these families—at least on the Salvini side. The marriage, in Italy, of Nicholas and Raphaella Salvini had been, typically, an arranged one. There were ten children from this union, five daughters and five sons, all of whom miraculously survived into adulthood. Billy's mother, Genevieve, was the youngest by many years. Little is known about the grandfather, Nicholas or "Nonnu." He was reportedly a fisherman, a hard worker, and something of a drinker, but the details of his life as well as his early death are only dimly remembered by current members of the family.

Billy's grandmother—"Nonna" as she was called—earned her living as a chambermaid in hotels and as a general domestic, but she was never at ease out in the new world, finding comfort only with her family and in the church. Language was a problem; to her dying day in 1946, Nonna never mastered English. When she was angry with someone she had this habit of biting rather than saying anything at all—a custom she brought with her from the old country. Billy and his brothers, sisters, and cousins have all told stories of Nonna from time to time nipping hand, ear, or limb to emphasize her displeasure.

She was also reported to be psychic. According to several members of the family, she had a method for determining the sex of a child while it was still in its mother's womb. "She did it with a needle on a thread, she'd hang the needle against the stomach of whoever it was who was pregnant, and depending on the way it moved, she would know," said one family friend. Billy's half-sister Pat Irvine, who remembers her grandmother—as do several of the other grandchildren—as a mysterious, almost eerie figure, did not recall the use of needle and thread in this manner but clearly remembered her ability to divine the sex of unborn children.

It was the grandmother, either by psychic power or otherwise, who somehow decided to move the family out of San Francisco to Berkeley around the time of the earthquake in 1904. According to Pat Irvine, the move was made three months prior to the quake. But another family member, Lucille Sabatini, insisted that the earthquake itself precipitated the move to Berkeley, because it was within easy reach of the refugee-laden barges that crossed the bay from the North Shore.

There is no dispute about what followed. The family settled in a house on 7th Street near Virginia Avenue. For a while, there were relatives all over the place, in all the rooms, "on the floors, under the tables, everywhere," recalls Pat Irvine. Eventually, the many relatives left, settling in and around the community. The house on 7th Street has remained in the family to this day.

There is yet another accident of design, one that was social more than geographic, that united these two families: poverty. The Salvinis and Martins were among those multitudes of ethnic arrivals who had not yet fulfilled the American dream when their paths crossed.

Nonetheless, in those early days, the area around 7th Street was barely populated countryside, enough like the old country to make settlers there feel comfortable. The few homes nearby, while not impressive, were perfectly functional wooden farmhouses that fit the terrain. Lucille Sabatini, in her eighties, just before she died, remembered a photograph she had of Billy's half-brother Tudo, older by ten years, at the age of one in 1919: The picture, taken from the front of the house on 7th Street looking across the way, shows Tudo sitting in grass. There are no other houses in view, only open fields all the way up to San Pablo Avenue—one of the area's main thoroughfares today.

"That house was like a farm," Sabatini said. "My grandmother had vegetable gardens and they made their own wine, they had everything . . . everything that they put in their own jars, it was all made at home: she baked all her own bread, so it was like we lived on a farm."

Decades later, the area around the house was still open. The children, Billy included, could roam through fields, tend to vegetable gardens, pick wild berries. "Then, all of a sudden it seemed like, there were all these houses," Billy's half-sister Pat said.

The neighborhood expanded rapidly in the thirties and the forties, particularly during and after the war. The area not just around Billy's house but on the whole west side of Berkeley from San Pablo Avenue down to the bay was working class and, according to boundaries marked by certain streets, was subdivided again by different ethnic groups. The predominantly Italian area where Billy grew up was, by any standard, modest but not dirt poor even in the worst days of the Depression when Billy was in his early years.

Jenny Salvini was in her mid-twenties when Billy was born, but she was already the divorced mother of a ten-year-old boy. Standing barely over four and a half feet tall, she was, according to her contemporaries, a formidable person, "a spitfire," given to quixotic and often violent outbursts of temper—a match for any man. Her speech was colorful and often abusive. And according to one friend, Ellen Vonitch, "She may not have been big, but she was physically strong. She had a punch."

Her temperament—often likened to Billy's—evolved over time. In her early years, Jenny seemed shy. Lucille Sabatini remembered her cousin as a girl who didn't talk much, was somewhat on the chubby side, and "was not especially pretty."

But she was always a determined person, particularly when she experienced anything she saw as unfair. When Lucille Sabatini's mother—Jenny's aunt—died in her mid-twenties, her children were scattered, sent off to other family members or else to foster homes. Sabatini was sent to a foster home—and Jenny, barely over ten years old, rebelled.

The foster home she was placed in, Sabatini remembered, was across town, miles from the neighborhood she knew. Jenny rescued her. "I wasn't allowed in the house, I was kept out in the yard during the days," she recalled, "and Jenny used to find me there. She walked all the way across town to find me and when she got to the gate, she called out, 'Lucy! Lucy!' And she took me by the hand and she led me away and we went back home together. Three or four days would pass, they'd return me to the foster home, and then Jenny would do it all over again."

Jenny's refusal to allow her cousin to be treated like an orphan eventually persuaded Nonna to intercede with the courts to gain custody of the child.

But Jenny came from a home and a background where family custom itself often seemed arbitrary and unfair—such as in the selection of a husband. As a teenager, Jenny was married, by arrangement, to a man named Donato Pisani, ten or fifteen years older than she. It was believed that Pisani came to the United States from Italy with the marriage plans already negotiated. And though Jenny dutifully accepted the arrangement, she eventually fought it.

The wedding was a traditional church ceremony with an outdoor reception at home afterward. "I remember the day they got married," Sabatini said, "because when they came back from the church, she was all dressed in white, and in the Italian custom you throw candy at the bride. There were almost no cars then, it was horse and buggy. There was a gate, a big gate—and we opened up the gate and the bride came walking down and where they started throwing the candy, all the kids scattered all over—but I tell you, she was pretty young, not much older than us kids."

The marriage to Pisani, which produced Billy's older half-brother, Tudo, lasted three or four years. In the course of that time, Jenny changed. Her rebelliousness no longer remained shrouded in shyness. She lost weight, acquired a certain attractiveness that later enabled her to tell her son Billy, "I have the best-looking ass in town and don't you forget it." She also acquired a new set of friends. Lucille Sabatini recalled that Jenny, when she was married to Pisani, had her eye on "the fella that used to bring the ice to the house, he was the one she wanted—but instead there was this marriage she didn't want." Her husband either left her or, more likely, was sent on his way. No one remembers what happened to Pisani or whether it was divorce or annulment that finally terminated the marriage. But there is no doubt whatsoever that Jenny had no intention of wasting her life on an arranged and loveless match—even if it meant defying her family.

When Jenny became single again, she ran with her new friends, a group of hard-living, fast-talking young people who quickened the pace of her life and brought her out of herself. There were four or five girlfriends, Mrs. Sabatini remembered, and a bunch of guys they used to go out with "who rode motorcycles. They weren't drinkers but they used to have picnics and they used to go to dances at these picnics."

Ellen Vonitch remembers going to the movies with Jenny and these new girlfriends of hers. "Jenny got in an argument with somebody on the ramp going up into the theater. It was over nothing. You should have heard her. We weren't allowed to swear when we were home. She said it like it was."

It was at one of these motorcycle picnics and dances that Jenny met Billy's father, Al. Alfred Manuel Martin (Billy's legal name also) was a truck driver for the City of Berkeley. Though he had been born on Kauai, he was called by some who knew him "the Por-to-gee." The Bay Area, because of its docks, was a logical settling place for the family looking to expand its economic horizons, and the picnic and dance where he met Jenny was an especially likely place for him, since his real interests then were said to be in music. He was a steel guitar player and he had a group of his own with whom he played regularly. Sabatini remembers that "he was a good-looking guy. Billy was passable, but his father was good-looking." He was around six foot tall, and his face looked something like his son's. He was easygoing and attractive to the opposite sex.

"Al and his cronies hung around—they all came from 23rd Street in Oakland," said Sabatini, "and they were just called 'The Twenty-Third Street Group'—fellas used to have their own groups to go with to these dances. The guys in the Twenty-Third Street Group were all good dancers and kind of popular."

According to Sabatini, Jenny Salvini fell in love with Al Martin. It was a match, a real one, and there the story—because it was so short-lived and violent—becomes somewhat murky. There is some doubt that the couple ever married. At least one old friend of the family, Ellen Vonitch, and one close relative seemed uncertain—although other relatives insist there was a marriage. This shadow of doubt, however, is important because it fell directly across Billy's life. According to Jill Martin, Billy's fourth wife, he was in severe turmoil at the time of his death because he had recently been told by an old childhood friend of his mother's that he was illegitimate. A marriage certificate, which Jill Martin says she discovered after her husband's death, apparently remained hidden till then.

There is no doubt, however, that the pair lived together as a married couple in a rented house not far from the grandmother. And some time later, the couple had their first and only child.

Like many children from old-world, low-income families, Billy was born at home—actually at his grandmother's house. Lucille Sabatini, in her late teens then and five years younger than Billy's mother, remembers assisting the doctor in the upstairs bedroom of Nonna's house that early afternoon of May 16, 1928. Jenny pulled on her cousin's hands and screamed from time to time until a cloth was placed over her face and drops of ether were administered.

"There were only the doctor and Jenny and I in the room when Billy was born," Sabatini said. "My grandmother was there when the labor started and the doctor had brought in a couple of oxygen tanks and was going to do something with them when my grandmother, seeing that, said, 'No, no, no, no, you're not going to use that on my daughter.' He said, 'Okay, but you're going to have to go downstairs.' She did—so I stayed and helped deliver the baby.

"Oh, I remember the sight of him being born. The doctor was great, he was explaining everything as it happened—first one shoulder came through and then the other and then he handed me the baby . . . he was a nice baby, not a great big fat baby. He weighed about seven pounds. How do I know that? The doctors in those days, they'd put them in their hands, feel them, and say in Italian, 'Oh, *dieci libre, dieci libre.*' You know, ten pounds. The doctor took Billy in his hands and said, 'Seven pounds! Seven pounds!' "

Sabatini also remembered being instructed in severing the umbilicus—she felt competent enough afterward to have been able to perform the services of a midwife if asked. And she remembered the circumcision that took place three days later:

"The doctor took the baby downstairs and circumcised him on the kitchen table," she said. "The baby screamed. The doctor put some cotton inside some gauze and tied it with some thread real tight and he dipped it with some whiskey and then put it in the baby's mouth. The baby sucked on it and quieted down."

Young Alfred also received a kind of knighthood in these first moments as well. The grandmother, cradling the infant in her arms, called him *Bello* (or "beautiful" in Italian). The name, repeated often enough, was later corrupted into "Billy."

It was storm, however, not beauty that actually surrounded the child. Billy's mother and father were on the verge of splitting even as he was being born.

The major reason given for the split—the view shared by Billy's sisters and brothers, by Lucille Sabatini, and others, including Ellen Vonitch—was that Al Martin was something of a rake and that his frequent infidelities and absences from home ignited Jenny's growing fury and led to a final break, in which Martin ran off with another woman.

But the end of this marriage was an event, not a process—a physical and psychic explosion that took place within range of a mute, uncomprehending three-month-old boy.

Billy, drawing on his mother's memories, reported the breakup this way in his autobiography, *Number One:*

> Apparently Dad was doing more during the day than just hauling garbage. One of the first gifts my mom gave him was a beautiful, expensive wristwatch. One day he came home without it, and when she asked him what had happened to it, he told her he didn't know. A few days later, one of Mom's many friends told her she had seen one of the students at the local high school wearing it. The girl was about fifteen years old, the woman said.
>
> After she left, my mom went into the closets, pulled out all Dad's clothes, stepped all over them to get them dirty, threw them in a suitcase, and threw the suitcase outside the front door. Dad came home and wanted to know what was the matter. Mom said, 'You're not chipping on me, you bastard. Out you go. And stay out.' She grabbed a hand mirror, went outside and broke every single window of his new car with the mirror. She had paid the five-hundred-dollar downpayment on the car, and wasn't about to let him get away scot-free . . .

Billy reported that shortly thereafter his mother, acting on a tip from a friend, actually discovered his father in bed with another woman: "She beat on his door, forced it open, and when she found him in bed with this girl, Mom started punching and hitting them both. She made such a racket, the neighbors called the police. She yelled at him, 'I'm still married to you, you son of a bitch. We're not divorced yet.' She felt better after she beat them up, Mom says."

Kelly Martin Knight, Billy's daughter, is the only person in the family who claims to have maintained a close relationship with Al Martin, her grandfather, over the years.

She says his version of the story was completely different. He, too, recalled one explosive day when he was thrown out of the house. He was thrown out, however, not because of his infidelities, but because of Jenny's—because "he had protested her working the streets as a hooker."

Kelly said that her grandfather eventually told her this story, waiting many years until she was old enough to hear it. "He waited till I was sixteen or seventeen years old before he told me, even though I knew something was terribly wrong and even though he knew how badly my grandmother had always treated me," she said.

According to Kelly, Al Martin told her one day "that [Jenny] used to be on the street. He'd go to work, then he'd have to go pick her up, bring her back home, she'd be fighting him all the way, then finally she just had enough. She said, 'If you don't leave right now, I'll kill this kid, I'll kill this little bastard kid.' She was actually holding a knife in her hand and pointing at my dad. 'And if you ever come back here again, I'll kill him, I swear it,' she said. My dad's grandmother, Nonna, was there and she said, 'Al, I will take care of him. Don't worry.' So he left and he stayed away. He would talk to my dad's grandmother, but he could never go around because he was afraid of what Jenny would do—and that hurt him very deeply. He never told my dad that, either, because he didn't want to hurt my dad's image of his mother. Because my dad thought his mother was the greatest."

The one common feature of these two irreconcilable versions of the story is that they both put Billy, as an infant, in the midst of a familial earthquake. Whatever happened, he was victimized by it in one way or another. Whether he was assaulted by screams and objects crashing around him or—though it seems implausible—he had a knife put to him, he was a tiny, totally helpless being in the middle of a blood feud between giants. It takes little imagination to wonder what sort of terror he experienced and how desperately his system must have wanted to reject it. There is today an ample body of professional opinion that holds that any kind of trauma in early childhood—from a raised voice to actual physical abuse—is doubly dangerous because at so early an age there is no way to deal with it. The likelihood is that, over time, such painful events are not lost but repressed, so that, never fully recalled nor understood, they reverberate into adulthood and beyond, compelling behavior that all too painfully remains bound to the original trauma. Child abusers usually turn out to have been victims of child abuse; the children of divorced parents are themselves more likely to have marriages end in divorce. What Billy, as an infant, was left with in this explosion of violence and retribution was immeasurable—but he was certainly then presented with an inchoate sense that the ground under his feet was not reliable, that the person he depended on most for nurturing could as soon kill as caress, that life between a man and a woman could be destructive, that anything like warmth and security—a family—was subject to sudden and violent upheaval.

The other question in all this is what Jenny was actually doing then. As Kelly recalled her grandfather's story, there was no doubt in her mind that Jenny had been a common streetwalker, making money any way she could. "That was the great secret in the family that everyone has tried to hush up," she said.

Even though others in the family are incredulous and angered by this story—which remains uncorroborated—what is intriguing is that everyone, relatives included, acknowledges that Jenny was then in the sometime employ of one of her sisters, Theresa, who ran a speakeasy and bordello on 66th Street. Billy himself, in his autobiography, noted the connection between his aunt and mother:

> Mom had a sister Theresa. . . . Theresa had a speakeasy, and she was making a thousand dollars a week during the Depression. . . . Mom would take me down to Theresa's place, and we'd sit on a chesterfield with my aunt, and Mom and Theresa would talk. I kept my mouth shut, because Mom always told me, 'When I'm talking don't butt in.' One time, my little brother Jackie went with us, and he interrupted, and Mom punched him on the mouth so hard she made his teeth bleed. He never interrupted again. We sat there, and during the day I would watch different men coming in and out, and I'd always wonder what those men were doing. The men would chat with my mom and buy me a Coke, and for several years Mom and I spent pleasant afternoons at Theresa's. The whole time I watched the men and wondered about them.
>
> I was about sixteen, and it was during the war, and a couple of my buddies and I went to a local cathouse. I didn't have the guts, and I certainly didn't have the money, to go upstairs with one of the girls, but

I enjoyed the ritual of the guy sitting there waiting for a girl to come, watching her take him away. It was very exciting for me.

A few days after I went to the cathouse, I was sitting down for breakfast, and I got to thinking about Aunt Theresa, and suddenly it dawned on me. 'Mom,' I called, 'does Aunt Theresa run a cathouse?' She said, 'Who told you?' No one had told me. I had finally figured out why all those men were coming in and out while I was sitting and talking with Mom and Aunt Theresa on her chesterfield.

Other family sources also acknowledge the connection between Jenny and Theresa, but all of those sources equally insist the employment did not involve prostitution. Jenny earned a few dollars helping her aunt serve drinks, cleaning up, keeping things running. But there are no other accounts of prostitution.

Billy's half-sister Pat and her husband, Ken, a retired firefighter who grew up in the neighborhood and who was an early schoolmate of Billy's, angrily deny that Jenny might have been one of Theresa's "girls," but there are certain qualifications in their version as well. For one thing, the main source of information for them, according to Pat, was Jenny. "My mother would never lie to us, she was the kind of person who if all that other stuff was true, she would come right out and say it," she explained. Her own childhood memories of Theresa and her house, though, were limited.

PAT: "Theresa was not a prostitute herself but she did have girls . . . and a bar . . ."

KEN: "That was during prohibition . . ."

PAT: "She had this great big house . . . and then on a little side street, an alley, they had the bar, the bootlegging, and about three girls . . . I remember it as a little kid."

KEN: "You made your money any way you could then."

PAT: "My mother would bring us all over there during the daytime and we'd sit downstairs and have our soda and water . . . of course we never knew what was going on in the evenings until my mother told us after we grew up. She told us everything. The story as I know it was this: My grandmother one time before I was born decided to go to Italy and she decided to take Tudo with her. Well, my mother was afraid to stay in the house. So Theresa said, 'Come and stay down here.' Well, my mother said, 'I'm not going to stay down there because you've got the whores.' Theresa said, 'Don't be silly, I have the room for you, come and stay there and earn a couple of dollars, work downstairs and serve the men.' "

KEN: "Serve the hootch. Your mother told me she used to work for your aunt a couple of times."
PAT: "But downstairs."
KEN: "But that other story . . ."
PAT: "That wasn't true."

Lucille Sabatini remembered Theresa and her establishment as well. She is certain that Jenny never worked the streets as a hooker or for Theresa as a prostitute. However, she pointed out that Billy, Pat—any of the children—had rarely if ever been in Theresa's house. "Billy and none of those kids was allowed in that house. And if it said that in Billy's book, it just wasn't true," Sabatini said.

Reminded of Pat's recollections, Mrs. Sabatini reluctantly added, "I don't think they were there two or three times in their lives. So what they said was whatever Jenny told them."

The common thread in all these stories is Jenny's personality and behavior. Late in her life, she struck people as a "character." Carol Lazaro, Lucille Sabatini's daughter, remembered a visit to Jenny's house several years before her death. She was old and infirm then, but she reminded Lazaro of Granny—Ma Clampett—in "The Beverly Hillbillies." "You know, she was sitting there in her kitchen, with a cigarette dangling out of the corner of her mouth, wearing heavy lipstick, swearing like a truck driver. She was talking about how the old neighborhood was running down—and I got the giggles. I kept thinking, 'Please don't look at me, because if you do, I'll burst out laughing.' "

Early or late, the picture of Jenny is consistent. She was an eccentric, an emotional dynamo, fast-talking, frequently foulmouthed, prone to using her fists if she had to. She went jaw to jaw with life as well as with any person, including her own kin, who got in her way.

How Jenny, a single parent barely out of her teens, managed to cope with two children, no money, and a bad temper is a real question. It is not clear what, if anything, she or her mother, whom she soon moved in with, did to earn sufficient money. The family's need was apparent. Ellen Vonitch remembers that she and her sister, who had a steady job, used to buy groceries and other goods for the family when they went to visit. There wasn't much around the house in the way of child-rearing equipment. "I remember," she said, "when we went over there, Jenny was there with Theresa and Lucille, and Billy was out in the yard with a beer bottle full of milk with a nipple on it." Other family members and local church officials also helped out.

Raphaella, the grandmother, did much of the child-rearing, housekeeping, and cooking. Her strength and character, very different from Jenny's, undoubtedly kept the young family together and functioning when they were most in need.

Her influence on Billy was at least as important as Jenny's. Sometime later, when Jenny remarried and the two women lived in separate and adjoining houses, Billy spent a great deal of time at his grandmother's. Lucille Sabatini maintains—but Billy's sisters deny——that he was actually raised by Raphaella. Whatever, Billy loved his grandmother devotedly and she in turn continued to treat him as a favorite—*Bello*, not Billy.

Billy's depth of affection for his grandmother undoubtedly stemmed from her generally kinder approach to him. A cousin who grew up with Billy, Mario DeGennaro, remembers resenting his grandmother for favoring Billy. "Billy and I were kinda close as kids, but I didn't go to my grandmother's too much, she was kinda like 'into' Billy. She thought he was 'pretty.' I kinda resented that. . . . When she died, Billy became unglued. He said, 'You're not even crying.' I said, 'Billy, that's me—I wasn't close to her, you were.' He slept in the same bed. I think I did once when we were really small kids—he lived right next door to me—he was at her house more than at his own house."

Billy—anyone—who stepped into his grandmother's house could not help being impressed by the obvious signs of her devout and old-world faith. Religious icons—crosses, pictures of Jesus and the Holy Mother—were everywhere. Pat Irvine didn't like to spend time in her grandmother's house because "her room was always dark and she had an altar in the corner. She was very religious and had this altar to the Holy Mother with candles burning twenty-four hours a day."

Lucille Sabatini, who adored Nonna, also recalled that "she was a religious lady. I remember sleeping in her room at night. There were so damn many holy pictures and she had an altar in her room. On this altar—it was made of marble with a couple of steps or ledges, set up on some kind of pedestal—she kept a candle that floated in oil and that was lit all the time. On the wall, she had all kinds of holy pictures. There was one that was so vivid: a picture of Christ, just his head, and he had the crown of thorns on his forehead with a couple of drops of blood. Well, with the light from the candle, the picture used to scare me."

Billy was impressed by what he found in his grandmother's house, too. From the earliest age to the end of his life, he was a regular churchgoer. This was a side of him usually ignored, but it came to him, first, with family love. From the interior of his grandmother's house, Billy took on this powerful, old-world Catholic faith, secured by obedience and catechism, that placed God and Church, matters of right and wrong, in simple patterns of thought that were also powerful and unassailable. Mario DeGennaro remembers how energetic Billy was about churchgoing:

"He'd come to my house on Sunday mornings," he said, "come around to the back and tap on the windows. 'What the hell do you want?' 'Come on,' he says, 'let's go to church.' 'Get outta here, I ain't going to no church!' 'Yeah, yeah, you are,' he says, 'get outta bed or I'll call your mom.' I'd tell him to go to church by himself and sure enough he'd go and get my mother and she'd come into the bedroom and get me up telling me that Billy was waiting for me to go to church and that I *had* to go with him."

But Raphaella's deepest influence was as a matriarch who held her family together. She did this not by command but by force of personality. She brought the old country with her and the old country—at least as Billy felt it—was about the strength and durability of family life. She had a wine press out back, Billy remembered years later, and the family used to stamp on the grapes to make the wine that would be stored in old barrels. Nonna used to preside over family dinners every Sunday and all the relatives would come—the uncles and aunts, nieces and nephews, all of those who had crossed the bay and settled in Berkeley and the communities nearby. "The kids would be fed first, and we'd get out of there early," Billy wrote in his autobiography years later, "and the adults would sit all afternoon eating and drinking . . . everyone would come, and they'd be so happy to see each other." The happiness, Billy remembered, would soon degenerate into loud and often vituperative quarreling, but such was the power of the grandmother's capacious table that these same battling relatives would all be back the following Sunday—restored, renewed, and ready for another round.

However, these were not Sundays in the Abruzzi but Sundays in Berkeley with the Depression in full swing. Raphaella was one woman alone—Billy's grandmother, not his mother—and the reality of everyday life, far from being secure and capacious, was fraught with want—and anger. Jenny, not Raphaella, was the most decisive person in Billy's life. And her teaching, first and last, was even more fundamental than any church creed: "Take shit from no one," she told her son.

He never did.

# CHAPTER 2

On Christmas Day 1929, a little over a year after the big explosion with Al Martin, Jenny remarried. Her new husband was a likeable, self-effacing man named Jack Downey, whom she met through friends. Downey had drifted to the West Coast from the Midwest, looking for work. He had a charming Irish tenor voice, and when Jenny met him he was a singing waiter on one of the ferry lines that regularly crossed the bay before the building of the area's bridges. Downey moved on from the ferries to truck driving, to working as a longshoreman, anything to make ends meet. He was hard-working, not always lucky, but always steady—steady in his willingness to work and support a family, steady in his willingness to defer to his wife. The couple married on Christmas Day because Jenny said it would limit gift-giving to one day.

Three children—Joan, Pat, and Jack—came from this union, soon filling the house with noise and activity. Downey seemed perfectly content to let Jenny rule the roost, and Jenny's temper clearly dominated things. Mario DeGennaro remembered Jenny as being "extremely bossy—used to tell her husband where to go, when to go, how to go. But he always took it with a grain of salt. Me, I would have bopped her one. But Jack—he laughed. Used to call her 'Patrone'—that's Italian for boss. She'd use the *F* word, any word that came to mind without thinking twice. She'd say, what the *F* you want, get your ass outta here. He'd laugh."

From the beginning, Billy seemed to have his mother's temperament. He was influenced little if at all by his easygoing stepfather, for whom he had affection without any discernible connection. Billy's instinct was to fight back rather than to laugh. If his mother's teaching was to take shit from no one, Billy not only accepted it but perfected it, often turning it against his teacher. All through his boyhood, Billy fought with his mother even as he followed her instruction. There are any number of friends from that time who remember a routine of hair-raising fights between mother and son. The fights were loud and physical, with screaming and yelling, objects flying across rooms.

Ruben DeAlba, perhaps Billy's closest childhood friend, remembers that "it was almost embarrassing listening to Billy and his mother fight. Sometimes I'd sit on the front stoop because I didn't want to go in there. I used to see Billy and his mom throw things at one another; toaster, pots, things like that. Billy'd come running out the door, saying, 'Let's go, Rube.' "

Billy had two retreats from this mayhem. One was his grandmother's house. The other was a park and playground up the street—James Kenney Park—which quickly became a home away from home. Kenney Park was an oasis for the neighborhood kids. It had a ballfield, a clubhouse, boxing equipment, basketball hoops—it was a center for sports and social life. It was also a battlefield. Years later, Billy said that kids spoiling for a fight would always be hanging around the park. If you didn't fight them, you couldn't use the park, it was that simple. Loving sports as much as he did, Billy said, made fighting back mandatory.

In fact, there was a lot Billy had to contend with in order to survive.

From the earliest age, contrary to his grandmother's belief that he was "pretty," he was taunted about his looks. He had an unusually large nose, floppy ears, and bad teeth. Billy's uncles—who regularly came to Kenney Park on the weekends to play ball—were particularly hard on him. "They had all kinds of names for him, you know, banana nose, flag ears, stuff like that," said Emil "Dootch" Firman, another close boyhood friend, "and it used to drive him wild." Later, the taunts, coming from others, ignited serious and bloody fights.

School was another early battleground. In grade school, the Franklin Elementary School, the taunting was an everyday occurrence. Jack Setzer, a year ahead of Billy, remembers that his friend was "not a particularly belligerent person but he was very intense and energetic—and you noticed that." There were fights—almost invariably over a remark about his looks—and then school itself was a problem.

By all accounts, Billy was never much of a student. Emil Firman, who thought Billy was smarter than people gave him credit for, said he earned Cs in school, "sometimes he'd bring home a B." Rube DeAlba remembered that Billy "was an average student, he had his moments in class, sometimes he applied himself, often he didn't." If he had a special interest in any subject, it was in history, his friends said. Firman recalled that "we were going to school right around the time the war began and we both got real interested in what the different planes and battleships looked like. He just loved that."

But Billy had a basic problem with his teachers and with authority. By the sixth grade, he was in continual trouble, never willing to accept what he believed was unfair treatment. Pat Irvine said that her mother's teaching was to respect adults, but only if they respected you in return. Not taking shit did not stop at the schoolhouse door. In that last year of grade school, the principal, a Mr. Cuttyback (euphemistically labeled as just a teacher in *Number One*) apparently took a ruler to Billy's hands one day. Cuttyback, according to Firman, was a particularly stern disciplinarian who had a habit of using corporal punishment to back up school regulations. Firman recalled that Cuttyback one day removed Billy from school safety patrol, rapping him across the knuckles, and sending him home to his mother. Jenny, observing welts on her son's hands, marched up to the school and confronted the principal.

"If you ever lay your hands on my son again, I'll come up here and break every bone in your body," she is reported to have told Cuttyback—a practical application of the basic philosophy.

Fighting, striving, competing was an inevitable part of Billy's growing up, even more so than for other children. Because of his unusual home situation, because of his small size and ungainly appearance, he constantly felt threatened. He had the misfortune to be thin-skinned and stouthearted, and the combination spelled endless trouble—and opportunity—for him. He had to learn to fend for himself at the earliest age. Even before he figured out quite who he was or where he was going, he seemed to have this urge to go one better than the next person, as though life itself was at stake any time he had to stand up for himself, whether in a classroom, on a playground, or on the street. He was a normal but clearly different child.

"Billy was extremely competitive, even in the fourth and fifth grade," remembered "Dootch" Firman. Firman recalled that every day at lunch break, he, Billy, and Rube—the best of friends—used to have a competition to see who could hit more balls over the school fence. For Billy there was something relentless in it. "Going home, he'd constantly remind you that he had sixteen that day and you had fourteen—but the next day when you reminded him that you had seventeen and he had fifteen, he'd get really pissed," Firman said.

Rube DeAlba remembers playing one-on-one basketball with Billy and that whenever he lost, he would cry. "I could laugh it off if I lost, not Billy, never, never," Rube said, "he couldn't take it. He'd leave the playground in tears if he lost."

What separated Billy from his mates was not his size or even his fighting skill. When Billy joined a community-sponsored boxing program, he lost as often as he won but this determination to win, DeAlba recalled, seemed almost crazy.

Secoro "Choke" Mejia, a childhood friend who remained close to Billy throughout his life, remembers an incident in Kenney Park that revealed just how far Billy could go:

"We used to play this game where you'd dive on the ground and take this little piece of land for yourself, and this kid Edward Piralto sticks a knife in the ground fighting over this little corner of turf," Mejia said. "This other kid, his name was Albert something or other, he and Billy were fighting for the same piece of ground so Albert sticks his foot down right in the middle of the area, saying he's got the land. Well, Billy reaches over, takes the knife out of the ground and sticks it in Albert's foot."

Usually friendly and fun-loving, Billy could instantly flash into fisticuffs. Though he was small—puny for his age—he was fearless. If someone, anyone—no matter how big or seemingly strong—challenged him, he would answer the challenge by striking first. Before he even reached junior high school, he had a reputation for street fighting that reached well beyond his own neighborhood.

In junior high there was another and more sophisticated kind of challenge to his self-respect. Billy went to Burbank Junior High, one of three feeder schools for Berkeley High in the city. Burbank was the school primarily set apart for the ethnic working classes. The program at Burbank clearly was on a vocational track, pointing students toward industrial jobs rather than careers or professions.

At Burbank, there was a wider pool of students around Billy—tougher kids, better athletes. For the first time, there were black faces in school. For the first time, there were sharper epithets to deal with—ones that tended to strengthen a fighting sense of "them" and "us."

Words like "dago," "wop," "spic," "nigger," were everyday triggers for injuries that were both emotional and physical.

The world was also in upheaval. The war was on when he entered junior high, and suddenly having a background that was Italian or German or Asian meant something. The Firman family—German by origin—had to move from the west side to a specially designed housing zone for "aliens." Billy named his friend "Dootch"—as in *Il Duce*—making him, for whatever it was worth, an honorary Italian.

The neighborhoods, as well as their unknowing children, were partisan, fiercely patriotic, and attached to the Democratic Party. Roosevelt was a hero in the working-class wards. Firman remembers that when Wendell Willkie, the Republican candidate for U.S. president, came to Berkeley to campaign in 1940, schoolkids attended his rally, "and Rube, Billy, and I threw eggs at him."

On the local level, all youngsters, especially those from ethnic areas like West Berkeley, began to understand that the city they lived in was divided into classes. Those who lived up in the hills, in the affluent parts of town, were regularly and snickeringly referred to as "goats" by those who lived below. The hill people, equally scornful, referred to their brethren down by the bay as "flatlanders."

For both goats and flatlanders, the dividing line in town was an absolute boundary: If you lived above San Pablo Avenue going up toward the hills, you were a goat; if you lived below San Pablo, say on 7th off Virginia in West Berkeley, you were a flatlander.

Billy's answer to the growing pressures around him was, again, both normal and different. He became, as many kids from the neighborhoods did, a member of one of the town's loosely affiliated gangs. Gang life then was more a form of social than criminal life, but fighting, turf fighting, was clearly at the heart of it. Gangs in Berkeley could be mean and tough. *Pachuco* gangs required all those under their domination to wear tattoos between their thumbs and forefingers.

Billy, small as he was, was not only a gang member but a leader before he ever set foot in junior high. His gang, "the West Berkeley Boys," enabled him to fight back on a group level as he did on an individual one. His gang enabled him, for the first time in his life, to create himself as someone larger, bolder, more accomplished than others might have considered him. Gang life for Billy had this extra component of imagination.

In his autobiography, Billy describes himself as a gang leader. He underscores the fact that he never started fights but that he never backed away from them, that he was forced to defend himself. When he came home through Kenney Park, for example, he sometimes, on his own, had to ward off forty or fifty toughs at a time, he said. And then, because he was the head of his gang, there were even larger battles.

What he remembers, however, is hard to separate from what he created. The gang he led—at times he referred to them as his "Prussian army," at times his "Chinese army"—consisted, he said, of hundreds of kids who ultimately discouraged other gangs from venturing into Kenney Park:

> I didn't want to get involved in gang fighting. I only went to one. One time a group of kids from East Berkeley, where the rich kids lived, came down to our park to fight us. They thought they were a bunch of toughies, but they didn't know what they were getting into. We beat them bad. When we went back to East Berkeley, instead of our having a gang fight, I took on their leader. I stood out in front of my Chinese Army, and he stood out in front of his army, and we went at it. After I beat him up, the fighting stopped. There were no more fights, and the East Berkeley kids didn't bother us anymore.

Billy's relatives and friends for the most part are amazed by these accounts of gang life. Billy's half-sister Pat and her husband, Ken, bridled at the notion that Billy was a gang leader of any sort, much less one who marched at the head of hundreds. Dootch Firman, one of the West Berkeley Boys, laughed and said the group was not so much a gang as a group of friends who simply used to hang out together. "There were never more than eighteen or twenty of us," Firman said. On the other hand, Rube DeAlba and Nick DeGennaro both remember gang fights, with Billy up front, where hundreds actually were involved.

The truth is that there was no gang of hundreds but the fighting was fiercely territorial and could bring out hundreds. Among the gangs, Billy and the West Berkeley Boys had a special reputation for toughness. They were never forced to wear tattoos, were never "conquered." On their own turf, these eighteen or twenty kids—Billy the toughest of them—were eventually left alone. Kenney Park was theirs, and when they were feeling lighthearted, they stopped local traffic and asked for tolls or else wandered on up to Henry's, the local drugstore and hangout where they could check out a goat girl or two, joust with a group of passing sailors on shore leave, talk their way out of a dispersal order by cops on the beat.

What was unique about Billy was not his leadership of hundreds but his ability in a street fight. He was tough, violent and willing—as others were not—to do almost anything to win. His reputation was built on his almost crazy, impulsive aggressiveness. In junior high, when he began to be taunted more frequently, the number of fights in which he was involved increased. So did his sense that winning a fight was about winning a place in the world, a way of being seen by others as a leader. Billy may or may not have started fights, but he built his reputation by getting into them.

Emil Firman remembers Billy having this thing about being "King of the Hill." He recalls that at Burbank, Billy had a couple of legendary noontime fights with another student named Orvin Lord. "The fight—there actually may have been two of them—between Orvin and Billy went on during one lunch hour, I think, or it may have been down at the YMCA, but it went on and on. Orvin Lord was this kid who thought he was King of the Hill and Billy didn't like that because he thought he should be the equal of anybody," Firman said.

As daring a streetfighter as Billy was, he also—especially in this period—learned how to use his fists skillfully. He acquired, as others did not, real technique to match his instincts.

In these early years at Kenney Park, one of the popular activities for the kids at the clubhouse was working out on the speedbag. All of the kids were into it, and some of them were better than others. Billy, for a number of reasons, became better than most. For one thing, he could simply hit. He had a strong throwing arm in baseball, which translated in boxing to punching power. As he himself acknowledged, he "could hit like a truck." Also, he was quick. He could get his hands going faster than others. And then he had another advantage.

Dick Foster, a well-known local pro boxer, lived in the neighborhood and was a close friend of Billy's half-brother Tudo. Foster was a frequent visitor to the house, and knew and liked Billy—liked him as a fighter. Foster liked Billy's hands and his power, but particularly liked his toughness, his willingness to stand up for himself under any circumstances. He trained him—how to use the speedbag, how to get his hands going, how to gain maximum power in throwing a punch.

"Dick Foster always used to egg Billy on," Emil Firman said. "He'd go at him all the time, tell him, 'You can beat anybody, you can beat anybody if you put your mind to it.' He just kept going after him to never give up, no matter what."

Billy, then, was just different. He knew it—and everyone else did, too.

"We all had this game," Nick DeGennaro, another cousin and one of the West Berkeley Boys, said. "We called it 'Copping a Sunday.' It meant getting in the first punch. You know, you'd be standing there talking to someone and—*boom*—you'd let him have it. We'd do it for fun, we'd do it in fights."

When Billy did it, it was dynamite.

At different times throughout his life, Billy casually, almost jokingly, acknowledged that had fate been only a little different, he might have wound up, as others he knew had, in jail or dead. What spared him wasn't family, church, or school, it was sports. Billy's saving grace, the one that moved him off both the vocational and criminal tracks he may have been on, was that he was an athlete. Beyond his fighting ability, he could play basketball and, most especially, baseball. But even more, he had luck on his side. As there had been someone to teach him how to use his fists in a professional manner, there was also available to him—as though summoned from his own Field of Dreams—a collection of professional baseball players who just happened to work out regularly in Kenney Park. Among those professionals was another one of Tudo's friends, Augie Galan.

The players began working out at the park in the off-season before and during the war years. Some of them were on the local Pacific Coast League team, the Oakland Oaks, and some were major leaguers who lived in the area. The Hafey brothers, Les Scarsella, Dario Lodigiani, Cookie Lavagetto, the great Ernie Lombardi, and Galan were regular members of this unofficial workout group. On weekends, the players took infield, shagged, hit, and played games. The neighborhood kids—and adults—crowded around to watch.

Billy was one of those youngsters who wanted more. From the start he made himself known to the players. He did small favors for them, kidded with them, tried harder than anyone else to let them know he was there.

Through Tudo, Billy had an entrée to these players that other kids did not. Emil Firman remembered that "of course we all wanted to hang out with these guys, but because they were older, most of us couldn't. But they sort of adopted Billy—and because of him, Rube and me. We'd go with them afterwards up to University Avenue or something, sometimes they'd take us to a show. It made an impression on us, believe me."

Galan was special. He lived in the neighborhood, just a couple of blocks away. He would turn up at Billy's house, have dinner there, spend time with the family, come in and out as a friend. Billy listened to his stories of life in the big leagues. He was a real-life hero.

"Billy even as a kid talked about one day playing for the Yankees," Rube DeAlba said. "But he was also a Cubs fan, Augie's team. The Yankees and the Cubs."

Billy ingratiated himself with Galan as he did with no one else. On Saturdays he wandered over to Galan's house and waited for him till he was ready to set out for the park. "He kind of took a shine to me," Galan remembered, "because I had known him since he was a kid. So he'd come over and carry my grip for me down to the park."

Galan worked with Billy, and then other kids as well. On his own, receiving no pay, furnishing his own equipment, he ran a children's program at Kenney Park. Billy was his ardent pupil. Galan said he taught fundamentals, "basic things that kids just don't know." Billy, he remembered, "was one of those kids you didn't have to say anything to twice."

But Galan saw something else in Billy—perhaps because he knew him better, perhaps because the signs of trouble and promise were so obvious. "I explained to him that when I played ball I had to fight for everything I got," Galan said. "All of us did then, I guess. But I kinda had a handicap myself and I told him about it. I broke my arm when I was eleven years old. I shattered my elbow and I didn't go to a doctor and it took about ten years to heal, but I could never let anybody know—you know—so I explained to him that, yeah, I had the handicap but goldarnit, if you have the determination nobody can stop you. I don't care how big you are, how small you are, what you look like, if you got it, you can make it. I was always a hustler when I played because you had to hustle or you weren't going to play—so I tried to insert that into him—just never give up, bear down all the time. Which he did, even though he had the ability not to need anybody to insert anything into him."

The most important thing Galan "inserted," however, was the most subtle: a sense of belonging. At an age when kids dream about playing in the majors, Billy already could feel himself a part of the fraternity. His sense of "them" and "us" had now been expanded to include the world of professional baseball.

So, by the very first day he moved on to Berkeley High School, that elite and sprawling school that served the entire community, the die was already cast. For most students coming from Billy's background, the way ahead was marked out, clear, and limited. For him, because he was an athlete, because he now was personally and constitutionally unable to accept anything that shunted him aside or put him down, the future was his to claim.

Billy began at Berkeley High in the fall of 1943 and was immediately placed on a vocational track. For 1945–46, Billy's senior year, the school yearbook, *Olla Podrida,* has a page of photographs illustrating "Our Shops in Action." In one of the pictures, Billy is the focus of attention, seated at a workbench, with two students standing to either side of him. He is busy measuring what appears to be a block of wood. Rube DeAlba, who intended to go on to college if he could, fought to get himself into an academic program. Billy never did. He took a lot of shop courses in metal and wood, all the way through school. That was never where the challenge lay for him.

Socially, there was a challenge, an acute one. Because he came from a poor neighborhood and because the school was filled with elites—the sons and daughters of U Cal faculty as well as those of civic and business leaders, identity was no easy matter. Money and clothes were not only signs of class but of status as well.

Ted Texeira, an old baseball teammate of Billy's at Berkeley, remembers that the school was filled with clubs. "The kids in one club all wore blue suede jackets," he said, "and in another, they wore these leather Glenn Miller flight jackets."

Billy's wardrobe was limited to a ubiquitous pair of jeans and a jeans jacket. It was something of a uniform for West Siders. Ken Irvine recalls that he used to place his one pair of jeans under his pillow at night "to get them so stiff they'd stand up on their own." Billy, acutely conscious of the way he looked to begin with, was even more sensitive to his appearance now. He had a habit, one friend remembered, of rubbing his shoes against the back of his jeans. "He always had polished shoes," this friend said, "and he just had this unconscious habit of rubbing them against his trouser legs to get them shinier when he was standing around."

He also had a big Hollywood mop of hair, swept back D.A.-style. It was a pride and joy to him, remembered Rube DeAlba, who sported his own big mop. The hair styles of these two friends got them into trouble right away. Billy's hair also revealed just how focused his ambitions were.

Billy and Rube came into the school as "bad boys," their gang reputations preceding them. They were watched by teachers and administrators. A current Berkeley High official, Dan Dean, then a fellow student, vividly remembered that Billy was a person "who everyone knew about. You knew he was someone you stayed away from."

When Billy and Rube went out for basketball that first semester, they were told—immediately—that they had to cut their long hair or be excluded from the team. They cut their hair. In the spring, when they wanted to go out for baseball, they had been enrolled in a physical education class that required swimming in the school pool. The boys had avoided the pool entirely because they did not want to subject their growing locks to the bleaching effects of chlorine. They were informed one day that they were going to receive failing grades for the course, which meant they would be ineligible for baseball. The failing grades would be rescinded only if they agreed to swim. "We cut our hair again," Rube said, "and then we went and put our heads under water every damn day in that pool so we could play baseball."

Billy became a star at Berkeley High the same way he became a gang leader: He saw everything as a challenge or an affront to be overcome. He made his mark from the very beginning. As small and nondescript as he was, as seemingly ungainly—he was never smooth at anything he did—he was as unavoidable on the courts and playing fields as he had been in the streets and alleys.

In the fall of that first semester, Billy and Rube DeAlba both went out for basketball. From the team pictures in *Olla Podrida* and from the reports of teammates and friends, Billy was an even less likely physical presence on the court than Spud Webb. Standing barely over five feet tall, hardly more than 110 pounds, his appearance scruffy, his easily caricatured features making him seem both baby-faced and vaguely unhygienic, he looked like a refugee from a Dead End Kids movie.

Billy and Rube both made junior varsity basketball. "The thing about Billy was that he had this supreme confidence," Rube said. "If he said he was going to do something he'd do it. It was uncanny. I know I was the better ballplayer, but he'd say before a game, 'Rube, tonight I'm getting sixteen points,' and that's exactly what he'd do. I'd be lucky if I got eight. I was smooth, I was out there as 'The Picture' but nothing I'd throw up would seem to go in. When he drove for a basket, he'd drive, didn't matter who was in front of him. Everything he said came to be."

Billy's stardom was based on his own proficiency, to be sure, but it came from his extraordinarily aggressive spirit. He hustled more than others, he risked more—and he fought more. From the start, fighting in team sports meant the same thing it did in gang combat: It meant, on a personal level, standing up, refusing to back down. Within his group it also meant leadership.

Billy's first big fights at Berkeley High were on the basketball court. Billy was the leading scorer on a JV team that won an Oakland area league championship. Inevitably, he became an easy target for opponents who, in the usual push and shove of the game, might have had an especially hard time believing that someone so small and funny-looking had done quite so much damage.

"There were a series of games where he had fights in the locker room after the game," Rube said. "There was taunting going on out there or someone might have hacked him going up for a shot. 'I'll see you after the game,' he'd say." DeAlba recalled one fight, in the eleventh grade, against a player from Piedmont High School. Billy and this player had gone for a loose ball near center court, there had been contact and scuffling, and a jump ball was called. "Billy and this guy got into an argument, I didn't hear how it started, there probably was some taunting, then Billy said, 'I'll see you after the game.' The other kid said, 'Fine,' you know, it was a challenge. He got him in the locker room just like he said he would. Billy cut him up so bad, he beat him to a pulp and it was over just like that."

Jack Setzer, another old friend and baseball teammate, remembered a fight Billy got into during another basketball game. In this game, Setzer recalled, a fan had been taunting Billy during the game, "kept calling him 'Pinocchio! Pinocchio!'—stuff like that," Setzer said. Billy asked Setzer at halftime to point out the agitator to him when the game ended and when Setzer did, Billy immediately went after him, "hitting him with the quickest barrage of punches I've ever seen."

Fighting accompanied Billy into baseball, too, but there his on-field skills were better matched to his temperament. The team's coach used him, Jack Setzer remembered, "as a kind of enforcer. When the coach wanted a guy straightened out, he'd turn his back, so to speak, and let Billy go to work."

There were fierce battles with opponents. Setzer remembered one game where Billy, playing third base, was hit high by a sliding base runner. When that same runner came into him again later in the game, Billy knocked him cold with the tag he applied. "We thought for a while the kid was dead," Setzer said.

Billy had no difficulty becoming a leader on a team that developed real camaraderie. Many of the players were West Berkeley Boys, the togetherness and identity of the gang transferring to the closeness of the team, with Billy as its fighting leader.

Billy did not begin as a second baseman. In that first year he played third and occasionally pitched. He was considered a good hitter, a hitter for average but not power, but he was clearly someone to watch because of his aggressiveness and heads-up play. He constantly exhorted his mates and he was the fiercest of bench jockeys at a time when verbal cutting and slashing from the sidelines was an art.

The team, because it was short on pitching, wasn't championship caliber, but still commanded attention. One year, it traveled out to Treasure Island to play a service team, filled with professionals and coached by Dick Bartell, the major league infielder. Berkeley High held a lead against the service team for much of the game, before yielding to a late-inning rally. Bartell, who had threatened members of his own team with transfers if they didn't beat the kids they were playing, praised the Berkeley team as one of the best high school teams he had seen.

Through the years, Billy's play constantly improved. He hit barely over .200 in his first season with the team, but then in succeeding seasons he hit .410 and .450. By his final season, he had moved from third to short, the position in high school usually filled by the team's best athlete.

But while Billy's play obviously improved, his reputation as a brawler grew, too. In one notorious game in his senior year, he got into an on-field brawl with a player from a rival school that wound up getting him suspended from the team—robbing him, he was sure, of his baseball future. This one fight seemed to bring together all of the forces that he was struggling with in himself and against which he was doing combat in the world.

The fight flared in a game with Hayward High School and involved a player named Pete Hernandez. In his autobiography, Billy typically pads his image in his description of the battle and its aftermath:

> One of the Hayward players, a kid by the name of Pete Hernandez, had told everyone at Hayward that he was going to whip my ass after the game. The kids from West Berkeley got wind of his threats, and we must have had a crowd of about four hundred of our kids at the game, because everyone wanted to see me and Hernandez go at it. During the game I singled. Hernandez was the first baseman, and a couple of times the pitcher threw over, and I dived back into the bag, and Hernandez slammed his glove into me. He said, "I'm going to get you after the game." Scare tactics. "I'm going to whip your ass." I said, "I'll be right there, pal." Everyone knew there was going to be a fight. I even told our

coach about it. He said, "Don't go after him, but if he comes after you, take care of him." The game ended, I was the shortstop and Hernandez came running my way. He took a swing at me, but I hit him three times hard to the face, knocked him cold. I tried to pick him up and hit him again, but the coach grabbed me and said, "Billy, he's had it. He's already out. Go to the locker room."

As we ran to the locker room, the Hayward fans threw rocks at me. My coach didn't want me to turn around or do anything. He rushed me into the clubhouse. Fights broke out all over the field. Our guys cleaned up on them, kicked hell out of their guys.

The school principal called me into his office the next day to tell me I was kicked off the team. He said, "You should have turned the other cheek." I said, "That's ridiculous. Turn the other cheek when he comes after you after he's told everybody he's going to beat you up?" When he told me I was off the team, I cried. How could I have turned the other cheek? The guy had come after me. It was cruel. I couldn't believe anyone could be so unfair.

Billy's cousin, Mario DeGennaro, was at that game and has another view of how the Hernandez fight developed. "I was down at the track practicing that day, you know, running around the outside of the field. This incident happened. Billy had this false tooth, I don't remember why, a plate or something. At any rate, I'm running around the track and they were playing Hayward High. This kid Hernandez was harassing them or something. I was going around and this other team was out in the field and Billy came over to me and said, 'Hey, we're gonna have a little fight here after the game. Be around.' He said, 'I'll give ya' the high sign. When I give you my tooth, get the hell out of the way, because I'm gonna go for this guy.' So I was the tooth holder. The game's over, he gives me the tooth, and then he goes over and belts this guy, knocks him for a loop. They were really going at it. Billy was a good fighter, but this other guy was no slouch. That was a good fight."

These two versions again point up Billy's tendency to create his own legend rather than coming to grips with his own complicated experience. None of Billy's friends, none of the former school administrators or people on the team, including assistant coach William Daoust, remembers an on-field brawl involving hundreds. On the other hand, everyone remembers the Hernandez fight because it was fierce and attention-grabbing and because in its aftermath Billy, Berkeley High's star player, was suspended from the team.

There are any number of explanations for why Billy might have resorted to exaggeration. He might have simply gotten his fights mixed up; he had surely been in enough of them to confuse one with the other—although there is no account from any source of that big an on-field battle at any time during his high school years. Another possibility is that Billy wanted to justify what happened in light of his suspension; he wanted to be seen as a victim.

But fighting—deadly fighting—was a part of his makeup as surely as any skills he had as a ballplayer. Both came from that unquenchable fire that he could neither contain nor understand.

Rube DeAlba, playing alongside Billy (he was the team's second baseman all those years), running with him from childhood, thought he knew where the violence fit in, where it became something far more than an undesirable character trait:

"Fighting, like everything else in Billy's life, was complicated," Rube said. "If you have one easy answer for it, the chances are you've missed the man. People really have multitudes of personalities; they aren't like compact little boxes where everyone has the same thoughts, the same motives for acting.

"One thing about Billy when he fought—not boxing but real fighting—was that his temper became uncontrollable. It was something that just seemed to come over him, like demons or whatever, and then when it was over, he would often get this look on his face like, 'What have I done?' As if it had been someone else who had done it.

"Then he was also someone who bore a grudge. He wouldn't let you know right away, either. It would just fester until one day it would explode.

"But the thing that's most often said about him is that he was trained mainly by his mother not to take anything from anyone. This is true. But Billy took it one step further. Because of his nose and his teeth and his size or whatever, he was very self-conscious. He really wasn't a bad-looking kid, but he was constantly belittled, so he built up this personality where he was gonna make himself, people were gonna accept him. This uncontrollable temper always arose from the feeling that he had to assert himself. In sports he could let it out and he could also excel, he could be accepted and idolized. He could make himself better than he was. So when we went out for basketball, right then and there, everything went into excelling. Boom, he was Billy Martin, athlete and star! Right there in the tenth grade. Never mind the fighting, he was becoming a star!

"Later on, they started writing about how he couldn't stand losing.

Well, right then, Billy seemed to see everything from the way he looked to how many points he scored to what people thought of him when he walked down the street in terms of winning and losing. Being a star meant the same thing. It meant being accepted. He used to tell me all the time, 'Rube, I'm going to the Yankees.' *This is in tenth grade.* I'd tell him, 'Yeah, sure, Billy.' He'd say, 'You watch me, Ruben, I'm going to the Yankees.' "

But suddenly, in the twelfth grade, when he could almost taste the dream of professional baseball, he was out on his ear. For someone else, being kicked off a team might have been painful, discouraging; for Billy it was devastating. He had a view of games and of winning that was different from the others. Being ahead, being on top—the leader, the winner—was about who he was as a human being. If he wasn't on top, he was nothing. He had not just been suspended. He had been canceled as a person.

# CHAPTER 3

Billy's senior picture is in the Berkeley High yearbook, *Olla Podrida*, for 1946. He graduated that year, say relatives and friends who attended the ceremonies with him at the University of California. But, strangely, Billy's school records at Berkeley are missing. School officials are uncertain why the records, kept under lock and key, are not there. Their absence, innocent or otherwise, is symbolic of Billy's final days as a schoolboy.

The night he graduated, Billy, Rube, and about seven other athletes—flatlanders—went up into the hills, going from goat party to goat party, eventually sleeping on someone's lawn. But the party had ended for Billy when he was thrown off the baseball team—at least so he thought.

He knew he had been a "prospect." He had made himself one. A number of Berkeley boys had gotten to know the trainer of the Oakland Oaks, Red Adams. But Billy's introduction to Adams, who devoted much of his life to helping area kids from troubled backgrounds, came from Augie Galan, who told him that Billy's talents were exceptional.

Adams encouraged Billy, and even introduced him to Casey Stengel, the Oaks' manager. It's likely that Billy, still in high school, got a tryout or at least worked out under Stengel's supervision—at Red Adams's prompting.

Many years later, Stengel recalled how Adams first introduced him to the player who shortly was to be known as his "pet." Stengel told a reporter from UPI in 1965, "I had this college shortstop I was looking at in a workout. He was neat as a pin. Did everything according to the book. Wore his pants just so, put his cap on straight and looked like something out of Spalding's guide.

"I made up my mind to sign him for $4,000 when the club trainer, Red Adams, came along and said I was signing the wrong guy. Told me he had a much better looking prospect. 'Show him to me,' I said.

"Well he brings this kid out and you never saw such a sight in your life. It was Martin here and you oughta see him. Uniform all dirty, one pants leg rolled up and the other falling down. Never saw anything like it before in my life."

Billy says that Stengel took part in several workouts that followed, hitting ground balls to him. "Red would keep telling Casey, who was the Oakland manager, about me," Billy wrote in his autobiography.

> I'd go out into the field and Casey would hit grounders to me and Red would keep telling Casey, "How'd you like him? See that kid out there, he's going to make it." Casey would say, "That skinny kid?" Red'd say, "You watch, Casey." Well, Casey kept hitting me grounders. I bet he hit between eighty and a hundred grounders, and I'd catch most of them, but some would bounce up and hit me, and I'd just throw them back, ready for some more.
>
> Casey told Red, "That little son of a gun. I've hit him so many grounders, I think he's trying to wear me out. He doesn't catch them all, but he doesn't back off from any either."

Though this moment of "discovery" has a touch of the apocryphal to it, Stengel did show up to watch Billy play. The occasion was a high school all-star game some time before Billy was kicked off his team. Billy didn't play particularly well, Rube DeAlba recalls, but he did hear encouraging words from Stengel at that game.

"We went to the clubhouse after the game," Rube said. "We walked down these stairs into a room—and there was Stengel sitting by himself. When he saw Billy, he called him over. 'You had a bad day, son, but keep on playin' ball,' he said, 'I think you have a future.' This was the manager of the Oaks telling him that. Believe me, I'll never forget that."

Billy didn't know it, but the Oaks had had their eyes on him for years. He was personally scouted by Johnny Babich, a team coach, who saw him play dozens of times over a three-year period—long before Stengel arrived on the scene.

"I began scouting Billy for Cookie DiVincenzo [the team's owner who sold the club to Brick Laws in 1946], never let him know I was scouting him at all," Babich said. "I told Casey about him, told him he's a fighter just like you. I told him he's a good ballplayer besides. He's got a good pair of hands and he's not a bad hitter. And he can run and he can field his position. And he got better, too. The only thing I told him I didn't like about him was his temper."

But Billy knew none of that. He was certain his chances for a baseball career had vanished when he was kicked off the high school team. He drifted that summer, working, hanging out in Kenney Park, playing for local league teams. And thinking of marriage. All through his school years, contrary to assertions he made in his autobiography, he had girlfriends—despite being sensitive about his looks; despite losing his virginity, he said, in a back-room encounter, accompanied by a buddy and a girl they were both after, in which "I didn't know where to put my peter."

From around the ninth grade on, he had a steady girl, Bobbi Pitter, a girl from a Canadian family who lived just on the other side of San Pablo Avenue, up toward Albany.

Bobbi's picture of Billy is in sharp contrast to the usual image of a dead-end kid. Billy, said Bobbi, "was terribly considerate to me—always. He was interested in me, of course, because of the way I looked, but what I liked most about him was that he was kind. He was a complex person. He was sweet and he was very protective. I knew all about his gang background, but he never showed me any of that. He never tried to be dominating as most boys in that time did."

Billy Martin met Bobbi Pitter at a church social club called The Ambrosians. The club was initiated and run by the St. Ambrose Catholic Church and was started by Father Dennis Moore, a priest who had been close to Billy and his family for years and who, it was said, prayed for Billy when he finally went off to play professional ball. Billy regarded him—as he did Augie Galan, Red Adams, and later Casey Stengel—as a kind of surrogate father. In addition to helping the needy, as he had the Downey family for years, Father Moore was immensely popular with young people; he was a good athlete, a junior high school basketball coach, and, according to one of the young women who frequented The Ambrosians, "a really good-looking guy who was a lot of fun."

The Ambrosians, though church-run, was principally set up as a recreational outlet for teenagers who were short on funds. "There was no attempt at indoctrination or anything to do with going to church, none of that," remembered Betty Firman, Dootch's ex-wife. "We danced a lot, we listened to records and jitterbugged a lot, we went there for boys."

Billy and his pal, Dootch, went there for girls—and met Bobbi and Betty. "We did everything together," Betty Firman said, "dancing, movies, shows, everything, all through high school." Eventually, Dootch fell in love with Betty and Billy fell in love with Bobbi. For both couples, marriage seemed inevitable. "I don't remember that we ever actually planned it," Bobbi said, "but it was assumed."

With Bobbi, Billy could be himself without having to prove anything to anyone. His soft side, which he felt comfortable showing only to people like his grandmother, he readily showed to his girlfriend.

Billy would stop by Bobbi's house every Sunday on his way to church. "He'd always stop in to see my parents. He'd stop and talk to my dad, who was a little frightening to Billy because he had thick eyebrows."

Betty saw something else hidden behind Billy's swagger: "I think there was something in him that always wanted a normal life, to sit in front of the fireplace, watch TV, read a book . . . the basics."

But there was this business of playing ball. That set Billy apart—from the basics and from Bobbi. One time when she and Billy were walking, he suddenly blurted out, "You know, one day I'm going to be a very famous person." She doesn't remember how she responded to this—whether she laughed or thought what he was saying was peculiar or even whether or not she believed him—only that she was struck by what he said. She had a brother who played professional baseball, and she knew enough about his world to know—when Billy did wind up with an offer to play professional ball that summer—their time together was coming to an end. She had no intention of being a baseball wife. He pursued her for a time, with passionate and jealous appeals, but no was no, and a door closed in Billy's life just as another opened wide.

The baseball offer seemed to come out of the blue. An Oaks official named Jimmy Hull came down to Kenney Park one day in July looking for Billy; the Idaho Falls team in the Class D Pioneer League, an affiliate of the Oaks, had had a rash of injuries and needed replacements immediately. At the urging of Johnny Babich, Red Adams, and Casey Stengel, Hull was dispatched to Kenney Park specifically to find Billy.

When he was offered two hundred dollars a month by Brick Laws, the Oaks' new owner, he readily accepted. That was more than he had ever earned at a job—he'd been an equipment man at Kenney Park, line worker at the Heinz pickle factory, cargo loader for a pharmaceutical company—and he was grateful to get it. But he had his wits about him, too. From the very first moment, he was hardly a lamb.

When Laws, who understood that Billy came from a poor family, asked him what kind of wardrobe he had, Billy said he told the owner that he had a suit, "but my uncle just died and they buried him in it." Did he have a suitcase? No, Billy said, no suitcase. The owner nodded and then added a three-hundred dollar bonus—for clothing and a suitcase.

Laws, according to several different accounts, then raised the issue of Billy's friends. The owner knew all about the West Berkeley Boys and Billy's high school suspension. In what would have been the first of many "good-boy" clauses in Billy's professional contracts, Laws asked Billy to agree to drop his "hoodlum" friends as a condition of employment.

Billy, as excited as he was about the prospect of becoming a pro, turned him down. *Take shit from no one.* Laws didn't care—at least not enough to press the matter. Billy was on his way to Idaho Falls.

Billy has embroidered the moment of his leavetaking into legend. It is Horatio Alger with a touch of Emma Lazarus. He told sportswriter Maury Allen, "I still remember that train station . . . It's a Chinese restaurant in Berkeley now. But that was some exciting day. I was off to play ball. I was a professional. I had dreamed about this day ever since I was a little kid. My family was very excited. Everybody came to the house to congratulate me, all my uncles and aunts and cousins, my brother Tudo, my uncle Ratcy, my uncle Sluice, my cousin Killer, they were all there. It was a great family night."

What Billy didn't include was the sense of loss and distress he felt over losing a relationship he cared about. Bobbi remembers that in the days before he left, Billy again reminded her that he was going to be famous. She remembered the tension and unhappiness between them. "He was eighteen and I was sixteen. You know, that's so long ago. Then he went away to play ball and I saw him off on the train when he went to Idaho Falls. . . . Oh, yes, it was difficult . . . I remember his getting on the train and that we were really upset. We might not have understood then that it was over . . . but it was . . ."

This was the first, but not the last, moment in his life when two different and irreconcilable dreams collided—and separated.

Billy played in thirty-two games with Idaho Falls, hitting an unspectacular .254, with no homers and only twelve RBIs in 114 plate appearances. In addition, he was something of a liability in the field. He committed sixteen errors, most of them on throws, an indication that he probably wasn't suited to the position he was playing. That alone must have weighed heavily on his mind. If he wasn't going to make it as a third baseman, then where? You needed an even better arm for shortstop—plus middle-infielder's range, which he did not seem to have.

The one on-field highlight anyone remembers from this month was a play Billy made at third one evening. With two out and a runner on first, a ball was spiked to Billy. The ball skipped just foul over the bag, but before the umpire made his call, Billy scooped the ball, flipped it to second, and then trotted off the field, drawing his team with him as he went. By quickness of wit rather than strength of arm, he had stolen one for his team.

When he returned to Berkeley that fall, his relationship with Bobbi Pitter was over. She had found someone else.

The following spring, Billy was shipped out to Oakland's Phoenix affiliate in the Class C Arizona-Texas League. It was a step up for him, but he didn't see it that way. He had had a good spring training with the Oakland Oaks and he was brash enough to let Casey Stengel know that he should have gotten a higher assignment.

"You sure blew one," he told the manager.

"Prove me wrong," the old man was reported to have returned.

"Wait and see," Billy answered.

The Arizona-Texas League was relatively new. It had started play in 1928, and its short history was already a colorful one. A couple of teams, Globe-Miami and, later, Bisbee-Douglas, were single teams representing pairs of mining towns that sometimes, as with Bisbee-Douglas, were at war with each other.

The strongest team in the league that year was from Juarez, Mexico, just across the border from El Paso. The Mexican connection, throughout the lower Rio Grande from Phoenix south into Texas, guaranteed sold-out ballparks and hot cross-national rivalries. The Mexicans remained a strong entry because minor league rules on eligibility in those days, which limited a player's time of service at different levels in the minors, didn't include experience in the Mexican League—which somehow was not considered "professional." The average age of the Juarez players, many of whom were grizzled, wily veterans of solid Mexican teams, was five to ten years older than the rest of the league.

In addition to a near-frontier atmosphere that prevailed, playing conditions were awful. A good portion of the games were played during the day when temperatures regularly soared above the one-hundred-degree mark. League fields were little more than brickyards, the infields harder than that. A player had to have unusual survival skills and a hide every bit as hard and baked as the turf. It turned out that Billy's survival skills—and his hide—needed no toughening that year. He had one of the best years any minor leaguer ever had. He hit an astonishing .393, leading all professional batsmen that season, and drove in an even more astonishing 173 runs.

Billy was determined and single-minded from the start. Poor playing conditions and housing conditions did not matter to him at all. "This was the one time in his life," said Buck Elliot, a teammate at Phoenix, ultimately its player-manager and a longtime friend, "when there were just no distractions in Billy's life. It was all baseball from day one."

The young players on the team, Billy included, were housed in a stifling barracks room beyond the right-field wall of the ballpark. Travel was done not even by bus but in two old station wagons hitched to trailer boxes filled with equipment. The first night at the ballpark, there was a near-fight between the younger members of the team and the older ones, players from the area who were there simply to fill the roster. There was a locker-room robbery—the team's bag of valuables had been lifted by a sneak thief while a team photo was being taken on field, and for hours afterward there were smoldering suspicions and dark hints among the new teammates. The matter was resolved when the thief was caught, but the tone was already set for the season.

But not for Billy. He took the uniform number one for himself and played that way right from opening day. He got off to a spectacular start. In his first sixteen at-bats, he had eight hits, including three doubles, two triples, a homer, and nine RBIs. He played errorless ball in the field and a week into the season, the local newspaper had already done a feature story on him.

Billy's Phoenix Senators were one of the best offensive minor-league teams ever. Taking every advantage of the hot dry climate, they averaged nearly eleven runs a game through the entire season. Three of their players, led by Billy, who usually hit third in the order, knocked in over 140 runs. By July fourth Billy already had over one hundred RBIs. "Any ball you hit," said one player, "seemed to bounce through on the kinds of fields we played on." The hits kept coming, and the averages kept soaring. For the longest time, Billy flirted with .400, and still had a chance—even with over five hundred at-bats—to get there till the last couple of games of the season.

Billy's potential was demonstrated by much more than numbers. He became the Senators' unofficial team leader. Supremely confident, totally fearless, his outgoing, combative nature just took over. He was alternately ebullient and fiery, friendly and feisty, becoming the team's principal cheerleader and, when the need arose, its chief enforcer.

There were two especially noteworthy career developments that took place during this season, the most important of which was Billy's being switched from third to second base about two-thirds of the way through. The move was totally unanticipated, having nothing to do with organizational plans for his future.

The team's regular second baseman then was the manager, Arky Biggs. Biggs was a hard-nosed, popular player-manager, a career minor leaguer who had an occasional weakness for the bottle and for a good on- or off-field brawl. One weekend afternoon, the Yankee affiliate, Bisbee, was in town for a series with the Senators. The Bisbee catcher that season was Clint Courtney, soon to be permanently engraved on Billy's all-time hit list. Courtney, long before he ever got to the majors, had a fierce reputation not only for hard play and fighting but also for bullying. He was a short, solidly built man, and his teammates referred to him as "Scrap Iron," but players on opposing teams worried about the scrap iron in his spikes. Courtney's trademark was to apply foot to flesh whenever he slid into a base.

On this particular play, Courtney sliced a clean single into right field but instead of stopping at first, he tried to stretch the hit into a double. The Senators' right fielder fired a strike to second base. Arky Biggs took the ball and waited for Courtney, who hit the ground, then raised his feet, cutting into Biggs who went down with him in a tangle. Biggs, grasping the baseball in fury, punched Courtney in the mouth. The force of the blow shattered a bone in the back of his hand, finishing him as a player for the season. The only other player on the team who had any experience as a middle infielder was Billy—though he had never till then played second. For the remainder of that game and then for most of the rest of his career, he was a second baseman.

The second development involved Courtney himself: Zale to Billy's Graziano. By this time, Courtney and Billy both had reputations on their respective teams. By then, Billy, though no bully, was like Courtney considered a ringleader whenever there was a team brawl.

In any event, the night following Biggs's run-in with Courtney, Billy's replacement at third base, an inexperienced reserve catcher named Eddie LeNieve, was spiked by Courtney, who was running from first base on a single to right. The play ended with Billy literally flying in from second base and leveling Courtney. "Billy was on Courtney before the dust cloud even settled," Buck Elliot said. "Boom, I mean it was instantaneous. And then it seemed like everybody on both benches got into it—it was one helluva brouhaha."

By season's end, the war between Billy and Courtney—and their teams—was so fierce that armed guards came out for the season finale between the two clubs at Bisbee.

"I'll never forget it," Buck Elliot said. "We went into Bisbee and Billy was hitting .400 with a chance to hold that for the season. We had a dressing room right behind the dugout with a little tunnel in between. Because I was the manager, I sort of went out first and here's this sheriff sitting on the edge of the dugout. He's the sheriff of Cochise County, name was Pruitt, and he was one of these mean, no-nonsense, little old guys.

"He said he wanted to talk to Billy Martin. I said, 'Oh my God, what did he do, what happened?' When Billy got out there, he then threatened him and me and the ballclub. He said there was going to be no horseshit going on of us fighting with their ballplayers, that he was going to have people armed with guns lining the field to see that that didn't happen. Well, right away, Billy starts *arguing* with him! So I grabbed him. Whoop! Whoop! Whoop! 'Billy, get back in the clubhouse,' I said. He went. I talked some more to this guy and when I saw that he wasn't about to budge, I got all our players off the field and back into the clubhouse and then went to the Bisbee office where I phoned the league president and told him what was happening. I let him know there was this goddamn sheriff and a whole posse of mean-looking deputies out there. Well, I guess he got ahold of the Bisbee ownership or something because when we got back out there, these guys weren't on the field. But they were everywhere throughout the stands. They stayed there through the whole game, cheering their asses off for Bisbee. That's how wild and wooly all that stuff between Billy and Courtney got to be."

Because Elliot got to know Billy well, he is one of the very few people able to furnish a clear picture of his state of mind in this early period of his career. More than anything, Billy was outgoing—outgoing about himself, his team, about life in general. All the hardships of minor league baseball were inconsequential to him. He was doing what he wanted and enjoying it immensely. He was a frequent visitor to Elliot's house, coming to regard the older player, his wife and young son almost as a kind of second family. "He was just wonderful with my son," Elliot said. "You can tell right off when someone likes kids or fakes it, and Billy really did enjoy kids—maybe because he was one himself. It was like he just enjoyed being part of a family."

And Billy was a dreamer. Although Elliot didn't believe then that Billy would ever make it to the majors—he just didn't have that kind of talent—he remembered that on long trips in the station wagon Billy almost never slept. He talked as Elliot drove, talked about his future, dreamed aloud about it. One night—this was 1947, Elliot pointed out—Billy, just chattering, began to broadcast a make-believe World Series game in the car. Everyone was sleeping except Elliot, who had his eyes on the road ahead.

"I kind of welcomed that on those long trips," Elliot said, "it was easy to get hypnotized driving hours on end on those roads. We were coming out of El Paso, I guess. I said, 'Billy, why don't you sit right behind me and I can hear you and that way I can keep my eye on the road.' Christ, you're going like hell on those roads and there wasn't no fifty-five-mile-per-hour speed limit then—and it's the middle of the night, 'cause the heat always made us travel at night, and everybody's asleep—and so I kinda looked forward to having him just talk, keeping me alert.

"Then this one time, he got to broadcasting this make-believe ballgame. It's eerie now when I think about it. But he starts broadcasting this game between the New York Yankees and I guess the Brooklyn Dodgers. But it's a World Series game, and he's playing second base—for the Yankees—playing second base and hitting fourth! That's when I said, 'Oh shit!' But he keeps right on. He was like Phil Rizzuto, describing the scene, making a joke or two, and a real Yankee fan, you know. He takes me right through the game, gets to the ninth inning, and sure as anything, he hits the home run to win it all. Then, of course, it was just Billy being full of himself—but Christ, five years later that's almost exactly what happened. I can never forget that. It's like he knew—he was with the Yankees, in the World Series, a star, the whole thing. But this is '47. Stengel was still in Oakland, Billy was just a kid buried in Class C. He made all of that up—and then he just stepped into it."

The Arizona-Texas League ended play that year with the season still running on the West Coast where weather permitted a schedule of almost two hundred games. Billy was rewarded for his spectacular season in two important ways. For one, he was named the league's Most Valuable Player. At an awards dinner, he was flushed with both excitement and gratitude but also ready to stand up for what he had done. When he was presented with a plaque that recorded his accomplishments, he protested, "Hey! I hit .393, not .390!"

But his great reward was that he was called up to Oakland for the final month of the season. To Billy, to any West Coast player, the Pacific Coast League in those days was a major league. All along the three-thousand mile strip from San Diego to Seattle, Coast League baseball was entrenched, with top-of-the-line young players emerging from strong college programs—like Jackie Jensen, the all-American football and baseball player from the University of California—mixing with older players who had once had substantial careers in the majors and who were looking to extend their playing days nearer their hometowns.

Billy later told an interviewer that when he got to Oakland he thought he was "in the highest league I would ever see." But he also assumed that he was ready to play there. He looked around and he saw players he respected, who had years of experience on him—players like Nick Etten, the old Yankee first baseman; Cookie Lavagetto, the ex-Dodger; Ernie Lombardi, the ex-Giant and Cincinnati catcher—and he believed he could play with them. All he needed was the chance. He arrived on the scene as he had left that spring, willing and unintimidated, but now even more convinced that he belonged.

The immediate problem was there was no place for him in the starting lineup. The Oaks, generally referred to by local sportswriters as "the Nine Old Men," were solid at every position. Billy was simply not regarded as a likely third baseman. Despite his season at the bat, he lacked power, a conventional requirement for the position. Also, his fielding remained suspect. Though he led all third basemen in the Arizona-Texas League in putouts and assists, he also led the league in errors—a reminder that, as strong as his arm was, it wasn't strong enough for third.

Second base was also filled. The team's second baseman then was Dario Lodigiani, a career .260 hitter with the A's and White Sox who at thirty-one still had good years left.

Even so, Billy did fit in his manager's plans for the future. Casey Stengel had taken an instinctive shine to the youngster, and he wanted to use him and other young players to break the comforting but limiting wall of age on the Oaks. The team had done well under Stengel but hadn't won anything yet. They had finished second in Stengel's first year as manager, and were on their way to a fourth-place finish when Billy joined the team that September. Stengel, better than anyone, knew that the Oaks' best chance of moving up in the standings lay with an infusion of youth—not youth for its own sake, but the kind Billy brought, the kind that might regularly kick up dust and awaken tired blood.

Billy provided an immediate lift. Though he was used sparingly that fall, his Berkeley background along with his well-publicized combativeness made him a popular figure before he ever set foot on the field. Fans, already familiar with him, even those only familiar with his reputation, applauded the move to promote him from Phoenix. Stengel himself saw in the young player something of a kindred spirit.

On the surface, the two men could not have been more dissimilar. The one was garrulous, laid back, wily, a raconteur, an eccentric who had been around long enough to know how difficult the game really was, and how winning, while essential, was only the flip side of losing; the young man, on the other hand, was pushy, unabashed, nervous, impatient, and too inexperienced to understand anything but winning—a trait that would stay with him for the rest of his life.

What initially drew these two men to each other was undoubtedly professional. Stengel followed Billy while he was in high school, as he would have any local player who was highly recommended. Billy, on the other hand, had a natural desire to ingratiate himself with the manager of the local professional team.

But beyond this purely opportunistic view, there was clearly affection between them, something that went well beyond the dugout and the field. Stengel was captivated by Billy's freshness, tenacity, and, above all, by his obvious appetite for the game.

But Billy was not just a young workhorse. What also touched the old man, what may even have reminded him of himself as a younger player, was a certain sense that Billy had of himself that allowed him to speak and act on impulse, as though he simply could not help himself. At eighteen, charming, raffish, pugnacious, even sweet beneath his street swagger, he was capable of off-field misadventures of many kinds, but never of betraying his absolute fidelity to the game. He was an original, like Stengel—someone who moved to his own drummer but whose dancing feet contained almost perfect baseball sense. Stengel, childless himself, did not find it hard to adopt Billy as both a professional project and a prodigal son.

From the start, he called Billy "kid." He had him sit next to him in the dugout; he explained different aspects of running a ballgame. And Billy willingly drank it in—and talked back to the old man whenever the spirit moved him.

One time, Stengel, convinced that Billy's chances of making it would improve if he played middle infield, knowing that he had recently played some second base in Phoenix, tried to work with him on making the double play at second base.

"I asked him how he makes it," Stengel told Norman Lewis Smith years later, "and he shows me and I say it's all right. So he says to me, freshlike, 'Show me the way you want to do it and I'll do it, but I still don't see what's wrong with my way. I got quick hands and quick feet.'

"I tell him, 'You ain't on the dance floor jitterbugging,' and he says to me, 'Don't knock it because you can't do it.' Another kid I'll tell to take off his uniform and get out of my sight, but not this kid, because he wants to play so bad it sticks out all over him."

Whatever insecurity Billy might have felt about not winning a position for himself, he remained supremely confident that things would work out. Part of that no doubt had to do with his own general cocksureness, but part of it, too, had to do with Stengel. Billy knew by then that the old man was firmly in his corner. He, as well as Stengel, knew that he could get away with behavior that others would not dare to indulge. He knew instinctively that his bond with the old man was based on their mutual passion for the game, a passion that excused hijinks and excesses. Stengel, more than anyone, had given Billy permission to be himself without penalty. He was the first baseball person who had ever done that—and Billy loved him for it.

# CHAPTER 4

In Oakland, playing first for Casey Stengel and then for Charlie Dressen, Billy came to belong in a way that was different from Phoenix, Idaho Falls, the Berkeley High Yellow Jackets, the West Berkeley Boys. For the first time, his deep familial longing was joined to the sense of belonging to an exclusive, skilled group of ballplayers. What had been awakened for him in Kenney Park, and thwarted and kindled in his own home, was answered in a new and very different way with the Oakland Oaks, his hometown team—as good as the majors for any West Coast kid. He was now a professional baseball man.

Stengel and Dressen were as different as night and day, and so were their teams—and Billy's place on each. First, with Stengel, there was the joy and the audacity of it. He was the old man's kid among those Nine Old Men. He could be fresh and cheeky—outrageous—and could get away with it because he was a pet and because, above all, he could play. He could play his position, and sometimes, when the old man let him—which seemed pretty nearly always, he could play provocateur and jester.

In his first spring camp with the Oaks, Billy—as he did throughout his career—sought to share his good fortune with others. He had his buddies from West Berkeley all try out with the Oaks, and some of them—Dick Sabatini, Dootch Firman, Howard Noble—came to camp with him in 1948, though only Billy stayed on with the team.

Dick Sabatini, a cousin, remembers how full of baseball that Stengel camp was: it was a boy's paradise of fundamentals, with special coaching in "all the little things" from great old players like Vince DiMaggio, Ernie Lombardi, and Cookie Lavagetto.

Sabatini also remembers the mischief. Billy, he recalled, far from being a greenhorn in this camp, cut a wide swath, apparently unconcerned about what anyone, even the old man, might think. One night during spring training, there was a party "with a lot of girls," Sabatini recalled. He wound up going off with a girl Billy had wanted. When he returned that night to the room he shared with Billy and Howard Noble, his roommates had sawed off the legs of his bed, hoisted it up on wastepaper baskets, short-sheeted his bedclothes, and filled the interior of the bed with shaving cream, lotion, and talcum. In the pitch dark, it all collapsed and engulfed Sabatini as he got into bed.

On another occasion, Billy, between workouts, brought a young girl—a groupie or a hooker—up to the room. His intention, Sabatini said, was "to share her among the three of us." The young players were staying in a team hotel, owned by Casey Stengel, so this daylight maneuver seemed risky to begin with. The young woman, however, had no intention of entertaining three men. She had accompanied Billy intending to be with him only. But Billy's notions of gallantry or even minimal consideration seemed not to apply when it came to women for hire. There was an argument, Sabatini remembered, and then "Billy just bopped her one—shut her up."

At that point, Howard Noble stepped in, Sabatini recalled, and said that he would quiet the woman down. He ushered his two roommates out of the room, closed the door, and then—time passed. Sabatini said that he and Billy figured out soon enough that Noble had merely moved in on this young woman for himself.

Billy plotted an immediate revenge. He ordered Sabatini to bring him a chair and then to unwind the long hose for the fire extinguisher that was on the wall. He climbed up on the chair, knocked in the transom, and then proceeded to flood the room in which Noble and the young woman were cowering for their lives. "He laid down two or three inches of water all over the floors," Sabatini said. "There was so much it went dripping down to the floors below—and this was Stengel's hotel, I mean he actually owned it, with those fancy gas lamps in the hallways—Billy must have caused thousands of dollars worth of damage."

Sabatini was sure all of them were going to be kicked off the team—at least. But he was wrong. Billy simply assured him the old man would be in his corner. "I told Billy, 'We're gonna get our asses sent home.' He just laughed and said not to worry."

Sabatini then recalled what happened next.

"So we go to practice that afternoon and sure enough Stengel found out about it. Billy's still laughing because he thinks it's funnier than hell. So then after practice, whaddaya think? Stengel says, 'Noble, Billy, and Sabatini, I want you three assholes in the back room right now.' So we go in the back room and Casey just reads us the riot act. 'You goddamned kids, you know how much your goddamn little prank is gonna cost, do you have any idea blah blah blah blah and so on—I oughta bust your asses and send you home.' Well, all through this Billy is sitting there with this big grin on his face. Casey looks up and finally sees this. You know what he does? He starts laughing, too. 'You dago son of a bitch,' he says, laughing, and he just turns around and walks out. I said, 'Billy, does that mean we're still here?' He says, 'Yeah, I told you not to worry about it.' "

Billy was there not just because Stengel loved him but because he felt he needed him. He believed Billy was a legitimate prospect, but, even more important, that he could be a real help in Oakland's quest for a pennant.

When the season began, the Oaks were not highly regarded. According to most observers, the San Francisco Seals were the heavy favorites that year and surged out to an early lead in the first months of the race.

When play began that season, though Billy still didn't have a guaranteed starting job, he fit into the team more like a settled veteran than an uncertain rookie. Some of that had to do with the confident relationship he had with Stengel and some of it with the composition of the team itself. The "Nine Old Men" were also, for the most part, old Kenney Park compatriots. There was infielder Dario Lodigiani, Cookie Lavagetto, Billy Raimondi, the longtime catcher, outfielders Mel Duezabou and Les Scarsella, and then Will Hafey, the left-handed pitcher, and Ernie Lombardi, the ex-National League catcher, both of whom were acquired in important mid-season trades. "Yeah, he was the same kid from Kenney Park we used to take around all the time," remembered Lodigiani. "We used to get quite a bang out of him—and he was quite a guy."

Initially, Billy rode the bench. The team opened that year with Merrill Combs at third, Ray Hamrick at short, and Lodigiani playing second. Billy occasionally pinch hit and filled in as a late inning replacement. Later, Billy was mixed into Stengel's new and provocative system of platooning. When the Oaks faced right-handed pitching, Cookie Lavagetto, who had been inserted at third to allow Combs to move to short, was benched, while Dario Lodigiani was moved to third, opening a space for Billy at second. Against left-handers, Billy saw no action at all.

Though Billy, from his usual seat on the bench next to Stengel, learned from him, he chafed mightily against the way he was used. "He used to yell at Casey all the time when he was benched," Dario Lodigiani said. "I mean, he would let Casey know that he was madder 'n hell. And Casey used to tell him, 'Goddamn it, you little guy, you're lucky you're on the club.' 'Course Casey used to get a big bang out of Billy. Billy was a young guy and a cocky son of a bugger, but not in an arrogant way—it was in a way where you know that whatever he said or did you had to laugh."

Getting Billy worked up was apparently one of the features of life in the clubhouse. The Oaks played in a ballpark with a short porch in right field, and Stengel wanted as many left-handed pull hitters as possible in the damaging slots of the lineup to take advantage of that. Hafey, even though he was a pitcher, hit well and could pull the ball, so he usually hit sixth in the lineup whenever he pitched—with Billy being dropped to ninth. Stengel regularly posted the lineup on a board in the clubhouse, and there was a certain glee, if not flourish of hand, in his placing Billy's name last on the board. Billy, no matter how many times it happened, used to erupt when he saw his name posted at the bottom of the lineup. "He screamed at Casey one time," Dario Lodigiani said, " 'Godarnit, you've got me hitting with the groundskeepers,' and the old man just laughed."

Billy was also teased about his nose, his clothes, his street manner. Mel Duezabou remembers that Billy—almost to the day he died more than four decades later—used to call the house and identify himself only as "Beaky Buzzard." "He'd always ask for Henry Hawk because I had a big nose, too," Duezabou said.

Sometimes the teasing went too far. Nick Etten, the ex-Yankee first baseman who was the Oaks' principal power hitter, used to needle Billy constantly. One time, the needling led to a near brawl on a team flight when he leaped to his feet and went after Etten. "This was forty thousand feet in the air," Lodigiani said, "but Billy went right after him. Nick, you know, liked to rib Billy—we all did, yeah, the nose, you know—so he jumps up and starts to go right after him. And we're all telling him, 'Hey, at least wait till you get to the ground—we're forty thousand feet in the air!' "

Stengel, like most of the team, knew that Billy had real deficiencies as a player. It was Stengel's system then—and always—to see that young players linked up with older ones in order to learn. He had Billy first room with Mel Duezabou, so that he might eventually learn to improve his hitting. Duezabou was a career .300 hitter in the minors, a student of the art, someone willing and able to explain things, someone who saw Billy's weaknesses. "I'll tell you one thing," he said, "when he first came up he couldn't hit his hat. I don't know what the hell happened to him. He hit real well in class C or D or whatever it was, but once he got here he hit terrible."

As soon as Billy's average began to climb, Stengel, who observed that student and pupil both seemed to have a shared love of late hours, had another veteran, Cookie Lavagetto, move into the picture. Lavagetto, at Stengel's prompting, went up to Duezabou on the field one day and simply announced that henceforth he would be rooming with Martin. "Cookie was a strange guy," Duezabou said. "He just walked up to me one day and said, 'I'm rooming with Billy from now on. You're thirty-one years old and not going anywhere, and this kid's going to the major leagues.' He became Billy's roommate—which was no problem for me."

Lavagetto and Dario Lodigiani then took Billy under their wing. The two men, both aware of Billy's physical limitations—stiff hands, limited range, no smoothness—but fully cognizant of his special appetite for the game, tried to show him some of the intricacies of middle infield play. "When I was playing second and Harry [Cookie Lavagetto] was playing third, we spent a lot of time with Billy during infield practice and during batting practice when we were out in the field," Lodigiani said. "We worked with him on how to shift his feet in making the double play, how to pivot around the bag. We tried to get him going into the bag at all times: Just stand a little short of the bag and then when you see which way the throw was coming you shift your feet that way. A throw that went to his right side, he'd step on the bag with his left foot; a throw to the left side, he'd shift over and hit the bag with his right foot. And then, you know, he used to kind of wind up before he threw the ball, so we taught him how to shorten his arm, so to speak, so that he could get rid of the ball quicker."

Billy became particularly attached to Lavagetto. The older man, who died in 1990, not only worked with him on the field but off as well. Dick Sabatini recalls that Billy shared with him stories of how Lavagetto worked with him in hotel rooms on the road. "Cookie'd put a pillow on the floor in front of a mirror and make him practice the double play pivot by the hour," Sabatini said. Billy later said that Lavagetto taught him how to cut a baseball on his belt buckle so that pitchers could throw illegal drops.

Lavagetto also taught Billy how to intimidate incoming runners at second base on double plays: Aim for their heads, drill them if you have to. In a Kenney Park softball game years later, Jack Setzer, playing alongside Billy that day, remembers actually nailing Lavagetto during the game—and Lavagetto's reaction:

"Billy was playing shortstop on our team—it's slow pitch softball—and all of the guys were playing. They could have hit the ball three miles but instead, they're just stroking singles and doubles," Setzer said. "Anyway, Lavagetto's the runner on first and they hit the ball to the other side of the infield and as I come across and catch the double-play throw, I'm doing just what Billy taught me. I hit the bag, I turn around, and I'm just about to let go of the ball—and there's Lavagetto bearing down on me. I drilled him right between the eyes with this softball. I thought, 'What have I done?' Everybody comes running out to see if he's hurt and he's laying there on the ground and he starts laughing. He looked up at me and he says, 'Don't worry about it, son, I shoulda been down. You did exactly the right thing.' I thought, Oh God—it made me feel good but I still felt so bad."

Lavagetto was apparently tireless in his willingness to teach. He took Billy into restaurants where he could make sure his young charge had a square meal and where, with a little time to burn, he could get him to work on odd things. "He'd make me sit in a restaurant and make me stare at a wall without blinking my eyes," Billy said years later "I'd practice that for hours. Try it sometime. It isn't easy. He had me do that because he felt that when you were up at the plate, the ball would go by so fast that if you accidentally blinked, that fraction of a second would be enough of a distraction to make you miss the ball." Lavagetto simply kept talking to Billy, using every opportunity to fill his imagination with the tips, shortcuts, little devices that any player—especially one whose natural gifts were limited—could use to extra advantage.

As the season progressed, Stengel increasingly found playing time for Billy, turning him into a solid regular. He was "the Kid" among the "Nine Old Men," a crowd favorite among crowd favorites. During the second week of July, the team climbed into first place and then proceeded to wage a seesaw struggle the rest of the way with the Seals and the powerful San Diego Padres—with Max West, Luke Easter, and Al Rosen. Billy by midseason had turned into a solid if unspectacular hitter (he finished the season hitting a respectable .277 with 3 homers and 42 RBIs), and a capable and aggressive middle infielder.

Most importantly, he was the exact sort of leader Stengel was looking for: an agitator and an enforcer. He was the team's "holler-guy," sometimes, to the amusement of his teammates, losing his voice in the course of a game. He was the fiercest of bench-jockeys in an age when hair-curling vituperation and insult spewed forth from the dugout in even greater quantities than tobacco juice. And as he had been everywhere else, he was a brawler.

There were classic fights—remembered by fans up and down the coast that year—between Billy and Lou Stringer of the Hollywood Stars, and Billy and Frankie Austin of Portland, a team managed by Jim Turner, later pitching coach for the Yankees.

Al Rosen had a fierce and memorable run-in with him. Rosen, aware that Stengel regularly used to order his pitchers to hit opposing batters in certain situations, had been nailed in this game following a homer by another San Diego player. When Rosen, trotting down to first, said something to the Oaks' pitcher, Johnny Tost, Tost shouted a racial slur at Rosen, who is Jewish. Rosen immediately went for Tost: "I made a left turn and went right up to the mound and disposed of him rather quickly," he said, "then all of a sudden I sensed something. It was Billy. He came up from behind and threw this punch that landed in back of me and missed. I tried to get to him and couldn't. He and I were oil and water after that. I always wanted a piece of him. I just didn't fancy sucker punches being thrown at me . . . and that's what he was into."

Rosen was sure there was nothing racial in Billy's behavior, just this uncontrollable fighting impulse. That was what drove Billy in everything. Billy fought others, he fought himself and his own limitations, he fought because that was the only way he was going to get where he knew he was going.

One time, after he had become a regular, he suffered what probably should have been a season-ending knee injury. On a hard, close play at second base, a runner hit him full force in the knee with his spikes. Blood poured all over his uniform. Billy was lifted from the field that day by Ernie Lombardi, the huge catcher, who cradled him in his arms and carried him to the locker room where, on the spot, Billy demanded that his wounds be treated immediately—no hospital stays, no encouragement for others to take his place.

Billy swallowed a couple of stiff shots of bourbon and then four players, one holding down each of his limbs, pinned him tight to the trainer's table as twenty-eight stitches were taken to close his wounds. Later, Billy bet with anyone who was willing that he would be back in the lineup in less than two weeks. It's not clear if anyone took him up on his bet. What is clear is that, even if he was only wagering against the force of his own fear, he won. He was back in the lineup six games later. No one and nothing—not even a major injury—was going to stand in his way.

In the days and weeks that followed, the Nine Old Men and the Kid won the first pennant for Oakland in twenty-one years, sweeping the two-game Governor's Cup playoff afterward. In appreciation for all that Billy had done, Brick Laws and the Oaks gave Billy a new car—a shiny black Chevrolet to replace the battered old one with its fender falling off that he'd been driving.

But even before the parade through downtown Oakland celebrating the team's championship was done, everything changed. Casey Stengel had received a very different kind of reward: He was named the next manager of the New York Yankees and, as much as he might have wanted to include the Kid in the package, he was leaving Billy behind. Baseball was baseball.

Billy later said to anyone who asked that he was "a little disappointed" by Stengel's decision, if indeed there was one, to leave him behind. But there was more to it than that. His benefactor, his "father," had abandoned him. His feelings were closer to devastation than disappointment.

"He was really upset with Casey back then because he didn't take him with him to the Yankees," said Ken Irvine, his brother-in-law.

"But he never would say anything bad about Casey," Billy's half-sister Pat Irvine said.

No one knew what that year had taken out of him. He had put everything into it. All the fight and fire, his high spirits, his leadership, his accomplishments had had a purpose and had come with a terrible price.

"He had wanted to do well so badly it just killed him when things didn't work out," his sister said. "If he did badly in a game, he'd be so mad, so disgusted. 'I popped out, I didn't do this, I didn't do that,' he'd say. It was like he didn't know how to leave it alone."

"The thing was," Ken Irvine said, "this wasn't the Arizona-Texas

League. He thought he could go directly to the major leagues, it was the logical next step. So he felt every time he booted a ball, it cost him his career."

Billy, nervous and jumpy, just hung out over that winter. Mario DeGennaro, his cousin, and Howard Noble traveled around with him in his new car. They went bar hopping a lot; Billy usually spent his time with different girls he knew, his friends having to wait for him till he got back from wherever he went.

Mario DeGennaro became tired of running around with a big shot and, literally, asked out of the car Billy was driving one day. While the car was idling at an intersection, DeGennaro spotted a help wanted sign in a store window. He got out of the car to answer it.

"Billy said, 'Don't be stupid, man, get back in the car.' I said, 'No, no, I can't be hanging around with you all my life. You're on your way and I'm on my way to nowhere."

But Billy was unsure that he was on his way. With Stengel gone, he now had to create himself all over again. And the Oaks' new manager, Charlie Dressen, was as different from Stengel as Stanley from Livingstone.

Where Stengel was easygoing and good-natured, Dressen was sharp-eyed, imperious, and at times arrogant. He ran a game by command not by suggestion, and his view of players was proprietary: They played for him and through him. "He was a strategist and a very shrewd manager," said George Metkovitch, the team's right fielder, who had been instrumental in Oakland's pennant drive the season before, "but the thing was he wanted everybody to know it."

Dressen seemed to bring into the clubhouse everything Stengel had kept out the year before. Tenseness and tightness were the rule not the exception. Stengel regularly rewarded his players for winning; anytime the team won, Mel Duezabou said, "there was a case of beer waiting for us in the clubhouse." He would reach into his own pocket and pass out five- or ten-dollar bills after important wins or double-header sweeps and tell his players to have a good restaurant meal on him somewhere. "With twenty-five or twenty-seven guys on the team, that came to some money, too," Bill Raimondi said.

Dressen rewarded no one. He expected performance because that was what players were there for. He demanded effort and loyalty because a team was an army, the game a war. When he didn't get what he was looking for there were fines. There were fines for everything.

"The only time I ever heard Casey mention the word 'fine,' " said

Dick Sabatini, "was when he talked to us about kids. Casey had this thing about kids. There used to be Kids Days at the ballpark and the first two or three hundred got in for free. 'They are the future of the game, the future customers,' he said. 'Anyone who doesn't sign an autograph for them can expect to be fined.' But that was it."

If a baseball season was a long military campaign, Dressen saw himself as a general. Where Stengel had grown up playing under, learning under, and, to a certain extent, suffering under John McGraw, Dressen, a small man who had battled his way as a professional football player before turning to baseball, had been a teammate and friend of Leo Durocher's at Cincinnati, later going to work for him as a third-base coach. Dressen, as well as Stengel, understood that the test of an army was its leadership. But where Stengel early on had learned that an army marches on its stomach, Dressen at an equally early age had learned that it marches to a winning strategy devised by the general himself.

Dressen approached a game with a plan and a highly elaborate intelligence system. He had perhaps the most intricate set of signs and signals any team had ever seen. There are a number of baseball people who insist today that current signal calling, with its baffling shuffle of indicators and semaphoric gestures, owes directly to Dressen. Sign stealing was yet another modern weapon in his arsenal.

"Dressen was a third-base coach at Cincinnati," said Johnny Babich, Stengel's third-base coach at Oakland and a former teammate of Dressen's, "and I'm telling you he used to say he could steal any pitcher's sign anytime. 'Course I never agreed with that approach because a pitcher can always change what he's going to do in his windup, but Charlie knew anyway."

Stengel, on the other hand, had an almost ludicrously simple set of signals. "God, did we have easy signals," Babich said. "If I had my back to first base, guy was on first, and I backed away from him, why he knew it was time to go. That was the steal signal. The take sign was when you walked toward the hitter from the coach's box. That was it. When we had three and oh on a hitter and we wanted him to swing away, we'd hold up both hands and practically yell out, 'Go to it!' There are so many damn signs today I don't see how a young ballplayer going up can even know what he's looking for."

But Dressen changed far more than the signals. He did not want Stengel's team, he wanted his own. He cut people, made trades, pickups. Gone was Nick Etten, the left-handed power hitter with his forty-three home runs; gone, too, was much of the pitching staff that had worked so closely with Stengel and Johnny Babich (also gone) the previous year. The Hafey brothers—Tom and Will—were sent on their way. Billy Raimondi came to the park one day and was told to walk across the field to the visitor's side because he had just been traded to Sacramento, the afternoon's opposition. And as for "the Kid," Stengel's "pet," Dressen decided, just because he was so young and had been so obviously favored, he was going to have to fight for a job like any other young player.

At first, Billy, like many of the other players on the team, felt turned off by Dressen. "When I first met Charlie, I didn't like him at all," he told Phil Pepe. "He had a tremendous ego and it was always 'I did this' and 'I did that,' never 'we' or 'they' or 'the team.' That pissed off a lot of people, especially his players, and I admit it pissed me off too."

But Billy had another problem. The older players had had their careers. He had not. He had to prove himself all over again, he had to make Dressen see who he was.

There is a widely told story about Billy in these early months that indicates just how he won Dressen over. The incident involved a spring exhibition game the Oaks were playing against the Cleveland Indians. Billy played through the game on a Sunday morning in Oakland, collecting a couple of hits, sparkling in the field—and then asked Dressen for permission to drive down to Stockton that afternoon to play another game for the team's "B" squad. "Cookie might need me," he explained to Dressen, referring to Cookie Lavagetto, who was managing the other squad for that game. Dressen gave permission for Billy to go and from then on never thought twice about who the team's second baseman was.

"Anybody who wants to play ball that bad belongs on my team," he is reported to have said in several different accounts of the incident. But Dressen quickly saw that he could get much more from a player who was that willing to play. Just as Casey had seen something of himself in the raffish and unpredictable battler who had this attachment to winning baseball games, so Dressen saw something of his own burning temperament in this wisp of a player.

As Casey had once seen that Billy could be an igniter, Dressen saw that he could go even further. "Take charge!" he used to yell at him from the dugout. "Talk back to them! Holler at them!"

And how Billy responded. It was as though Dressen was another manager who had given him permission to just be himself.

"I'll tell you one thing about Billy," George Metkovitch said, "when he put that uniform on, all he wanted to do was play and play hard. . . . He wasn't even the manager then but he'd come right after you. 'We want to win,' he'd say to somebody, 'the majority of us want to win. If you don't, take a powder.' "

Even though Billy fought for Dressen, he also stood up to him. This was no relationship of father and son. It was more like fighter and fighter. There was one incident, during the first months of the season, when Billy nearly came to blows with Dressen. The incident, recounted by Dressen himself years later, marked the actual turning point in their relationship.

In this particular game—against Sacramento—Billy had a serious run-in with Walt Dropo, Sacramento's huge first baseman. Following an early-inning single, Billy jockeyed into a lead off first base, with Dropo holding him close. On one of the pitcher's pickoff throws to the base, Dropo quite methodically crunched Billy beneath him in an effort to block the base. Billy was enraged, but with a mountain of muscled flesh lying on top of him he was hardly in a position to do anything. He swore to Dropo that he would get him if he had the chance later in the game.

With the Oaks ahead by a run in the last inning, Billy had his opportunity. Dropo singled with one out. The next batter then hit what looked like a sure, game-ending double play ball to the shortstop, Artie Wilson. Wilson whipped the ball in plenty of time to Billy who, instead of immediately relaying to first to complete the double play, took aim at the slow-moving Dropo, lumbering toward second base. Firing the ball as hard as he could, he tried to hit Dropo right between the eyes. He missed. The ball whistled past Dropo's head and then past the first baseman, skipping over toward the stands. Instead of the game being over, the tying run had been allowed to reach base. Fortunately for Billy, no further damage was done. But the matter did not end there.

Following the game, Dressen confronted Billy in the dugout and then again in the locker room. Billy listened for so long but then no further. He told the manager to shut up and then that he knew nothing about baseball. He stalked off to the shower—with Dressen following almost on his heels. The argument resumed in the shower stall itself with Dressen, splattered by water, shouting at Billy that unless he immediately apologized, he was fined two hundred dollars.

Billy gave Dressen his answer the following day. He marched into the owner Brick Laws's office and proceeded to peel off two hundred dollars in small bills.

"What's that for?" Laws was supposed to have said.

"I'm paying my fine," Billy told him.

Laws declined to accept the money at that point, telling Billy that it would be deducted from his next paycheck. A team meeting followed later that afternoon, and at it Billy asked to speak and offered an apology for what he had said to Dressen the previous day. Dressen accepted the apology, forgave the fine, and—in telling the story years later—indicated that the incident had somehow cemented his relationship with Billy.

"That Martin was such a fresh kid," he told a reporter years later, remembering what happened with an affectionate smile.

Billy, for his part, wound up having a better year for Dressen than he had had for Stengel. While the team faded from the race during the last month and a half of the season, Billy hit .286, drove in ninety-two runs, even showed some pop in his bat with twelve homers. In over six hundred plate appearances, he struck out only forty-nine times and he stole eleven bases.

"I wound up liking Charlie a lot," Billy said, years later. "I found out what a nice man he really was. He loved to cook and he was always cooking something up in the ballpark. His favorites were crab claws and chili and he would cook up batches and invite the players to come in and feast."

Dressen, over time, came to have something like paternal feeling for Billy, although it is not clear that Billy ever fully reciprocated.

Mel Duezabou recalled an incident from the '49 season that seemed to reveal Dressen's feeling for Billy. Just prior to one of the team's road trips, the crusty manager came up to Billy, concerned that his dress might be an embarrassment to him. He wanted to help Billy out. " 'You can't go off on a road trip with shoes like that,' Charlie said to Billy. 'Here, let me help you.' " Duezabou recalls that Dressen then went to his own locker and pulled out a pair of two-toned green and lizard shoes, which he handed to Billy. " 'You wear these,' he said. Then when Charlie walked away," Duezabou said, "Billy says, 'I'm not gonna wear those shoes. If I wear those shoes in my neighborhood, they'd kill me.' "

This time with Dressen was at least as important as his time with Stengel. His legacy to Billy was not a pair of shoes but a managerial style. Dressen hated losing—just like Billy. His post-game tirades were almost identically duplicated by Billy decades later. Dressen believed that other teams lost games more than his own team won them, and that those losses were set off by unsettling and aggressive play—exactly what Billy followed. Billy picked up the same terms of leadership—the team as an army, the manager as a general, the game as a war—that Dressen showed him. Billy saw how much advantage could be taken with sign stealing and with an intelligence system. Billy also saw that it was possible to reach people even if they didn't like you. It was possible to manage well without the lovable social graces of a Casey Stengel.

One evening in early September, with the Oaks slowly sinking out of the race, there was a nice hometown crowd at the old wooden ballpark in Emeryville. One of the ballpark's charms was a slowly circling blimp with a light belt of different messages, usually advertisements, sometimes news flashes. On this particular night, there was a news flash: Billy Martin had been sold to the New York Yankees! The players on the field were apparently alerted to the news by the gathering roar of the crowd. Though rumors had been circulating for weeks that Billy was headed for the Yankees, this was the first that anyone had heard it officially.

There are several differing accounts of how Billy reacted to the news of what, after all, was the fulfillment of a dream. On the one hand, there was obvious ebullience, carefully noted by the local press, the public side of feelings which, in private, turned out to have some edges. But Billy had some reservations about signing a contract with the Yankees. The premier major league team in the game was offering him less money than he was making with the Oakland Oaks. The Yankee offer was $7,500 for one year—$1,500 less than he was making with the Oaks—with no bonuses, no clauses, no incentives to sweeten the pot. A teammate of Billy's, Jackie Jensen, was purchased with Billy at the same time, part of the same package. Jensen received $65,000 as a signing bonus, befitting his status as a potential superstar but also reinforcing Billy's as a throw-in.

What Billy did not know then was that some very knowledgeable baseball people—including Casey Stengel, who had never forgotten Billy—regarded Jensen as the throw-in. Jensen's big price-tag was a sort of disguise for these people, enabling the Yankees to pick off Martin before other teams did.

There is another story about Billy's mind-set as he joined the Yankees. Sometime during the following spring, long before the season began, he was approached by one of the New York sportswriters. The writer was not quite sure who he was and wanted to know how he wanted to be addressed.

"Billy," said this youngster on the threshold of all that he had dreamed about. "The name's Billy Martin and don't you forget it."

# CHAPTER 5

Everywhere he had been, in everything he had done—from the effort of simply surviving his first months on Earth until the present—he was not supposed to make it. In each place where survival had been called for, he had not only done that, he had triumphed. In the storm of his birth he was called "Bello," he had won in the streets, he had won in the parks, in the schools, in the minor leagues, against long odds and even friendly opinion. This ability of his had nothing to do with God-given gifts; he could not hit a ball like Babe Ruth, run like Jesse Owens, think like Einstein, buy his way like J. P. Morgan. At each step along the way, his task had been the same—to make himself better than he was or at least better than people thought he was. His gift was one of heart and imagination: he could, no matter his size or the shape of his features, create himself in the unlikeliest circumstances. And his most formidable challenge loomed: to make it as a New York Yankee. A boy's dream was one thing, a man's work another.

Billy's first contact with the Yankees came in January 1950, a month before spring training. The Yankees that year ran a hush-hush training camp for their top minor league prospects and best young major league players. The camp, held in Phoenix, was run on the sly because it technically infringed on rules mandating official dates for the beginning of spring training. Long-term, however, this camp actually initiated what later turned into organized instructional league training.

Unlike other wide-eyed prospects at that first camp—including Mickey Mantle—Billy carried himself almost like a veteran. He was brash, friendly, generous, playful. "He'd just give you the shirt off his back," said his roommate, Syd Thrift—a very shy minor league first baseman. He was also enormously confident, to the point where he seemed, to a young player like Thrift, almost beside himself.

"The thing I remember about Billy was that he was more than just a cocky guy. He had this glove with him that he kept soaking in a bucket right there in the clubhouse. And he'd strut around that clubhouse and tell people that he was gonna show those guys in New York what he could do," Thrift said. He told the young players, the older ones, anyone who would listen that he was going to take Jerry Coleman's job from him. Coleman was the team's regular second baseman and that previous season had been named American League Rookie of the Year.

Billy seemed to know exactly where he was and who he was dealing with. He was dealing with Stengel again—and he knew Casey well enough to enjoy himself, well enough to work like no other rookie in camp. At nights, Thrift remembered, though there was only one rule in camp—stay away from the dog track—Billy, usually with Yogi Berra as his sidekick, went off to the dog track, arriving back in camp sometime in the middle of the night. During the day, he was all baseball. In the clubhouse, said Thrift, the talk was endlessly of baseball; on the field there was something called the Yankee Way. Billy, because he had already played for the old man, and because of his own savvy, was way ahead.

The Yankees assembled not only their top young players but also a coaching staff that could begin to teach fundamentals in a uniform manner so that up and down the organization—from Bisbee to the Bronx—there would be something like a Yankee Way of playing baseball. Jim Turner was the pitching coach, Frank Crosetti trained the infielders, Bill Dickey the catchers, and Stengel himself took the outfielders and was the camp's presiding spirit, locating himself everywhere and nowhere—unannounced, unbidden, his eye and his mind never-failing.

Stengel's new Yankee lore was fascinating. Billy knew all about the old man's seven ways of sliding, but when Stengel had his young players standing around the sliding pits in left field, he illustrated everything he said by talking about Joe DiMaggio—the best base runner he had ever seen. DiMaggio was a master of every slide: straight in, hook slide left and right, the sweep wide past home plate taking the base with the hand, or flopping completely over back-to-stomach so the reach in with the hand would be quick and surprising.

The old man talked—preached—baseball awareness, but now he did it with Yankee stories. "There was a game we had against the Browns in St. Louis," he told his young players. "Ned Garver was pitching, who beats us all the time—and this funny little guy comes back to the dugout and tells me that he can call all of his pitches. I said, 'Whaddaya mean?' and he says, 'Well, I can see the shadow of the catcher's hand on the ground.' This is about the fifth or sixth inning and when the word got passed we knocked that guy [Garver] from one side of the field to the other."

The funny little guy was Yogi Berra, but Billy had learned about shadows in the dirt and a lot of other little things sitting next to the old man in Oakland.

Out in the field, Billy helped and hollered—and kidded. He absorbed everything, because he knew he would need everything, but even as he made himself indispensable he lightened the load for others. "During a game or a drill, if he threw a ball in the dirt," Syd Thrift said, "he'd wink, you know, and say, 'I just did that to make you look good.' He'd get you to laugh, loosen up, even as he got himself to do that. He was always helpful, always asking how you were doing."

This camp in the Yankee Way, which included Thrift and a very young Whitey Herzog, was important for Billy because it had carrying power. He had a taste of being a Yankee, and it was different than anything he had experienced.

But then spring training itself carried him to another and higher level; school was over, and life at the top began. Spring training with the Yankees was like no other.

Just as he had let every young player in the Phoenix camp know who he was and how far he was going to go with the Yankees, so, from the first day in Florida, he let his new teammates know, too—non-stop.

"A lot of the guys just thought he was a wise guy," Phil Rizzuto remembered. "It took quite a while before people understood that all of that came from how much he loved the game and how badly he wanted to win."

While Billy was secure in his sense that Stengel wanted him, he was sure of nothing else. He set out to conquer the Yankees, the summit of the baseball world, his rivals and teammates the most celebrated baseball players in the game. Miller Huggins Field filled with names and faces he knew from his dreams and fantasies. Each station on the diamond was filled by another all-star; each reserve fighting for a place on the team was an all-star in waiting.

Billy listened, he worked, and he challenged. When Jim Turner saw Billy throwing batting practice one day, he ordered him off the mound—he wanted his pitchers to get the work. Billy told Turner that, so far as he knew, Stengel was the manager of the team. He wasn't about to move.

Then there was a celebrated *contretemps* with Frank Crosetti. Mickey Mantle and Billy say the episode took place the following spring, but others remember it happening in 1950. Crosetti was showing the infielders how he wanted double plays turned. His model for second baseman was Jerry Coleman. All through the preliminary camp in Phoenix, Crosetti had talked about Coleman. He continued to emphasize Coleman's exemplary skills and technique. Coleman approached the base correctly. He understood that you had to cheat in rather than toward the base, that you had to move quickly to the base so you could stop by the time you received the throw. To do this, the trick was taking little tiny steps at the end so you could bring your feet set just as you reached the base. Then it was possible to straddle the bag, which in turn allowed a quick relay throw, so quick that it looked to others that you were almost pushing the ball from your hands rather than throwing it.

"That's not the way I learned to make a double play," Billy finally snapped one day, stopping everything. He then actually demonstrated for Crosetti—and all the other amazed infielders standing nearby—the way he had learned to make the double play from Cookie Lavagetto.

There was no intention to be insulting. Billy, above all, was fighting for his own place, just standing up for himself—as his mother had taught him. Crosetti ultimately became indispensable to him in learning his craft.

Billy pursued Crosetti—and anyone else with real knowledge. "I remember in that first spring training we were all afraid to ask questions," Whitey Ford said, "but not Billy. He was always after people. He used to talk to Crosetti—'when do you hit and run, when do you steal, why did you have him bunt'—all these things."

Crosetti taught Billy as much as anyone. He taught him that if he got down on a ground ball he could make his throw without having to drop his hands below his belt, that he then could control his throw with a quick snap of the wrist rather than any time-wasting motion of the arm; he taught him that there were many ways of winning baseball games even if he wasn't able to chime in with the big hit: he could push the ball, deaden it one way, roll it another, he could shorten up and hit behind a runner, he could take a base on balls or learn to be hit with a pitch. And then, because Billy really was that curious, he watched, learned—and never forgot—just what effect a third base coach could have on a game.

Crosetti made his runners think. He taught them that they, not the coach, had to determine for themselves whether they could actually get from first to third on a base hit. So many things went into that. It was Crosetti's view that if there were none out in an inning, you didn't want to take risks; if there was one out, you did; with two out you didn't run yourself out of an inning. Who was playing outfield, what arm strength did the outfielder have, where was he positioned? By giving the runner this leeway, the third base coach not only kept his head in the game but also helped him technically. A runner going from first who looked toward the third base coach as he approached second unconsciously slowed himself, making it more likely that he would be cut down if he tried for the extra base.

And then Crosetti had a way of bringing runners home that seemed flamboyant but was really something more. On a hit to the outfield, with a base runner coming around to score, he left the third-base coach's box entirely, venturing far down the line, sometimes within feet of the plate itself, before waving in or holding up the runner. When Billy saw his coach standing nearer home than third the first time he rounded third trying to score, he took note of it, and later asked about it. Crosetti told his players—and Billy always remembered it—that the fan sitting up in the stands had the best vantage point of all in seeing a play develop. A third-base coach could see more getting away from the base. Ultimately, a spy-in-the-sky coach sitting in the press box with a walkie-talkie—a favorite device of Billy's as a manager—could control the action even further.

Billy made his way not by breaking into the starting lineup but by making himself indispensable: by doing things like pitching batting practice, helping out in every way he could, hustling, hanging around. Stengel praised Billy's virtues to the media, and other players heard that praise to the point where they knew that this young player mattered to the old man, to the point where it was understood that his presence on the roster was in all likelihood due to Stengel's insistence.

But Billy was going to make it on *his* terms, no one else's. The Yankees put their pants on the same way people did in West Berkeley.

That went for all those Yankees—including the very magisterial DiMaggio.

One of the biggest surprises for Yankee veterans and youngsters alike in that 1950 camp was the odd-couple friendship that developed between Billy and DiMaggio, who normally befriended few, keeping quietly to himself. That friendship, eagerly pursued, brought Billy into the heart of the Yankee family.

No one is quite sure how he did it, but Billy not only broke through DiMaggio's shield of aloofness, he was even able to tease the great man with an irreverence incomprehensible to others. DiMaggio, to him, was not "Mr. DiMaggio" or "Joe" or "Clipper," but "Dage" or "Dago"—as in "Hey, Dage, let's go to dinner?"

Billy regularly entered the locker room walking behind DiMaggio, imitating the way he walked. When DiMaggio sat at his locker, Billy sat at his. When DiMaggio asked for coffee, Billy asked for coffee, too. He took off his pants when DiMaggio did, he mirrored the great man with such comic glee that DiMaggio, caught in whatever mood, looked up and could do no more than laugh.

DiMaggio, to be sure, was not simply a mountain trod upon or a king amused by a would-be court jester. As he had in the past with other young players from Italian backgrounds, he extended himself to Billy. Following practices and, later, regular season games, DiMaggio spent hours in the clubhouse nursing a beer, talking baseball with his young friend. It was only natural that these clubhouse get-togethers extended to further socializing. Billy and Joe subsequently became regular dinner companions in New York, hitting the best clubs and nightspots. In a sense, DiMaggio, with his elegant manner and his acquired sophistication, became Billy's mentor not only in the fine points of becoming a Yankee but in learning how to cope with celebrity life in New York as well.

For DiMaggio, the rewards of this relationship, seemingly so puzzling, made perfect sense. Billy, the noisiest and most unlikely rookie to hit the Yankees since Gerry Priddy, made the dour DiMaggio laugh. And even more than that, Billy simply talked to him, without fuss or flattery, just person to person, friend to friend—the way it might have been before there were headlines or cameras or reporters or fans.

For Billy, the rewards were simply incalculable. One time he came hustling up to DiMaggio in the clubhouse, flourishing a pen and paper—an autograph for someone, perhaps something else. Whatever, Billy contrived to stumble, or somehow mishandle the pen, squirting ink from it all over DiMaggio's freshly starched, expensive shirt.

"Oh, he was in a rage at that," Rizzuto remembered, "he was mad enough to hit Billy." But the ink was invisible ink, the clumsiness, as in a thousand other japes, contrived. Before DiMaggio's anger could harden, the ink vanished, and the absurdity of the moment quickly became as clear as the erstwhile stain on DiMaggio's shirt. Billy wasn't disrespectful, he was lovable, and by the sheer power of feeling and effort, he made this greatest Yankee of them all see that he, too, was a teammate, a brother—a Yankee.

"I think the reason they became such fast friends," Rizzuto said, "was because Billy would do anything DiMaggio wanted, anytime. You had to want to do anything Joe wanted to do and, you know, that's hard to do. But Billy was the type who wasn't bothered by that and Billy loved Joe, he idolized him."

Billy swept through that Yankee spring training as though he had hurled himself through the Arizona-Texas League. He stood in with the big Yankee hitters like DiMaggio and Tommy Henrich and Johnny Mize and he hit—he hit .350 for the spring, among the team leaders, and he fielded, if not well enough to take Jerry Coleman's job, at least well enough to take George Stirnweiss's. By the end of that spring camp, Stirnweiss, who in true Yankee fashion had helped this brash young competitor to secure his place on the squad, had seen his own become expendable. By June, the popular veteran would be gone. Billy was that much closer to making it.

Or at least, so he thought.

The first time Billy saw Yankee Stadium was during an exhibition series against the Brooklyn Dodgers before the opening of the 1950 season. Whatever awe he might have felt, the first thing he noticed on that initial game day was that his name was not on the lineup card. He was not about to be discouraged. Far from burying himself on the bench, Billy took a seat on the top step of the dugout, as close to the action as he could get, and then, to the further amazement of his teammates, already aware of his ability to make himself known, stepped over yet another line. Tommy Henrich, "Old Reliable," remembered:

"The first time, as far as I know, that he had ever been in Yankee Stadium, we were playing the Dodgers in an exhibition game—before the season starts. It's a chilly day and guys who aren't playing are sitting on the bench with their Yankee jackets on. Billy is on the top steps—without a jacket—right up at the very top step.

"Jackie Robinson grounded out in the first inning—it's only the first inning remember. Routine ground ball out. Jackie goes down the line past first, makes his turn to the right, and passes in front of our dugout. Billy Martin has his hands cupped and he's screaming out at him, 'You big clown, it's a good thing you're not in my league, I'd have your job in a week!' We all did a double-take at that, I'll tell you. That's Billy Martin. That's true. The reason I say it's true is because I saw it. I was right there."

For Billy, the fury of the moment was the game and the fact that he was not in it. With his jacket off and his competitive fires blazing, he was on his way. "Yankee Stadium is just a ballpark," he later told one reporter. "As long as it's a ballpark, I can play in it and hit in it."

Billy got his chance to play and hit in a major league game for the first time in Fenway Park that year. He was sent in as a pinch hitter in a seemingly lost game and stayed on for a memorable Yankee comeback from a 9–0 deficit. In the decisive eighth inning in which the Yankees scored ten runs, Billy had two hits—the only time in major-league history a first-game player had done that.

When the game ended and the press swarmed through the Yankee clubhouse, looking for someone to adequately define what had happened from the winners' perspective, they naturally went to DiMaggio. DiMaggio, in turn, referred them to Billy:

"Talk to him," he said, "he's the real star."

But he was no star, and his place on the team, for all his efforts, was tenuous at best. He saw action the following day, but then went an entire month before he was used again.

Through this time, Billy tried as best he could to keep a handle on the pressures that were rising in him. When the team was at home, he roomed with the reserve catcher, Charlie Silvera, and Hank Bauer. The three lived at the Concourse Plaza Hotel, frequented in those years by Yankee players, just a couple of blocks' walk from the stadium. Silvera remembered that Billy was not at all wild in this time. He was nervous and determined to do well. The roommates were all aware of the pressures of playing for the Yankees. They had a routine, Silvera said. They got up early, and each day the team was home, they went down to the stadium and took extra batting practice. A coach left them a bag of balls because he knew they would be coming in, and each day they emptied the bag hitting.

"I really got to know Billy when he, Hank Bauer, and I roomed with each other in 1950," the catcher said. "It was really tough on Billy because he wasn't playing and Coleman was the second baseman. It was tough for me because I played behind Yogi and I was getting used to that, to be a role player. But Hank was playing regularly so there was some tension built up between the two of them—but we got along. We were all close friends."

Silvera also recalled that the trio, plus an extra, spent a good deal of time at the stadium after the games as well:

"That year, Hank, Billy, DiMaggio, and I would hang around the ballpark, especially after day games—we only had fourteen night games—and we'd sit around and have a couple of beers and talk for two, three, four hours. It was all baseball. We'd listen to Joe. As a matter of fact, after I became a coach, I told Billy, 'I never thought you were paying that much attention.' But he was."

Bauer remembered Billy vividly from the period, too. He recalled that Billy in many ways was a typical rookie, but that he had a hard time eating. And he is the first who seemed to have noticed that Billy drank—not so much to call attention to himself but still enough to notice.

Phil Rizzuto, who wound up rooming with Billy on the road, said that "Billy was great. One reason was that he stayed out so late. I had time to come in and go to sleep and then he'd come in and I wouldn't see him till the next day."

Rizzuto knew something else about Billy, something he observed on the field but then saw up close as well:

"He was ready to fight from the first day. The least little thing, anything would set him off. He was just so jumpy about everything. Guy'd throw close to him, just say something the wrong way, he'd explode."

Rizzuto, along with many others, knew that not playing ate Billy alive.

The person who probably knew better than anyone what the young, volatile rookie was going through was Stengel. He had been through this before with Billy at Oakland. At the end of the '47 season and through a portion of '48, he had seen what not playing did to him. But where he had been able to tinker and tamper in order to find room for Billy in the minors, he was dealing with a very different situation here. The Yankees were not the Oaks. And that, ultimately, is what Stengel—always able to choose baseball over sentiment—and the front office acted upon. Stengel, knowing that Billy was not able to contribute and that he needed playing time, decided to ship him back to the minors, to the team's Triple A farm in Kansas City.

On May 14, Billy was summoned into Stengel's office. The old man told him he was being sent down and then tried to console him, assuring him that he would soon be back. He pointed out that the team was trying to make a deal for George Stirnweiss and that when it was done he would surely be recalled. Billy wept. Stengel, seeing his distress, confided to him that he, too, did not like the decision:

"You go up to the front office and tell Mr. George Weiss and Mr. Dan Topping that you don't think this is fair," Stengel reportedly told his "pet."

And that, strangely, is precisely what Billy did. Instead of minding his rookie business, he challenged the front office. Billy went upstairs and confronted George Weiss, the team's general manager. He ended a stormy meeting with him by shouting at him, "You'll be sorry for this!"

Years later, Billy became convinced that this single episode forever marked him in Weiss's eyes, made him expendable as a Yankee even before he had become one. In any case, it did not save him—nor did it stand in his way when he was finally recalled from Kansas City, as Stengel had predicted, a month later.

Ultimately, Billy got into thirty-four games for the Yankees that year, spending nearly all his time on the bench—next to Casey, listening, fuming, joking. "Is widda Biwwy mad?" the old man kidded him one day. Billy, who was angry and upset at not playing, could only laugh.

When the season ended, though, Billy had made it through a Yankee year, which meant a World Series. Never mind that he saw no action; he returned to West Berkeley a hero, and something of a good-natured braggart. He turned up at Rube DeAlba's house one evening brandishing his World Series check for $4,700. Rube, who had recently quit a baseball career to get married, was appropriately impressed. "Everything he predicted came to be," he said. "I'll never forget the look of him whipping out that check. That was big money in those days and he just had to push that in my face."

Billy did cash his check, though—and he did need the money. First, he had his nose fixed. He did this surreptitiously, checking in and out of a local hospital on the same day. He was supposed to be in longer, but he called Mel Duezabou that night, wanting very much to escape the hospital environment.

He also needed money because his family was expanding. He got married that fall. He had been dating a local girl, Lois Berndt, ever since he had broken off with Bobbi Pitter. Lois, like Bobbi, was from the "other" side of San Pablo Avenue and had known Billy for years, attending the same schools, though four years behind him.

Lois, Billy said, was "a doll," but the reasons why he later said he married her seem open to question:

"My best friend was Howard Noble, and Lois was the best friend of Howard Noble's girlfriend. They used to hang out together, and Howard used to tell me how ideal it would be if I took Lois out. So I started dating her.

"We got married because Howard and his girlfriend got married, and Lois kept telling me how depressed she was with me away from home playing ball, and all that same old baloney you always hear. To be honest with you, I didn't want to get married. I was twenty-two years old and in the major leagues. But when I got back home at the end of the season, I felt sorry for her, and we ran off and got married."

Billy may or may not have wanted to get married at the time. But he did not run off with Lois. He married her on October 20, 1950, at the St. Ambrose Catholic Church, where he and his family had worshipped and socialized throughout their lives; the possibly distinguishing improvisational feature of this wedding was Billy's dress. He had apparently been involved that day in an Oakland Oaks all-star game, and he appeared at the altar wearing his tux—but with a pair of sneakers or shower-slippers (there are different versions of this) that he had worn from the ballpark, apparently meaning to change before the ceremony. That Billy may not have nearly been ready to settle down with anyone was another question, but marry he did, with the expectation that his jumpy, risky life would now be more stable and secure.

Billy and Lois barely had time to settle down or even prepare for the upcoming season. The Korean War was then in full swing and twenty-two-year-olds were being drafted, even when they were members of the New York Yankees. Billy received his draft notice, passed his physical, and was sent off to Ft. Ord for basic training before he even had time to worry about what role, if any, he would have on the 1951 Yankees.

In the time he was at Ft. Ord—less than a couple of months—he wound up in an off-base altercation with a civilian that cost him $3,000 in damages, and with an on-base case of severe poison oak that made him, according to Jackie Duezabou, who visited him on weekends with Lois, "totally miserable." An old Berkeley High teammate,

Ted Texeira, also remembers that Billy in the army was a sorry sight. Texeira, recently drafted and shipped to Ft. Ord, set out to find Billy on base one day and actually did—in a deserted barracks building. The sight of him sitting there that day has remained with Texeira ever since:

"I knew he was at Ord because I read about it in the Berkeley *Gazette,*" Texeira said. "I found the barracks—all barracks look alike, but I found him. He was just sitting there this one day on the bottom bunkbed that he had, shining his boots. He just kept shining his boots. We chatted about Berkeley, what we were doing, where we were going, and so on. He didn't like the army one bit—but who did? I can still see him sitting there polishing his boots."

Billy put in for a hardship discharge, citing his stepfather's failing health, his new marriage, and his family's continuing need for his support as reasons, and he got it.

The discharge was granted prior to spring training, but this short stay in the army changed things in his life far more than he might have anticipated. From the day he got out, he was no longer quite the same person back in the neighborhoods. Local papers, including the *Gazette* in Berkeley, received numerous complaining letters about the preferential treatment Billy had received. Far from a favorite son, he was now just one of a number of ballplayers who had been able to use their privileged status to avoid service. Back in West Berkeley, friends Billy had grown up with—some of the West Berkeley Boys, in fact—had gone to war, Rube's brother among them. It created bitterness and resentment where there had been none before.

"Billy got the deferment on the grounds that he was a breadwinner and that it would be a hardship on the family for him to remain in the service," said Rube DeAlba, "but there were people at home who were wage-earners. Everyone at that time knew that his brothers, Tudo and Jackie, were at home, his stepdad was at home. So we resented that."

The sense of resentment and separation was not only local but reached across the country itself, as the entire matter of deferments had become a highly charged one.

Still, he was out and glad of it—and back with the Yankees. But, once again, he had no place on the team in 1951. Though he had been released from the army in time for spring training, he was still facing a set Yankee infield, with Jerry Coleman very much in his way at second base and a promising rookie, Gil McDougald, versatile in the field as well as a strong hitter, claiming time at third. Billy wound up appearing in only fifty-one games, many of them as a pinch hitter or a late-inning replacement in the field. When the Yankees made it into the World Series that year against the Giants, Billy made his first postseason appearance as a pinch-runner in one game. In all, whereas he had thirty-six at-bats the previous season, he had fifty-eight in 1951. Where he had eight RBIs in 1950, he had only two in 1951. He was, even giving full scope to the meaning of the term, not even a utility player. But he belonged more now, he was more a Yankee.

He was no longer a rookie. He was not only back with the club—proof that, however limited his playing time, he really was wanted—but he had started to make friends within his own age group. The year before, toward the end of the season, he had become friendly with Whitey Ford who, joining the Yankees in August, quickly established himself as one of the team's best pitchers. Billy, having already done his tour of duty at Kansas City, was there as a veteran of sorts to initiate Ford when he arrived in Boston one summer day.

Ford remembered coming to the Yankee hotel, knowing only Billy on the squad, and then being treated—at breakfast no less—to a pair of stunning blondes, apparently attached to his friend.

"We go to the lobby and standing there waiting for us are two of the most beautiful blondes I have ever seen in my life," Ford said in *Slick*, his autobiography. "A couple of knockouts. Now, here we are, two rookies, one just up from the minor leagues that day, and we're parading through the lobby of the Kenmore Hotel with these gorgeous blondes. And the older guys like Allie Reynolds and Bobby Brown are standing there glaring at us because it looks like the girls have just come with us from our rooms. I haven't even checked into my room, but it was a nice impression we made."

Beginning in 1951, while Ford was in the army, Billy had also befriended Mickey Mantle. Mantle was a rookie, shy, and someone Billy could help—and, in turn, find companionship with.

Mantle's eruption on the Yankee scene has been amply described. He was a hayseed god, everybody's next superstar after Joe D. He was the Yankee future in a frame that was only 5'10" and 160 pounds when he first turned up at that Yankee instructional camp in 1950. He could run faster and hit further than most players who had ever played the game. In foot races with teammates, he finished yards ahead of everyone else. In batting practice, the balls he hit just traveled harder, higher, farther than they did off the bats of other players. Everyone stopped to watch him.

Mantle made the team in 1951 as an outfielder. It was clear by the end of spring training that his best position was going to be the outfield. His speed, his throwing strength, his offensive potential simply dictated that. The fact that Joe DiMaggio was clearly in his last days as a player only increased the attention—and the pressure—heralding Mantle's arrival.

There was more. All through this period, Mantle was involved in a well-publicized and often-criticized running battle with his local draft board. It was not a battle, really, because Mantle had done nothing more than present to the board proof that he had a degenerative bone condition, osteomyelitis, that he had acquired as a result of an old football injury. News of his deferment followed him wherever he went, and he became subject to the kind of criticism on a national level that Billy had tasted locally in Oakland. Mantle, because he was such a celebrated rookie, seemed to become a symbol and a scapegoat for all the discontent people felt toward perceived inequities in the draft system. Letters to the editor invariably singled out the Mantle case, death threats were received, Congress was getting into the act.

In any case, Mantle withered under all the pressures he was dealing with, and in July of that year was shipped down to Kansas City so he could regain his hitting stroke and his confidence. When he returned later that summer, he had an experienced friend to help him out—Billy.

Billy took to Mantle as he had to no other player, including DiMaggio. Mantle clearly was the Yankee future, but he was also a buddy and even a younger brother. Billy, though he was married, though Lois was there with him in New York, had a running mate the likes of which he had not found since he had been in the East. Bauer and Silvera had moved downtown to an apartment over the Stage Delicatessen, and now Mantle and Billy, in love with the city's bright lights and gaudy charms, joined them regularly. On the road, Billy and Mickey began rooming with each other.

For Billy, this infusion of fun and games was, in reality, another step up the ladder. If Billy was not indispensable to the Yankees, he was to the living but naive embodiment of its future. Billy, needed as much as he was, was more a part of the Yankee future than he had been before Mantle arrived.

Back home in Berkeley, that hardly seemed to matter. As much as he wanted to go on being accepted as just another one of the guys, that was no longer possible. Some of the less fortunate West Berkeley Boys had been killed in Korea. Rube's brother had fallen in combat and his body had been shipped home that fall.

There was an honor guard of the Boys at the DeAlba funeral—"Sort of like the Hell's Angels when they were burying one of their own," Rube said—and Billy was one of the honor guard.

But this death, and the others like it, tended to move him further away from his roots even as he was making it big. He was a man in between. Bitterness, palpable but only subtly manifested, surrounded him. Rube teased him, as he always had. But the teasing now had an edge. Billy never thought of himself as a shirker. He was, then and always, keenly patriotic—yet his privileges and his ambition said something else to old friends who knew him better than anyone. Anger and resentment built up in him. Rube and he, and other West Berkeley Boys, continued to see each other that fall—but it was all different.

One night, coming back from a round of partying and drinking, Rube remembers that he and Billy got into it. At first there was teasing—Rube was the only one of the Boys who had ever been able to get away with kidding him—but the edge behind the teasing and Billy's sensitivity to it were all heightened and different. The old friends were in a car, and drunk. The teasing degenerated into quarreling. The quarreling became physical. Billy and Rube had the car stop. They got out, walked a few paces to the side of the road, and then fell into a short, bloody, and terrible fight. Billy, said Rube, punched him "eight, ten times so fast I never knew what hit me." It was as though, "through all those years, he had been carrying around this grudge, which he never said anything about but which he had never forgotten about. It was like he was waiting to explode."

There were subsequent apologies, but never any discussion of what had happened—nothing remained except the unspoken understanding that beyond the fight, beyond the measure of a friendship that actually survived until Billy's death, the feeling of being best friends had been lost, never to be regained.

In this brief, climactic moment, Billy, whether he knew it or not, had bloodied far more than a friendship. He had cut himself off from a part of his own past.

# CHAPTER 6

The United States military, which had so complicated Billy's life, in one drop of an envelope suddenly uncomplicated it. The army did for Billy what Casey Stengel couldn't—it found him a starting position on the New York Yankees when it called Jerry Coleman into service in 1952. The army's move could not have come at a better time.

To say that Billy was ready is an understatement. He had *always* been ready. Even while he was deep on the bench, he was in the midst of the action. Phil Rizzuto remembers that "even before he was a starter, whenever he was out there, he'd get on the pitchers something terrible—he'd just yell at them and guys like [Vic] Raschi, oh my, they hated that, told him to get away, but he didn't care, he'd be right on them, all he was interested in was his team winning. Nothing fazed him."

He was also interested in erasing whatever doubts anyone had about his supposedly limited skills. As in the past, he just did more than others: hollered more, put out more, fought more. He also healed faster.

On March 12 of that year, as a favor to Joe DiMaggio, recently retired, he appeared as a guest on his new television program. Demonstrating a sliding technique for DiMaggio, he broke an ankle in two places. He was back in the lineup—to stay—on May 12.

Billy played all out. From his position in the field, he chirped and harangued just as Stengel wanted, his high-pitched voice providing a never-ending stream of chatter. He was, as he had been at Oakland, the old man's straw boss, the enforcer. He lashed his mates, but he protected them, too—particularly his middle-infield partner, Phil Rizzuto, through his utter fearlessness in turning a double play. On offense, he could handle a bat in many different ways. He could bunt and hit and run; and the funny, floppy way he ran the bases caught the fans' attention. He was a crowd pleaser from the start.

The 1952 Yankees moved sluggishly through the first two months of the pennant race, trailing Cleveland and Chicago. There was nothing wrong with the Yankees that a good wake-up call wouldn't provide. Billy then provided it.

Prior to a game in Fenway Park, Billy, the bench jockey, and Jimmy Piersall, rookie outfielder and bench jockey for the Red Sox, got into a battle under the stands. The fight started with a few insults exchanged by the two volatile players and then adjourned to an area behind the dugouts.

With coaches as seconds, the two men bloodied each other. Billy's Sunday best sent Piersall sprawling to the floor and then, when the outfielder rose and came at him again, Billy hit him with a flurry of punches too fast for anyone to count that left Piersall semi-conscious.

Billy later was highly distraught, because the fight ultimately led to Piersall's demotion to the minor leagues and his subsequent nervous breakdown. But Casey Stengel, far from upbraiding or even reining in his fiery second baseman, praised him for what he had done.

"This should wake my other tigers up," he told the press. "It's about time they realize they got to fight harder this year. I just hope that Martin's fighting spirit spreads to some of the others."

Then because the old man knew so expertly how to work a room, he took the edge off what he was saying, emphasizing with merriment and euphemism what otherwise might have seemed simply ugly: "I'll have to ask [Billy] to confine his fighting. He knocked Dickey's cap off and damned near spiked him trying to get to Piersall again. I don't want to be losing any of my coaches."

Stengel was obviously not in the fight promotion business, but he knew the value of a good old-fashioned fistfight on a baseball field.

A month later, Casey's boy was in another brawl—the first of two—with his old nemesis from the Arizona-Texas League, Clint Courtney (the second, even bloodier fight took place the following season). Courtney, ironically, had been a Yankee farmhand, working his way up through the system, briefly catching on with the big club before being traded to the St. Louis Browns. With the Browns—as with every team he had played on—his reputation went with him.

In June at the stadium, the Browns came in for their initial series of the year with the Yankees. Prior to the game, the Yankee players, particularly Billy, talked about the likelihood of Courtney starting something. Billy indicated in the clubhouse that he had to be stopped.

In the second inning, Courtney, following a single, broke up a double play by successfully kicking the ball out of Billy's glove. In the eighth inning, following a hit, Courtney tried to steal second, spikes raised. Billy planted his tag in the catcher's teeth; when Courtney came after him as he was trotting off the field he leveled him. Courtney rose and was decked again and then, after the umpires had separated the players, insult was added to injury: He—but not Billy—was ejected from the game for fighting.

Stengel again was quick to take Billy's side. He argued long and hard with the umpires to keep Billy in the game following the fracas and then, talking to the media afterward, defended the right of his second baseman to respond when attacked by another player. Through this incident, as with the earlier one, Stengel did what he could to spur on his team, its fans, even the sportswriters covering the club.

Billy did *anything* for his team, for Stengel. Prior to one game, when the Yankees were up against Harry Byrd of the Athletics, a particularly tough pitcher, Stengel offered any player on his team one hundred dollars if he let himself be hit by a pitch. Billy took three for the team (and three hundred dollars, happily given, from the old man).

Billy just inevitably became the sparkplug that Stengel craved for this machine of his. He was outstanding at nothing but good at everything. He could bunt, hit and run, occasionally hit for power; he could fearlessly turn the double play, he knew how to position himself well enough to more than make up for the step that he might have lacked in the field; he was quick, not fast; he was smart in everything. He spent time reading signs—the signs of third-base coaches, the signs he picked up watching the movements of managers and others in opposing dugouts. He continued to be a shadow at Stengel's side as well as an occasional thorn in it. He was, said all the players who knew him then, a kind of second manager.

"I think Casey admired what he got out of Billy's ability," said Tony Kubek, who came to the team later. "Casey let him be a leader in the field, like he was a manager. Billy'd go to the pitcher all the time and tell him what to do. He'd control the infield. I think Casey felt if somebody screwed up on the field, it was always better that a member of the peer group straighten him out. He'd not only get on the pitchers, he'd get on everybody. Even if it was Yogi, you could hear Billy's loud, shrieking voice—it was almost squeaky and soprano-like, 'Aww, Yogi, you dummy . . .' I'm just using that as an example, they were good friends. But Billy didn't care, because 'Win At All Costs' was so important to him, and I think that Casey just liked that he could set guys straight on the field—and Billy knew that Casey wanted that from him and let him do it."

Unbeknownst to Stengel or any of the coaching staff, Billy became a kind of personal coach and manager-in-hiding to Mickey Mantle. He gave Mantle advice, tips and pointers on the little things. Eventually, he flashed signs to him during game situations.

"We didn't talk too much baseball away from the field," Mantle said. "Only if I messed up—the first thing he'd do before we got to drinking too much is he'd say, 'You know, I got to tell you something—you remember that ball you caught in right center, the one you threw over my head? From now on you better be sure to hit the cutoff man.' Hell, he could tell me stuff like that anytime. Like I told you, it was like he was my big brother. See, I was never known for bein' very smart as a baseball player. Like people ask me if I'd ever want to manage? Well, there's no way I could manage. I didn't know when to bunt or steal or hit and run or squeeze or take a pitcher out. I was just . . . I could run and throw and hit. That was it. But I didn't know the game. He did. He taught me a lot about baseball, yeah. He'd even tell me when to steal sometimes, like if Casey didn't give the signal to steal second. I hardly ever got thrown out. . . . If it was like the eighth or ninth inning and we were one run behind or tied or something, I'd look in to the bench and Billy'd give me the go-ahead. He'd tell me to go ahead and steal and I would."

Billy cut and slashed his way, making the best of the opportunity that had come his way. He hit .267 in that first full season in 1952 (he would never hit higher again as a regular, finishing with a career average of .257), but he made his mark by the "inside" things he did: the timely hit, the big play, the propensity for being in the middle of things when it counted. Billy was the anchor of an infield that backed up its pitching staff with a league-leading 199 double plays. And then there was the World Series against the Dodgers. Other players were stars, but Billy was ultimately the reason they won.

The record book shows that he went 5 for 23 in that series, hitting a not-so-gaudy .217. But his five hits were big ones, including a three-run homer that broke open the second game. It was what he did apart from the box scores and averages, however, that was decisive. In the fifth inning of the critical fourth game at Yankee Stadium—the Dodgers had won two of the first three—the Yankees clung to a 1–0 lead. The Dodger left fielder, Andy Pafko, opened the inning with a single to left and then moved up a base when the next batter walked. The two runners were then sacrificed—the tying and winning runs were in scoring position with only one out. Because it was early enough in the game and because he could handle the bat, Joe Black, the pitcher, was allowed to hit.

The Dodger third-base coach then just happened to be Charlie Dressen, the master signal-caller and sign-stealer Billy knew so well. He picked off Dressen's sign for a squeeze and, just as the Yankee pitcher, Allie Reynolds, went into his windup, screamed out that the play was on. Pafko, on a pitchout, was dead by yards at the plate.

Billy's catch of a wind-blown pop fly off the bat of Jackie Robinson in the seventh game remains one of the great moments in World Series history. The catch came in the seventh inning with two out and the bases loaded, the Yankees leading at the time, 4–2. With the runners going, and against all propriety, Billy came streaking in, losing his cap as he flew, and made a last-second catch at knee level before the ball hit the ground. He saved the game and the series. The play, as no other, also epitomized what it was that this Seventh Samurai brought to the New York Yankees.

Frank Crosetti, the wily and respected infield and third-base coach of the team, said that Billy was "alive" to the situation, a way of saying that he took responsibility on his own shoulders without being directed to—the Yankee Way.

Mickey Mantle said that Billy was the only player he had ever seen who was able to raise the level of his game through his fury. "Other players lose it when they get mad. Billy had this knack of becoming better, he would get angry in clutch situations and anger seemed to make him that much better."

When a game was on the line, Billy was *always* in a fury.

Undoubtedly, if brackets could be put around the year 1952, they would show that this was the year in which Billy gained—and lost—a family.

The family he gained was the Yankees. As never before, he belonged—team sparkplug, best friends with the team's best player, favorite of the team's manager and with multitudes of its fans.

Mickey and Billy and Whitey became a trio like no other.

Singly and together they shared a passion for baseball, drinking, and women. They indulged all three without apology or disguise. They were, like rock stars or actors, aware of the perks of the trade and simply cashed them in as they went. From the start, and all through their lives, they found strength in each other: a hayseed from Oklahoma, a street kid from Berkeley, a worldly-wise son of a New York tavern owner. They egged each other on, boy daring boy, man daring man, middle-aged person daring middle-aged person—to be sillier, cruder, more outrageous than any one of them might have been otherwise.

Billy's Berkeley friends occasionally passed through New York. When they did, they called him—and Billy, still wanting to connect, as gregarious as ever, invited them into the heart of this new world of his. Mel Duezabou made a trip to the city and Billy brought him out to the stadium where he was reunited with Casey Stengel. Then Billy took him out to dinner:

"We went to the Harwyn Club that night," Duezabou said. "The night I was there, Grace Kelly and Prince Rainier were there. It was a big place. Jeez, all those celebs—and they loved hanging around them. We had dinner with Rocky Marciano. Can you believe that? He sat right next to me. . . . Before he got there, Mantle was there with some contractor, supposed to be some friend of his, and he had one of those whoopie cushions—he blows this thing up and he slips it under the contractor's seat before the guy gets there and, jeez, Billy and Mickey . . . I thought they were gonna fall on the ground laughing. . . . And then after that, after dinner, we were going to this cocktail party. We go to this real fancy place, like on the twentieth floor, and there are only about ten people there, and I look and here's Teresa Brewer sitting there. I loved her voice—and Billy told me after she kinda liked Mickey a little bit."

On another occasion, Jack Setzer, one of the West Berkeley Boys, passed through at World Series time, and Billy took him to dinner at one of those clubs. Setzer remembers reading the menu right to left, prices first, and Billy laughingly telling him to forget it, to order anything he wanted.

"That place—I was like a kid in a candy store. I met Joe DiMaggio, Leo Durocher, Charlie Dressen, some umpires—I don't know who—and I met Sid Caesar, Jo Stafford and her husband, Paul Whiting, Imogene Coca, Carl Reiner—the whole 'Show of Shows' cast. Anyway, we're at the bar, we have a few drinks, and we went upstairs for dinner. And all those people came up for dinner, too! It was just one big party. Billy was so popular with these people—of course, when he wanted to be he could be the most likeable person in the world. He didn't have a chip on his shoulder with those people. To them, he figured, 'Hey, I'm the second baseman of the New York Yankees. I'm Billy Martin from West Berkeley to anybody who's from West Berkeley, but I'm not Billy Martin from West Berkeley to those people.' Oh, God, it was one big show up there. Guys would get up and do a few jokes, then somebody would tell stories on somebody else. It was such a good big laugh for everyone.

"And then the other nights on my trip . . . I'm having dinner with Yogi Berra and Mickey Mantle and Billy. Whitey wasn't there because he was from New York and was home with his family—but the first five or six nights, Mickey's with a different gal every night and each one's better-looking than the last. Gorgeous gals. I couldn't believe what I had seen."

When Mickey and Billy—and their wives—shared adjoining apartments at the Concourse Plaza that year, the men regularly snuck out on the ledge between their adjoining balconies to see if they could catch the other couple in bed. On the road, when they roomed together, they found others to spy on. One night at the old Cadillac Hotel in Detroit, after a solid round of drinking, Billy and Mickey crawled out on the ledge, barely a yard wide, twenty-two stories above ground, and edged along toward a nearby window where their best information had led them to believe they would catch a teammate in a compromising position with a woman friend. Mantle, who was and remains terrified of heights, crawled right behind Billy, inch by traumatic inch.

"That's a true story," Mantle said. "One of the other ballplayers had a girl and he was gonna leave the window blind up and we was gonna crawl out there and watch—like it was only two or three windows down. 'Course you gotta know that we had had a few . . . so we're crawlin' down this ledge . . . if you looked over it you could see the ground way down there. We crawled about four, five windows and the damn blind was down. I said, 'Billy, we can't see nothing, let's go back.' He said, 'I can't back up.' So we had to crawl all the way around the building, around the whole twenty-second floor, to get back to the window we came from."

But these escapades mask rather than reveal the closeness of friendship. The pressures of playing in New York, the unheard-of advantages and enticements to young people—each one so different—were all part of it. These men were expected to produce, to bring pennants and world championships to a team already laden with championship tradition. They were also expected to comport themselves like Yankees, like the champions they were; to be role models. They were not. They were talented kids.

Mickey and Billy spent hours reducing clubhouse pressures to the level of child's play. They regularly lugged water pistols around—six-guns—and had shootouts, silly, meaningless waterfights, like kids at camp. They constantly played practical jokes on each other—and on anyone else who was in their way, including the manager. Billy, knowing that Stengel limped from an old automobile accident that had crippled one leg, used to place a baseball under his uniform sock and walk around limping, imitating Stengel, who merely growled and laughed.

Then they made a game of the game. They outraged the old man by pretending to make light of strikeouts during games. Mickey and Billy had a rubber ball on a string which they shot back and forth, fielding and hitting in the clubhouse.

More than anything, they found in each other something that told them they more than belonged to this very special world that was out there beyond the dugout steps and beyond the glittering fronts of the clubs and bars and hotels.

But the cost of all this for Billy was his marriage, which came to an end in that first year of near-stardom. All through the long season, Lois had spent much of her time alone. Billy, she said, was the first at work and the last to come home. As young as she was, Lois was also a woman whose eyes were open and whose mind worked. She was ready to be a wife and a mother but not a pushover. If Billy had expected to have an uncomplaining, docile, and submissive wife, willing to wait upon him whenever he came home—no matter where he had been, no matter with whom—he was mistaken. Lois was nineteen, and though she was pregnant, she was still very much interested in having a life beyond baseball widowhood.

In his autobiography, Billy says he never saw the divorce coming—only that Lois seemed increasingly to dislike him. He was sure she was cheating on him. Yes, he had been on the go all the time, he had been away from home much of the time, but still he couldn't understand why she wanted a divorce. He wrote:

> When she came home from the hospital, I could see that she even hated to see me. She hated everything about me. I accused her of

> having a boyfriend, and one time I did catch her on a date when she told me she was going out with her girlfriends, but looking back, it really didn't matter. We really shouldn't have gotten married in the first place.
>
> I was living with her and her parents in their home, and there was a knock at the door. She said, "Go see who it is, there's someone to see you." I opened the door, and this guy handed me my walking papers. Lois had filed for divorce.

Lois, of course, saw all this differently.

"You can just say there was too much baseball," she said. "One thing I liked about Billy's second wife, Gretchen, was the statement—and I had always wished I said it—'Play me or trade me.' Someone said she said that and at any rate I thought it was a very good line. It's one thing for a man to be that involved in his job. Men are known for going to work, I know, but they also come home in their time. But he was always the first at work and the last to come home, talking about the game with just about anybody, till everybody was gone, then he'd come back and replay it over and over and over again."

Jackie Duezabou, friendly with both Billy and Lois, particularly with Lois, wondered how Billy was unable to see what it was in himself that might have contributed to the split.

"When he and Lois went on their honeymoon, they came back early because he missed his friends," she said. "But he was always a man's man. I know he's had a lot of marriages and a lot of girlfriends, but he was really a man's man. . . . I don't remember what he wrote in his book but he made it sound like Lois wasn't the best wife in the world. I think Billy always felt that, if you loved someone, you would never have to lie. I know other young people who think they have to be perfect, but I've always felt it was better to be honest—the people who love you are going to love you anyhow and be forgiving if you're honest about things. Instead, he'd kinda make up fibs that made him more of a hero than he really was, or made somebody else out a villain, because he seemed to think he had to be perfect or people wouldn't accept him."

At the end, several months after the birth of their daughter, Kelly Ann, in 1952, Billy may have been surprised when he was served with divorce papers, but Lois remains skeptical about that. "I remember the time very well because my dad had just passed away," she said. "At that time we were together and he was here, hadn't left for spring training yet. It was right then that the papers were served. But no one gets a divorce and is not aware. Things that are not very pleasant, you have a way of putting them out of your head, I guess."

But Billy could not put the divorce, the collapse of his personal life, out of mind, despite the fact that 1953 was his best season in the majors. He hit only .257, but he had fifteen home runs and drove in seventy-five runs. And then he truly led the Yankees to their fifth straight world championship, hitting .500, with a record-tying twelve hits, as he was named Series MVP.

But all through his great year, he had problems keeping his food down or being able to fall asleep at night. He told reporter Al Stump that he had had to use sleeping pills just to get through the season. "I was on them all season," he told Stump, "two a night. I took over three hundred goofballs. Even then, most nights I'd be walking the floor till daylight." He became so thin that any uniform he wore seemed to swallow his jumpy, taut body. His playing weight dropped from 165 to 130 pounds. He wrote later, in his autobiography, about this period:

> I had an empty, terrible feeling. I loved Lois, probably more than I realized, and I wanted her back and I wanted to be able to be with my baby, and I could not accept the reality of her wanting a divorce. I wouldn't give her the divorce right away. I held back quite awhile, because I was praying she'd change her mind. I guess I should have realized there was no way I was ever going to get her back.
>
> During the season when we were in New York I went to St. Patrick's every day to say my Hail Marys. I used to say this one prayer to the Virgin Mary to "help me in this need." I was hoping through my prayers Lois would come back to me. Through the entire 1953 season, which was my best in the majors . . . I was on the verge of a nervous breakdown. Only my friendship with Mickey saved me from going over the edge.

Billy did not go over the edge, but he did not then—or ever in his life—make sense of the seemingly irreconcilable split in his nature that on the one hand made him crave winning and success and the excitement that went with them, and on the other wanted a durable and stable loving relationship. It was as though one came at the expense of the other. Both were essential to his well-being, but were opposite poles of a single magnet, of his own personality.

At the end of the '53 season, he sought refuge from his personal woes—first by barnstorming, then by escaping his hometown, where Lois was, to spend time with Mickey Mantle in Oklahoma.

Shortly after the season finished, Billy joined the Eddie Lopat All-Stars for a brief series of exhibition games in Japan. With little pressure on him, he could enjoy himself, celebrating on and off the field, always on the go. During the days—even in places like Hiroshima, strange and eerie in its post-war newness—people seemed to accept and like him, as they seemed, almost inexplicably, to like all American ballplayers.

At night Billy cut loose, good-naturedly indulging himself to the hilt. His roommate on tour was Hank Sauer, the National League slugger. Sauer remembered a Billy who was far from breaking down.

"He was just fun to be with," Sauer said. Billy had struck up a friendship with a beautiful Japanese actress and one night, as this friendship progressed, Billy asked Sauer to stay away from the room they shared until around midnight. "So of course I did," Sauer said, "but when I came back and unlocked the door, Billy's still there with this actress—and someone was sitting at the foot of the bed. Billy couldn't speak Japanese and this gal couldn't speak English—so they had an interpreter there with them! It was a helluva sight!"

Billy's friendship with Mantle, which also extended beyond the season, provided a more complex kind of retreat. Mantle lived in cowboy country, loved country-western music, and was surrounded by open spaces, the rhythms of another kind of life. Over time, Billy, the city slicker, became increasingly captivated by the music and the culture of the small towns, the lonely prairies.

Years later, he told his friend Bill Reedy that if he ever could have lived in a different time and place, it would have been in the old West where he might have been a gunfighter, relying only on himself to survive.

In Commerce, Oklahoma, Mantle's hometown, Billy felt free to pursue a life he wanted, a man's life—good times at night, guns and hunting during the day. Billy loved hunting and guns, but Mantle, though from the region, was not so taken with them. He remembered that on one hunting trip he had mortally wounded a deer and that he and Billy had to trail the animal for four or five miles. "We found the deer sittin' on its haunches, on its front feet with its tongue hangin' out," Mantle said, "and it was lookin' at me like 'What the fuck did you shoot me for?' You know. And I told Billy, 'I ain't shootin' another deer—but I'll go with you.' And he liked that because he got to shoot mine."

One story Billy told in *Number One* that has become an oft-repeated part of the Martin apocrypha is about visiting a ranch owned by a friend of Mantle's. The friend was going to allow them to hunt on the property and asked Mantle, in exchange, to put down a lame mule which he had in the barn. Mantle pretended to Billy that his friend had refused permission for them to hunt and that he was going to get even with him by shooting one of the guy's mules. Billy, backing up Mantle's "anger," proceeded to blast two of the rancher's cows that were also housed in the barn.

The story was fabricated. "I heard it from a hillbilly comedian one night and told it on Billy at a dinner. Billy nearly fell off his chair laughing and he used the story [from then on]," Mantle said.

But there was much more to this new wild West that Billy had taken to. It was a strange and soft place as well as a simple and violent one. Mantle's family touched Billy's heart. Poverty that made his own seem inconsequential by comparison had gripped this family—as had disease. Mantle's father and several of his siblings had been struck down by Hodgkin's disease.

Over the years, Mickey and Billy had code names for each other. Billy's favorite for Mickey was Often Jackson; Mickey's for Billy was Waco Turner. The names literally came off the front porch of Mantle's home. A severely retarded village resident gave the friends their aliases.

"This guy's name was Roy Crow and he knew that I was a baseball player," Mantle said. "I gave him a baseball cap and a glove and he was always over at my house. He'd get the paper and be sittin' on the front porch with it every day when I got up. Anyway, he got to know and like Billy—called him Bill Bottoned. He knew his name was Billy Martin but he couldn't pronounce it. He had this imaginary group of people that traveled with him. I asked him one day to introduce these people to Billy. He says, 'Bill Bottoned, this is Waco Turner'—there's nobody there—'this is Hal Tuna, this is Often Jackson'—that's me. Every once in a while, one of these people would die. We'd come outside and he'd be standing there with his cap off—you knew that he was burying one of them."

But Billy could no more slip back into another era than he could fast forward to the next one. Over that winter when he felt his life had come apart, Billy made an extended trip to Commerce. A cousin, Nick DeGennaro, who accompanied him on the trip from Berkeley, recalled that on the first night there, they went out for dinner, to a place called Lloyd's Diner. It was run by an Indian woman and was the only eating place in town. Though Oklahoma was a dry state, drinks were readily available. "Everybody congregated there, had a ball drinking and dancing, all the booze under the table," Nick said. But this was not where the action really was. Afterward, after dinner and a few drinks, they all went back to Mantle's house to change and then set out again, this time traveling up toward the Missouri border, stopping just short of it in Miami, another small Oklahoma town.

At first, Nick was puzzled—Mantle had taken them to a place called the Stable, and that is exactly what it seemed to be from the outside: a horse barn and paddocks. "It was a real horse stable, see," Nick said, "till they opened the door to the inside. It turned out it was a big nightclub and everybody there was going crazy, drinking and dancing, having a ball."

For Billy and Mickey, this was a continuation of the roaring good times they regularly had in each other's company during the baseball season. And while Nick might have been too dazzled to see it, there were shadows in this nightclub in the woods for both Mickey and Billy.

Mantle, young as he was, drank a lot—so much so that he later acknowledged that he had a serious problem:

"That past winter, 1953–54, when Billy was with me, I fell into the routine of getting out of the house by saying we were going fishing," Mantle said in his autobiography. "Instead, we would go into Joplin, have a few drinks, and before I knew it I was drunk. I wouldn't even think about going home." Mantle, with years of hindsight, subsequently acknowledged how his drinking then got worse, becoming, in his own words, "a bad problem. I know it took a toll on Merlyn and the kids. And I'm sure it took a few years off my baseball career."

Billy, his companion, might well have said the same thing about his own career.

In 1954, the United States military once again intervened in Billy's life. He was drafted for a second time—and this time he served an almost full term, a year and a half. He once again protested, but with congressional committees investigating the entire question of privileged deferments, he got nowhere. He was lucky to get an eventual stateside assignment in Colorado.

Billy played—and, more importantly, managed—an army team at Ft. Carson. The post team had great success in the area, compiling a 25–4 record, winning the 1954 Colorado-Utah area championships. In addition, Billy, with some other army players, was allowed to join a semi-pro team in Goodland, Kansas, several hours away by car. Goodland, with Billy playing some center field, shortstop, second base, and even pitching, went to the semi-final round of the National Baseball Congress semi-pro tournament in Wichita, losing to a team led by Daryl Spencer, which eventually won the championship in 1954.

In the '55 tourney, the Goodland Tigers, led again by Billy, who also doubled as the team's manager, lost to the Wichita Boeing Bombers. Billy, angered by that tournament loss, says that he learned then, as a manager, never to allow a pitcher to talk him out of removing him from a game. In this game, he brought himself in for a scoreless five-strikeout stint only after the team's pitcher, Jaques Janneau, had surrendered a decisive three-run homer on the way to an 8–4 loss.

By all accounts, Billy, knowing his job with the Yankees was secure, enjoyed himself during this hitch. He roomed off base with some hard-partying local college athletes, including the hockey player Andy Gambucci.

Gambucci remembers that Billy "had his beers but was never excessive," that he was generous to a fault ("the key to his caddy was available to anyone who needed to go get a six-pack"), and that, above all, he was Billy Martin: feisty, angry, funny, willing at any time to stand up for himself. Gambucci remembers that his group of friends, Billy included, used to drag race through the center of town—for fun, no harm intended. One time, he and Billy were stopped by a local cop who observed their cars weaving back and forth on the street. Billy pointed out to the cop, Gambucci recalled, that they were breaking no laws and should not have been stopped. The cop hauled them into the station house where Billy, still protesting, challenged the chief of police:

"Billy told the chief we were not driving recklessly and the cop had no business stopping us or hauling us in," Gambucci said. "He pointed out that if we had been driving recklessly we would have been given a ticket—which we weren't. The cop got really upset and said that Billy wasn't telling the truth. 'I don't lie,' Billy said, 'I'm a Catholic.' I nearly fell out of my chair. The chief had all he could do to keep from swallowing his cigar. . . . He dismissed all charges, patted the cop on the back and . . . I realized later that Billy wasn't really trying to be a smartass, he just had this thing about never taking crap from anybody, always standing up for himself—even when it was no big deal."

The Yankees—and his position—were waiting all the while for him when he returned to the team in August 1955, a month earlier than his scheduled discharge date. Inserted into the lineup almost immediately, he seemed to pick up where he had left off, hitting over .300, becoming a driving force, a second manager in the field, providing exactly the sort of spark Stengel had been looking for. By mid-September, though, the Yankees still trailed the Indians and seemed to be playing sluggishly. At a team meeting that month, Stengel turned the floor over to Billy, who did not lecture his mates so much as remind them, in true Yankee fashion, that by playing poorly they were messing with his money.

"I don't know about you guys," he said, "I don't know how hungry you are, but I'm hungry. I need the money. I want to win this pennant real bad."

Billy, according to writers covering the team then, was the missing ingredient for the Yankees. But as overjoyed as he was to be back, Billy was no fool; he knew that his team, especially this one led by George Weiss, had not been idle in his absence. He knew, as every veteran player did, that there was always someone at your back ready to move up and take over. There was a new, promising young middle infielder in the organization—Bobby Richardson—and he, too, was there at the end of the season, getting his first taste of life on the big team.

When the Yankees lost to the Brooklyn Dodgers in a taut and thrilling seven-game World Series that fall, the most devastated player on the team was Billy. Following the seventh-game shutout loss to Johnny Podres, he was the last player to leave the clubhouse. His eyes were red and swollen when he passed by the manager's door. Stengel sat in his room, naked, talking to the last two reporters who had gathered after the game. One of them was Howard Cosell. Billy, trying to explain his feelings to Cosell, began crying again. He jabbed a finger toward his manager. "A man like that," he said, "shouldn't have to lose."

For Billy a loss was never just a loss—and never was that so clear as in this instance. This rush of feeling for Stengel was really the first time he had publicly shown his attachment to the old man—something that went beyond games.

Billy returned that summer to far more than a team or a job. The Yankees were his circle of safety, his home. He had been accepted there as nowhere else in life. He was important and needed. His contributions added up; his words, his actions, his way of seeing things were valued by these people he valued most in life.

At the same time, though, he had seen that the guard was changing, the great machine was in the process of being re-tooled. Teams were families whose sons were traded, cut, terminated according to need, not blood. The game was pitiless and unpredictable.

Bobby Richardson was in camp that following spring, just as young Billy had been years before. Billy, unlike his brothers who were stars, returned to this team with the feeling that nothing was guaranteed and everything had to be proven all over again.

Billy held off Richardson for a season—as Jerry Coleman, whose skills never returned after his army stay, had held Billy off. But at the beginning of the 1957 season, Billy lost his starting position to Richardson, a player whose skills were simply superior to his own.

Richardson was never the enemy. The enemy was upstairs in the front office—and, more painfully, in the limitations imposed on him by his own body. Billy worked as furiously as ever because he still had the old man in his corner, and he was still very much a man at the center of things, the life of the Yankees' party.

In fact, it was a party, not Bobby Richardson, that finally did Billy in, that destroyed his great dream and his spiritual family—or at least, so Billy believed.

On May 16, 1957, a group of Yankee players, including Mickey Mantle, Yogi Berra, Whitey Ford, Hank Bauer, and Johnny Kucks were out celebrating Billy's birthday. They began the evening at one club and then shifted to another—the Copacabana—to watch Sammy Davis, Jr., perform. A commotion broke out between several of the Yankee players and a group of patrons at an adjoining table. Racial slurs directed at Davis may or may not have been involved (members of the Yankee party today do not recall such remarks), but eventually the words led to blows. One of the patrons was knocked cold by *someone*. Hank Bauer was singled out, though the Yankee players all said a club bouncer had thrown the punch. George Weiss and the Yankee front office concluded that no matter who threw what or why, the person principally to blame was Billy—who always seemed to be there whenever midnight troubles and escapades involving Yankee stars occurred.

There were fines levied, stern warnings issued, even a farcical grand jury investigation into the matter (one which cleared all the Yankees involved), but in the end there was just Billy—and George Weiss.

The day following the incident, Billy had all his bags packed at his locker. Mickey Mantle was surprised and asked his friend what was happening.

"I'm gone, pard," he told Mantle. He was certain that Weiss, who he knew hated him and who had warned him in spring training that he would no longer tolerate any of his off-field misadventures, had already traded him. He had not.

But, in fact, there was a deal in the works—a big one that had been initiated before the Copa and was not completed until weeks later. In George Weiss's mind, no matter what he thought of Billy—he didn't like him because he had never seen him as a true Yankee—feelings and even personal habits were beside the point. If Billy could play like his buddy Mickey there would not even have been the whisper of a trade.

Still, as the June 15 trading deadline approached, there was no trade. Billy knew, as everyone else did, that if he passed that date, he would be safe—at least for the time being. He was, with each passing day, wound tighter and tighter.

June 13, in Chicago—just forty-eight hours prior to the deadline—he seemed to snap. In a game against the White Sox, a brush-back incident between Sox star Larry Doby and Yankee pitcher Art Ditmar led to a lengthy, ugly, bench-clearing brawl. As order was finally being reestablished, Billy asked Ditmar what it was Doby said that set him off. The pitcher told him that Doby had threatened to knife him if he ever threw at him again. Billy then went berserk, rushing Doby, swinging wildly at him. His outburst seemed totally incomprehensible.

Billy never liked Doby, but his actions had nothing to do with what had or hadn't taken place on the field. The clock was still ticking.

On June 15 itself the Yankees were in Kansas City. Billy came to the park early convinced that the lineup card that day would tell him whether or not he had been traded. If he was not listed, he thought, that meant he was traded. He was not listed.

Billy later said in his autobiography that, to safeguard himself from the bad news, he went down to the bullpen that day and, in the seventh inning, Stengel walked under the grandstand to the bullpen to let him know the bad news—that he had, in fact, been traded.

But the Yankee pitchers in the bullpen that day, Bobby Shantz and Bob Grim, remember no such trip to the bullpen. One of them recalled that Stengel never came to the bullpen during a game, the other that there was no access to the bullpen from beneath the grandstand in Kansas City—that Stengel, if he had made the trip, would have had to cross the field in full view of the crowd, something that never happened.

In fact, Stengel never told Billy. It was Lee MacPhail, the Yankee farm director under Weiss, who informed him after the game—in the locker room—that he was being sent to Kansas City.

MacPhail, under instructions from Weiss, left his official box in the grandstand at game's end and made his way to the Yankee clubhouse where he found Martin at his locker. He spent about fifteen minutes with him, he said, informing him of the trade, explaining as best he could the reasons for it. It was a difficult and most unwelcome task.

"I remember it very distinctly," he said nearly thirty-five years later. "Billy's reaction was extremely emotional. I didn't stay long—about fifteen minutes—and some of the players came up to me and asked what had happened. I wasn't particularly liked by the players but I know that Billy didn't blame me then or afterwards for the trade. What I wanted then was for him to go and talk to Casey Stengel because I knew how close they were and I thought Casey could explain it best to him."

And that, apparently, is what Billy decided to do—on the spot. Go to the old man, let him deliver the news personally, father to son, so that he might, beyond understanding it, begin to cope with it. Billy crossed the locker room, MacPhail remembered, where a second and even more devastating surprise was awaiting: The old man closed the door in Billy's face.

"For some reason, and I can't explain it," MacPhail said, "Stengel just closed his door—wouldn't speak to him, wouldn't talk to him at that time."

For almost seven years following this day, Billy Martin refused to speak to Casey Stengel, until, at Mantle's prompting, they were reunited at the baseball winter meetings in Houston. In all his explanations, Billy never could bring himself to mention the humiliation of that closed door. There was only the depth of the hurt he felt—as though it was the force of his feeling, not the old man's cruelty or weakness, that was involved. It was true that Stengel could not have saved him. He was, after all, only the manager who also took his orders. But he was, at the very least, Billy's friend, if not more. He knew better than anyone what playing for the Yankees meant to Billy Martin. He alone knew that this was family Billy was being sent away from. He alone knew that this player had looked to him as a surrogate father, and that in this most painful place of all, what he most cried out for was not a reversal of the decision—Billy knew the pitilessness of the game as well as anyone—but the simplest of gestures: an arm around his shoulders, the sharing of sorrow, anything that might offer him some small measure of comfort. Instead, there was just a closed door that would not open. Billy would have to find his comfort elsewhere.

# CHAPTER 7

Mickey Mantle and Whitey Ford, Billy's closest friends on the Yankees, spent the night drinking with him. In the immediate hours following the trade, they shared his tears and rage. Each of them had his own George Weiss stories—Weiss, the penny-pinching blue blood who compiled dossiers on his players and who looked down his long nose at people like Billy.

The three men laughed, too, as they had on so many other occasions.

"If I happen to throw you a curve ball tomorrow," said Ford, who was scheduled to pitch against the team Billy had just been traded to, "I don't want you hitting one out off me."

"That's just what I'll do," Billy said.

The friends carried on and on into the small hours. They reminisced about their years together on the Yankees. Mantle emphasized, "We were like family, the Yankees were like family. I know people say that about sports teams, but it's very different today than it was then.

"I mean, when I joined the Yankees it was like I was the little brother. Hank Bauer, Gene Woodling, Allie Reynolds, Vic Raschi, those were the big brothers. Whitey and Billy were like my best friends but they were still like my brothers."

Around one or two in the morning, Ford, because he did have to pitch the next day, left. Mantle and Martin remained, closing down the bar where they were drinking.

Hours later, the Yankees took the field against the Kansas City A's and their new second baseman, Billy Martin. With the Yanks safely ahead in the late innings, Ford faced Billy in a bases-empty situation. He threw him a big, slow curve ball. And then another. Each time he made sure he signaled his friend so he would know what was coming. And then Billy hit one out. He measured the pitch, practically counted the stitches on the incoming baseball, and then whacked it far over the left-field wall. The members of the family, watching Billy circle the bases with his head down, could have sworn that he was biting his lips to keep from laughing.

But then the Yankees moved on—and Billy stayed right where he was.

Lou Skizas, a friend and former Yankee teammate who then happened to be with the A's, believed that the Yankee strategy in trading Billy "had been to depersonalize the guy, to get him away from Mantle and Ford and to send a message to anyone else on the team that the same thing could happen to them if they didn't watch out."

Skizas also had a first-hand view of Billy when he came over. "He was angry and bitter," he said. "He showed up but his heart just wasn't in it. You could just see a demoralized person. I think he just went through the motions, ya know? I think he wanted to get out of KC from the start, it was a halfway house for him. There was no way he was going to stay there."

But Billy played hard for Kansas City—the only way he knew. Like most of the players on the team, he did not particularly like the team's manager, Lou Boudreau, but that didn't matter. In seventy-three games for the A's, he hit .257—his career average (he wound up hitting .251 overall for the year, with nine homers and thirty-nine RBIs). His hustle and drive, though, were now more technical than inspirational components of his game. His old teammates, as well as his new ones, acknowledged that the spirit just seemed to go out of him. Mantle and Ford both said Billy was never the same player once he left the Yankees. Ultimately, Billy acknowledged it himself.

The A's were a new experience for Billy. They expected to lose. The players, even though some like Vic Power and the aging Gus Zernial were talented, wound up mostly playing for the numbers, suspicious of anyone who wanted more.

"In Kansas City, you just never won," Lou Slizas said. "The talent that we had—we had some—didn't matter. We played in that dinky ballpark, we're thirty games out of first place, just going through the motions. You go out to play just to get the game over with and hopefully next year get traded back to the Yankees. The manager? Lou Boudreau was kind of an individualist. He wasn't honest or fair. He had a kind of elitist attitude—you know, he was Lou Boudreau—he wasn't particularly close with any of his players, you didn't see him a lot of the time, you had the impression he didn't care too much himself."

What was left in Kansas City, then, was a nightlife. Billy lived in the Berkeley Hotel, the one place in Kansas City where everything really was up to date.

"It was a beehive of activity," Skizas said. "It had all the showgirls there, and all the airline hostesses, all the ballplayers—and there was a smorgasbord. I mean, you walk through the lobby of that place and you see some dolls, some real dolls."

According to Skizas, Billy kept to himself a lot in Kansas City; he didn't seem to have close friends. "There was a guy, Jimmy Robertson, used to be a catcher on the team, hung with him a little, he was dating Janis Paige." And then, Skizas said, "I think Billy and Janis kind of got close there for a while."

Occasionally, Billy would call Skizas and they would go out. Skizas wasn't a drinker—and Billy was, he said—but they enjoyed each other's company. "Billy liked to drink, that was no secret. He had a problem in his life but I don't know if it was really noticeable in Kansas City. He got into a couple of fights there. One, with Mickey McDermott, happened on the bus. McDermott was totally smashed—I think, but I'm not sure, it was over some broad."

Billy was a maverick to Skizas—the real reason why he didn't fit the Yankees. He had played well, and he knew the game the way few players did. "He could tell you just how to cheat coming across second base, he knew how to sneak in behind a runner, how to suck you in, pick you off . . . and he'd get ya from the bench, he knew how to really do that, he'd get on ya about your nose, how big it was, something like that, so that you'd let your concentration slip for just a second . . . he just knew what it was to be a streetfighter. He had an instinct for the game."

Because he had been with the Yankees for two years previously, Skizas also had a particularly opportune view of Billy's relationship with Casey Stengel. Among those passions in Billy that would now harden into a grudge was the one he bore for Stengel. But Skizas believed that Stengel had not really cut Billy off.

"He had a love affair with Billy. . . . He really liked his flair, his fisticuffs—because Casey was a brawler, too. Casey would punch your face in. I saw him grab hold of Don Larsen one night in Baltimore. Larsen had come in with a couple of beers, held up the train for about twenty minutes—he was gonna pop him right in the chops. . . . Oh, he loved Billy and Mickey and he loved them together. He liked their ability, he liked the way they played so hard, and he liked their rascaliness—the dead-end kids—he loved their youthfulness and exuberance. Billy would have been gone a long time before then if Casey hadn't been in his corner all the while."

Skizas knew that Billy's fury was loyalty betrayed, disappointed love. His strongest memory of Billy, even in this dark corner, had far more light than shadow in it. Billy touched Skizas's life in such a way that he would remember his capacity for generosity, his exuberance of spirit more than the moods, the booze, the hates. "Lemme tell you something about Billy," he said, "if he ever liked you, he would really take care of you. Ask anyone that, they'll tell you. Billy liked me, he always did. And he always tried to help me out any way he could. If I needed a couple of bucks, anything, he'd always be in my corner."

Skizas was also one of several players, including Mickey McDermott, who was traded with Billy from Kansas City to Detroit at the end of the 1957 season. For Billy, the trade was what he was waiting for—a chance to escape from Siberia, to once again be with a contender. But first there was some endgamesmanship to take care of.

Billy was informed of the deal, he said, not by the A's but by the Tigers' general manager, John McHale. The deal was an elaborate one, involving a dozen players, negotiated over many months. But Billy, who had remained behind in Kansas City after the season to augment his income by selling cars (he got no World Series share from the Yankees that year), saw an additional opportunity in the trade. Why hadn't he been properly informed? he said to Kansas City reporters. Was he merely a traveler from one club to another? There was a perception for a brief time—aided by his indignation—that Billy might somehow torpedo the deal, unless some sort of cash payment from the A's was worked out. It apparently was, and Billy moved on.

The Tigers, at least on paper, were the sort of club Billy could help. They had finished fourth in 1957, twenty games behind the Yankees. But they had talented players, led by Al Kaline and Harvey Kuenn, and might, with the addition of a sparkplug like Billy, have a chance of moving up in the standings. The promise was only on paper, though; the paper Tigers turned out to be no more than another stop along the way for Billy, a man whose legs, whatever the condition of his broken heart, no longer worked.

Because the Tigers already had a second baseman—Frank Bolling—doing a solid enough job, Tiger brass decided that Billy would be able to play shortstop. Their reasoning was that he had enough arm and that, as a second baseman, he knew middle infield play well enough to make the switch. The decision, even though it was made with Billy's consent during spring training, was a poor one. Billy had neither the range nor the hands for the position.

"He just couldn't play the position," Lou Skizas said. "When he got to Detroit, he was feeling a little better, that was true. But he played poorly—and eventually they had to move him to second."

The move to second was the prelude to his being moved out of the organization. The Tigers went nowhere in 1958, finishing fifth. Billy's abrasive, rah-rah style, on a team whose stripes were conservative and whose bite was something less than fearsome, was ultimately unneeded. A year to the day after he was traded from the A's, the Tigers sent him on to the Indians. The story, with variations, was the same there.

The Indians had been in decline since 1954, when they won 111 games and the American League pennant. The reasons for their decline were beyond the reach of any one player's assistance. The team's success had been built on great starting pitching—the quartet of Early Wynn, Bob Lemon, Mike Garcia, and Bob Feller. But 1954 was really a last hurrah for an aging staff. It was the final season of effectiveness for Feller, who retired two years later; injury all but ended the careers of Bob Lemon and Mike Garcia as well as that of Cleveland's hoped-for replacement for Feller, Herb Score; Early Wynn, though he pitched effectively into the next decade, was traded at the end of the 1957 season.

Billy's fundamental problem in Cleveland, he maintained, was a clash of temperament with Joe Gordon, the team's manager. Gordon, an ex-Yankee second baseman himself, had his own continuing version of the Yankee Way—one which Billy took to with little enthusiasm. Gordon knew how to turn the double play: you kept your right foot on the bag, then you went airborne, quick release, avoidance of injury. Dozens of second basemen since Gordon had successfully copied the style—but not Billy, who knew, from the time of Cookie Lavagetto and Dario Lodigiani, that you wanted to be moving toward the bag when you took a double play, that quick release came with that single step across the bag, one which increased the danger of injury but which would also give the second baseman a chance to intimidate the runner coming toward him. It wasn't just a matter of style, it was a matter of heart and fighting spirit.

Joe Gordon was exactly the sort of manager who unsettled Billy most. He was a battler himself, but one who seemed to hold no brief for his players, especially those whose egos conflicted with his own. He sometimes talked critically about his players to the press. Billy was nearly undone by Gordon's sniping about the number of errors he was making at the position. Billy, as a result, had some research done on Joe Gordon, turning up the interesting stat that Gordon, in his eleven-year career as a second baseman, had committed 260 errors, as opposed to Billy's 45 in seven seasons plus. Needless to say, Billy's research did not sit well with his manager.

But ultimately, the clash of temperaments had little to do with Billy's tenure in Cleveland. Gordon himself was gone within a year, a major disappointment to management. And Billy was management's prize. Frank Lane, the team's general manager, had been outmaneuvered for Billy's services the year before by the Tigers, and had coveted him ever since. He consistently took Billy's side in his quarrels with Joe Gordon. He remained clear, afterward, why he wanted Billy so badly to begin with: "He's a feisty little son of a bitch," Lane said. "He's the kind of guy you'd like to kill if he's playing for the other team, but you'd like ten of him on your own side. The little bastard."

But Lane had wound up dealing for Billy as though he was worth those ten players, surrendering good young pitching—Ray Narleski and Don Mossi, Cleveland gold—to get him. The deal had done far more damage than good.

Billy's savvy notwithstanding, his body seemed unable to take the punishment any longer. Early in the year, he took a tumble fielding a bunt, falling heavily on his right shoulder. The shoulder was separated and he was out for a few weeks. When he returned, he found that he could not throw. There was no pain in the arm, he said, just no zip on the ball when he threw it. It was as though his arm strength vanished overnight. He kept checking himself, throwing as hard as he could—but it was useless.

Then his knee—the one that had been ripped apart in the Coast League years before—kept locking on him. There had been just too many hits added to that prior structural damage.

Finally, in a game against the Washington Senators, Billy came close to losing his life. It was the second game of a doubleheader, the light was bad, and Billy was leading off against Tex Clevenger. The Senators' pitcher threw tight—Billy eventually became satisfied that Clevenger had not thrown at him deliberately—but the pitch, a high riding fastball, tailed in and caught him directly on the left side of the head.

Without a helmet to deflect the blow, the injury was devastating. A portion of Billy's cheekbone was driven into his face. Clevenger, rushing to the plate, reported that there seemed to be a hole in Billy's face and that he looked dead. Blood was pouring from his nose, ears, and mouth. He was placed, unconscious, on a stretcher and removed by ambulance to a nearby hospital where he remained for weeks. His shattered cheekbone was operated on, his jaw was wired shut, and he received daily doses of morphine for the pain, which he said was the most intense he ever felt in his life. The goal of the morphine, Billy reported in his autobiography, was to enable him to stand the pain "five or ten minutes longer each day" until the drug was gradually withdrawn.

Ultimately, Billy made his way back—but it was too late. Cleveland management, as much as they liked him, knew that his playing days were all but over. Even though his value had clearly been diminished, the Indians jumped at the opportunity to trade him to Cincinnati at season's end for Johnny Temple, a solid second baseman whose best years were also behind him.

The year in Cleveland, however, was not wholly unfortunate. He was a year past his thirtieth birthday now—still Billy the Kid to the baseball world, but to himself, a person who, whether he wanted it that way or not, had some age on him. The view ahead suddenly contained shadows not visible in that period of his life when he really was a youngster and a pet, able to simply let his energies fly. At the end of that 1959 Cleveland season, on October 7, he was married for the second time; his new wife was Gretchen Winkler, an airline stewardess he had met two years before in Kansas City, when he was residing in that Xanadu of the Plains, the Berkeley Hotel. The wedding was in Las Vegas, that Xanadu of the Desert, and Billy meant for it to be an SRO celebration.

It didn't quite work out that way. Because of conflicting schedules, travel arrangements, and other excuses, some of Billy's closest baseball friends did not attend. Even though they had been invited, Mickey, Whitey, Jimmy Piersall, Bob Lemon, and some others all stayed home. Woodie Held was the only baseball player who turned up.

This marriage really was meant to mark a change. He was determined to make something of a real life for himself, to have the stability he had not been able to secure in his earlier marriage. Just because he was now over thirty, because he knew the business of baseball so well, because he and his bride really did know each other so well, it might work.

Gretchen was not only a beauty, she was smart and ready to be involved in all of the practical areas of his life. Decisions about money, home, family—she was eager to deal with all of these. She had been around enough, had acquired the sort of experience that enabled her to read the rough and tumble of Billy's world pretty well—to let him have his life, and be part of it, too. Billy loved her, loved her looks—to the point where he would always have a suspicious eye out for the attention other men paid to her—and loved her intelligence and practicality that promised him the basics he had so sorely missed.

But as had been the case the first time, Billy was married first to the chase of the game, to its peculiar and privileged fraternal culture of nomadic life and high times. The next stop was not really home life so much as Cincinnati, home of the Reds, the first of two National League teams he played for.

The Reds were then managed by Freddie Hutchinson, who had taken over the team in mid-season the year before. Hutchinson knew Billy from playing and managing against him in the American League and he was eager to have him on the ballclub. Hutchinson intended for Billy to arouse his team and then keep it going. The Reds were in fifth place when Hutchinson took over in 1959, and they had finished in a fifth place tie with the Cubs. Still, the National League race had been close, with teams tightly bunched all the way to the end. Only thirteen games separated the first six teams. Moving up was more than just a perennial hope. The Reds had good, young players—Frank Robinson and Vada Pinson among them—as well as veterans like Billy who could give them a boost.

But Billy, no matter what his manager projected for him, was really unable to do much. He had a poor spring and everyone knew why. "His legs just weren't in good shape for a guy his age," said Lee Walls, a teammate, friend, and later a coach on several teams Billy managed.

"He was a good scrappy player," Vada Pinson said, "but he didn't do nothing that year; at least I didn't see anything he did from my position."

Walls remembered that Billy was scrappy, too—on and off the

field. The first opportunity Walls had to spend any time with him was after spring training one day in Tampa when they went out for a beer together. It was in the middle of the day, after a workout, and the bar was nearly deserted when they entered.

"There was one guy sittin' at the bar, and when we came in the bartender bought Billy and me a drink. Well, that one guy sitting there said, 'Christ, Fred, I been coming in here for twenty years and you never bought me a drink. Who the hell are Billy Martin and Lee Walls anyway?' So Billy sends him a drink. The guy comes back and throws it in Billy's face. The next thing I know is that that guy was layin' dead out on the floor. Billy got him with a right hand. That was my first introduction to him. He could throw it. You better believe it."

Billy was in an on-field brawl in June that season that Vada Pinson remembered—with laughter. Pinson had grown up in Oakland, had followed Billy when he was with the Oaks, and had always admired his baseball sense and his fighting spirit.

"This fight was a big one—in Philadelphia. Gene Conley, the pitcher, big tall guy [six foot eight, a pro basketball player in the off-season], and Frank—Frank Robinson—got into it, and then Billy stepped in and tried to hit Conley on the top of the head. It was funny," Pinson said.

"Gene just came right down and hit *him* on the top of the head because he was so tall. Next thing I know, Wally Post had Billy and was squeezing him. I told him, 'Let him go! Let him go!' Wally looked at me because he was just traded over there from our team; he said, 'All right, you take care of him.' So I grabbed him. I dunno, I was just a young kid—and so all we did was dance out there behind second base. I was just trying to keep him from going back in there . . . but it was just so funny to see Billy trying to jump up and hit Conley—he needed a step-ladder just to get to his belt buckle."

There was far less laughter in Billy's celebrated fight with Cubs' pitcher Jim Brewer. The fight occurred at Wrigley Field in the second game of a June series between the Cubs and Reds. But in reality, the fight had been building long before then and had little to do with Jim Brewer as such.

In that first game, Billy had taken a number of close pitches. He believed he was deliberately being thrown at—something that teams had taken to ever since his beaning—and he was upset about it. Better than anyone, Billy knew what effect this was having on him. Against his intent, Billy had discovered that he was bailing out, and that it was happening almost as a reflex. To counter it, he had on several occasions taken special batting practice, having his own pitchers throw at him. He padded himself in four coats and held himself still as pitched balls thudded against his body. But none of it had worked.

When Jim Brewer began throwing close to him in this particular game, Billy began a verbal battle with him. On a subsequent close pitch, Billy threw his bat, which slipped from his hands and sailed toward first rather than the mound. When Brewer came toward him, shouting at him, Billy, looking as though he was trying to pick up his bat, came upright and leveled the pitcher with a solid right hand.

When the melee that ensued was finally quieted, Brewer's face was a gory mess. He had received numerous heavy blows in and around the head area; an orbital bone above one eye was shattered, an injury that cost Brewer his rookie season and required two operations and a lengthy hospital stay. Brewer ultimately wound up suing Billy for a million dollars, winning a court judgment of ten thousand dollars, which, with expenses, finally added up to twenty-two thousand dollars—paid by Billy out of his own pocket.

Billy then and ever afterward contended that while he struck the first blow—to the jaw—he was not the one who caused the grievous eye injuries suffered by Brewer.

He told *Sport* magazine in March 1961 that the Brewer fight was the first in his life in which he had taken the first swing, but Billy said, "My punch landed on Brewer's jaw. It was no sneak punch—I'd telegraphed it when I turned down the first-base line. Chicago newspapermen, however, claim I swung without warning.

"I wasn't the only Cincinnati player in that fight, either, but nobody seemed to know that. Cal McLish, my roommate last year and one of the greatest competitors in baseball, was right out there with me. Cal sprinted to the mound to get Brewer and I understand that Cal belted him, too. I'm told that Cal's punch hit Brewer just below the eye.

"Still, I've been blamed for everything—for starting the fight, and for Brewer's caved-in cheek and damaged eye. A lot of the blame I'm sure is simply because of my reputation."

Billy's reputation, not just as a brawler but as a sucker puncher, had preceded him and undoubtedly entered into the consensus opinion that it was he and no one else who had wrecked Brewer. But Billy's teammates—including Cal McLish—rallied to his defense. McLish, in several subsequent statements, acknowledged that he indeed did strike Brewer in the region of the eye and cheekbone; Vada Pinson and Lee Walls, to this day, retain similar memories.

"Years later I was working for Kaiser Aerospace and Electronics and Billy called me and wanted me to come in and testify in the lawsuit against him," Pinson said. "We were in the middle of some things and I couldn't get away but I said I'd be glad to give it over the phone or in writing. . . . What I had to say, McLish had already said the same thing. Billy threw one blow and that was it. And it was a good blow. But McLish came in and McLish said something to him and McLish hit him at least three good ones and then it seemed like everyone was beating up on him."

Lee Walls had the same impression along with a theory about why Brewer sued Billy and not McLish:

"Calvin McLish hit him. Sure. And Billy got sued and took the rap. But it was McLish that did the damage. Hell, I was in the game, I was right there. Billy got sued because, you know, one pitcher wouldn't sue another pitcher—but a pitcher would sue an infielder . . . if you know what I mean."

The designated hitter rule has probably never received a subtler argument, but that notwithstanding, Billy remains the one associated with the Brewer brawl to this day. His denials, perhaps because they were so familiar, seemed to fall on deaf ears—as though he was the Little Boy Who Cried Wolf. He had acquired a reputation, and it would follow him like a spotlight or a hangover for the rest of his life.

The Brewer fight kept the image of Billy the Battler fresh. But Billy, perhaps better than anyone, knew that the end of his playing days was drawing near. Because he knew the game so well, he could not fool himself any longer about what he could and could not do on the field. There is never a tougher time in a player's life than that coda of final activity before retirement. All of one's senses are marshaled against the day, while all of one's doubts and fears underscore the closeness of the day; all of the hurts, the fatigue, the body parts that no longer seem to function as they did, become a kind of chorus reminding a player that his once gifted body is, after all, finite and mortal. Athletes rarely die young but they have an unusually hard time fading away. Their mid-life crisis happens at a time most other people's lives are just taking off.

Billy, unlike many other athletes nearing the end, had an option or two. He knew the game so well, had learned and retained so much simply as a matter of survival, that he could see himself as a coach or manager. In his autobiography and elsewhere, whenever the question came up, Billy maintained that the idea of managing never entered his mind until he was suddenly offered the opportunity to manage the

Twins' Triple A affiliate in Denver in 1968. But it was clear, even in his rookie year with the Yankees, that he had thoughts about managing. He made a vow to Charlie Silvera—one he kept—that if he ever became manager later in his career, he would hire him as a coach. And then, from his actions on the field as a "second manager" in his Yankee playing days, even from the way he thought about the game—wanting to take control of it rather than simply being in it as a single player—the idea of managing was always a kind of star against which he might set his course.

In Cincinnati, the wheels were already spinning. "I don't know if Billy's heart was in playing then, but it definitely was in managing," Lee Walls said. Walls said he knew this because Billy told him—flat out.

"He just told me, that's all. 'I'm gonna manage someday,' he said, 'I'm gonna win this and I'm gonna win that'—he just would lay it right out. And he did everything he said he was gonna do, too," Walls said.

But he was not there yet. The endgame of his playing career was something he could neither predict nor control. The Reds did not want him. He simply did not fit their transition to speed and power. The Reds were a pennant-winner in 1961, but Billy had already moved on. The Reds sold him to the Milwaukee Braves the previous winter, another contending team but one that also had no place for him. The Braves, nearly alone among major league teams, showed interest in Billy—not because they were unable to see how much he had deteriorated as a player, but because the team's manager was Charlie Dressen.

Dressen had all the scouting reports he needed on Billy, knew his reputation better than anyone, and was even aware that in bringing him to the Braves he was probably bringing a potential managerial rival into the fold.

"Don't think he won't help us," he told *The Sporting News*. "They warned me against buying him because he has ambitions to be a manager, but I don't care. I got him because I think we can use him."

For his part, Billy was overjoyed to get a stay of execution.

"I never had a chance with the Reds," he said. "Every time I looked around they were sending up a pinch hitter for me. It was the same way in Cleveland the year before. You can't ever get going that way. It was different with the Yankees. Casey Stengel never used a pinch hitter for me. He had confidence in me and he let me hit with men on base.

"Being with a better ballclub will help, too. That's why I'm so happy to be with Milwaukee. Charlie was one of my original teachers—he and Casey and Cookie Lavagetto. He knows baseball and he loves teaching it. All he wants is to know you like it and want to play."

Dressen wanted more. As he did in Oakland and everywhere else along the way, he wanted a winner—and the Braves, in 1961, were supposed to contend. They did not. And, more to the point, they just had no room for Billy. Four days after the Braves picked him up, they were able to trade for Frank Bolling, the Tigers' second baseman—who had once before bumped Billy from a job. By June, Billy had seen action in only six games, and when the Minnesota Twins—Cookie Lavagetto was the manager there—had a chance to pick Billy up in what everyone knew was a meaningless utility player trade, they did. Billy finished the season with the Twins, hitting .242, the lowest season average of his career, playing in 106 games, impressing everyone with his hustle and his knowledge but also his inability to continue as a player. When Cookie Lavagetto was fired midway through the season, the end seemed near.

Still, he returned to the Twins the following spring, hopeful that Sam Mele, the new manager—someone Billy knew and liked—would give him a chance. But Billy's playing career no longer was about opportunity given or denied. He simply could no longer play on the major league level. One day, late in spring training, Mele took Billy aside. The clubhouse at Tinker Field in Orlando had emptied. As usual, Billy was the last to leave. Mele walked over to him and put an arm around his shoulder. Mele and Billy went way back together, to when they were rivals—and friends—on the Red Sox and Yankees. The two players used to bet with each other on who would hit more home runs during the course of a season. Billy usually did and Mele used to complain about it.

"Ah, you're hittin' down the left field line in New York, it's about 290 feet, and I've got a 315-foot shot and a sixty-foot-high wall," he had needled his friend.

There was no needling now. Mele remembered the conversation he had with Billy, informing him of his release, as though it had taken place only the day before.

"I put my arm around him and I said, 'I don't know how the hell to do this really,' " Mele said. "Billy looks at me and says, 'What? Something's wrong?' He knew right away. I says, 'Look, it's not only my decision, but I'm the guy who has to tell you. Calvin [Griffith, the

Twins' owner] and I got together and we think maybe your career has been a great one but it's time, maybe . . . look, you have to go.'

"Christ. He started to cry. 'Why?' he says. 'I think I can help you.' I'm crying with him. 'Jesus, Billy, I wish you could but it's time . . . every good thing has to come to an end.' "

But Mele would not let Billy go. He promised to intercede for him, to find another job for him in the Twins organization. It was a friend's promise—but also a baseball man's. Because, Mele said, "I knew just how much he knew about this game."

Billy, though, was unable to think then about anything beyond the terrible reality of the moment. For the first time since 1946, he was out of baseball, with nowhere to go and another season coming up. He was not yet thirty-three years old.

# CHAPTER 8

Billy was determined to come back as a player. "I will eat humble pie," he said, vowing to change as a person, to prove to baseball people that they were judging him not on his playing ability but on his character. An offer did come: Billy was offered a reported hundred thousand dollars to play ball in Japan. The offer was tempting, not only from a financial standpoint but from a personal one. He had enjoyed himself enormously the two times he had been in Japan. The more recent trip—with the Yankees following the '56 season—had been triumphant. The Yankees swept their games and were greeted everywhere by the baseball-mad Japanese in a manner befitting their status as World Champions. Billy, as he had done before, had a ball. He pursued the pleasures of the country as hard as he did anyplace, even taking a stab at the language. Depending on which admiring observer was doing the observing, Billy learned either the language or at least one hundred or so useful words and phrases, enough for him to take his chances without needing an interpreter at the foot of his bed. Whitey Ford—of the hundred phrases school—remembered that on one occasion, they were on their way, by car, to Hiroshima and had paused briefly in a small town on the way.

"We stopped off at this little grocery store in this tiny town, and this old Japanese guy is playing this game of Japanese checkers—go or whatever it was—and Billy went in and began to watch for a while. They didn't know who he was. Then he started talking to them—in

Japanese—and they talked back to him. Billy went over, bought them all some peanuts . . . the old Japanese guy thought Billy was the greatest."

But playing ball in Japan was not what he had in mind. For an American player, the decision to play in Japan was an acknowledgment that he did not have the skills to play major league ball. Even though he had already been told that by Sam Mele and by his own worst fears, he was reluctant to accept such a verdict, no matter what form it came packaged in. Eventually, though, he did, and he chose to stay in the United States not because he hoped that his playing career might be extended but because common sense pointed toward a far more promising career in management. Whatever damage had been done to his playing skills over time, nothing had affected his ambition.

True to his word, Sam Mele talked Twins owner Calvin Griffith into hiring Billy—not in an on-field capacity but as a scout. It was not exactly what Billy hoped for, but it was not a throwaway offer either. The job meant being around the ballparks, rubbing shoulders with former rivals and teammates, being a part of the scene even as he was, for the first time, apart from it. Scouting at the major league level was a big first step toward a career in managing. Billy took to it with all the gusto and ambition with which he had played.

The Twins, in a way, were the perfect club with which to begin this phase of his career. They had just arrived in Minnesota, the old and ridiculed Washington Senators suddenly transferred into this shiny new vehicle in a brand new territory. The Twins played their games in upgraded Metropolitan Stadium, but there was a long and honored baseball tradition in the area and the coming of the major leagues seemed to carry with it almost endless promise.

Billy "sold" the ballclub as much as anyone, and in the process sold himself. As a sidelight—and an income enhancer—he became a sales representative for a local brewery. He pushed the Twins as hard as he did his company's brew. "Every bar in Minnesota knew him," Calvin Griffith said. "He became known and loved maybe because he was always buying free rounds for everyone, and he was always promoting the Twins."

Scouting, though a new area for Billy, was one he took to as though he were a player rather than an executive. He performed this new job of his beyond expectation. He got on well with everyone. As a bon vivant and recently retired player he was welcome almost everywhere he went, no questions asked. He was straightforward and fun-loving.

Above all, he knew his boss, knew whom he was ultimately playing to.

"I always thought Billy was a person who could manage a ballclub," Calvin Griffith said. "You always have somebody in the background somewhere along the line to become a manager." Griffith was satisfied with Billy's work as a scout and promoter, and came to rely on his judgment. "He did a real good job for us there. He recommended ballplayers, told us to take this guy and not to take that guy—and he was nearly always right on the money."

Twins scout Herb Stein first met Billy during that 1962 season, shortly after Billy began his front-office work. The occasion was a general organizational meeting of the scouting staff in Minneapolis while the team was away on a road trip. The purpose of the meeting was to run a monitored workout for the top prospects each of the scouts was currently working with. Billy was in the middle of this because he was management's man, their top evaluator.

"I didn't know Billy till then. I knew about him, seen him play and all that but I didn't know the man," Stein said. "Anyway, we all checked into the Radisson hotel—it was June 1962. I was the New York City area scout then and I brought this kid along with me—I think he might have been from Hofstra University—name was D'Oca, something like that. We reported to the ballpark, had a little meeting and I met Billy Martin then. He more or less oversaw everything besides the farm director and the scouting director. . . . Well, we work these kids out for three days and afterwards, after it's all over, we convened in the conference room to make some decisions. Every scout there had been evaluating all the players for three solid days. Which of these kids were we actually going to sign? Sherry [Robertson, the farm director] began and went over each ballplayer—some of the scouts would say, 'Yes,' others would say, 'No'—that sort of thing. When it came to my player, all I heard was 'No,' 'No,' 'No'—all around the whole damned conference table—maybe ten, fifteen scouts. I said, 'Yes,' what else? I had a good reason why I said, 'Yes.' Sherry says, 'Well, looks like most everybody here don't like him.' They move along to the next player. All of a sudden I heard somebody say, 'Wait a minute.' It was Billy. He said something to this effect: 'There were two balls hit out of the ballpark and Stein's player was the only one that did it. I'm with Stein.' That was that. All that was left was to go sign the turkey, who turned down $1,000—I mean he was lucky he got offered ten cents—but the thing was Billy took his job seriously, and it was clear he had the ear of the front office."

Stein also observed something else about Billy. He was warm and gregarious, he liked good times, liked baseball people especially, and didn't mind throwing his money around.

"After maybe the first workout, before the business meeting, Sherry comes up to all of us and says, 'Listen, you guys, Billy Martin is taking you out tonight. So you all meet at the hotel, he'll get you around eleven o'clock or midnight'—maybe this was the last night we were there—so a whole bunch of us met Billy in the lobby. Where are we going, we asked him? 'Aw,' he says, 'wait till you see where I'm takin' you.' He took us to one of those after-hour joints. It was one of those places where you couldn't get in unless they knew ya. They opened this door, saw Billy, swung open the doors, and we all walked in; everybody in the place, when they saw Billy Martin—now remember, he's only in the front office—they ran after him. Oh those people, those beautiful people, they were something to see! They just ran after him! It was such a friendly gathering, everybody was coming over to see Billy Martin. And you know something, I don't think he had two beers the whole night! When it was over—whenever that was—we all walked back to the hotel."

Stein, like everyone else in the organization—and around the league—knew what Billy was doing in the front office. Calvin Griffith knew, perhaps more than anyone, about Billy's popularity. He was a star—not necessarily a star player, but a star nevertheless, someone with name recognition, the sort of personality that just seemed to draw people in. He was box office.

"Oh, they knew Billy's background," Herb Stein said, "they knew the type of player he was, they knew how fiery he was, that he was an inspiration on his own ballclub, didn't have to motivate anybody—that's a misused word—just stayed on the game all the time and made everyone else that way, too."

As nearly all of those following the team knew, Billy Martin was not going to remain a scout forever. He was a man on the move, getting ready to prove the original judgment of his employer, that he was "a person who could manage a ballclub."

At the beginning of the 1965 season, Calvin Griffith moved Billy from the front office back to the field, installing him, with manager Sam Mele's consent, as the team's third-base coach. The Twins just happened to win the pennant that year and Mele himself gave a large part of the credit to Billy.

All through that year, area writers emphasized the hot and palpable breath of Billy's—and Calvin Griffith's—ambition. Once out of his office and back on the field, writers seemed to say, Billy was no longer a manager-in-hiding but one ready to take over for Sam Mele if the team suffered through another disappointing season. After a close second-place finish under Mele in 1962, the slow, heavy-hitting Twins slipped to third in 1963 and then to seventh in 1964. It did not take an expert to know that an axe with Mele's name on it had been fashioned in 1965. Likewise, neither acerbity nor malicious intent was needed to believe that Billy Martin was after Sam Mele's job when he began his coaching duties that year.

Mele, who was fired two years later, had a very different view of Billy. He had no sense at all that Billy was maneuvering to take his job.

"In '65 we won the pennant, but all year the writers kept writing how Billy is after my job, he's gonna stab me in the back, which was the furthest thing from the truth because he's helping me win games, and if I'm winning he's not gonna get the job."

Billy was, before anything else, a professional baseball man, part of the fraternity. His personal as well as his professional creed was to win at all costs. Everything he did from the moment he set foot on Tinker Field was devoted to that end. And he also happened to like Sam Mele.

Mele, Billy later said, was one of the two great third base coaches in the game (the other was Crosetti). He learned from him, he said, but Mele was equally insistent that he got every bit as much back from Billy—and then some.

Billy had been coming to spring camp for several seasons to work with the Twins' infielders. Mele knew from watching him that he was not only a good teacher but a likely manager as well.

"Oh, you knew he was going to be a good one right away," Mele said. "Because he was such a stickler for fundamentals, you knew he would do that as a manager himself when he got the chance. And he had judgment. He knew talent, believe me. He took Rod Carew over before anyone really knew about him. He worked with Bernie Allen and Rod, who was in the minors then, and he showed 'em stuff about middle infield play you wouldn't believe. Yeah, he did all that stuff about drawing lines in the dirt, here, here, and here, to teach the guys where to make what kind of throw to the bag—but I can still hear him telling them that when they were middle men on the double play they had to always anticipate a bad throw, get to the bag as quick as possible and then anticipate a bad throw."

Straight from Frank Crosetti and the Yankee Way.

Mele remembered that Billy spent endless hours with Carew, who had stiff hands to begin with, having the young player handle balls that were caromed off a wall at different speeds and angles. Billy was ready—and, Mele said, "he was a helluva third base coach."

In the beginning of the '65 season, still in spring training, Mele said that he talked with Billy about the absence of a running game on the team. He wanted, if possible, to have this side of the game more developed in the hopes of at least achieving a more aggressive and opportunistic style.

"Billy ran 'em all and they were getting thrown out and thrown out," Mele remembered. "Christ, four feet, five feet, close plays, the whole thing, and I just told him to keep doing it because it's gonna help us in the long run. And sure enough, towards the end of spring training, they started to take the extra base and now other teams were starting to rush their throws and didn't hit the cutoff man . . . and the players started seeing that they could win by doing this."

Mele not only gave Billy credit for establishing a running game among players who were not used to running, he credits him with being intimately involved in every facet of the team's success that year.

"How high a percentage can you put on his contribution to the pennant? I don't know, but how can you measure it? This guy made me a better manager. I could turn the team over to him any time, and I did. He was always there for me. This guy didn't sit back and let anything pass him by. Christ, this guy'd be on the bench and he'd be stealing their signs, everything else . . . I don't know how he did that, he wouldn't say too much about it but he was good, I'll tell you that. He used to get it from the pitcher or the catcher, watch an infielder give a sign behind his back to an outfielder; if the guys are moved in a certain way, even slightly, he knew it was a curve ball or a fastball. Joe Nossek, who's now on the White Sox, is great—but he was with us then, while Billy was doing all that. You know what? If Billy was after my job and they gave it to him, I would have been happy because it was he who got the job."

Because Mele became a close friend in that period, he had a chance to see Billy very differently than those Billy was trying to impress by promoting and creating his own career. To Mele, Billy was a man who loved and respected the game to the point of near-obsession. "We used to stay behind after a game, we'd have a few drinks and we'd just talk baseball. Baseball, baseball, baseball. He'd never tire of it, never stop talking about it, coming up with things. We'd lose a game and he'd want to go over it and over it. I'd tell him, 'Bill, it's just one game,' and he'd say, 'Yeah, but if we pick up just one thing we shouldn't have done, we might win tomorrow.' "

Because Billy was really a man of the fraternity, as Mele was, the manager knew—as those outside the fraternity couldn't know—that even if Billy one day might succeed him, it would never be because of anything he did behind his back. There were coaches and organization people who were like that—but Billy was not one of them.

At the 1966 All-Star game, Mele, manager of the American League team, selected Mickey Mantle as his centerfielder. At the last minute, Mantle asked to be excused, citing the need to rest his damaged legs. Mele excused him and named Tommie Agee, the White Sox centerfielder, in his place. The selection of Agee, a black player, prompted a serious death threat against Mele and Tony Oliva, one of the Twins' young stars. Mele was scared, he said, but his sense of humor remained intact—particularly with Billy Martin, whom he had named as an All-Star coach, around.

"Christ, when we got on the bus to go to the ballpark in New York, there were FBI men, cops, security people. They took us right to the stadium and when we got out they had these policemen all lined up to let us go through," Mele remembered. In the clubhouse, Mele called his coaches together to advise them of the latest information he had received and to ask them whether or not they thought Tony Oliva should be informed, withheld from the game, or allowed to play. The coaches unanimously recommended that Oliva not be told, that he be allowed to have his game. Then as the coaches left the room, Mele asked Billy to remain behind.

"I told Billy to shut the door," Mele said. "He did. I looked at him and said, 'Now look, Billy, I know you've always wanted to manage in the major leagues, manage the big teams, the big games. Here's your chance. You put my uniform on and you go out there and take the lineup right to home plate.' He said, 'You lousy sonofabitch, I know what you're driving at and you can forget it.' And then we both cracked up."

Another time, the manager and his coach were out fishing together on one of those ten thousand lakes. They did this frequently. They spent hours on the water, drinking and fishing and talking baseball.

"Of course, we overdrank in the boat," said Mele, "I made a cast and as I did I leaned forward and did a perfect dive into the goddamned lake. I had this rod of Billy's—he always brought the equipment—so when I came up I showed him I still had his rod, not to worry about it. But now I'm in this muck. The water wasn't that deep but there was this muck like quicksand. I said, 'Chrissakes, come on and help me.' He said, 'You know they're always writing about me wanting to manage the ballclub. I got a good spot right now.' He says to me, 'I'll throw you the anchor!' The sonofabitch. Of course, we laughed like hell and he got me back in the boat and the next day Calvin Griffith says, 'Jeez, I hear one of your coaches fell in the lake.' I says, 'Yeah, can you imagine one of them dumb coaches of mine doing something like that!' "

Billy's work progressed as the team's did not. The 1965 pennant was followed by a second-place finish in 1966 and a sluggish start in 1967. Fifty games into the 1967 season, Sam Mele was fired and replaced by Cal Ermer—a surprise to some who had expected Billy to be named immediately. In the years following the Twins' first pennant, Billy had impressed everyone with his relentless and infectious enthusiasm. He was credited for his work with Rod Carew, who was an immediate All-Star and Rookie of the Year in 1967, and with another of the team's young and "difficult" stars, shortstop Zoilo Versalles.

But Calvin Griffith was not as eager as others in and around the team to move Billy into a position of leadership. However successful Billy had been on the field, he had his detractors. Billy did not get along with some of the older players, among them the pitcher Jim Kaat, and some members of the coaching staff—Johnny Sain, the pitching coach, in particular.

Sain jealously guarded his pitchers, treating them as a unit within the team. He would often exempt them from workouts and drills imposed on other players—something that Billy, as well as other coaches, resented. The resentment between the two men led to a dugout quarrel in one instance and a kind of continual smoldering in the clubhouse.

And then there was Billy being Billy.

"Billy used to get me in trouble, the sonofabitch," Mele said, "because he used to come in late all the time, a half hour before game time—and you know, Sain and those other coaches, they all dressed in the same room, and they would see that and they would look at me and you know what was going through their minds."

Calvin Griffith, who understood the dynamics of baseball teams as well as anyone, ultimately replaced Johnny Sain with Early Wynn as his pitching coach, but he kept an increasingly wary eye on Billy, whose off-field habits seemed, at least, to represent a challenge to authority.

In 1966, Billy was involved in a serious brawl with the team's traveling secretary Howard Fox who, unfortunately for Billy, also happened to be a close friend and confidant of Calvin Griffith. Preexisting bad feelings between the men were exacerbated during a charter flight to Washington that the Twins wound up sharing with the Yankees. As Billy reported it many times afterward, the background mattered little if at all, and the foreground was an early morning wait in a hotel lobby for room keys that angered and frustrated Billy because he was the last served by the road secretary. Angry words were exchanged and then, Billy said, Fox threw his room key, which struck him in the lip. The fight immediately ensued.

Tom Mee, the team's press officer and a champion of Billy's in the Twins' inner circle, recalled the fight somewhat differently. He was on the team plane when the quarrel had its start and was there, on the bottom of the pile, when it ended hours later.

"The flight was supposed to take off from the Twin Cities Airport at eight o'clock but was delayed getting in. So the guys spent four hours at the bar in the airport—which is never best," Mee said. "And Billy could tend to get mean when he drank. So now he's drinking with his buddies, the Yankees—Ford, Mantle, Clete Boyer. Anyway, we get on the plane and up in the front on the right, Mantle, Billy, and Ford, and I don't recall who the fourth one was, were sitting in seats facing each other, just to the right of the pilots. Right across the aisle from them were Boyer and Hal Reniff—they're all mean drunks.

"Well, there was this gay steward on the plane and the guys started to get on him—because he asked them to buckle up or something. So right away they took a dislike to him. They started riding him pretty hard and pretty soon the steward had enough. So next the pilot came back, but instead of telling the guys to settle down, he went back in the compartment to speak to [Yankee manager] Ralph Houk and Sam Mele, who were sitting a row apart halfway back. Mele was asleep so the pilot said to Houk, 'You better straighten those guys out or I'm gonna set the plane down and kick 'em off.' And Howard Fox was sitting directly across the way from Houk and he gets up from his seat and gets Billy's attention up front by shaking a finger in his face. That was the worst thing he could have done. That really set Billy off. Now Houk gets up . . . and tells the guys to knock it off and they did. Except Reniff, sitting over there with Boyer, made some smart remark and Ralph Houk starts leaning over Boyer and starts pounding his fist to his chest to Reniff, challenging him to fight right there on the spot—and of course, Reniff slunk down in his seat. No one wanted any part of Ralph Houk. So that was the end of that.

"Now we get on the bus after they drop us off in Washington—it's about a forty-mile ride from Dulles and my wife and I were sitting . . . about halfway back. Billy is sitting right in front of us . . . and Howard Fox was sitting up front on a side seat with his wife across the way from him. At some point during the ride, Howard got up and grabbed a strap so he could lean over and say something to his wife. As he did, Billy hollers out, 'Kiss ass, Howard!' Howard doesn't respond, so Billy hollers again, 'Kiss ass, Howard!' Then he does it a third time, 'I said, kiss ass, Howard!' Howard glares at him this time and just sits down.

"Now we get to the hotel. Fox always gave out the keys to everybody. I knew there was going to be some trouble, so I said to my wife, 'Let's get out of here, just in case.' Fox was caught up in a problem of some kind having to do with Jim Perry's parents coming up from North Carolina and needing a room or something; meanwhile Billy is over there waiting. The desk clerk is there, Billy's standing at the end of the desk—about twelve feet away from Fox and Perry. Finally, Billy says to Fox, 'Did you have to wait till last to give me my key?' Fox doesn't answer. Billy says it again, 'Did you have to wait till last to give me my key, Howard?' Fox doesn't answer again, so Billy turns away from the counter and says, 'I'll tell you one thing, I'd like to get you outside, you sonofabitch.' And he starts to walk away. At that point, Fox takes off his glasses, puts 'em on a counter, and says, 'All right, you loud-mouthed bastard, you want me, come and get me!' So, jeez, in a flash Billy was on him—landed a real good one and Fox landed one back, and by this time I got Billy around the shoulders, and the three of us fall in a heap, Killebrew and Earl Battey grabbed Fox and pulled him away.

"And I'm laying on the floor and somehow—I don't know how this happened—I'm laying there on my back, Billy is between me and Bob Allison and he's looking me right in the eye about three inches away. There's fire in his eyes and he's throwing punches. I yelled at him, 'Billy, it's Tom, it's Tom'—and I'm trying to avoid his punches. He's driving his hands into the concrete, into the tile floor—he had no idea who he was swinging at, he was just blind with rage. . . . Anyway, Allison finally gets him off and drags him across the room, bends him back over a counter on the other side of the room—he has him by the tie: 'Are you gonna quit, Billy? Are you gonna quit?' 'Yeah, Bobby, yeah, Bobby, I'm okay, let me up.' So he let him up and he's standing there talking with his back to the other side of the room. And by this time, Killebrew and Battey had let Fox go—which was a big mistake. Fox was all bloody, but as soon as they let him go—zap!—he flies across the room, pushes Allison out of the way, and lands a Sunday on Billy. Luckily, Allison was able to jump in between them again before Billy could throw a retaliatory punch."

Jim Kaat, an eyewitness to the fight—and no friend of Billy's—remembers Fox throwing a key toward Billy and then fisticuffs immediately following. But whatever the exact details of the fight, its aftermath proved to be far more troubling. With this fight, there was no next-morning forgiving and forgetting. Fox and Billy were two very different people. Fox, college educated, from a well-to-do family, might as well have been from the Berkeley hills with Billy forever eyeing him from the flatlands. Worse, he was official family—and he was not about to have his position in the hierarchy compromised.

When Calvin Griffith flew into Boston on a peace mission, Fox was sure, Tom Mee said, that Billy was going to be either fired, suspended, or leveled with a huge fine. Instead, Griffith's immediate interest seemed to be damage control. He fined Billy $150, tried to shrug off the incident—and instead wound up infuriating Fox who, having Griffith's friendship and ear, never let up until Billy was actually fired as the team's manager three years later.

More immediately, what the fight with Fox did was slow Billy's climb within the organization. Griffith knew, perhaps better than anyone, just how talented his fiery coach was. Because he himself was from the old school, he was not about to let anything as meaningless as a life-threatening, blood-spilling brawl stand in the way of building the strongest possible ballclub—but he was not about to hastily turn the wheelhouse over to someone as unpredictable and as uncomfortable within the chain of command as Billy obviously was. There are any number of people who believe that Billy may well have sealed his fate in Minnesota with that fight because, even though he was eventually named the team's manager, it was done as much with breath held tightly as with hope for the future.

In any case, the question of Billy as a manager, something on Griffith's mind all the while, now seemed to move to another track—to one off to the side of the main route. Instead of moving Billy directly into line, Griffith more and more realized that his temperament—his temper—demanded testing and experience rather than simple opportunity. In 1967, when Sam Mele was fired, Billy was passed over as a successor. In 1968, when the Twins' Triple A team in Denver got off to a horrible start, Calvin Griffith gave Billy his chance—in the minors.

A number of accounts from that period suggest that Denver management itself was the moving force behind Billy's being hired. On the surface, that would seem to be so. There were discussions between Denver and Minnesota officials on a whole range of moves—including a managerial change—that might be made to strengthen the minor league team. A group of Denver executives led by team president Jim Burris had campaigned for Billy as a manager, but the deal was clinched only after Calvin Griffith had decided, for himself and *his* organization, that it was in their best interests to send him along. "Sending him to Denver was our idea, not theirs," he said.

For his part, Billy was not sure whether he was once more being sent packing or actually being given an opportunity. When the offer was made to him early in the 1968 season, he did not give an immediate answer. Instead he consulted Gretchen, and came around only reluctantly. For Billy, the question was never one of belief in his own ability nor even whether the Twins would really give him a fair shake, but whether managing in the minors would ever lead to a job in the majors. What Gretchen told him was that, regardless of the Twins, the time was right. Expansion was coming, there would be jobs, there would surely be a need for someone with a name who knew the game.

The Denver Bears had to make Billy wonder, however. When he took over on May 27, the team was 8–22, dead last in their division with the worst record in the league. Local papers ran headlines like "Indians Cuff Teddy Bears," and "Bears Blast Six Singles in Loss to Indy." Worse, the team itself seemed to have lost any sense of cohesion. Denver writers made a point of letting their readers know that Johnny Goryl, the team's manager, had lost control of the team, and that his successor would have a real job on his hands. "The Bears need a collective kick in the tail," wrote columnist Jim Graham, "and maybe 'Bad Boy' Billy Martin can provide it."

If Billy needed time to think before taking the job, he needed none to figure out what he wanted to do once he got there. As he had from the day he first realized his dreams were contained in a stitched white ball, he was determined to win, to use the very limitations and obstacles in his way to better his own cause. Whether it was the Kenney Park regulars, the Phoenix Senators, the New York Yankees, or the Denver Bears, Billy Martin had the ability to make more of himself than anyone expected. He had this uncanny capacity to create himself—powerful, effective, triumphant; a star—in places where only eclipse and defeat might have been anticipated.

Billy hit town wanting, initially, to make the best impression possible. He told newsmen on arriving that managing was really new to him and that he was just there to learn. He had been satisfied being a third-base coach, he said, because he liked the idea of "becoming another Frankie Crosetti."

Within a day, though, his competitive teeth were bared. "I'm here to win," he said, "my managerial education is secondary. . . . Right now my job is to convince the players that this is a dog-eat-dog business. I'm sure they know this in a general sense. But I'm starting with an open mind on individuals. . . . The only thing I'll demand is hustle and loyalty. I consider loyalty a two-way street."

Charlie Dressen couldn't have said it better, and, at first, the Denver Bears took to Billy rather the way the Oakland Oaks did to Dressen: They disliked him intensely.

"I couldn't stand him at first," Graig Nettles, the team's third baseman, said. "I would say for the first weeks it was like that. He'd scream and rave and rant and he just turned everybody off. Until we realized that he could teach us how to win—which is what he did."

Billy was actually at an advantage because of the team's previously wretched performance. When he took over, they had lost nine straight, including seven at home. Almost any positive thing he did or said would be to his credit. The first game under his direction was an 11–1 walloping at the hands of the Oklahoma City 89'ers. But Billy caught some ink by saying that the team's problem really was not talent. "Our problem right now is to taste a little blood and get the confidence of these guys up. Most people miss the great part mental outlook plays in this game."

Blood and confidence came sooner than anyone expected. When Billy took over, the team had yet to have even a winning homestand. Their nine-game losing streak had set a team record. But in an 18-game homestand, the team divided its games, winning nine, losing nine. And then, on a long road trip, the Bears went 5–7 but only after losing three of their final four games.

Billy let everyone know that winning was on his mind, and that he would do things differently to get there. After an early June loss to the Seattle Angels, Billy praised his team for their hustle but made a point of letting people know that a failed cutoff play cost the team the game. After a tough defeat to the Tulsa Oilers, he went wild in the

1

*Alfred Manuel Martin, age three.*

2

*Billy's reputation for battling with umpires goes way back; this cartoon appeared in his high school yearbook.*

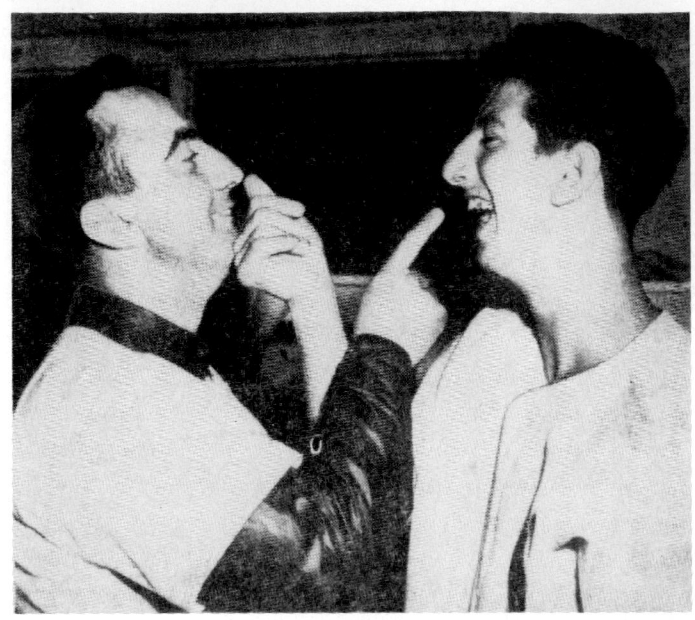

3

*Billy compares noses with his Oakland Oaks teammate Dario Lodigiani (left)—one of the few times he found the subject funny.*

*Billy (the newspaper caption called him "the Oakland Ball Club's brilliant young infielder") signs a contract while Charley Dressen (center) and Brick Laws, team president, look on.*

4

5

*Newspaper cartoon, 1949.*

6 *Billy and Casey Stengel after Billy drove in the runs that clinched the 1952 pennant.*

7

*Billy rushes in to snare Jackie Robinson's popup in game seven of the 1952 Series, as Robinson and Phil Rizzuto look on.*

*Billy in the locker room after his two-for-five day capped a twelve-hit performance in the six-game 1953 World Series.*

8

9

*Billy kisses his mother goodbye as he heads off to face the Draft Board in 1954.*

10

*Now a Cincinnati Red, Billy tangles with Cubs pitcher Jim Brewer.*

11

*A young-looking Billy prepares to take over as manager of the Minnesota Twins.*

*Billy and Ed Brinkman plead the Tigers' cause in Billy's next managerial stop.*

12

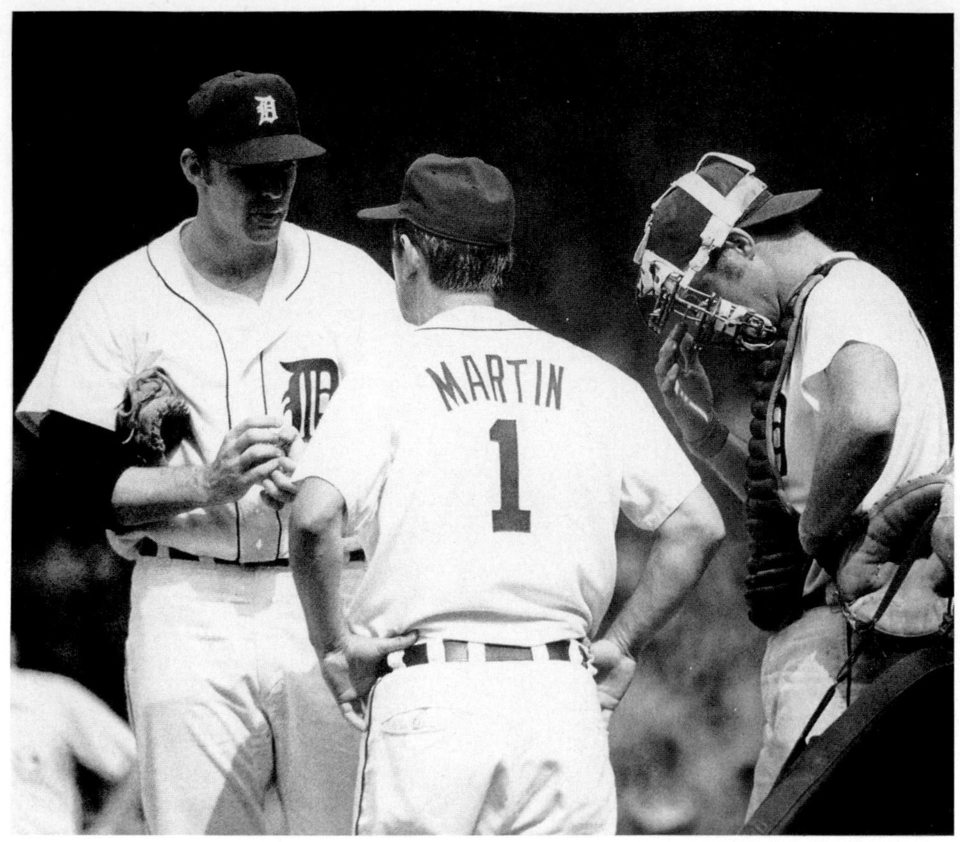


13 *Billy, here with Dean Chance and catcher Bill Freehan, was always very demanding of his pitchers. Occasionally, those demands included hitting batters, with fines for those who disobeyed.*

*Billy's return to the New York Yankees meant many dugout reunions, as here with Mickey Mantle and Whitey Ford.*

14 *Next stop for Billy was Texas, as manager of the Rangers from 1974–76, the Texas experience furthering his growing gunslinger image.* 15

16

17 *Billy's most famous confrontation as Yankee manager was with Reggie Jackson in Fenway Park. Reggie was slow to react to a bloop single by Jim Rice, and Billy pulled him from the game in the middle of the inning. Players and coaches had to jump between the two to prevent an all-out fight on national television.*

18

*Billy's next (and next-to last) managerial stop was back home in Oakland, where the A's promoted BillyBall, featuring adventurous baserunning, daring managing, and as always, Billy's running battles with the umpires.*

19

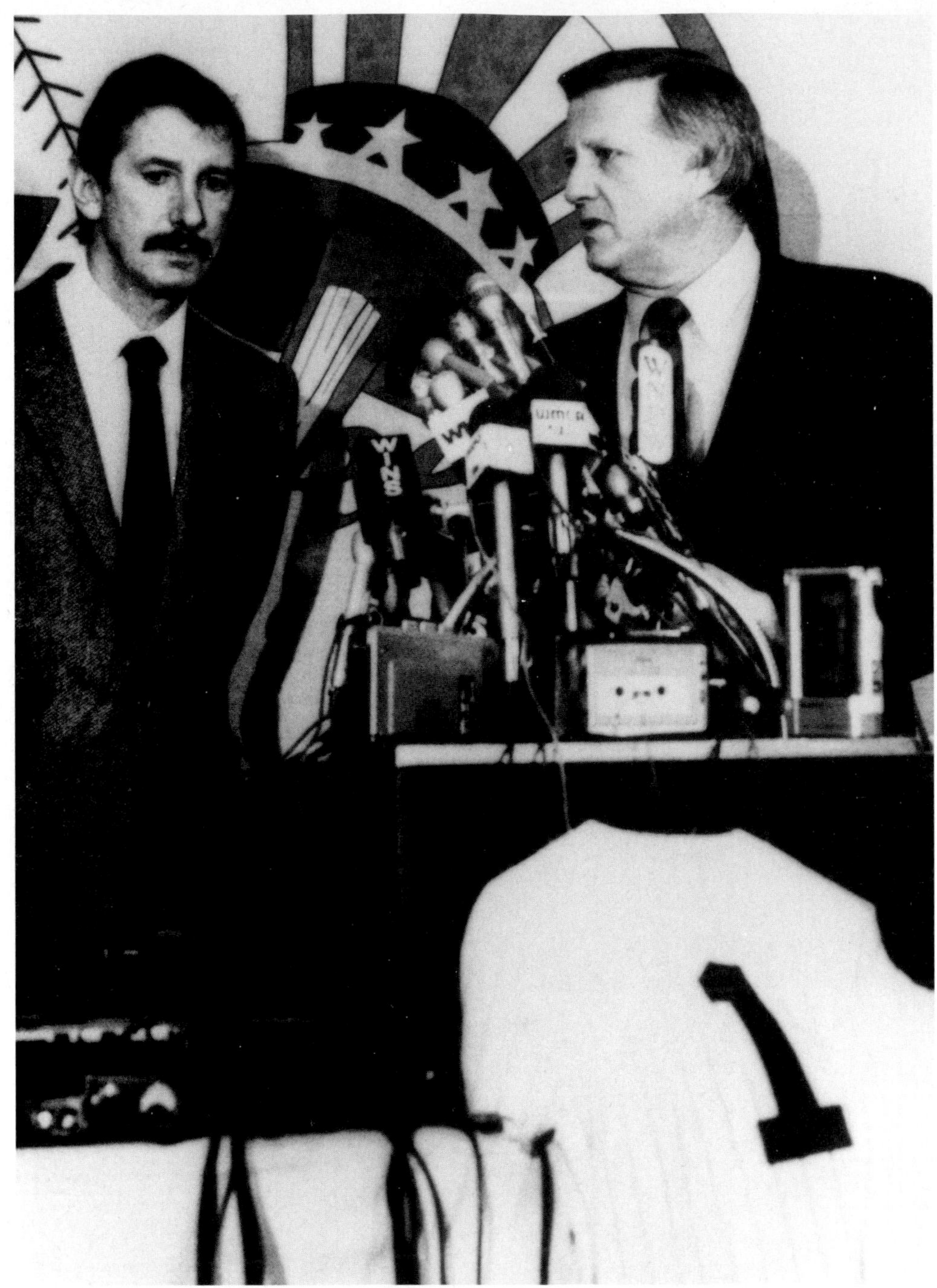

20 *Billy and George. The could never help looking uneasy with each other, even on happy occasions like this, when they were announcing the retirement of Billy's number.*

21

*For all the comic opera buffoonery of the hire-fire-hire-fire-hire of Billy's last years as a manager, he was never so much in control as when he wore Yankee pinstripes and commanded the game from the steps of the dugout.*

*Billy tries to hold back tears as his mother and sisters look on proudly on Billy Martin Day at Yankee Stadium, 1986.*

22

23 *Billy and Mickey at Yankee Stadium, 1985.*

24

*Billy with his fourth wife, Jill.*

25 *Billy with Bill Reedy.*

26 *Billy's casket is carried down the steps of St. Patrick's Cathedral as Jill Martin, flanked by Billy Joe Martin and Richard Nixon, looks on.*

27 *Billy and his mother while he was managing Oakland. The two died within weeks of each other.*

clubhouse for half an hour following the game, letting his players—and anyone within earshot—know that four of the Oilers' seven runs were the result of walks, that a poorly played bunt—bad judgment—cost another and then that two passed balls resulted in two more runs. All of these mistakes, Billy thundered, came from lapses of attention. Little things win games—and lose them as well.

Within his first weeks on the job, he had his first run-in with umpires, protesting an extra-inning loss to Seattle which, Billy said, was the result of an umpire reversing a "judgment" call (not allowed under the rules), permitting Seattle's winning run to score; days after that, he took the first of his eight ejections that season, protesting a balk call and, in the process, kicking dirt all over the home-plate umpire.

Billy was ubiquitous. While he was powerless to change the personnel on his team, he could lash, coax, wheedle, and intimidate his players into doing things his way. "You knew pretty quickly that he couldn't stand losing," Graig Nettles said, "so that as a player you became scared to lose."

Billy did things differently, unpredictably. The running game he had developed for Sam Mele, he instituted immediately for the Denver Bears. Bob Oliver, the slugger, stole home not once but twice that season. The old first-third double steal, with the runner on first falling down and drawing a throw while the base runner on third scampers home, became a part of the attack—at least to the point where other teams worried about it, changed their defensive alignments and pitch selection, and sometimes hurried into errors and sloppy play. The team hit and run, won games with squeeze plays, set up winning runs with sacrifice bunts and steals. In one come-from-behind win, the tying run was scored on a steal of home, a daring gamble with the game on the line.

Billy taught people how to win, Graig Nettles said, by impressing on them that everything they did was for the team: the team was the unit—a family, an army—and its undisputed leader and general was the manager. "Billy used to have this thing about college players on the team—maybe because he didn't go to college himself—but he'd bench us," Nettles said, "and then tell us that we'd learn more on the bench next to him than we did in college."

One time in San Diego, Nettles's hometown, Billy pulled his third baseman from the lineup at the last minute, a provocative and deeply embarrassing move. "He waited until I was in the field," Nettles said in his autobiography, *Balls*, "then he called time, and then he sent someone else out to replace me. He was letting me know that he was going to be the boss of the ballclub, that the players were not going to run the team, that he was."

Billy gave the same message to everyone: This was *his* ballclub, and it would do things the way he wanted them done. But he was never so far removed that he wasn't right down there with his players, as though he was one of them before he was anything else.

In one game, he batted Tom Tichinski, a catcher, eighth. Tichinski exploded, complaining that a hitter of his caliber shouldn't be dropped in the order that way. Perhaps remembering his own travails, but surely remembering an old trick used by Casey Stengel, Billy suddenly inaugurated his version of the names-in-a-hat trick. He tore up paper scraps, dropped them in a cap, and had the players draw them out in what would be the day's batting order. Strangely, Tichinski's name still came out eighth, but it hardly mattered. A troublesome situation had been defused, and the team was being drawn still closer to their leader.

Billy brought the fans into the act as well. At one Bears home game, he rounded up a few of the players, joining them himself, for a pre-game hitting exhibition against a superstar softball pitcher. The players, including Billy, were easily dispatched, and the fans loved it, loved Billy's Bears—and loved Billy.

The team played an exhibition game against the Minnesota Twins. Billy played right field through half the game, won by the parent club, 8–2. But Billy *really* played. He left the game because he swung so hard at one pitch, he pulled muscles in his rib cage.

Billy was also on the field in a players-and-wives game—it was all for fun, and for promoting his idea of one team, one leader. He ran clinics for kids, teaching them proper techniques for different fundamentals, but also speaking over their heads to an increasingly fascinated and captivated media who continued to report that the once moribund Denver Bears were not dead after all.

The Bears, under Billy, were not only resuscitated, they were rejuvenated, and turned in a completely different direction. By midsummer they were out of the cellar. By season's end, they were the hottest team in the league, winning twenty-six of thirty-five games down the stretch to finish in fourth place, one game above .500. The team's overall record under Billy was 65–50, an astonishing accomplishment, and one that obviously caught the attention of many people beyond the city of Denver, including, most importantly, Billy's employers.

By season's end, there was ample speculation that Billy would soon be moving on to a major league managing assignment. There were openings in the American League expansion cities, Kansas City and Seattle, as well as with old-line teams who were looking around for new field leaders—including the Twins.

Charlie Metro, the director of player development for the new Kansas City Royals, went out of his way to publicly praise Billy. "I've never seen a manager develop as fast as Martin," he told the *Denver Post*. "I think he's the outstanding big-league prospect in the minors."

Calvin Griffith, heavily involved in speculation about the future of his own team after a clearly disappointing season, continued to brush aside speculation that he would soon replace Cal Ermer, the incumbent manager, with Billy. Griffith had let it be known in August that Ermer would not be back, but he played a waiting game with Billy, still entirely cognizant of what he had accomplished.

"We may make up our minds by September 22," he said as the Bears season was coming to a close. "Billy has done a fantastic job at Denver. . . . I let him go to prove to himself and the baseball world that he can do it and, yes, he has proved that."

For all that, winning had come with a price. Not everyone who played for him was taken with him. His pitchers groused about the way they were treated. One pitcher, Joe Grzenda, complained about being used while he had a sore arm. Other pitchers, as the team made its push through the final weeks of the season, were used on unusually short rest. *Post* columnist Frank Hardaway noted that the team's most effective pitchers—Danny Morris and Jerry Crider—had been obviously overworked. "Martin has called on Morris to start seven times with only two days of rest. Crider has been called on six times—twice with a relief stint thrown in for good measure. . . . It is amazing that each has posted 4–2 records in these thirteen third-day starts."

Calvin Griffith's reservations, perhaps strategic as well as personal, were more significant.

"The big thing is his temperament," he told a Minnesota reporter. "He's got kicked out of eight games, and you don't help your team getting kicked out of the game. Of course, my uncle Clark got kicked out of fifty games one year.

"I'm looking for a take-charge type of manager. Martin was a tough coach. I'm sure he'd be a tough manager. But you've got to realize there's a difference between being tough and obnoxious."

Still, after the season he had, after he had so obviously "proven to himself and to others" what nearly everyone knew anyway, the Minnesota Twins on October 11 made Billy Martin their next manager, offering him a one-year contract at an estimated $50,000, which he quickly accepted.

A new era in the game was about to begin—one largely fashioned in the mind and imagination of Billy Martin.

# CHAPTER 9

There is a standing cliché about managers: that they are only as good as the players they have. Like most clichés, this one is rooted in truth. But also, like most clichés, this one has exceptions. Billy Martin was one of them. As a manager, he of course coveted talented players; he fought to have them and then keep them on his teams. But he, possibly more than any manager of his time, was able to make something of whatever talent he had. Possibly because he learned, as a player, just how far limited ability could be taken, perhaps because he knew just how much the game yielded up to those who observed more and tried harder, he never approached any managing job with the assumption that he couldn't win.

Billy's greatest asset—and liability—as a manager was that he believed he could win on the spot: any time, anywhere, with any group of players. There are managers who approach teams with five-year plans, who work hard to bring players along slowly, letting them ripen through defeat into playing maturity.

Billy was never that way. For all his knowledge of the game and of what players could and could not do, his one approach—wherever he was, whoever the owner, whatever the payroll—was winning. His views of strategy, of psychology, of handling pitching staffs and temperamental players, were all subservient to this one goal of winning.

He once impatiently brushed off a reporter who did not know him very well but who asked him why he managed so differently with different teams.

"You manage the team you have," he said, in that short manner he reserved for unknown and uninformed media people who might, after all, have agendas he knew nothing about. "You use whatever you have to win."

At Denver, Billy had a couple of home run batters—Bob Oliver and Graig Nettles—and a handful of other everyday players (Pat Kelly, George Mitterwald, Rick Renick) who wound up with major league experience. But the team was surely not greatly blessed. There were no consistent hitters, and the pitching staff—with the exception of Tom Hall—was painfully deficient (the team's ERA leader was forty-five-year-old Art Fowler, who became Billy's unofficial pitching coach, confidant, and drinking buddy). It didn't matter. Another manager's goal might have been respectability or player development; Billy's goal was to jump-start his team, immediately, into winning—which he did.

The Minnesota Twins were another story. Not only were they major league, they had real (if frayed and underachieving) talent. They had been in the hunt in recent years, following their 1965 pennant with a heartbreaking four-team rush to the wire in 1967, in which they ultimately lost to the Boston Red Sox on the final day of the season—a defeat painfully etched in then third-base coach Billy Martin's mind.

Billy chose the Twins job from among several he might have landed because, in purely practical terms, it was the best one around. The Twins, compared to the expansion teams and the shabbier old-line teams, including the Yankees, promised the best chance for winning right away. The Twins went into the 1969 season with as much chance for a divisional title as any other team in the West.

There was still another reason to choose the Twins. He had made a home in Minnesota, the first real one he had had since he left Berkeley in 1946. Though he was only forty, he had been on the road for almost a quarter of a century. Pit stops, bars, hotel rooms, the flash and dash of celebrity hijinks, were all part of baseball's high-pressured culture of one-night stands and endless travel arrangements. Through it all, through a failed marriage and then a second try, he had been looking for this balancing act between a home life and the game.

His Berkeley roots continued to remain problematic for him. He returned there nearly every year, spending brief time with old friends, particularly Lewis Figone, a cousin of one of his mother's oldest friends. Figone and Billy had briefly gone into business together, opening a bar in 1959–60, which failed with a great deal of fanfare. The two men subsequently shared a love of good times, spending part of each winter duck hunting, camping, drinking. But he saw fewer and fewer of the West Berkeley Boys, and spent less and less time with his family. From the time he had had his falling out with Ruben DeAlba—about the same time his marriage to Lois failed—there was just less pull to that side of San Pablo Avenue.

Minnesota was new and different. He had a comfortable rented home in the Twin Cities, in the Hillsborough section not far from the ballpark. His second child, Billy Joe, had been born in 1962 and was beginning to attend school. With his wife's help and that of local businessmen he had befriended, he had begun to think about making investments in the area, which might help him defray the unusually large tax bills he had carelessly accumulated—the result, usually, of his forgoing withholding payments throughout the year.

Yet this new home was still just a promise, the roots shallow rather than deep, the marriage to baseball still more compelling than any other. Billy had never been able to work out a coherent parental relationship with his daughter from his first marriage, Kelly Ann, now a teenager. Kelly would visit Billy briefly over the summers while he was a player, and now she tried to fit into this new family. It didn't work. Her father was not around much, and when he was he was usually occupied.

"Art Fowler used to come over all the time," Kelly said. "My dad and Art would sit around and tell stories and jokes and then I'd have to leave the room because Art was gonna tell one of those jokes where girls couldn't be present."

Kelly often served as a baby-sitter for her younger brother when Billy and Gretchen were not in the house, and that proved difficult because she had a wild streak not unlike her father's—or her grandmother's. Even though she was underaged, she would put the baby in the back of one of the family cars and then drive around town, replacing the car in its exact spot, marked off by lines, in the driveway. Then she would play in the basement, in Billy's specially constructed bar, having to explain to her father why some bottles were short, some beer missing. Eventually, she said, she had a physical battle one time with Gretchen—frying pans flying, pushing and shoving—and following a fierce quarrel she overheard between Billy and Gretchen concerning this fight, she stopped visiting entirely.

Tony Kubek, broadcasting NBC's "Game of the Week," got another and even more intriguing view of just how precarious Billy's home life was in this period.

"Mickey [Mantle] was working with us that year, pre-game stuff, and we were supposed to get there Friday, go to Billy's house to do the show," Kubek remembered. "Well, Mickey had had a few beers, maybe more, and so we waited and waited, finally we're waiting at Billy's house, and they had like a semi parked in the driveway at the house next to Billy's and there was probably a crew of fifteen people there. . . . Finally it's one o'clock, we go down to Billy's rec room, Mickey has finally shown up. Billy says, 'Come on, Mickey, let's have a couple of drinks.' . . . Now we get in the rec room and there are these pictures all over the wall, a lot of them with him and Mickey. Billy says, 'Start with this one, I want to tell a story.'

"The picture was of a log cabin somewhere in Texas—and Billy had a .45 revolver, a pistol, to Mickey's head. So I introduced the thing and Billy comes in and says, 'Here's what kind of buddies we are, we were just kidding around . . .' and then Mickey comes in—this is all on tape—and says, 'The only thing is, we found out later that the gun was really loaded.' He's pulling the trigger, it was like Russian roulette and they were just laughing and laughing about it. I sat there for four hours trying to get just seven or eight minutes I could use on tape and it was really something. The language got totally out of hand and unbelievable but the thing was, all the while, Gretchen, without Billy's realizing it, was sitting upstairs in that mobile unit watching and listening to the whole thing. She didn't care for Mickey because she thought he was leading Billy astray, and Merlyn [Mickey's wife] didn't like Billy for the same reason. But Billy and Mickey could have cared less, they were just two little kids having a good time."

On the field, in spite of taking over a good team he was already familiar with, there were many uncertainties. Billy was suddenly thrust into a situation where he had limited control and a strong and often quirky front office to answer to.

Even at this early stage of his career, Billy had definite ideas about managing. Managers were bosses, generals. The only problem was that that was not the ticket that had been written for him by Calvin Griffith, who considered himself, if not an absolute dictator, at least the commander-in-chief. Managers could call themselves generals, but they moved at his bidding and not vice versa. They certainly had to make themselves available for consultation. Billy's deal was for a year, even though he wanted long-term security, because that was the way Griffith did things. In addition, no matter what kind of input Billy said he wanted, player development—key in Billy's idea of generalship—was absolutely off limits. And he had to report regularly to Griffith every afternoon around four—not later, because Griffith began a daily nap at five—to go over what moves he made on the field. Billy, said Griffith, "is a personality who has the ability to be another Casey Stengel," adding, just to be sure people knew exactly where he was coming from, "My brother Billy [Robertson—a Twins executive] says that Billy is either going to be the greatest manager in baseball—or the worst."

Even down on the field, among the ranks, generalship was not as automatic as it might have been—as it had been, say, when Casey Stengel was managing the Yankees and felt free enough, as actually happened once, to slap a player like Mickey Mantle if he thought he was out of line.

The Twins were not the Denver Bears. The big home run hitters were not the youthful Bob Oliver and Graig Nettles but the aging Harmon Killebrew and Bob Allison; the pitching staff had tough, smart, and independent-minded veterans like Jim Kaat, Jim Perry, and others who had been close to Johnny Sain rather than to Billy. And then, added to this already combustible mix, spring training opened with sixteen players unsigned and unwilling to come to camp. It wasn't a strike, but the Players Association had urged veterans not to sign their contracts and to skip the early days of training camp. Billy, according to one beat writer, urged fans coming to the team's first exhibition games to buy programs, because "they won't recognize anybody on our team."

Still, Billy went about drawing in his team as he had in Denver. Whatever problems there were with the front office, with contract negotiations, with the status of veterans (not to mention the manager), the Minnesota Twins were still going to play baseball the way Billy Martin wanted them to. His approach to his players from the start was both demanding and easygoing. In no uncertain terms, he told the team—everyone on it, including the pitchers—that they were going to run; all of the things he had done when he coached for Mele he would do again. Taking the extra base would be the rule not the exception; stealing bases would be an everyday part of the attack; fundamentals were to be stressed. "Billy plans to have his team play 'Inside Baseball,' " wrote columnist Dick Cullum. Steal, double steal, delayed steal, the squeeze, the sacrifice were all to be used. Smart, aggressive baseball was the style; winning was the goal. As if to underscore this, Billy had his team go for the jugular even during those spring games. In one game against the Washington Senators—managed by another rookie skipper, Ted Williams—the Twins took a come-from-behind win using a safety squeeze and a steal of home, something that infuriated the Senator players and manager but which pleased Billy enormously.

"It was the first time I've seen Ted since he got the job," he told newsmen later. "Our salaries don't bring us into the same circles." But the game did. "Of course I was trying to win," he said. "You can say what you want about exhibitions, but the name of the game with me is winning. Don't you think Ted Williams was trying to win when he brought in a left-handed pitcher to face one of our left-handed hitters?"

But Billy was no taskmaster. He wasn't running a boot camp but one in which his players could feel free to do what they wanted—provided they took care of business on the field. In fact, Billy, borrowing a page from Casey Stengel perhaps, instituted a system of little rewards for his players. After one victory over the Braves in West Palm Beach, Billy arranged for the team bus to take the players downtown for, as he put it, "ninety minutes of fun and libation."

Billy also courted and coaxed his players, particularly those he knew could be an integral part of his success. Rod Carew, who had followed a spectacular rookie season in 1967 with a troubled one in 1968, was particularly glad to have Billy back in the fold. Carew gave much credit for his own success to the time Billy had spent with him years before. Billy—dispelling organizational talk that Carew might be converted to shortstop—told him he was the team's second baseman, period.

"We'll be a different ballclub with Billy managing," Carew said. "I went downhill from the time he left the club. He was a great influence on me. I'll be glad to play for him."

But no one really knew whether or not the Twins would be a different ballclub when the season opened. The contract hassles, the mini-boycott of camp, and a freak hand injury to pitcher Dave Boswell prompted Calvin Griffith to declare that that spring had been the worst he had known in baseball, but that Billy had been great: "He has run the best spring camp I have ever seen."

Billy approached the season desperately wanting to get off on the right foot. People familiar with his game all stress the importance to him of winning right away, particularly on opening day.

"I feel like there's a one-hundred-pound weight on my shoulders,"

Billy said on the eve of the new season. "I've been trying to inject so much into the players and my coaches this spring. I know I've been tough on some people. Now we're ready to see if we've done any good down in Florida."

The Twins did not win on opening day—or the day after or the day after that or the day after that. They lost four straight to open the season, and the most noticeable thing about the club was the tautness of its manager's nerves.

There is no doubt that it was doubly difficult to begin by losing two games to the expansion Kansas City Royals. A friend of Billy's was overheard telling him, "I would have bet my house and wife that we wouldn't lose both games to Kansas City."

"I'll go you one better," Billy retorted, "I would have bet my life on it."

The losses were especially galling because the team just seemed to go to sleep, and was impervious to the wake-up call Billy had been sounding from day one. The opening day loss, 4–3, was in extra innings and was the result, Billy said, of mental mistakes: a blown outfield call, a pitcher—Tom Hall—going with a fastball in a situation where a breaking pitch had been ordered. The next day's loss to the Royals, another one-run extra-inning game, was again plagued by blown opportunities.

When the Twins finally won their first game at the close of a three-game set against the Angels, Billy was visibly relieved. Why had he taken so long to win, he was asked. "I wanted to bring it home to my mother as a present," he said. The team's next stop was Oakland.

It took awhile for the Twins to kick into gear, and in the meantime Calvin Griffith kept watch on Billy. When Billy made a point of barring a *Sports Illustrated* reporter from the team's clubhouse in Oakland because the magazine had run an article critical of Billy's off-field behavior, Griffith, the day following, reminded a Minneapolis columnist that the odds on Billy's being selected to manage the Twins just a year ago had been "1000–1." Billy's temperament and reports of his off-field behavior had stood in his way, Griffith reported telling Billy then, and he had only promised Billy that he would have a better job in the organization if he did well at Denver. The reminder, though not specific, was clear enough: The front office expected its manager to comport himself at all times in a manner acceptable to the front office.

When the Twins came off the road, they were greeted by the largest home opening crowd in their history—and it was for Billy, said one local headline. He was box office even before the team had established itself.

When the Twins won then and on the day following, it was already clear that Calvin Griffith had a countervailing force on his hands as well as an unpredictable employee. Billy almost immediately turned the fans on—as well as the media.

"They just didn't play baseball that way at Metropolitan Stadium in 1968," began one story detailing the Twins' fifth straight victory, a 6–5 come-from-behind win over the Angels. The game report acknowledged that there were many heroes in this victory—Rod Carew stole home to tie the game in the seventh, Harmon Killebrew hit a game-winning single to right field (previously he would *never* hit to the opposite field)—but, said the article, "this win should go to the Twins' colorful new manager. It was strategy, sometimes audacious, that turned the game around. It was the kind of victory that constantly eluded Minnesota in 1968." Nine games into the season, the Twins were in a three-way tie for first place in the American League's Western Division, noted the somewhat overheated beat writer who, in ignoring their lackluster 5–4 record, was only picking up on the excitement that Billy seemed to inspire.

During the last week of April and the first week of May, the Twins surged to the top of the AL West by winning eight games in a row. More importantly—for Billy—they established themselves as *his* team. Fans, writers, and opponents all became aware that the team not only was playing unusually well, but with a style clearly identified with its new manager. Attendance swelled at the ballpark—as did ink in the hometown papers. As they never had before, local writers suddenly found themselves treated to a seminar on "inside baseball" so long as the Twins kept winning.

Why did the manager call for a bunt with the bases loaded and three runs already in in the first inning of a game that the Twins wound up winning 12–1? "Because," Billy said, "I wanted that one more run. If we had scored only one run at that point, I'd have had the batter hitting away—but in this situation he could have hit into a double play." Billy called for the bunt, it was clear, because he was going for the kill—right away, never mind the niceties.

Why a delayed double-steal with two out and the pitcher hitting? Wasn't that a sure invitation to terminating a rally and an inning? On the contrary, said the willing professor, "I don't worry about a man being thrown out and the pitcher possibly leading off the next inning. All I'm interested in is the run and we got it on the catcher's bad throw to third base attempting to get Graig Nettles. He scored on the error."

Whatever people wanted to know, Billy seemed willing to explain. Why did hitting seem to be "infectious"? There wasn't anything seeming about it; one hit lessens the pressure on the next hitter, Billy pointed out, "and the next man doesn't want to be outdone. Hits lead to runs and runs lead to runs. That's what we want!"

Why always go for a bigger lead, why pile it on?

"Because a lead takes away so much from the club that's behind. They can't bunt and steal, they can't play with reckless abandon. It limits the things they can do."

Everything was for winning. There had been nothing like it in the state of Minnesota since George Mikan—and he was big and slow and a perfect gentleman.

By April's end, no one confused Billy with George Mikan. You did *anything* to win. When the Oakland A's, with their formidable young slugger, Reggie Jackson, came to town for the first time, Billy was ready. The A's won the series opener easily, 7–0. Billy got himself tossed by arguing a safe call at home plate with rookie umpire Larry Barnett, whom he had been needling for three innings. The Twins took the second game of the series 6–4 and then, in the finale, all hell broke loose. With Mickey Mantle in the stands, the A's jumped to a 5–0 lead after four innings. Jackson homered in each of his first two plate appearances and was the leadoff hitter in the fifth.

The Twins pitcher, Dick Woodson—an unsettlingly wild and hard thrower—uncorked a pitch at Jackson's head. It was not just high and tight, it was behind him—behind his head, the surest sign, any baseball person would say, that the hitter was being thrown at intentionally. Jackson dusted himself off and stood in again. The next pitch sailed at least four feet over his head, crashing against the backstop. Jackson seemed to explode in segments. For a moment he just stood there, gazing at Woodson. Then he threw his bat aside. Then he charged the mound. By the time he got there, every player on the field and those in both dugouts and bullpens had seemed to converge there with him. The fight—no less than the incident that precipitated it—was ugly and disturbing. But even at this early stage of Billy's stewardship, perhaps just because of that, it came off like theater; even this was part of the new show, staged by a unique master.

*Minneapolis Tribune* writer Dave Mona, far from recoiling from what he saw, seemed to join the general chorus of aroused approval, cheering their new champion on:

"So unusual are full-scale brawls in these parts that not only the dugouts but the bullpens emptied onto the field. . . . It should be noted that Minnesota manager Billy Martin, a veteran of one or two fights, conducted himself admirably. He grabbed Oakland catcher Dave Duncan by the throat when Duncan tried to join the scuffle around the two principals. Martin passed Duncan to Bob Allison where the catcher spent the remainder of the melee in an uncomfortable and unbreakable full nelson.

"Martin was unimpressed with Jackson's display. 'You don't come after a guy when he throws behind you and six feet over your head. I didn't tell Woodson to brush Jackson back, but when I do order a brushback it won't be where either of those two pitches went. I may call for a brush but I'll never tell one of my players to throw at a man. . . . When they finally got Jackson off Woodson, he yelled at me that he was going to get me. I want somebody to write that so that if we ever get in a fight, he won't be able to sue me and say I started it.' "

For his part, Reggie Jackson had no doubts about the origin of the incident. He did not need a column in a newspaper to tell him something he already knew about Billy Martin. Even though this was 1969, a full decade before these two would come to far more celebrated loggerheads, it was clear no love was lost between them:

"When I came out of the dugout in the fifth inning," Reggie explained shortly afterward, "I knew I was going down. That's the kind of manager Billy Martin is. If someone is beating his club, he's going to put a little fear in his heart. I've been thrown at before but not like that. And I can't sell popcorn. Baseball is my business. At moments like that, you get lost in anger. Thoughts go through your mind about Tony Conigliaro getting hit and almost losing the sight of his eye. I was scared after that second pitch. I don't blame Woodson. He pitched under orders. But I blame the manager."

More than twenty years later, Jackson still recalled the incident much as he did then. It was not Woodson who threw at him, it was Billy—because that was how he played the game. "You knew he would do anything to win a game," he said. "I don't know where exactly I learned that he threw at guys, it was just something you pick up—it gets out on the grapevine pretty quickly and you know."

The major thing that Billy accomplished in these early weeks was that he got his team to believe in itself and, perhaps more importantly, in him. The Jackson incident, Billy told columnist Sid Hartmann, recalling Casey Stengel again, helped mold his team. But throwing at hitters and fighting was not what it was all about. It was about establishing an aggressive and unpredictable approach to the game, throwing fear and uncertainty into the hearts of opponents and into the minds of opposing managers. The Twins won a game against Seattle in early May with a triple steal, led by Rod Carew's third swipe of home in three tries. The spectacle of three men taking advantage at once was just as important as the desired result—like the purpose pitches at Reggie, it struck fear, wonder, and uncertainty into the minds of the opposition. Ultimately, it made them play differently.

And then there was Carew, the moody young player who only a year before, angry and withdrawn over being benched, had actually left the team at one point. With Billy, he had not only regained form but had risen to leadership. Billy told Carew early in the spring that he not only had a starting position, but his speed was going to be a fundamental part of what the Twins did. He would steal bases, Billy said, and particularly he would steal home. Billy was aware of the major league record for steals of home in a season (eight), and he simply informed his young star that he was going to break it.

For Carew, his manager's confidence was more than appreciated. "I learned something from Billy that I never forgot. I used to think about stealing bases in terms of speed, in terms of my legs. Billy taught me that you steal with your head," Carew said. "In stealing home, you watch the pitcher, you take your lead in a certain way, you get into the minds of the pitcher and the catcher, you watch what they do. You don't have to be particularly fast to take advantage."

For Billy, winning Carew over involved far more than confidence-building. It was team-building. Billy saw in Carew a spearhead for the game he wanted to establish. The kind of thinking he wanted from Carew, he wanted from his team. He wanted all his players to be "alive," as he had once been taught, to become baseball-aware every second they were on the field, to win games with the extra initiative and aggressiveness that awareness brought. It was not only hitting that was infectious, but anything anyone did to win games. It was winning that was ultimately infectious and Billy had his team winning in such dramatic fashion, at such an early stage of the campaign, that it set a tone for the rest of the league and, most importantly, within the team itself.

"The big thing was that Billy had more balls than any manager I've ever seen," said Charlie Silvera, whom Billy had hired as a coach, true to his word given almost twenty years earlier. "He wasn't afraid to make a mistake. They say, 'Save your trick plays for the road, play conservatively at home.' Stealing home, suicide squeeze . . . if they failed on the road there wouldn't be the same impact. But Billy didn't give a damn. He had the guts of a burglar. He'd do just what he wanted to do and if it didn't work, too bad. He upset other players, other managers by his aggressiveness—they'd wind up saying, 'Oh my goodness, what do we have to do now?' He'd make a defensive ballclub out of the other team. He did that right away. And our guys saw it and believed in it. They saw they could do it and they made it work."

But as surely as Billy unsettled opponents on the field, he had an equally unsettling influence on his employers. Within the first couple of months of the season, a simmering source of conflict between Billy and the farm department came to a full boil and then to an explosion.

"The keg of dynamite that Calvin Griffith has been sitting on . . . exploded yesterday . . . and did most of its damage to the Twins farm department, headed by Griffith's brother, Sherry Robertson," began a lead in one of the local papers.

The triggering incident was the demotion of a Twins pitcher, Charley Walters, to the low minors. Billy had been high on Walters during the spring and had all but promised him that if he did not stick with the big team, he would be pitching at least at the Triple A level. When the decision was made to option Walters, Billy assumed it was to Denver. He told newsmen that that had been his understanding following a meeting he had with Calvin Griffith. Then Billy said, "By the time I walked from Calvin's office to mine, my phone had rung four times. It was George Brophy [the assistant farm director]. He told me Walters was going to Charlotte. He had already talked Calvin into it.

"I may be old-fashioned," Billy said, letting everybody in Minnesota have a peek at the family laundry, "but I thought that when you went from the big leagues, you went to Triple A. How the hell am I supposed to tell something like that to Walters? Here he is almost good enough to pitch for us and he's not good enough to pitch for Denver? Brophy says he hasn't got a curve ball. The kid's been working on it and for the last six days he's thrown one helluva curve ball. But Brophy never goes down on the field. How would he know?"

Billy was careful in his mortar attack on the front office to avoid aiming for Sherry Robertson, a genuinely close friend. But this was no isolated incident, no sudden fit of pique. Billy had been feuding over personnel matters with the farm department ever since his days with the Bears. And now, grandly and indiscreetly, it was out in the open. While he'd managed the Bears he had wanted pitching help, and the front office promised but didn't deliver or delivered late; in turn, when the front office wanted someone from Denver, that player—without consultation—was gone the next day. Then there were these decisions made over his head when he took over the Twins. Beyond Charley Walters was Bill Zepp, another young pitcher, demoted to Red Springs or Charlotte (Billy wasn't sure) when, Billy said, two pitching coaches, Early Wynn and Art Fowler, recommended keeping him. Billy's assault on the front office was no guerrilla attack in the middle of the night; it was more like a kamikaze raid. He didn't blame Calvin Griffith, he said, but then took aim right for the smokestacks:

"I don't know what the fascination is with Charlotte except that it's run by Phil Howser, one of Calvin's fraternity brothers," Billy said, adding, "I'll never call up a player from Charlotte if I have anything to say about it."

Whatever Griffith may have felt personally, he was far more disturbed by the breach of organizational etiquette. There were two principles, beyond any personal feeling (and the evidence remains even today that Griffith all along admired the pirate in Billy), that just could not be overlooked: An organization man did not go to the press with complaints about the organization. And an organization man never bit the hand of the man who fed him.

"I guarantee you, he didn't have a goddamn thing to do with any of that stuff as far as I was concerned," Griffith said years later. "We had our farm director and everything else—my brother—and he certainly had enough knowledge to make those decisions. Billy may have wanted that authority but he never got it from us. Yeah, he may have been fiery, but you can always ignore it, you know. Like the ballplayers you come north with; he may not have wanted someone on the ballclub we put on there, but we didn't give him that kind of authority, because we were the ones that were paying him and we had to do what we thought was best for the ballclub."

The Walters affair, it turned out, was only a preview of coming attractions.

In early August, the Twins, clinging to a narrow lead in the AL West, opened a three-game series against the World Champion Tigers in Detroit. Not available because of a blister on his throwing hand was one of Billy's key pitchers, Dave Boswell, a fierce competitor but a free spirit. The day after an exceptionally tough extra-inning loss to Detroit, Boswell was asked by Billy's pitching coach, Art Fowler, to do some running. Boswell refused—rudely and crudely. Fowler, easygoing but utterly loyal, reported the incident to Billy. After the game that night, in a players' hangout called the Lindell A.C., Boswell and Billy came to blows—with Boswell winding up hospitalized, his face nearly torn off. The fight was not only horrifying, it was, in the manner of *Rashomon*, mysterious. It was a different fight depending on who was speaking about it.

Billy then and later, in his autobiography, maintained that he stepped into a fight that had broken out between Boswell and another player, Bob Allison, and that he retaliated after being struck by Boswell, inflicting admittedly heavy damage, for which he was subsequently apologetic. But Boswell reported that he had been held and that Billy had pummeled him into near-oblivion. Allison and Sonny Eliot, the TV announcer who had been sitting at Billy's table and was an eyewitness, corroborated Billy's version, but Calvin Griffith, though he ultimately supported his manager and wound up fining Boswell, leaned toward the player's account. A meeting in Washington between the principals clarified little for the owner, but the sight of Boswell had been convincing to Griffith:

"I went to Washington and tried to have a meeting," he said, "but, hell, I didn't find out anything. I knew goddamn well that something was wrong, though, because Boswell could never have been beaten up like that by Martin because he would have been able to take Martin and tear him in half in a real fight."

The Boswell affair touched one of Griffith's deepest fears: that his temperamental and fight-prone manager would somehow wind up battling and injuring his own players. Beyond that, there was the question of Billy simply not following guidelines; the manager was not supposed to drink in bars frequented by players. Billy did so often. The Boswell affair only underscored a growing sense Griffith had that Billy's success on the field was matched only by his unreliability off it. There were other, less publicized incidents. Jim Kaat, one of the team's top pitchers, was called on the carpet by Griffith for being absent for a couple of days between starts. Kaat acknowledged that he had been missing, but said that it was because his father had just suffered a stroke and Billy had given him permission to leave the club for a few days.

"I went to visit my father, and then when I got back to Minneapolis, I got a call from Calvin's secretary to come in and see him," Kaat recalls. "And when I got there he was pretty irate. He accused me of jumping the club . . . he went on for about ten minutes, and when he cooled down I told him Billy had given me permission to visit my father. When he heard that, he kind of scratched his head, and then all of a sudden it was like a light went on because this was evidently the third or fourth time a player's story and Billy's story were different, and he began to sense that he wasn't getting a straight story. What had happened is that, when I was visiting home, Calvin went down to the locker room and asked to see the player reps. I was a player rep and wasn't there, so he asked Billy where I was. Billy told him that he didn't know, that he guessed I missed the plane—because he didn't want to get in trouble. He didn't have the balls to tell him that he had given me permission to go home."

Then there was the celebrated and deeply embarrassing Humphrey affair. Following a late August loss to the Washington Senators, former vice president and presidential candidate Hubert Humphrey, with an NBC camera crew in tow, showed up in the locker room of his favorite team. What Humphrey didn't know—and what any baseball fan remotely familiar with Billy Martin might have told him—was that visiting Billy after a loss was probably going to be even more unpleasant than having to visit Lyndon Johnson after he was denied a driver's license by the Texas Motor Vehicle Bureau. Billy simply told the vice president to get his ass out of the dressing room, the command given in tones forceful enough to widen the clubhouse and tunnel walls.

"That's one scene that won't make 'Huntley-Brinkley,' " noted beat writer Dave Mona.

Billy's explanation following the event was completely straightforward, but probably did little to enhance Griffith's sense of his reliability.

"I've got nothing against Humphrey," he told the assembled and wide-eyed press corps, "he's a good fan and I like the guy. It's fine with me if he wants to talk to the guys. But there won't be any pictures after we lose. This isn't a three-ring circus. I don't care if it's Nixon or the king of Italy, I'm trying to get these guys into the right frame of mind to get into the World Series. Everything's fine if you win, nothing goes if you lose."

The problem—at least to the front office—was that the Twins were winning and everything was not fine. Down on the field, the Twins charged into September leading the West by three and a half games.

Rod Carew was closing in on a record for steals of home to go with an almost certain batting title (he won the batting title but, nursing a leg injury, only tied the record for steals); Harmon Killebrew, having his best season in the majors, was on a pace to hit fifty home runs; Tony Oliva, Cesar Tovar, and Rich Reese were all hitting near or above .300; Jim Perry and Dave Boswell were on course to win twenty games. At the summit of it all was Billy, riding a wave of adulation that was almost inexplicable. He had captured the heart and imagination—as well as the pocketbook—of the entire region. The Twins were drawing fans to the ballpark in record numbers as they made their stretch drive for the pennant.

The problem for the front office was that Billy, in the process, had become a great guerrilla chieftain rather than a general who also took his orders. His constituency no longer seemed to be the front office but the ordinary fan, multiplied by the tens of thousands.

"I used to have Billy come up to my office two or three times a week and talk baseball," Griffith remembered. "We'd go over what he did the day before or what he was going to do, you know, his ideas against mine. . . . But then he got so good, he wouldn't come up to the office. He'd come up at five o'clock and I'd tell him, 'I'll be goddamned if I'm gonna have you come up here at five o'clock. I take a nap between five and six.' I told him, 'If you can't get here before four o'clock, I don't want you around.' "

Griffith concluded long before the season ended that Billy was intent on establishing his own authority. The surprise was that he had done so without changing a word, period, or comma of his tenuous one-year contract. Billy, much as if he were a skilled politician, had been able to go over heads and convince multitudes of ordinary people that his success was theirs, that what he promised he would actually deliver.

The Twins clinched the West on September 23, beating the Royals in Kansas City—where it all began. Harmon Killebrew hit his forty-seventh homer of the year in this division-winner, which was won by a little-regarded pitcher, Bob Miller. But for those who had followed the team all season, there was no doubt who the man of the hour was: "Billy Martin, who promised a pennant when he took over a year ago," read the lead in the *Minneapolis Tribune*, "was clearly the moment's hero."

The euphoria seemed to sweep everyone up—everyone, that is, except Calvin Griffith, who, though gratified with a first-place finish, retained his skepticism.

"Billy Martin has done an outstanding job as manager," he said. "He has played daring baseball, had the players on their toes all the time and been a real inspiration to the club. But he has had a lot of good players."

Billy, for his part, was not content. He had miles to go. Ahead were the Baltimore Orioles and the first-ever American League Championship Series.

"When we win that one, you'll see a big celebration," Billy said. "The World Series? That one will be celebrated with gold."

The series with the Orioles, led by arch-rival Earl Weaver, opened in Baltimore on October 4. The Orioles, who had taken eight of twelve games from the Twins during the season, were heavily favored—a fact that pleased Billy, because it once again cast him in the role of underdog.

The opener of the best of five series was one of those classics baseball fans talk about. The Orioles jumped out to a 1–0 lead in the fourth inning on a solo homer by Frank Robinson off twenty-game winner Jim Perry. The Twins tied it in their next at-bat. In the bottom of the fifth, though, light-hitting Mark Belanger, with two out and the pitcher coming up next, hit another solo homer. The score held into the seventh when Tony Oliva, following a walk to Harmon Killebrew, hit a two-run shot for a 3–2 Twins lead. The lead held into the bottom of the ninth. With the right-hander Perry still pitching effectively, Billy chose to let him finish the game rather than call on his top reliever, lefty Ron Perranoski, who was fully warmed in the bullpen. It was a mistake. Left-handed hitting slugger Boog Powell, the O's leadoff hitter in the ninth, broke his bat on an inside pitch but still managed to lift a game-tying homer over the right-field wall. The Orioles eventually won it, 4–3, in the twelfth on a daring two-out bunt by Paul Blair.

The following day, the Twins' luck was no better. Dave McNally threw an eleven-inning 1–0 shutout at them. Through much of the game, Dave Boswell—fully restored to favored status with his manager—dodged trouble. The Orioles had lead runners on in six different innings, placing runners in scoring position in the second, third, fifth, eighth, ninth, and eleventh. In the top of the tenth, the Twins catcher, George Mitterwald, missed a home run by inches down the left-field line. A pinch single by Curt Motton won it for the Orioles in the next inning.

Billy was taut but not really angry with the two defeats in Baltimore. His team had played hard and well, had given him all he had asked. In the end, his only complaint was losing. "We battled them all the way but it was still a bitter pill to swallow," he said.

Perhaps because he was not really angry, perhaps because he simply wanted relief from the terrible tension of the opening games, Billy let himself relax on the team flight back to Minnesota. He had a couple of drinks and began to listen to music on a portable record-player he had with him. The music attracted the attention of Calvin Griffith. The sight—and sounds—of his manager enjoying himself in the midst of defeat seemed odd and out of character. Griffith ordered Billy to turn the music off. He complied. But he did not at all comply with Griffith's expectation about how to deal with the Orioles in the next game.

Griffith, along with almost everyone else, expected Billy to start Jim Kaat in the third game. Instead, perhaps borrowing another page from Casey Stengel, he turned to little-used Bob Miller to preserve the season. As soon as Billy revealed his intention, the front office interceded in an effort to make him change his mind. Griffith, reported Sid Hartman, wanted Kaat to start. "Kaat won two games versus Baltimore this year," Griffith told Hartman. "He allowed them only twenty-one hits in twenty-five innings. He was the logical man to pitch." Howard Fox, now Griffith's closest advisor, told Billy the same thing. But there was no way Billy was going to be headed off. Miller, who had won some key games for the team but who also happened to be one of Billy's occasional drinking partners, went to the mound—and was hammered. He lasted just an inning and a third as the Orioles went on to an 11–2 final game victory.

There is the chance, of course, that if Miller had won, Billy's move might have been seen more generously, as one more example of great daring under pressure paying off. But as it turned out, the loss—for game, match, and season—left a bitter aftertaste. Rather than seeing daring, Griffith saw insubordination. Griffith denied that this pitching choice entered into his thinking, but Jim Kaat, the pitcher who had been passed over, thought otherwise.

"Billy made that decision early on. I remember Calvin Griffith telling the story sometime later that what irritated him most was that Billy had actually called him and said, 'Who would you start in the playoffs?' And Calvin said, 'Boswell, Perry, and Kaat.' And Billy said, 'I'm starting Boswell, Perry, and Miller.' "

As far as he was concerned, Billy's choice was a fair one, Kaat said, because he had been struggling with injury problems throughout the season, as Billy knew. But Calvin Griffith had other ideas. Sometime before the World Series, Griffith began to think about whether or not he should retain his mercurial and unpredictable manager. Griffith, to this day, swears that he never actually made a decision to fire Billy—that Billy did that himself.

"I never fired him," Griffith said. "I told him to come out to the ballpark this one Saturday morning before the World Series began—I think it was around eleven o'clock—because I wanted to sit down with him and go over all these stories that I had condensed in a whole shelf, pros and cons—I wanted to sit down and go over all those damn things with him. He came in an hour before he was supposed to come in. I said, 'Billy, I'm not ready to talk to you, I got all this stuff I gotta double-check first.' Well, he said, 'I'm going hunting'—or fishing or some damn thing like that. I said, 'Go ahead, goddamnit, I'll sit down with you after I get back from the World Series.' Well, what happened then was that I got a call from Sid Hartman, the columnist, who told me that Billy Martin said he was fired. I said, 'If he feels that he's fired, then he's fired.' "

As eccentric as Griffith was, the decision to fire Billy in the face of his obvious success and popularity was not a casual one at all. Hartman's story came out on October 13, a Monday and a traveling day in the Series between Baltimore and New York. The decision to fire Billy was indeed taken, according to Tom Mee, who was present at the meeting—in New York—where it occurred. Mee contends that Griffith was actually undecided going into the meeting and that he was ultimately swayed by those in the meeting, including Howard Fox, who very much wanted to see Billy go. If Billy had had one additional strong advocate, Mee suggested, the ax might have been spared.

"Fox, myself, Calvin, Brophy, and Clarkie [Griffith's nephew] were at this meeting, called for eight A.M. Sherry Robertson had gotten drunk the night before and slept in that morning," Mee said. "If he had been there, Billy wouldn't have been fired. The meeting could have gone either way. It went on for about forty-five minutes. Brophy and Clarkie didn't say anything—Billy Robertson may have been there, too, I can't recall, I certainly don't remember him saying anything."

The two speakers were Mee, a very junior executive, for the defense, and Howard Fox, holding the brief for the organization. Billy was gone. In spite of his having taken the Twins to a first-place finish, in spite of everything he did to boost attendance to record levels, to sell the team and himself, he was out. Calvin Griffith might have been Harry Truman sacking General MacArthur—an analogy Billy might not have minded—but the decision was taken, and roughly for similar reasons: the chain of command was sacred. No one, not even a popular general with an adoring public, could put himself above the commander-in-chief and expect to get away with it. The Griffiths came from Washington, and though they knew all about being last in the American League, they also knew very well where bucks stopped and generals got off.

# CHAPTER 10

This was a firing that should never have happened, one, certainly, that Billy neither anticipated nor understood. Managers, it was true, were hired to be fired; that was part of the trade. But Billy had won in Minnesota—as he had in Denver—in spectacular fashion. In both places, he had taken teams he could have easily and blamelessly gone down with and gave them surprising new life.

"If Billy Martin is not the manager," columnist Dick Cullum wrote on the eve of the firing, "Calvin Griffith has dealt a blow to his fans by failing to appreciate the importance to the organization of Billy's popularity. Martin is the people's choice, their only choice."

But Griffith knew all about Billy's popularity and, even more than the average fan, appreciated the success he had brought the team. He let Billy go because he was no longer willing to tolerate Billy's unpredictability and insubordination.

There were many explanations given for the firing: Billy's off-field behavior, his clashes with the front office and Howard Fox, his willingness to tolerate high-stakes poker games in the clubhouse, his conflicts with some of the older players who, one writer suggested, had been going over Billy's head to the front office with their complaints—but none of them outweighed Calvin Griffith's sense that this was a relationship ruptured beyond repair.

The Twins, in firing Billy, indeed brought on an open rebellion from their fans. Attendance plummeted following Billy's departure, even though the team won another divisional title the next year. Boycotts were organized, talk shows deluged with complaints.

For Billy, there could only be denial. The blame for what happened, as the fans well knew, lay with the front office, especially those in it—like Howard Fox—who all along had been out to get him.

But there was a great sense of loss, no matter who was to blame. Eight years of home- and career-building had suddenly come crashing down. At the end of the 1969 season, he had continuously been part of the Minnesota organization for nearly a decade —the longest uninterrupted stop he would ever enjoy in his nomadic professional life.

He had a real home and family in Minnesota, he had business opportunities and a professional future that any other manager in baseball would have envied. And now, in one seemingly perverse spasm of pride and temperament, it had all collapsed.

The closest Billy could come to self-criticism was to acknowledge that he did not blame the man who fired him and that, in fact, he liked him.

"Calvin gave me the chance to manage and I'm not going to blast him," Billy said. He shifted the grounds for the firing, however, as though it all was somehow a baseball argument, a wrong-headed intrusion of "artistic differences" from which no real manager could back down. "Calvin faulted me for getting Tony Oliva caught stealing eight times with Harmon Killebrew up. Isn't it a known fact," he said, "that once you establish . . . that a runner might steal, the pitcher is more apt to throw a fastball to the hitter—Killebrew in this case—to give the catcher a better chance to throw out the runner? Harmon hit a lot of those fastballs out of the park this year."

But he was arguing with himself, and perhaps for himself, because he had nowhere to go, nothing to do. If Billy was anticipating that doors would swing wide open for him, he was disappointed. The winter meetings came and went, and there were some queries—nibbles but no bites. Other owners, it seemed, were reluctant to hire someone as "difficult" as Billy. He was shocked and undoubtedly shaken; spring training in 1970 came and went without Billy Martin for the first time since 1947.

Billy spent the early part of the new season trying to make a life for himself outside baseball. He continued to live and work in Minnesota, nursing the unabated popularity he enjoyed in the area. He did some public relations work for Grain Belt, the local brewery; he worked for a radio station for a while . . . and he waited.

During that summer there was, finally, a break. Billy wrote in his autobiography that Charles O. Finley, owner of the Oakland A's, was interested in hiring him as a manager. Billy says that he met Finley in Chicago, and was offered the job immediately. "It was a Sunday, and [Finley] said, 'Monday's a day off. Will you take over the team Tuesday in Washington?' "

His response, he said, was to tell Finley—about whom he had reservations—that he would take over on one condition: that the team's current manager, John McNamara, who was a friend, be retained as a third-base coach. Finley, Billy said, then agreed to contract terms and the deal was set—only to be put on hold the following morning when Finley called and told him that, after a conversation with his wife, in which she told him he had already fired too many people, he wanted Billy to wait until later in the season before taking over.

Finley has a completely different version of this story. He had not in any way contacted Billy, he said, nor had any third party on his behalf. "Billy called me up and said he was interested in having me hire him," Finley said. "He said he could win a pennant for me that year if I fired John McNamara and hired him." It was unusual for any out-of-work manager to make contact that way, Finley said: "It never happened before or afterwards with me."

There was a meeting in Chicago—arranged at Billy's request, in which Finley did acknowledge what Billy had picked up on the grapevine—that the A's owner was unhappy with John McNamara—except that Finley was not about to fire him. At least not then. "I gave Johnny my word that he had the team for the season and I wasn't about to break that word," Finley said. "I told Billy I would take him for the following season, he agreed, we shook hands on it. I thought we had a deal. What are those words, 'categorically deny'? What he said was a damned lie. I never went to him, never said I was going to fire McNamara then—and I never consulted my wife, ever, about anything having to do with baseball."

The point of agreement between Billy and Finley is that there was nothing on paper. Whatever Billy was waiting for, a more lucrative offer surfaced in the meantime. Weeks later, in early August, there was a call from Jim Campbell of the Tigers. The Tigers, World Champions less than two seasons before, were going nowhere in 1970; the team was top-heavy with age, but it still had talented and veteran stars who, Campbell said, "maybe could do it just one more time with the right kick in the butt. I was debating whether to try to get one more win out of 'em or trade 'em off and rebuild it. I may have made a mistake, I might have been better off to start tearing the club apart and trading them while they had some bats. But, I thought, well, Billy could come in here, whip 'em in, win one more time, then do it—and we damn near did it."

Campbell, as shrewd and knowledgeable as any executive in the game, had measured Billy as fully as Calvin Griffith—and, like Griffith, wound up believing he could "handle" him.

Campbell described the August meeting with Tigers owner John Fetzer that resulted in Billy's hiring. Twenty years later, the sense of charm, apprehension, and amazement were still palpably present.

"Mr. Fetzer had a cabin up in northern Michigan and Billy came down from Minneapolis and I came up from Detroit; Mr. Fetzer was already there. I went to the airport to meet Billy," Campbell said, "and I didn't see the guy anywhere. Then I see someone standing over in a corner, he's got this huge mustache, wearing dark glasses. It's Billy. He's got a disguise on. Guess he wanted to be incognito. I said, 'You wily sonofabitch.' He just grinned. So we went out to the cabin. I remember Mr. Fetzer had said, 'You know, you may have a tiger by the tail here, always keep that in the back of your mind.' I said, 'Yeah, I know, I'm willing to run the risk because I think the guy can do for our club what has to be done.' If I were rebuilding a ballclub, no, but to take an older club that needed straightening up, I thought he could do it."

The meeting with Fetzer went so well that the unlikely rapport between the owner and the new employee became a later source of speculation when Billy was fired. There were intimations—laughed off by Campbell—that he ultimately let Billy go because he was jealous of the relationship between the owner and the manager.

" 'When are you going to ask me, Mr. Fetzer, to call you John?' " Campbell remembers Billy saying as they sat around the fireplace in the cabin. "Mr. Fetzer said, 'Billy, whenever you think it's apropos.' Mr. Fetzer laughed," Campbell said, "and Billy said, 'What the hell are you laughing at?' Fetzer goes, 'You don't even know what the fuck "apropos" means!' Boy, did I needle him about that. I'd say to him, 'Hey, Billy, whenever it's apropos.' "

But the deal was done—spelled out and crystal clear. Billy placed no demands on the club, Campbell said; there was never any indication that he wanted control of personnel decisions, player development, anything that might put him in conflict with the front office.

The task of guiding the Tigers on the field—to Billy and to Campbell—was daunting enough. Not only were the Tigers a year older and a step slower, they were a team, Campbell said, of "personalities," pulling in different directions. One of the major reasons why Mayo Smith, a well-respected field manager, had been relieved of command was that Campbell had come to the conclusion he could no longer hold the team together.

It was no easy task. The World Champions of 1968 had had a great fall: second in their division in 1969, fourth in 1970. The anchor of the 1968 pitching staff, Denny McLain, who had won thirty-one games that year, had become enmeshed in a betting scandal and then traded away; the veterans who had powered the Tigers in '68—Norm Cash, Al Kaline, Jim Northrup, Dick McAuliffe, Willie Horton—had all faded in the previous seasons but were still strong individuals with their own ideas about the team and their role on it.

There is no question that Billy, like Casey Stengel, felt more comfortable with veterans. He felt he could work with them, that they were known quantities, able to understand what he wanted from them, able to withstand what might have only confused or bruised younger players. Billy gave a speech on one of his first days in spring training that year—on pride. He wanted the players to wear their English letter *D*s with pride, as the Yankees years ago had worn their classic *NY* logo. There was a difference, Billy said—taking yet another page from Casey Stengel—between knowing and hoping that you were going to win when you stepped on the field. Pride mattered, the general said, along with the way the campaign was waged.

Billy told the old Tigers that they were going to run. They had stolen thirty-five bases in 1969, and a nearly arthritic total of twenty-nine in 1970. But they were still going to run. The Tigers, as if they were Berkeley High kids rather than a collection of Grey Panthers, were to steal bases—the first-and-third double steal of home was in, so were the suicide squeeze and the taking of extra bases—and to prove that he meant it, Billy installed himself as the team's third-base coach when the exhibition season began. It was a move he had made at Denver and Minnesota before Calvin Griffith had put a stop to it. The front office in Detroit, insisting on managerial etiquette, stopped it as well.

But Billy knew what he could and could not do on the field as well as anyone. His goal was not to challenge the front office, but from the start to incite his own players and even his coaching staff.

"Billy really came down hard on us, I'll tell you," said Charlie Silvera, who again was one of the staff. "But it was like the coaches were the buffers between the players and Billy. He wouldn't directly confront a guy if he felt he did something wrong, but he'd come after us—right in the clubhouse—and the guy'd overhear it, he'd know. Billy did that right off, to let people know it was his team, that he wanted things done in a certain way right from the start."

Billy's temper, his unpredictability, his inability to accept losing were all part of the ignition wiring, but the key to the switch was his leadership. He couldn't make old legs new, but he could get them into lockstep behind him. "Billy Blasts Tigers For Poor Spring Play," ran one mid-March headline in the *Detroit News.* But all Billy wanted was to make sure his troops were going to follow when the season began.

The Tigers' direction at the outset was not nearly as clear as Billy's. The team lost seven of its first eleven regular season games, floundering its way through April. But Billy was the one who made news. His control of the team, rather than what the team itself was doing on the field, seemed to preoccupy those who came to the ballpark. It was as though he had this extra dimension—as though he was actually a tenth player—that made a difference.

In one losing game, Billy used Kevin Collins, a light-hitting, little-known reserve, to pinch hit instead of using the more popular, more powerful Gates Brown. Asked about it afterward, Billy explained that he was after a fly ball in that specific situation, and "I thought Collins had the best chance of hitting a fly ball because he's a low ball hitter." The answer, whatever the merits, carried a weight of thinking and strategy with it—people were impressed.

Following another game, Billy went out of his way to praise the team's large and skillful catcher, Bill Freehan—not for the game he called or for his hitting, but for the way he broke up a double play sliding into second.

In another game, he allowed Mickey Lolich, the team's ace pitcher, to choose his own reliever. It was a daring but typical gesture—reward and encouragement, like Casey handing out meal money. And it paid off, in terms of newsprint and desire. Lolich, in his next start, pitched a complete game, a 2–1 extra-inning win over the Royals, knowing that his manager intended to start him again on three days' rest. Lolich jokingly—and happily—made a point of confronting Billy after the game in the clubhouse. "You told me you weren't going to let me go more than six innings today—you lied!" Lolich said. "Just remember that Italians don't count too good," the equally happy manager shot back. Teammates, reporters, and the principals all loved it.

But then Billy equally made a point of coming down hard, on some of his players, on opponents, on a variety of real and imagined enemies. He benched Willie Horton, the team's moody slugger, for not hitting, and because Billy questioned Horton's attitude. When Horton criticized him in the media, Billy held firm—also publicly. On another occasion, he fined one of his players for carrying beer onto the team bus—it was a fine, needless to say, that was announced in the papers, as were Billy's quarrels with scoreboard operators in Baltimore for spying for the Orioles, with the organist in Oakland for deliberately distracting visiting players, and with umpires wherever and whenever the situation arose. Billy even let himself be drawn into quarreling with the media. Columnist Jerry Green, with whom he would feud throughout his time in Detroit, questioned Billy's baseball judgment for saying that the Orioles' success was somehow due to more than skill on the field. Billy clipped the article and posted it on a clubhouse wall, attracting the attention of his players and, of course, the media itself.

Billy, in that first losing month, established himself as firmly in control, creating a mirage of winning—before there was any actual winning to talk about.

Throughout the first half of May, the team continued to struggle. The Tigers, everyone knew, did not have much pitching. After Mickey Lolich and Joe Coleman, there were no reliable starters. Dean Chance and Dave Boswell, both sore-armed and erratic, had recently arrived from Minnesota, but they were unable to help. The bullpen, with John Hiller gone, had candidates but, as yet, no one to close a game. And then there was the continuing problem of "personalities." Willie Horton, the hometown hero, who had been the team's leader and on whose shoulders much of the current team's offensive potential rested, seemed distracted and alienated.

During the second week of May, Horton, slumping and playing only sporadically, told the press, "I'm trying too hard . . . I tighten up at home, maybe they should get rid of me."

Billy's answer was to send Horton to the bench once more. Following a day out of the lineup, he inserted the slugger again—only this time Horton said no. He told Billy he had a shoulder injury and wasn't available. Billy exploded. Horton was challenging his authority, something which could never be tolerated. He blasted his star—in the press—immediately: "He hit a dozen balls in the seats and then went in and told the trainer his shoulder hurt so much he couldn't play."

Billy was then called into conference with Jim Campbell, who wanted the conflict settled quickly before it got out of hand. But two hours later, neither the general manager nor the manager had resolved anything.

"I wish I was smart enough to know what to do," Campbell said.

Billy, who obviously was not about to give an inch, invoked his Yankee past.

"This is something I can't understand," he said. "I played for the Yankees when I had the flu, pneumonia, broken bones, and a few other things wrong with me. My salary was $20,000 and I was hungry."

No one needed a calculator to catch Billy's meaning. Horton's well-publicized salary was $80,000—more than the manager's, and more than enough to convince the fans of this workingman's city who was in the right.

An unidentified friend of Horton's told the *Detroit News* that the star was actually hurting financially. "He's not as mixed up as Denny McLain was in Detroit but it might be close," this source said.

Horton, for his part, reiterated his desire to play elsewhere—telling a post-game TV audience that it might be better for everyone if he simply got out of his hometown.

In fact, Horton did get out of Detroit—along with the rest of his teammates. The Tigers went out on the road during the third week in May and caught fire—with Horton, back in the lineup, suddenly beginning to hit. The struggle of wills had not ended but the headlines mercifully changed.

The Tigers won seven in a row to surge to third place, just four-and-a-half games behind the division-leading Red Sox. Even more important was the way they won. The old guys were doing just what their manager said they were going to do. They won one game when Dick McAuliffe, the veteran second baseman, stole third on his own—because, Billy pointed out, that was what his players had been urged to do from day one. The steal of third, he said, was not about legs but about brains; McAuliffe, moving to third, changed the task of the hitter, Al Kaline, who—with a runner on third—was able to swing away rather than trying to hit the ball to the right side to advance the runner.

In a 1–0 win over the Senators, Billy again raised eyebrows when he ordered an intentional walk to load the bases in the eighth inning. The move brought slugger Frank Howard to the plate, but even more unorthodox was the decision to keep the catcher, Bill Freehan, in his crouch behind the plate rather than having him step aside while the intentional walk was being delivered. The strategy of pitching to Howard was understandable, if risky; keeping Freehan in place was something else:

"On that kind of walk," Billy said, "you don't mind if the hitter tries to swing at a bad pitch." No one had ever heard that before. It was new, it was different. It changed the way writers wrote, fans watched, players played the game. Above all, it helped solidify the way everyone thought about Billy Martin as a manager. Between the lines there was no one better. Follow him and winning was sure to happen. And the Tigers, suddenly, were winning.

The Tigers closed out the month with a Memorial Day loss to the Twins in Minnesota. It was the first time Billy had been back to the Twin Cities in another uniform and the huge ovation he received cheered him, even in defeat.

The Tigers, it was increasingly clear, were for real. Of their first thirty wins, ten were fashioned after they were trailing going into the seventh inning, an unheard-of number. The team was scrapping, fighting, taking every advantage—pure Billy Martin style—and the league had again taken notice.

"The two best managers in the American League are Earl [Weaver] and Billy," said Frank Lane, the Brewers' general manager, acknowledging that the Tigers' success, unexpected as it was, was really Billy's.

The players on the team during this first year were as caught up as anyone. Aurelio Rodriguez, the flashy-fielding but usually light-hitting third baseman, discovered that he was a good hit-and-run man. Billy, he said, was the difference because he made him understand that he could hit the ball where it was pitched rather than, following conventional wisdom, trying to go to the opposite field. "It's just become easier here," Rodriguez said. "The manager tells you to hit the ball somewhere rather than just to right field—and I do it." And he became the team's master of the squeeze—and again, Rodriguez gave the credit to Billy:

"I didn't have a single bunt last year when I played for Washington," he said. "When I played there, Ted Williams told me to forget about the bunt and come out swinging." Through the first half of the season, Rodriguez had, in numerous bunting situations, failed only once.

The anonymous pinch hitters, the bench players, the forgotten middle relievers joined a chorus of approving starters and regulars in giving credit to Billy, and he in turn spent much of his time praising his players, making a point of letting them, as well as the baseball world, know what was possible when a team played together, doing "all the little things" in order to win. Even Willie Horton came around. After one game, in which he went four for five and twice drove in go-ahead runs, good feeling abounded.

"Hey, Willie, how many?" Billy shouted across the clubhouse. Horton, grinning, held up four fingers. "If they pitch him outside, he'll go to right; if they come in, he'll lose it," Billy told the press. "That was a week's work when I played."

Even Jim Northrup, another one of those "personalities," and eventually an arch antagonist, acknowledged that "in that first year, he had us all on his side."

The Tigers went into the All-Star break trailing the Orioles, still everyone's choice, by six and a half games. But the team had won three in a row going in. Bill Gilbreth, a rookie, pitched a complete-game victory over the Yankees, promising better things for the second half; Joe Coleman, on his way to a twenty-win season, beat the Senators 1–0 in eleven innings, the winning run scoring on a suicide squeeze; Mickey Lolich wrapped up the first half by winning his fourteenth game.

But then, instead of reaching orbit, the rocket seemed to fall back to Earth. The Tigers fell to nine games back during the third week in July, and to nine and a half by month's end. The team's problems, no matter what the manager did, could not be finessed away. The pitching remained thin, the bullpen unreliable, the offense weighted down by feet that were simply too heavy.

Still, Billy had control of the clubhouse. Losing remained intolerable for him; tirades and icy silences followed defeats. But there was tolerance, if not outright sympathy, extended to him; he had the benefit of the doubt. Watson Spoelstra, the veteran columnist, noted that Billy "is the hardest loser we've seen in 35 years in Detroit sports." The owner of the team, John Fetzer, declared, "Billy's a teacher by instinct, he's the nearest thing I've ever seen to Charlie Dressen." Mickey Lolich, Billy's principal cheerleader in the clubhouse, said that "player-manager relations couldn't be better. I'd do anything for the guy managing this club."

For his part, Billy was interested in doing anything he could to get his team back on course. In early August, after campaigning with the front office, he secured the services of Ron Perranoski, the Twins reliever who had starred for Billy in 1969 but who had since become an odd man out in Minnesota. And he did whatever he could to interject himself into the action—whether with umpires or opposing players—whenever he could.

In a tough three-game series with the Red Sox in Boston, the Tigers won a pair to climb back within seven and a half games. The series was marked by several hit batsmen, the most flagrant involving a sixth-inning pitch in the final game thrown by the Tigers' Bill Denehy (the team's designated "hatchet man," according to one player) that found the middle of Reggie Smith's back. Following the game, Smith and Billy nearly came to blows.

As Billy told it, Smith was waiting for him under the stands as he left the clubhouse. When he saw Smith, he acknowledged, he put down a package he was carrying and asked the Red Sox star, "You looking for me?"

"What's your problem?" Smith reportedly replied.

"You're the one who has the problem," Billy said, "your mouth." Billy explained that Smith, from the safe distance of center field, three hundred feet away, had been taunting his players after being hit with the pitch; he wanted him, now, to back up his words "instead of crying like a little kid." When Smith, powerfully built, younger and stronger than Billy, moved forward, policemen standing nearby interceded. Nothing happened, except the chance to stir things up and fan some flames—in print.

"I wish the cops had let me hit him," Billy told reporters. "He would have been a sucker for a right-hand punch."

The near-fight, though, as Detroit writers unearthed its background, was not personal but was about Billy standing up for his players, three of whom had been hit earlier in the series by Red Sox pitchers. But it all made no difference; no matter what the manager said or did, the Tigers just did not have the personnel to win.

By the end of August, the team had slipped twelve games behind, hopelessly out of it. It had become obvious that mid-season trades for Tony Taylor, the veteran infielder, and for Perranoski had not corrected fundamental problems still plaguing the team.

Still, it was just as obvious that Billy had made a difference. The Tigers were on their way to winning ninety-one games, a twelve-game improvement over the year before. Out of it as they were, they still played as though they were in a race. For three weeks into September, they were playing better than anyone in the American League. Individual players pursued individual records as though they belonged to the team. When Mickey Lolich won his twenty-third game of the season in Washington, he threw a wild party for his teammates—to which Billy was invited—at the downtown Shoreham Hotel.

Behind it all was Billy, who daily received the sort of press that might have been reserved for a maker of miracles rather than someone who had guided a basically good team to a distant second-place finish. Everyone knew now that he did not know when to quit. For good or ill, he would always fight to the last, do anything, anytime if there was even the remotest chance of winning.

When Willie Horton was seriously beaned in a game with the White Sox at the end of August, Billy was the first one at his side. Never mind that he had feuded with him, he was a professional ballplayer, and a career was at stake.

"I know what Willie's going through," Billy said. "I got hit like that near the end of my career, and the doctor said it was like coming out of an automobile accident at over 100 miles an hour. You just can't realize the pain involved."

Billy made a point of cheerleading, even when all hope seemed to be gone. With the Orioles ahead by eleven games heading into the final weeks of play, a reporter asked Billy if he still felt the team had any chance.

"Back that up a little, pal," he replied, "we just won a ballgame today so now it's ten and a half games—and we still play Baltimore seven more times. Sure, we have a chance."

But when the team showed up in Baltimore in mid-September for their showdown with the Orioles, Earl Weaver was able to declare that the war was over even before the series started. "All I'm concerned about is having four pitchers on my team win twenty games," he said.

The Orioles eventually finished the season with 101 wins, twelve games ahead. But even given the ease with which Baltimore took the pennant, everyone knew what Billy had done. The kick in the butt Jim Campbell had been looking for had been delivered. When the Tigers won the American League East the following season, even the experts, including the majority who had picked the Orioles in the spring, were not really surprised—because by then all of them knew that Billy Martin, the manager, could do all the things Billy Martin the player could never have done. In only his third year in the dugout, there were those who knew that this manager, out of all those in the game, was the only one who could wave his hand over a shabby baseball cap and pull from its depths one toothsome tiger.

# CHAPTER 11

The Detroit Tigers in 1972 were having their best spring since 1968. The team's younger pitchers, Fred Scherman, Mike Kilkenny, and Chuck Seelbach, had looked good, promising needed support for mainstays Mickey Lolich and Joe Coleman. Willie Horton was not only hitting, he seemed relaxed and happy. "Willie's having fun," Billy said after one especially productive spring game. "That's what baseball is all about—winning and enjoying it."

The Detroit media noticed that Billy was also having fun. He lived in a houseboat on the huge lake beyond the Tiger camp and was able to do a lot of bass fishing. The crowds at Joker Marchant Stadium were friendly, large—just as in '68—and hugely disposed toward Billy. He was mobbed by fans, who called out to him as he patiently and gratefully shook hands and signed autographs: "You're a scrapper, Billy, keep it up!" "God bless you, Billy, good luck!" He was a star and he knew it—and he enjoyed it.

Except for one notorious—and possibly calculated—outburst, his temper seemed to be held in remarkable check. He made a show of losing his cool one day when Jim Bouton, the ex-Yankee pitcher, celebrated author, and now TV announcer for ABC, turned up on the field with a camera crew. Bouton, the Yankee, had savaged his old Bronx teammates—particularly Mickey Mantle—in his book, *Ball Four*. Whatever Billy felt personally, the tight bonding and discipline of a team or an army could not withstand the work of a traitor; it was necessary to make an example of such people.

"Schultzie," Billy said to Joe Schultz, his third-base coach, loud enough for reporters nearby to catch every word, "get out there real quick and run the man off the field. I don't want him around my players, I wouldn't go on his show for $25,000. I didn't read his book but he's a Benedict Arnold. He'd sell his team out or do anything for money. I don't like to hurt people, but this man is just no good."

But things were going well. Billy was in mid-season form, bench-jockeying, arguing from the dugout, running games as though they counted but, nearly always, easing up off the field. After a nice 3–1 win over the Yankees, he gave his team a day off—a little reward for the players—while he took a few hours to be with Mickey Mantle, who was about to undergo gallbladder surgery.

But this view of ease and harmony was deceptive. Baseball, like the rest of American society in the Vietnam-Watergate era, was about to undergo upheavals that no one in the game, much less an ordinary field manager, could control. At the beginning of April, virtually on the eve of the new season, the newly strengthened Baseball Players Association, after failing to reach agreement with management on pension contributions and other matters, voted to authorize a players' strike. Management responded by closing down training camps and all other major-league facilities, effectively locking the players out.

The issues involved in this first general players' strike were obviously about more than winning or losing games—but not to ordinary fans, and not to Billy. "We worked hard to get this team ready. For what? A summer vacation?" he asked, after only five of twenty-five players showed up for an informal workout scheduled at a local high school field. Local and national media lambasted the selfishness and greed of the players in colors far more vivid than anything seen in the subsequent era of multi-million dollar salaries and high-powered labor battles.

But what could anyone say? The players, at that time, had starting salaries of $13,500. The average major-league salary was $29,000; meal money was $18 a day. A twenty-year veteran at age sixty-five received a pension of under $1100 a month. These really were bread and butter issues that could empty the dugouts, making any manager's convictions about leading a team as though it were an army completely irrelevant. This first labor strike—if only subtly at that point—forever changed the nature of relationships in professional baseball. The ballpark was a workplace—a concept shocking to fans, owners, writers, perhaps even to some players. In this single stroke, the dugout and clubhouse became places where loyalty and brotherhood were more likely to be determined by ink than blood.

The strike, perhaps because the reality of it exceeded anyone's preparations for it, was settled within two weeks. Billy remained in Florida, away from his family, for most of the strike, and when he returned to Detroit ready to launch the campaign, he was clearly on edge. The last weeks had been terrible for him, he acknowledged just prior to the season opener. "I can't sleep anymore," he said. "I didn't get over three hours before I came to the park today."

There is a continuing notion that winning teams, like happy families, are all alike and that only losing ones are different in their own ways. The Tigers won the division in 1972—and were different in doing it. They were, imperceptibly but surely, coming apart at the seams even as they were in the process of surprising the American League and the baseball world.

Most people expected the Orioles to win again. They were that era's super team and on paper they looked unbeatable in 1972. But the Orioles were not the same team they had been. Though they still had a powerful lineup and strong pitching, they had blundered into one of the worst trades in their history when they sent the inspirational Frank Robinson to the Dodgers over the winter for a cluster of younger players, only one of whom—pitcher Doyle Alexander—returned any kind of value.

On the surface, the Tigers—clearly Billy's team—scrapped and clawed as they had the year before. Billy, the chief cheerleader, talked pennant from the first day, and the writers following the team picked up on it, emphasizing the team's first-place standing even with only a handful of games played. A mid-April series with the Orioles was greeted with near-playoff hysteria in Detroit. When the Tigers took the first game of the series, a game in which Billy had been tossed and continued to manage from the tunnel leading to the dugout, his post-game comments became a headline:

" 'We'll stay on top,' vows Martin."

Bill Freehan was quoted extensively on the importance of the early win and lead:

"Billy was all keyed up . . . and we were," he said. "That's all we talked about in practice Monday. Look, we know we're going to play them later but if they sweep us or we sweep them, it's going to set a lot of people thinking, and I'd like them to look at our heads for a change."

Earl Weaver, with a sure nose for the moment, had his own view:

"Did they pop the champagne?" he asked, barely concealing a smile.

Still, there was sound strategy behind this seemingly inexplicable use of the whip at the starting gate. Pennants were won by teams that got off to a big early lead. The Yankees had done it when Billy was a player, and so had the Orioles in recent years. Second-place thinking was different than first-place thinking down to the particulars of inning-by-inning strategy.

The Tigers never got that big early lead. The Orioles wound up taking that first series and the two teams, along with the Red Sox and Yankees, battled right through the summer, leap-frogging each other, usually within a game or two of the other, right down to the wire. At the All-Star break, the Tigers led the Orioles by a game and the fans in both cities—particularly those in Detroit—were roused and excited by a real pennant race and by two managers delighting in a kind of two-city, back-page vaudeville rivalry in which insults, jibes, horseplay, and first-rate baseball talk spun through the air like so many colored balls.

Beneath the dash and splash, however, all was not well. The Tigers, though nearer the top than the year before, were still a year older. Ron Perranoski, a favorite of Billy's at Minnesota, had to be released during the season. It was not one of Billy's happier moments, and because he undoubtedly did not want to face getting rid of someone he liked, he had someone else inform Perranoski. Like Casey Stengel, he sometimes kept his door shut.

"I didn't hold it against Billy. It was just one of those things where my arm was going and I didn't know it," said Perranoski. "It was the hardest thing he had to do—but he didn't do it. He had Jim Campbell do it. I called him afterwards, and I said, 'Billy, don't worry about that, I love you and that's our business. The time has come and that's the way it is.' He was more embarrassed than anything to hear from me."

The players were harder to deal with in this second year. A number of them chafed under a system of platooning that cut into their playing time. Willie Horton's productivity continued to decline, and he wound up with fewer at-bats that season than at any time since 1965, his first full season in the majors. Jim Northrup was in similar decline—and wound up resenting Billy bitterly as a consequence, blaming him directly for a nasty feud that finally erupted between them.

Northrup, who was moved up and down the order from his accustomed power position in the lineup, maintains that the loss of position and playing time was never a real issue with him: "I didn't care if he hit me first or eighth so long as I played—and let's face it, every manager has the right to play or sit who he wants."

The sticking point was Billy's humiliating him, Northrup said. The incident that sparked the trouble was a game at Yankee Stadium where, Northrup remembered, Billy criticized him to the press for not running out a ground ball. Northrup maintains that the play in question was actually a one-hop liner to the first baseman who stepped on the bag before he had a chance to move out of the batter's box. "He was looking for someone to blame because we lost the game, that's all," he said, "so he went after me—in the papers. Everybody could read that, my family could read it. I told him he knew better than that. I told him, 'You've pulled enough of that shit, that's the end of it.' " Northrup maintains that for the rest of Billy's time in Detroit—a year and a half—he refused to speak to Billy, or Billy to him. "Whenever he wanted to communicate with me, he sent one of the coaches," he said.

Twenty years later, Northrup's view of Billy remains corrosive, as unshaded as it must have been under the lash of that immediate moment. But because Northrup never tried to conceal his contempt for Billy, what he said about him had reverberations—in the clubhouse and, said one of Billy's coaches at the time, in the front office.

Northrup thought that Billy handled a team much like a seducer and a betrayer, winning players over only to shatter them later with relentless and wearying pressure, blaming them when things did not go well, taking the credit for himself when they did. He lied to the players, to the press, to the front office—to anyone from whom he sought advantage of any kind. He was a browbeater and a tyrant, coming down on players and, even more, his own coaches:

"It was awful, a real shame—he'd go after those coaches with all of us around. Joe Schultz especially took a horrible beating," Northrup said. "No man should have to put up with what Joe Schultz took. No matter what Joe did, it was wrong. We used to say that they were the whipping boys. He had to blame somebody, anybody, whoever was there—that was it. He actually blamed the ground crew for losing a game one day—grass was too high, or too low, there was too much sand."

The pitchers, especially the younger ones who were least confident and most concerned about their jobs, were under constant duress to do things Billy's way. Though Billy's nominal pitching coach was Art Fowler, there was no question, Northrup maintained, that Billy was his own pitching coach, "because he knew better than anybody—better than any pitcher, better than any coach—what to throw in any situation."

Young pitchers were under standing orders to never allow themselves to be beaten by throwing fastballs in a two-strike situation unless they were overpowering fastball pitchers to begin with ("like the kind of pitchers that were on the Yankees when he was a player"). A catcher—even Bill Freehan—was always under special pressure. "Billy was the kind of guy who'd second-guess the catchers but he wouldn't call the signals himself. He'd second-guess the pitcher, the catcher, on everything that happened. If you didn't get 'em out, it wasn't right. If you got 'em out, he was right," Northrup said.

The pitchers were also expected to throw at hitters when ordered. "Billy told 'em he'd fine 'em two thousand bucks if they didn't throw at 'em—you better knock 'em down or it's two thousand bucks," said Northrup. There were a couple of marginal pitchers on the team who were "hatchet men," he said. "We knew whenever they came into a game, we better get ready to fight because they were going to throw at people." (One of those pitchers, who remembers being fined for not hitting batters, corroborates Northrop's story, though he could not recall any fine being as large as two thousand dollars; his own, he said, was five hundred.)

Northrup emphasized that he was not talking about pitching inside, either, which he knew was part of the game, but of deliberately going after hitters. The older pitchers, he maintained, did not often throw at hitters—they didn't need to. It was the younger ones, those who could be intimidated, "the hangers-on or your mediocre pitchers," those who could not deal with being lit up—or with intimidating pressure from Billy.

Then there was the matter of privileges and rewards. These were not distributed equally, Northrup said. "There were two or three guys that thought he was a really good manager and really were enjoying themselves—but those were the guys that had special privileges. The rest of us didn't."

The system of privileges particularly favored the team's best pitcher, Mickey Lolich, who was regularly allowed to leave the park early and to take days off between his starts, Northrup asserted. The result was that the pitching staff—like the team itself—became resentful and divided.

Then there was Billy off the field. His drinking, Northrup charged, ultimately interfered with the team's ability to play.

"He drank an awful lot. Of course, all of us were guilty of doing our share of drinking, but Billy Martin drank a lot. I've seen him, I've known when he came to the park extremely hung over or even pretty well pie-eyed, I mean I know that for a fact," he said. "That's tough on a ballclub. He tried to manage from the phone one time when he was so sick—from Minnesota. He was at the hotel calling in to the dugout. I never heard of anybody trying to do that. You can imagine having to go through that kind of stuff. The last game when we lost the playoffs to Oakland in '72, in the fifth game, he shows up forty-five minutes before the game and nobody knows what the lineup's gonna be or who's gonna play. We took batting practice the way we did the last game because nobody knew who was going to play—these are the playoffs against the Oakland A's! An hour before the game, forty-five minutes, no lineup, no nothing—the most important game we had to play all year. So then he puts Duke Sims in left field, a catcher, and Billy Freehan behind the plate with a broken thumb, and both guys wind up being involved in plays that cost us the game."

Northrup might as well have been talking about Captain Queeg as the manager of the Detroit Tigers, but he was not alone on the club. Joe Coleman, the team's other big pitcher—and its player rep—also faulted Billy for favoring Lolich and for placing undue pressure on other pitchers. One time, because a number of players on the team were complaining about it, Coleman went to Billy—as the player rep.

"There was this instance where some of the players got so upset that preferential treatment was being given to Lolich that some people asked me to go to him as the rep and talk to him. There were a lot of times I had to go and talk to him about certain things," Coleman said. "I had to tell him it isn't right, isn't in the nature of good team spirit or team aspect. So now all of a sudden, Billy gets pissed off at me, and he said, 'Well, you can do the same things as Lolich can do, and you come in here complaining about it?' I said, 'Hey, I'm complaining about it because I don't think it's right—but there are some others on the club who don't think it's right either. Secondly, I wouldn't do the things he does. It's got to the point where it's gone overboard,' and I said a lot of people on the club feel it has to stop."

Coleman corroborated charges that Billy would interfere with pitch selection and also noted the negative effect his life-style seemed to have on the rest of the team.

"It got to the point where there were just too many distractions, there were a lot of off-field things going on, there were times he was late to the ballpark. . . . We'd go into towns, go out and have a drink or something—he'd have too many and before you know it he's fighting or arguing with a player."

But Coleman, who had difficulty with Billy throughout his tenure there, also believed that he ran the game well, that he was an impressive field leader.

"He knew how the game should be played. He was a winner. He came out of the Yankee organization and everybody knew he was a winner. And he managed to win—not just for the sake of managing. But the one thing that happened there," Coleman said, "was that if we started to lose, he would come back trying to be more right with his next moves, so instead of staying with the basics when we went through a losing streak, he'd try to do a little bit more—little things that a lot of guys didn't think necessary. We had a veteran ballclub, let us come out of it on our own and we'll be fine."

Because the team won in '72, a lot of the dissension and friction that had developed within the club was pushed aside, Coleman said, but there was no mistaking that trouble existed—even as the headlines and acclaim for Billy grew.

Al Kaline, already a legend if an aging fixture on the club, kept his distance from Billy, and Billy seemed to keep his distance from him. But Kaline, even in praising Billy, acknowledged the buildup of tension in the atmosphere around the team:

"I never saw anybody who hated to lose as much as Billy Martin," Kaline told Maury Allen. "If there was anything worse to him than just losing, it was looking bad. He hated sloppy play, careless play, games lost because guys weren't alert. He would go into a rage. . . . He never really yelled at the players much, but he would scream at his coaches, abuse them, take all his anger out on them. . . . At the same time he would force these players to play better than they ever had. He could motivate men. I think a lot of the players were physically afraid of him. He was a tough little guy and they knew he could kick their ass in a fight. If Billy got down on a player, he was finished."

There was general agreement within the team, and from the media and the fans, that the mid-season acquisition of pitcher Woodie Fryman along with the play of veteran Tony Taylor made a decisive difference in the Tigers' drive to a divisional title. Fryman won ten games and lost only three down the stretch, frequently putting the brakes on losing skids, giving the starting staff the balance it had so obviously lacked. Taylor became the team's super-role-player and general handyman, able to fill in where asked, providing the sort of timely hitting and veteran leadership that any team in a pennant race hopes to have.

But winning simply was not enough. The relationship between Billy and the front office, as it had in Minnesota, grew testy. Increasingly, Billy wanted a say in personnel decisions and, just as increasingly, Jim Campbell, the GM, made it clear that he, not Billy, ran the front office.

In his autobiography, Billy outlined the battles he had with Campbell going into the '72 season:

"Over the winter, I kept telling Campbell that we had to get rid of some of the veterans and some of the guys I didn't feel were going to help us win a pennant. I was pushing Campbell to trade [Les] Cain and [Joe] Niekro and Kilkenny, and McAuliffe had a bad year and I felt we should trade him. Also I felt we could get a top starter if we could trade Northrup. But Campbell for many years had been the farm director for the Tigers, and these were all kids who had won the pennant for the team in '68, and though some of them might have been going downhill, he wouldn't listen to me because they were his babies."

Campbell, who acknowledged that he eventually wearied of fighting with Billy, said that he was used to managers coming through his office steaming about personnel matters. The difference with Billy was the way he went about it, Campbell said. "All managers, you see, one day or another want to get rid of somebody and bring someone else in—to me, it goes in one ear and out the other. But sometimes Billy would go to the press with it. The press would say, 'Billy wants to get rid of this guy,' and you have to jump in and say to him, 'Hey, don't goddamn do that.' Other managers, Ralph Houk, would never do that."

Campbell, who made a habit, as many general managers did, of staying away from the clubhouse and of giving his manager latitude, still was in a better position than most to know what was going on within the club—if only because Billy's critics, like Jim Northrup, were so vocal, and because Billy himself never went to lengths to remain discreet.

At one point in the season, the Detroit papers carried a story that the Yankees were interested in luring Billy to New York as a manager. The story, which seemed to emanate out of New York, involved reports that CBS, the current owner of the Yankees, was interested in selling the team, that a likely new ownership group had indicated that it would be looking for a new manager when it took over the team—and that Billy was the group's prime candidate. Watson Spoelstra, the veteran *Detroit News* baseball writer, noted that for the Yankees—new ownership or old—to have approached Billy would have amounted to tampering, and also indicated that "June rumors run a little deeper than usual with this story." The reason was that no one—Billy included, who was pushing the front office for a contract extension—seemed at great pains to deny the story.

Billy's personal habits and the ways he put pressure on his team—orthodox or unorthodox—were also well known to the front office. Anytime Billy came late, and usually anytime he drank, the front office knew about it because other players and coaches were inevitably there as eyewitnesses if not drinking companions.

When a player was thrown at in a game, whatever the newspapers reported, the front office was already aware of the background of the situation. There was another Reggie Jackson story during June that year; in the course of a 5–2 A's win over the Tigers at Detroit, Jackson was hit by Mickey Lolich, normally a pitcher with pinpoint control. Jackson had to be walked to first base by his manager, Dick Williams, to keep him from charging the mound. Afterward, Reggie told the media, "I don't dig getting hit. I don't like it. Brushing the hitter back is part of the game. But it makes me mad when I get hit. I have respect for Lolich. He isn't known for throwing at guys." The real, the only, culprit as far as Jackson was concerned was, again, Billy Martin. "Some of the things he does," he said, "are uncalled for."

When the Tigers won their division, there was another, far more ugly, far more serious episode of batter bashing during the League Championship Series against the A's. Reggie Jackson was not involved in this one; the principals were Bert Campaneris, the A's base-stealing shortstop and sparkplug, and little-used Detroit reliever Lerrin LaGrow.

The series opened in Oakland, and Billy was keenly aware that he was taking center stage in his hometown. Old friends and family were there to greet him; it had been some time since he had spent more than travel time in the area—usually during regular season stops or for brief post-season visits. When reporters suggested that he might, on a regular basis, be able to fill the Oakland Coliseum with his friends, he jokingly shot back, "Or with my enemies."

But there is no question that returning in this way was special. Whatever his ordinary incentive to win, there was that much more because he was home.

In the opener, before a solidly partisan A's crowd, the teams went to extra innings in a tensely matched pitching duel between Mickey Lolich and Catfish Hunter. In the ninth inning, with the score knotted at 1–1, the Tigers blew a huge opportunity by getting a runner to third with none out and then stranding him—the failure to execute a squeeze bunt, Billy later said, costing the team the game. But the Tigers got another chance in the eleventh when Al Kaline hit a solo homer for a 2–1 lead. But the A's rallied. Two Texas League singles started the inning, but a great defensive play by Aurelio Rodriguez on an attempted sacrifice bunt seemed to break the back of the rally. Then an obscure pinch hitter, Gonzalo Marquez, lashed a single to right, scoring the tying run, and when Al Kaline threw wildly to the plate, the winning run scored as well. The loss, hard to take under any circumstances, was doubly so for Billy, whose experience with extra-inning playoff losses was already excruciating.

Jim Northrup maintains that Billy's determination to win at all costs made him decide to go after Bert Campaneris in the following game. With the A's leading 5–0 late in the game, the Tigers' chances in the series all but on a precipice, Billy brought in Lerrin LaGrow to pitch to Campaneris. "Billy ordered LaGrow to throw at Campaneris—at his feet. 'If you don't,' he said, 'I want you to hit him someplace so that he's out of there,' " Northrup maintains Billy said. Campaneris got hit in the legs and then threw his bat at LaGrow. "He knew exactly what we were trying to do," Northrup charged.

Campaneris, whose bat-flinging horrified a national TV audience and league officials—was ejected from the game (as was LaGrow), was fined and, more importantly for the A's and Tigers, was suspended for the remainder of the series. The possibility that Billy deliberately went after Campaneris was never investigated, but there was plenty of smoke nevertheless. Northrup was, it turned out, not the only one who suspected what Billy was up to. The night before the game, Billy had dinner with Tony Kubek, no great personal friend, who was announcing the series for NBC. During the course of dinner, Billy suggested—strongly enough for Kubek to warn his viewers the next day of the impending incident—that Campaneris had to be stopped.

"Billy and I were sitting there, we had dinner and stuff, a couple of drinks, and he said, 'We gotta stop Campaneris,' " Kubek said. "I didn't say anything, he goes on: 'We gotta stop him. He's beating us with his feet. We gotta get him.' LaGrow goes out and throws at Campaneris's legs—I think it was twice—and the next thing you know Campaneris slings the bat. On the air, I never said that Billy told me this, because it was a confidence. But before it happened, I said, 'This little guy right here, you might look for something to happen.' And it did, the fight ensued, and Campaneris was suspended.

"The Tiger people were very upset," Kubek said. "I had a letter from them, and some local DJ took off on me; one of the real popular broadcasters in Detroit was saying how we instigated this because how could we have known what was coming? Things got so bad we had to change hotels."

When the series shifted back to Detroit, Campaneris indeed was out of the lineup and the Tigers were prepared to make their last stand. That was all anyone cared about.

The Detroit Tigers of 1972 were a success story and there was no doubt about why. The banner headlines that had greeted the Tigers' division clinching proclaimed Billy the man of the hour. "How did the Tigers do it?" asked one lead. "One man made the difference." Billy was not just a hero in Detroit, he was a *Detroit* hero, peculiarly fashioned after the gritty, hard-working, blue-collar residents of the town who knew all about battling and scrapping and making the most out of the least. This was no ordinary handler of men. He had run his team with only two players—Aurelio Rodriguez and shortstop Eddie Brinkman—as regulars, skillfully platooning everyone else. Never mind those who from time to time had expressed dissatisfaction; Billy was a winner wherever he went, the hardest loser in any sport—the team lost sixty-nine times, which meant the players had to look Billy in the eye sixty-nine times afterward—and it was as though he willed them to win in spite of themselves.

"The assembly-line worker, the office manager can identify with Martin, a scrapping, snarling type when things go wrong . . . but when he's winning, he can charm anyone with remarkable personal warmth," said the article in the *News*.

Columnist Jack Berry was even more effusive. "Billy Martin is the only one left in the game who plays Gas House baseball. In an age when players are named Randy and Scott, rather than Butch and Rocky, when they no longer come from the alleys and pool halls, Billy, who did, still plays tough baseball." Berry managed to corner Reggie Jackson, who put his own flourish of icing on the celebratory cake:

"I don't like Billy Martin because he plays tough baseball," he told the writer, "but I'd probably love him if I played for him."

The Tigers fought back in the third game of the series, getting a complete-game shutout from Joe Coleman. The following day, it got implausibly better. Fate, which had seemed to have definite ideas about Billy Martin since he became a manager of baseball teams, seemed suddenly to switch sides. Mickey Lolich, pitching on short rest, carried the Tigers on his portly frame, allowing only a single run through nine innings. The Tigers, unfortunately, had been able to do no better. When Lolich left in the tenth, the A's jumped all over reliever Chuck Seelbach, scoring twice to virtually ice the game—and the champagne.

But in the Tiger tenth, two singles and a wild pitch put runners on second and third with no one out. The A's elected to walk pinch hitter Gates Brown, loading the bases, and then Bill Freehan, a powerful hitter but slow runner, bounced a certain double play ball to short. The A's wisely elected to allow a run to score, going for two outs—but there was no double play. In fact, no one was retired. Gene Tenace, the catcher, filling in at second base, dropped the throw from short as the runner from first was bearing down on him. The Tigers were a run closer and the bases were still loaded. With two left-handed hitters coming up, the A's brought a left-handed pitcher, Dave Hamilton, into the game. Hamilton walked Norm Cash, allowing the tying run to score, and then faced Jim Northrup. Northrup won the game by lining a ball over the head of the drawn-in right fielder.

The Tiger dressing room afterward was the city in microcosm. Country music blared through the stalls and dressing areas crowded with throngs of wildly happy players and writers. It seemed as though everyone in Michigan—from the front office to the last cubbyhole at the end of the radio dial—was simultaneously discovering Billy's music: Merle Haggard's "No Reason to Quit," "Every Fool Has a Rainbow," "The Fightin' Side of Me." Suddenly, the series that the Tigers had lost was a single game from their grasp—at home, in front of all those adoring, unquestioning fans.

The finale might better have been staged one day later, Friday the thirteenth. Billy's team went down, 2–1—and the agony of it could not have been more exquisite if it had been designed by the Marquis de Sade. Billy's lineup changes—Duke Sims, the catcher, in left field, the injured Bill Freehan behind the plate—came back to haunt him.

The Tigers scored a first-inning run, but the A's answered in the second when Reggie Jackson stole home—pulling a hamstring muscle in the process. The tie held into the fourth when George Hendrick, Reggie's replacement, bounced a routine ground ball to short leading off the inning for the A's. The throw to first was in plenty of time to get Hendrick—but umpire John Rice said the first baseman, Norm

Cash, removed his foot from the bag too soon. The argument that followed carried through the inning and beyond. Sal Bando, the A's third baseman, sacrificed Hendrick to second, a play the Tigers' broken-thumbed catcher, Bill Freehan, could not head off. With two out, Gene Tenace dumped a single into left, in front of weak-armed Duke Sims, allowing Hendrick to score the tie-breaking run. The fact of the run, its irony and its obvious importance, was too much. The low-level protest that had simmered through the inning boiled over as the Tigers came to bat in their half of the inning. Frank Howard, the very large Tiger player-coach, confronted Rice. He followed the umpire up the first-base line, toward right field:

"You see that play every day during the season—what's the matter with you!" he barked.

"Are you calling me a liar?" the umpire responded.

"No sir," said the mammoth Tiger, "but you are full of shit!"

"What did you say?" Rice barked.

"I said you are full of shit!" roared Howard.

Rice fired a fist into the air, Howard was gone, Billy's coaches were holding him in restraint—none of it mattered. The single, aberrant run was enough. The Tigers, despite a brilliant, gutsy pitching performance by Woodie Fryman, fell to the A's, 2–1. The loss, as devastating as it was for the team and its fans, was doubly so for Billy. Of course, he had wanted this as he would have craved any championship—any victory—but this one carried all of that unseen baggage. All the troubles that had been dragging at his leadership might, with this one win, have been eased. He would have been in an extraordinary position to consolidate his place in an organization that could never be comfortable with having him do things his way, any way he wanted. At game's end, he now had to answer not to the charge of a blown umpire's call, but to why he had played a catcher in left field while Willie Horton was sitting on the bench, and why he used Bill Freehan, with a broken thumb, behind the plate. He now had to answer not for a championship team but to the swirl of dissatisfaction and complaint that had accumulated on a team that had gone, almost certainly, as far as it could go.

Charlie Silvera, Billy's old comrade-in-arms, his bullpen coach at Detroit, remained with him in the clubhouse following the game. Silvera, who had seen Billy many times in the wake of defeat over the years, remembered this as one that stood apart:

"Okay, now we lose this game, lose the playoffs to Oakland in Detroit—controversial play at first with Rice, fifth game, all of that—so we went back to the clubhouse after the game and went back to the training room," Silvera recalled. "There was champagne there—and we had some. Everybody left and Billy said, 'Come on, I gotta go see Campbell.' The office was up behind the right-field corner, so we walk up there and suddenly he stops me and says, 'Wait a minute.' And he just came into my arms and started crying. He said, 'This is the one I wanted, this is the one I really wanted.' He just cried in my arms up there in the stands before he went in to see Campbell. The man is dead now, he probably wouldn't want me to say that—but that's just what happened."

Silvera's affection for Billy has, if anything, deepened over the years. But his very closeness allowed him to see sympathetically what less well-disposed observers might have seen more clinically.

Silvera knew that there was friction between Billy and Jim Campbell. "There are a lot of things that can't be mentioned," he said. "I think it had mostly to do with off-field stuff. But I think Billy thought Campbell was always trying to take a defensive position in everything. Between you and me, Billy came into the Detroit organization and they didn't want to shake it, everybody was making money, everybody was having a good time—don't shake it, just win. Well, that's what Billy was into. So incidents happened. I remember one the night we won the division. You know, people went crazy and tore up everything, including the bullpen phone. Well, Billy told this ballpark guy, 'You better make sure you have that fixed by the time we get back from Oakland.' We got back and the phone wasn't fixed. I told Billy about it and he just blew his stack—went after the guy, called him in—Campbell had to intervene in that one, too. So there were a lot of little things going on all the time, probably more things than I know."

In any case, the Tigers' near-win had only limited carrying effect. Billy received a contract extension from the team, but it was clear that none of the internal tensions he was dealing with had been relieved. Early in spring training the following season, columnist Milt Richman published a piece on a new and mellower Billy, more likely to use his head than his fists to deal with problems, a man able to communicate in a new and troubled age.

"Today, people say 'right on,' " Billy told Richman. "We simply said it another way twenty years ago. Today they ask why and how come? You have to answer all those questions. If you can communicate, you can. Times have changed. A leader can't fake his way through anymore."

But within days of this portrait of the "new" leader, some old and not very pretty problems surfaced. Willie Horton, moody and depressed again, complained not to his manager but to the media about his lack of playing time. He placed the blame squarely on Billy's shoulders:

"I don't know how I got in the clink with him but I'd sure like to get out of it," Horton said. "I'm only twenty-nine years old and platooning is for guys who are thirty-nine."

For his part, Billy shot back. "All he's got to do is hit. I've been here two years and I've heard what a good hitter Willie is, but I've never seen it. He's the only player I know who can go 0 for 35 and still expect to play."

Then, two weeks later, Billy was in an ugly bar incident with another Tiger player, Ike Blessitt. The incident, which possibly involved a woman and almost certainly included one drink too many, resulted in a near-brawl between the manager and player. A close friend of Billy's said a knife was pulled, though no one was quite sure—except that both men were briefly detained and then released by police. News of the fight spread through the organization—though, for the time being, it was kept from the newspapers. There was enough going on in Tigertown for Jim Campbell to intercede.

Late in March, with papers back home printing stories about Billy's use of a new video machine in camp, Campbell called Billy and Willie Horton into a meeting, ostensibly to settle the question of a fine Billy had recently levied against the star player for leaving a pre-season game early. But the whole question of Billy's leadership style was also obviously involved. According to Campbell, Billy had reached the point where he wanted Horton removed from the team for insubordination. Campbell acknowledges that he did most of the talking in this meeting and that his intention was to get a number of things straightened out—principally that he was willing to back his manager, but not by getting rid of Willie Horton. The meeting, he maintains, was low-key—no raised voices, no quarreling—when suddenly, Billy jumped up, threw down a pipe Campbell had once given him as a gift, and announced that he was quitting.

"He just walked out," Campbell said. "He was pissed. He had a terrible temper, so I didn't go after him, didn't try to call him—nothing."

Billy spent the entire day in the bar of the local Holiday Inn—"Having a few shooters," Campbell said—and then at 5:30 the next morning, called him. "Billy asked if he could talk; I said, 'It's five-thirty. Yeah, come on, you SOB, I'm in bed, for chrissakes.' "

A day after banner headlines in the Detroit papers on his quitting, Billy was back at the helm—but the damage to him, beyond the organization itself, was considerable.

"As usual, Billy will say that he was misunderstood," wrote the nearly always friendly Dan Ewald.

Jack Berry, another key press ally, cautioned readers that "someday, Martin will erupt once too often." In his article, Berry took an unusually harsh view of the popular manager. "Vincent van Gogh cut off his ear but it didn't diminish his talent as an artist." Berry underscored that Billy was a kind of split personality—a great manager but a drunken brawler, an intense, often boorish celebrity in the manner of George S. Patton, Frank Sinatra, and others whose violent tempers seemed forever crossed with their abilities.

There was a curious and completely unreported sidelight to the episode, however. Between the time he left the team and the time he returned, Billy visited Willie Horton in his hotel room. The meeting, Horton said, forever changed his view of Billy.

"He basically apologized," Horton said, "and he explained some things to me, and my whole life actually turned around. He told me that as a leader, as a manager, like the captain of a ship, you're never wrong. If you show players that you're wrong, then you lose the respect you need to run things. A fine had been levied against me—a thousand dollars. Eventually, he gave it back to me but told me that if I let on that he had done that, he would deny it. He was telling me that he was wrong but that he had a team to lead, and from that day on I thought differently about him—and about myself. It was the same as my father had once taught me: to have dignity and self-respect in life. Billy added eight years to my career and he became a close friend."

But for the front office and the rest of the team, nothing so positive came from the incident. The damage had been done, and what should have been a long and glorious reign for Billy in Detroit ended miserably for everyone involved. The aging Tigers simply could not repeat their success of the year before. For a while the team stayed close to the Yankees and Orioles who battled at the top of the standings through the first half of the season. But it was clear they simply did not have the guns. Woodie Fryman, so crucial to the team's success the year before, couldn't overcome chronic elbow problems and became all but invisible on the staff. There was no one to take his place. Mickey Lolich, who had a "tired arm," according to opponents, was also ineffective. Eddie Brinkman, another key the year before, had spinal surgery over the winter and was never the same player; the unhappy players were unhappier, the old ones even older. By midseason, local columnist Jerry Green was calling for the breakup of the team as later he would call for a firm disciplining of Billy Martin.

But Billy did everything he could to win with what he had—and didn't have. The year 1973 saw the amazing culmination of relief pitcher John Hiller's return from a heart attack. With Billy's constant encouragement, Hiller, against the worries of management and suggestions that he retire, turned in an American League–leading thirty-eight saves.

The year 1973 was also the season when the Tigers signed Ron LeFlore who, but for Billy, would almost certainly never have found his way to the major leagues. LeFlore was in the middle of a long prison sentence when Billy heard about him through a Detroit friend, Jimmy Busakeris. Busakeris had been told that LeFlore, whatever else he was, was an outstanding baseball talent—and Billy was unorthodox enough to find out for himself. He visited LeFlore in prison, and arranged thereafter for him to come to Tiger Stadium for a tryout. LeFlore was so impressive that, with Billy's strong backing, he was ultimately paroled and signed to a Tiger contract in 1973.

But the team's fortunes could not be reversed. There are those who argue that when it became clear by the end of August that the Tigers could not repeat, Billy was already campaigning for a managing job elsewhere. Detroit papers reported a strong rumor that the Mets were probably going to fire Yogi Berra and were interested in hiring Billy. Jim Northrup swears that one night in a restaurant he was present when Billy asked an unnamed Yankee official to consider him for the Yankee job—immediately placing that official in a situation where, if he had responded, charges of tampering could have been brought.

The reality was that Billy's job was in jeopardy. There is simply no proof that he was looking to give it away. "If Billy was looking to get out, he sure went about it in a funny way," said longtime Detroit friend Bill Reedy. The facts seem to bear him out. The Tigers surged in August, coming from well back in the standings to actually take first and hold it through the middle of the month, only falling behind afterward. With armies of fans again rallying to the team and the manager, with a pennant possibly in the offing once more, it would have been completely implausible for the manager or the management to do anything to rock the boat.

But losing not only rocked the boat, it finally capsized it. By the end of August, with the team slipping further and further behind, Billy again was in the press with his criticism of the team, telling reporters that morale on the team was low and that he was no longer sure how to revive it. "It's a question of how to come across to the players and right now, I'm not sure what to do."

He went public again with his unhappiness with the Tiger farm system; he was noticeably—press-noticeably—late to a game with the White Sox after he had been missing from the team for a day with a reported tooth ailment. Then, in a game between the Indians and Tigers on August 31, a spitball war broke out.

The Indians pitcher was Gaylord Perry—proof enough to the Tigers that Vaseline was lubricating the proceedings. With Detroit trailing 3–0, Tiger pitchers Joe Coleman and then Fred Scherman began loading up. All of this might have remained a damp skirmish but for Billy's post-game comments.

"My pitchers were deliberately throwing spitballs the last two innings on orders from me," he said into the teeth of baseball authority everywhere. "I did it to prove a point that it can be done without the umpires doing anything about it. They're making a mockery of the game by not stopping Perry. Everyone knows he does it and nobody does anything about it. We're going to keep on doing it every time he pitches against us."

An astonished Joe Coleman then told the press that he was deliberately throwing spitballs, that he had a gob of Vaseline on his wrist and that he marked the balls exactly as Perry had, across the signature of the American League president. It did not matter that later, different players said that the idea of throwing spitters originated with them, not Billy—that he had merely interceded for them. Jim Campbell had had enough. Billy was suspended the following day and fired two days after that.

Campbell maintains to this day that the spitball incident was not the reason Billy was fired, that the triggering reason was one he promised Billy he would never disclose. "But it doesn't take a genius to see that no one incident was responsible," he added.

The Detroit media and fans were predictably in high turmoil, fiercely divided, partisan and acrimonious. Talk show hosts and local DJs seemingly could focus on nothing else, prompting one writer to note that it was simply ". . . amazing that Billy could absorb so much attention with everything else that was going on in the world."

For a day or two, the only comments Billy made were on his privately contracted local radio show, where he was able to say what he wanted while remaining insulated from reporters' questions. He need not have been apprehensive, however; if he was no longer universally admired in the media, he was still overwhelmingly supported by ordinary fans—many of whom began to deluge the airwaves, op-ed pages, and Tiger offices with their complaints. In his time in Detroit, Billy had, as never before—including Denver and Minnesota—created this sense of identification with ordinary people. Somehow his passions and aspirations were theirs, his disappointments and wounds theirs as well.

Jim Campbell knew what Billy had created in Detroit and, better than anyone else, knew what firing him meant. Billy hadn't been hired because he was a "genius," Campbell said, but because he was a solid professional baseball man, "highly aware of the way the game worked." He had taken an old, slow team and awakened it, awakening the passions of an entire city in the process. But he was just not an organization man, and working with him had become impossible.

For all the distress and rubble in their broken relationship, Campbell retained some affection for Billy—along with a ray of gallows humor concerning those last nerve-shattering days.

"I fired Billy that Sunday and man, right away, everyone was up in arms," Campbell recalled. "He had a lot of fans. Billy was their hero—and I knew this was going to happen, that I was going to get my ass ripped: not so much in the press, but the fans. Billy was popular, and rightly so—he'd won for us. But that was Sunday. Monday, we finished our game here . . . and I'd been getting phone calls, from everywhere, from out-of-town writers, the works. . . . I went home that day, and I walked in the door and did something that I'd never done before, and never done since. It was about five o'clock and I was beat and tired, and I poured myself a drink: Cutty Sark and water. I sat down at a dining room table—come to think of it, maybe this was Tuesday because it had taken time for this to build up. Well, anyway, suddenly I hear this goddamn noise and the plaster over my head was falling out and then, just like that, all the windows in my apartment were shot out. And I hear this loud screaming: 'Now you did it! Now you did it! You killed him! Now you did it!'

"What the fuck is going on, I'm thinking, they're coming after me because I got rid of Billy? . . . I lay there on the floor, I still had this drink in my hand . . . and then I got over to the telephone and called 911, you know, 'Hey, I'm calling from such and such and such and such—there's a shootout here in my building. . . .'

"It turned out that none of this had to do with me, it was some drug-related thing. . . . When things finally got cleaned up, there were three body bags out there in the hallway. . . . Then when the police came into my apartment, saw me and the bullet holes, this guy kinda looked at me and said, 'You're Jim Campbell, aren'tcha?' I said, 'Yeah.' He said, 'You've had a helluva week, haven't you?' I said, 'Yeah, Jesus Christ, tell me about it!'

"Of course, all of this made the papers and then, you know what? I get a call from Billy. 'They're tryin' to shoot ya for firing me, huh?' he says, laughing. 'Yeah, goddamnit,' I say to him. I never had a week like that in my life."

It was an even more implausible week for Billy, though. Within days of his firing, he had been hired as the new manager of the Texas Rangers.

# CHAPTER 12

Accepting field leadership of the Texas Rangers at the end of 1973 had all the appeal of being given eleventh-hour command of the Alamo with the strains of Santa Anna's death trumpets wailing in the air. The Rangers, when Billy took over, were 47–81, last in the American League West and by consensus the worst team in baseball. By season's end, they would lose 105 games, the most in the majors. Attendance for the year was a little over 600,000—lowest in the majors.

But Billy, perhaps like that last Alamo commander, saw something else. The owner of the Rangers was Bob Short, an old friend from Minnesota. Short and Billy had become friends in the mid-sixties and after he was dismissed from his managerial job with the Twins, Billy had briefly campaigned for Short in the Minnesota Democratic primary for governor. He liked the man, trusted him and came to believe that he, almost alone among sports executives, actually understood him.

Short, when he took over the Washington Senators, had wanted Billy to manage his Triple A team under Ted Williams, a job Billy refused. Short had liked and admired Billy and had wanted to hire him ever since. When Detroit fired him, Short had another chance—one that Billy jumped at.

Because the team had done so poorly, and because Short admired Billy as much as he did, he gave him the sort of free hand he never had before. He was offered a five-year contract at around $65,000 annually, and, more importantly, there was a handshake understanding that control of personnel was his. The agreement was that Billy had final say on the makeup of the team's twenty-five-man roster which, in effect, gave him veto power over trades, the farm system, life on the team in general.

There were, of course, raised eyebrows when Billy was hired. Short fired a young Whitey Herzog, acknowledged even then to be topflight managerial material, to get Billy. Only days before, he had given Herzog the sort of public endorsement that would have suited any cynic's notion of the perfect kiss of death. Four days before firing him, Short called Herzog the best rookie manager in baseball. One day after cashiering him he simply said he had made a mistake.

Because the Rangers had done so badly, Billy had some advantages coming in: The team couldn't do worse. There were no stars here, few veterans or established "personalities." The talent, needless to say, was also questionable. The pitching was the worst in the American League; no one on the staff won more than nine games in 1973, and the team's ERA was the highest in the majors. The hitting, with the exception of Jeff Burroughs, was not much better. Among regulars, there wasn't a single .300 hitter.

But from the day he was introduced to the press—his first day on the job—Billy said he was there to win. Whitey Herzog, as most managers would have in those circumstances, talked about winning as an eventual goal, the result of long-term planning and building. Billy talked about winning right away. "Managers don't win games, teams do," Herzog said after he was fired. Billy said, "I know what the record is now, but I didn't come here to lose. I detest losing. Losing eats at me. I take every loss personally. If I didn't think I could win, I wouldn't be here today. And I want to win in this final month."

Billy knew that he was perfect for Texas. Not only was this an ideal team for him to be taking over, one that he could mold in his own image, but it was in a perfect place. It wasn't just the Alamo he was being handed, but the whole state of Texas—wide open, wild, uncharted.

Billy loved the imagery of it as well as the challenge. It was as if he was already an honorary Texan, someone with the culture and the challenge already in his blood, someone on speaking terms with Sam Houston, Jim Bowie, the remnant desperadoes of the Dalton gang.

Billy loved the West, its music, its culture. He was a regular reader of the Western romances of Louis L'Amour and Zane Grey; "those were about the only books he read aside from Civil War books," his son Billy Joe recalled. Almost from the moment he set foot in Texas, he began dressing like a Texan, remembered Randy Galloway, who had only recently begun covering the team for the *Dallas Morning News*. It was as though Billy not only had been given a new team but a chance to create himself anew.

"Texas was so much like Billy—wild and loose. He loved that image, that atmosphere," Galloway said. "He immediately started wearing boots and everything; he got down here and right away he became a Number One Cowboy. You can check, but I don't think he ever did that before."

Billy's office at Arlington Stadium had a huge framed picture of Stephen F. Austin, the founder of the actual Texas Rangers. He packed a pistol to go along with his valuable collection of rifles and, said any number of people who knew him while he managed the Rangers, he would from time to time take target practice under the stands when the stadium was deserted. Bill Reedy remembers that Billy, who shortly afterward became proprietor of a couple of Western wear stores, "at one point wanted to get all his friends into wearing those long leather Western coats, you know, like butcher-block coats—be damned if I'd ever do that," he said.

Texas, then, *should* have been perfect—and for a time it was. In the beginning, it was as if he had actually found a whole new life. He bought a home—the first he had ever owned—in the suburbs of Arlington. Gretchen was not only a wife, a mother raising his son, but she was also a partner in his success. Increasingly, she entered into his business affairs, helping him decide which investments were worth his time and which weren't. She even had an eye and ear out for the way he came across to the public. At one of his early press conferences, he referred to the writer "George Pimpleton." "*Plimpton*," Gretchen, sitting at his elbow, corrected with a whisper.

He watched his players, studying them, he said, not only for the talents they had, "but for what was in their heads—in their hearts and souls." And he talked winning through that final month of the season, into the winter, and in the following spring, convincing the players on the existing squad that things were about to turn around in ways they might not believe, convincing the writers that there would be "trades that will knock your socks off," convincing fans that it was now time—whatever the standings or the experts said—to head back to the ballpark with hope in their hearts and cash in their hands.

Because the Rangers were, for the most part, young and because their fans were, for the most part, used to losing, almost anything Billy did or said in the beginning was received as though he was already a legend.

"There was an aura around Billy Martin," reported second baseman Dave Nelson. To Nelson, Billy didn't look or sound imposing but "whenever he spoke, thirty pairs of ears would listen. I think we're going to be a winner," he said, sounding as much hypnotized as convinced.

"Growing up, the Yankees were always my favorite team," said Toby Harrah, the team's twenty-four-year-old shortstop. "Guys like Whitey Ford, Mickey Mantle, Yogi—and, of course, Billy Martin—they were the only team you could watch on the weekends, and then to have him just walk in the clubhouse like that!"

The whole team, the organization, the area seemed to take to Billy that way. It really was as though the long mysterious reaches of the Great Plains opened up for a moment to permit one of those old Texas heroes to step out of the shadows for the sole purpose of putting the big baseball team right.

Bill Ziegler, the young Ranger trainer then, still the Ranger trainer today, recalled the day Billy first walked into the clubhouse at Arlington Stadium. "I had never met him before. I'll never forget the day he walked into the clubhouse the day he got the job with the Rangers and I was there, just a trainer, thinking 'God, I've heard so much about Billy Martin'—and he walked over, put out his hand and said, 'Doc, my name's Billy Martin' as if I wouldn't have known or something."

Ziegler, who valued Billy's friendship till the end, also saw Billy up close, in ways that others within the organization may not have. Occasionally, Billy called him after a fight; the details of the fight never mattered, but the injuries did. Ziegler would see Billy from time to time in the training room when he had taken a beating and needed treatment—and someone to talk to.

But even that side of Billy's life, which came with the name and the legend, fit the mystique—at least in the beginning. "Billy was probably not welcome in half the bars in Texas," Toby Harrah said with a touch of pride. Everyone knew Billy fought and drank and lived as hard as any mythic Texan of the past.

Because the Ranger situation was as unpromising as it was, almost any improvement would have been welcome, but Billy was after more. He spent the last month of the 1973 season hyping his team to local writers, hoping that they in turn would generate the beginnings of

Ranger-mania for their readers. Billy swore his team would not only improve, but would contend the following season. That was worth a story. He bet a local writer a suit that the Rangers would draw over a million people and would be in the thick of the pennant race; that was worth a bigger story. He analyzed the Rangers talent player by player, position by position, arguing that the ingredients for a pennant already were in place—bigger story. Finally, he managed. He played the last games as if they meant something—not in the standings, because he could do nothing about that, but to the players.

Jeff Burroughs, the team's one big hitter, still had a remote chance of catching Reggie Jackson for the home run title. He let Burroughs lead off through the last games of the season so that he would have more at-bats, more opportunities to catch him. "Having Jeff Burroughs lead off," said Randy Galloway, invoking the gods of Dallas Cowboys football, "is akin to having Bob Lilly as a punt return specialist." He was not being critical at all. In a few short weeks, Billy Martin, said Galloway, did and said things "that made you forget your next question."

True to his word, Billy did hit the trading markets over the winter. He did not exactly open the pens and drive out the herd, but he did, in a single stroke, improve the team's prospects. For little-known Bill Madlock and another player, Vic Harris, Billy lassoed the Cubs' great Ferguson Jenkins. True, Jenkins had slipped to only fourteen wins in 1973—the first time since 1966 that he had failed to win twenty—but he was the sort of pitcher a team could build a staff around. Along with Jim Bibby, the Rangers just like that had the sort of one-two pitching punch that made the prospects of a .500 season at least plausible, if not likely.

More than fifty players were invited to the Ranger camp that next spring, far in excess of most teams, and more than was practicable, thought some of the writers. For Billy and his coaching staff—which again included Charlie Silvera and Art Fowler—the numbers only reflected his commitment to finding that exact combination of players, no matter their previous experience, that would enable the team to win immediately. Two of the players in camp, Mike Hargrove and Jim Sundberg, had only low minor league experience, but had been personally scouted by Billy and invited to camp. When the season opened, they had both won starting positions.

Billy had also brought in some old hands with fast legs, chief among them Cesar Tovar, a key player for Minnesota in 1969. Billy's camp, everyone said, was wide-open, exciting, unpredictable, daring—just like Billy himself, who clearly was in charge.

The atmosphere was completely different than any he had ever seen in spring training, Toby Harrah said. "We worked hard all right, but it wasn't ever grim or long, we were outta there by one o'clock in the afternoon. Everything was just fun to do, it was fun to play baseball again."

Fundamentals were stressed. Art Fowler, rumpled and red-nosed, concocted Rube Goldberg boxes of strings to help train his young pitchers to throw strikes.

"Ain't no Babe Ruth around no more, so y'all just throw strikes," he'd say in that slow Carolina drawl of his that often turned his words into an incomprehensible mush, making others laugh—even when they didn't understand him. One writer remembered that Fowler, when asked about the thinness of Ranger pitching, reached into his pants and pulled out a worn, crumpled ball of paper which, the writer said, he thought contained the names of some of the team's pitchers. "Fowler smoothed this thing out and then began reading off these names, which I couldn't make out. Then he looked up at me and said, 'That should tell y'all we're as good as anybody in the league.' "

But everyone in camp knew that Billy meant business, that fun was the reward for hard work and winning. When country and western singer Charley Pride, an old minor league ballplayer, who was to the Rangers what Jack Nicholson has been to the Lakers, took his annual turn working out with the team, Billy really had him work. Pride stayed for a month, and worked as though he was a rookie ballplayer instead of a celebrity singer.

The players knew, the writers reported, that speed would be the basis of Billy's game this year—as it had not been in Detroit. Billy had players in camp—Dave Nelson, Tovar, even the moody Alex Johnson—who could run. One player, Lenny Randle, a marginal player in the organization for the past couple of seasons, had reported late to camp—a certain invitation to oblivion with Billy Martin, said the writers—but because he came prepared to hustle and, above all, able to run, he quickly established himself in his manager's plans.

What all of the work, all of the fun, all of the imagery added up to was that, going into the season, Billy somehow had been able to convince his players, the writers who followed the team, and the fans who paid the fare that things were going to be very different. He apparently even convinced the hard-hearted men of Las Vegas. The year before, the Rangers began play looking down the long barrel of 100–1 odds; the odds on the Rangers in 1974 had dropped to 50–1.

There is a numbing sameness to the fate of Billy Martin's teams. Billy could jump-start a team the way no other person who ever managed could. Denver, Minnesota, even Detroit were not accidents. Billy in those places not only set the cables to the right nodes and threw the switch, he got these machines going more like high-speed rockets than revived jalopies. The typical flight path was that this vehicular bullet carried everyone with it in the beginning, climbing toward a level of space no one could finally predict, but then, when the burn had gone on for a while, the engine slowed, wobbled, and those aboard or watching it came to realize that the great climb was the result of overload, too much stress and strain. The rocket ultimately nose-dived, crashing back to earth in a self-destructive and clamorous ball of fire.

Each of these managerial thrusts and crashes had, with variations, seemingly similar causes. The postmortems inevitably pointed to the excitement Billy first engendered on his team, the fierce loyalties created and the equally fierce resentments; then, with the progression of pressures, there was conflict and trouble with the front office, turmoil and sometimes fisticuffs off the field (sometimes on), and eventually a hopeless and wearying division of energies, as animosities and just plain fatigue led to another ending—and, just as typically, a new beginning somewhere else.

The master shot, equally applicable for each of these managerial stops, even had interchangeable particulars. There were always reports of insubordination; of drinking and rules violations getting out of hand; of headline quarrels with stars, obscure younger players, umpires, a writer or two; someone always remembered how hard Billy came down on his coaches, or how he inevitably came to blame one or two of them for being front office spies—especially if they wound up succeeding him in the dugout, as was the case with Joe Schultz in Detroit and Frank Lucchesi in Texas; there were, at each stop, charges—sometimes *sotto voce,* sometimes loud and clear—that he mishandled his pitching staff or abused his catchers, especially those with little experience; when it came to the barroom fights, there were always denials of responsibility from Billy coupled with a wearying litany of explanations, complaints, and counter-claims from Billy.

On the other side, there was always someone there to point out that no manager in the game was better between the lines than Billy

Martin; there were genuine testimonials to his genius and leadership, the particulars nearly always involving his extraordinary savvy and field awareness, the seemingly endless repertoire he brought to bear in unsettling the opposition and in finding ways to win.

All of that was present in his stay at Texas, which consisted of one late-season fragment, a complete season, then most of a season following. There were some significant variations here, but the script followed true to form.

The conflicts with management were different in that they changed even as Billy was settling into his new job. The spring following his arrival, Bob Short, the owner who had hired him and given him a more or less free hand, sold the team, coming to see more opportunity for himself in unloading a money-losing franchise than in waiting for it to achieve success in the standings. The new ownership, headed by businessman Brad Corbett and a Metroplex group of associates, though happy to have Billy as the field manager, were ultimately unwilling to have him operate with the latitude afforded him by Short.

Another important difference was the team itself. The Rangers really had no business winning—but they did. And everything Billy did became that much more magnified, not only in and around Arlington but across the baseball world.

The Oakland A's were the odds-on favorite to win everything again. They had been divisional champs each year since 1971, pennant winners and World Champions since 1972. At the end of that first month in 1974, the Rangers had traveled to Oakland, taken a series from them, moved around the league, won some more, and, improbably, sat atop the division—something that not only made for headlines but for believers. Jump-starting, like getting in that first punch, meant taking it to the opposition right away, surprising and confusing them.

"The days when the Rangers are patsies for everybody are over," Billy said after the team's very first road trip. "That's all in the past now. The most progressive thing I have seen on the field is the attitude of this team. The players believe they can win. They're playing like winners, they're acting like winners, they're talking like winners."

And so it went. The team stayed close through May, June, and early July, dropping, finally, to fourth place, eight games back at the All-Star break—but still a considerable accomplishment. Attendance at the ballpark, true to Billy's bet, nearly doubled from the year before, heading toward a million paying customers; the team, which really consisted of two strong veteran pitchers, both on course to win twenty or more games, and a band of no-faces, continued to surprise on an almost nightly basis. Of course they ran—but they also hit, leading the American League in team batting average, hovering near the top in several other offensive categories. Players like Lenny Randle, all but forgotten the year before; the rookies Mike Hargrove and Jim Sundberg; the younger veteran players, Toby Harrah, and the powerful Jeff Burroughs—all were having spectacular seasons together. DJs spun out records. Jukeboxes and radio stations were alight with the mid-summer smash, "Billy's Turnaround Gang," the flip side of which was "I Want to Play Ball for Billy."

"The whole thing was magic," Randy Galloway said. "The team responded to him like I've never seen a team respond. I don't know what it was, he had something, there was something in his personality."

At the Rangers old-timers game that year, the opposition was the All-Time New York Yankee team. One by one, the great Yankee stars of the past—Joe D., Mickey Mantle, Whitey Ford, Allie Reynolds, Gil McDougald—trotted out onto the field in their classic pinstripes. Finally, Billy joined them, wearing Yankee pinstripes, too—the perfect, if incongruous, image of the new pride of Texas that had come to define this reborn Rangers team.

The Rangers, even more incongruously, battled back in the second half, moving from fourth to second place, staying within hailing distance of the A's who, for the most part, looked at their upstart challengers with disdain. When the Rangers took three out of four games in Oakland to move within five and a half games of the lead in early September, Reggie Jackson had the sort of words for his challengers that probably found their way to the clubhouse bulletin board.

"Oh, I'm concerned about Texas but I'm not worried," he said. "I'm sure their win today gave them some hope of catching us but with that five and a half game lead, we're in good shape. I don't think we'll be caught but again we are capable of losing it ourselves."

A week later, the Rangers, at home, took the first two games of a three game set with the A's, but then lost the final game, seemingly ending the race. Billy appeared almost—but not quite—resigned:

"For the first time since they won two championships, the A's really had their backs to the wall. They really had to go out there and bust their asses against us tonight. They were concerned, real concerned. We needed this game, of course, but beating the World Champs five out of the last seven games and going 10–8 for the year isn't too shabby—it's up to the rest of the division now," he said.

The rest of the division kept the A's pinned down while the Rangers, a week later, were still coming through the tall grass with their bowie knives at the ready.

"Billy goes into the final two weeks of the season as feisty, as confident, as arrogant as if it were April and he had 162 games to overhaul the A's," wrote Randy Galloway.

But he didn't have 162 games left. When the team dropped both ends of a doubleheader to the Royals on September 22, the impossible dream was over—but the reality of what had been accomplished remained. The last-place team that had gone 57–105 the year before was runner-up to the best team in baseball in 1974. With a record of 84–76, the Rangers were five games from actually winning the division.

As in Detroit, victory meant the papering over of difficulties that went beyond limitations of talent on the field. Conflicts with the new management team, principally with Bobby Brown, Billy's old Yankee teammate, who had been brought in by Brad Corbett to administer the baseball side of the operation, and with Corbett himself, occasionally caught the attention of writers during the year. There were notable quarrels over the disposition of the young pitcher David Clyde, a Texas schoolboy phenom who had been prematurely rushed to the Rangers the year before in an effort to boost attendance but who was clearly unable to pitch effectively at the major-league level. Billy wanted him demoted, Corbett and Brown did not—and then, during the next winter, there was an even sharper dispute over the acquisition of Willie Davis, the ex-Dodger, a favorite of Corbett's but someone unwanted by Billy. The real quarrel, of course, was the usual one concerning chains of command and control of the team, with Billy maintaining that Short had given him, as a condition of his coming to Texas, the kind of authority now being denied him.

Billy maintained that all it took was losing—which came the following year—to provide the excuse to fire him. It was true that the Rangers could not duplicate their success of the year before. Several of the players, notably Jeff Burroughs, Cesar Tovar, and Jim Sundberg, were dramatically less productive; the great pitching tandem of the year before did not hold. Ferguson Jenkins slipped from twenty-five to seventeen wins. Nineteen-game winner Jim Bibby, ineffective and sore-armed, was traded to Cleveland with Jackie Brown and Rick Waits for Gaylord Perry, who wound up winning only twelve games in 1975.

Billy was fired in July with the team struggling, well below the .500 mark. The cause for the firing, ostensibly, was a final quarrel between Billy and Corbett over the refusal of the front office to sign a backup catcher Billy wanted. In the course of this argument, Billy says he told Corbett, whose business background included pipe manufacturing, "that you know as much about baseball as I know about pipe."

But it was the full and familiar accumulation of tensions exacerbated, behind-the-scenes explanations, relationships strained and finally broken that made Texas just one more inhospitable stop along the way. The tipoff was, finally, Billy's effect on the team: For good or ill, the team seemed to slip away from him, worn out either from having to continually play over its head or from simply having to deal with Billy Martin on a daily basis.

Within any of Billy's teams, regardless of what may have been going on with the front office, there was always a kind of powerful core energy, like the interior of a highly volatile, unstable atom. Unbelievable potential, creative as well as destructive, seemed located in it, depending on how this atom was split.

Billy maintained throughout his career that on any team, there would always be a handful of players who loved you and an equal number who hated you. "The manager's job," he said, "was to keep everyone else from going over to the side that hated you"—a variation of an old saying of Stengel's. At Texas, as elsewhere, this division became untenable. But because the team really had been carried in the beginning as if by magic, and because it accomplished as much as it did, the failure to reach the balance that might have meant stability is especially noteworthy.

Two players on the team—Toby Harrah, who clearly was among those players who loved him, and Jim Sundberg, who was one of those in the middle, capable of moving one way or the other—together underscore how Billy could hold and then lose a team.

Harrah acknowledged that playing for Billy was probably easier for veteran players than younger ones—and that, young as he was, he fit the former category.

He was excited, thrilled when he heard that Billy was going to take over the team. It was something that went well beyond having stars in his eyes; he was a professional ballplayer and had followed Billy's career—as a professional—through his Minnesota and Detroit phases. "The thing was he always won wherever he went, and of course everyone likes to identify with a winner," Harrah said. "I was really excited because I knew, being a major league ballplayer, he was going to make me a better baseball player. I knew without a shadow of doubt that if I played under him, I was going to improve. And I felt that I did. Not only as a player but mentally, I got a lot tougher and played the game a little better."

Jim Sundberg, a teenager in Double A ball in 1973, remembers the day that Billy came to scout him—but doesn't remember meeting him. "Billy came down to Instructional League in '73 to take a look at me, and from what I understand, when he saw me down there he decided I was going to be his catcher," Sundberg said.

He did remember going to that first spring training under Billy.

"I guess I was so much in awe of being in the big leagues, the only thing I really remember was that I didn't have a really good spring—but I didn't have to because I'd already been told that I'd made the call, he'd already determined I was going to be there."

But Sundberg remembered the atmosphere of the camp very well, its special quality, in his opinion, attached clearly to Billy. He allowed his players the flexibility to "really do their own thing," Sundberg said. "When you got on the field, between the lines, you played hard—in the spring. And then he let up on you.

"In all the spring trainings I ever went to in the big leagues, I never saw the kind of luncheon spread Billy had for his players—it was something to see. Man, we had five different kinds of meat, salad, garnishes, everything. I always thought the way to lose weight was to have a terrible lunch but man oh man you should have seen that. . . ."

Sundberg was aware from the start that Billy had a special relationship with his coaches. All the players knew that Merrill Combs, the first base coach—one of Billy's old teammates from the Oaks—was there so that he could get in a couple of years in order to get his major-league pension. But Combs, he said, "was scared to death. He lost thirty-five pounds during the course of the year."

And then there was Arthur—to Sundberg and everyone else in camp, Fowler was not only Billy's sidekick and drinking buddy, but someone who lightened the load.

"Art was absolutely a comedian. He'd come walking out and say, 'Jimmy, I've got this pond back home. I've got so many fish in this pond I've gotta hide behind a tree to bait my hook.' What that had to do with the ballgame, I don't know. On the other hand, he used to come to the mound forty times a year and say, 'Billy is in there chewing my butt out because you're not throwing slop. Anybody can throw slop. My grandmother can throw slop. Babe Ruth's dead so you don't have to worry about him. So just throw the damn ball in there and if you don't hit the bat you'll be just fine.' We all knew about this fight that Arthur started in Denver when he was pitching for Billy. He hit a guy in the head, both benches emptied, the fight went on for forty minutes, and three quarters of the way through it Billy noticed Art sitting over in a corner of the dugout smoking a cigarette. Yeah, it was fun in the beginning."

Both players were astonished and caught up in the winning, only differently. Harrah was aware that Billy could be tough, that he kept the pressure up constantly so that the focus on winning was never lost.

"If he was tough on you, it was for a reason. I remember one time Jim Spencer hit a home run," Harrah said, "and I was the next batter up. We were playing the White Sox and Stan Bahnsen drilled me—hit me square on the elbow and I was lying there in the dirt. And Billy comes runnin' up—I thought he was gonna say, 'Hey, Tobe, howya doin', ya gonna be all right?' He never even asked me if I was all right. He said, 'Listen, when you get up, I want you to go down to first and steal second on the first pitch!' I thought I was gonna have to come out of the game, but, no, he didn't even care. He just made me a little tougher. Funny thing was, every time I got hit after that, I didn't think twice about looking in the dugout for sympathy. I just went down to first and knew, no matter what, I wasn't coming out."

Billy toughened him in other ways as well. Harrah had the feeling from the start that he could never loaf, that he always had to be ready—for Billy. When he got on base, because he was a base stealer, he was under orders to watch the bench, not the third-base coach. Billy never wanted him to relax for a moment. The situation did not matter, the book did not matter, being unpredictable did—and that meant constantly being on the razor edge that Billy set for him.

"Listen, I was never Rod Carew but I had stolen a couple hundred bases so he wanted me to pay attention to him—and I did. I had usually taken a steal sign off the third base coach but, no, Billy said, 'You watch me.' And he'd let me know when he wanted me to go—what count, what pitch—and you had no way of predicting it, either. He'd give me just a little nod of the head—and I'd go, never even thought twice about it. Every day with Billy was a new ballgame and you never knew what to expect."

Billy, at Texas and elsewhere, used to ask his hitters to write down the names of pitchers they found especially difficult. Harrah recalls that he wrote down the name of Luis Tiant.

"He did that with me," he said. "He didn't do it with a sheet but he came up to me and said, 'Tell me the pitchers who really give you trouble.' I said, 'Tiant, man, Tiant.' So I was sure he was gonna sit me whenever we faced Luis Tiant. But, no, he played me every time. I even asked him about that, I said, 'Why do you even need to know who gives me trouble if you're gonna play me anyway?' Didn't say anything, just kept playing me against him till I understood. I was tougher for standing in against Tiant, and I actually wound up hitting him better toward the end of my career."

Harrah named other areas—the hit-and-run, bunting, hard baserunning, positioning—where constant pressure from Billy was toughening and helpful, and fun.

"I looked forward to getting to the ballpark and being around him. He had charisma, ya know? He's the type of guy who could be all over you one day and the next day it's forgotten. I mean he could get in a screaming and yelling match with anybody and the next day you started all over. That's neat. A lot of people aren't like that."

Jim Sundberg was not only newer to the team than Harrah, he also had an entirely different nervous system—winning and toughness were words that were just as important to him as to Harrah, but they acted on him differently. He took to the pressure Billy put on him differently.

"Billy was really tough—he felt like the game centered around the catcher and the catcher really had to be on his toes," Sundberg said, "and being a first-year player, he put a lot of time into me."

Sundberg detailed the way Billy would ride him about pitch selection.

"Billy evidently was not a good breaking-ball hitter when he played," Sundberg said, "so he had this thing—whenever the game was tied or there were men in scoring position, if we didn't throw a breaking ball, we were in trouble. If we ever got beat on a fastball, I got my rear end beat out. He always had to go out and talk to the pitcher and remind him when the count was 0 and 2. My rear was just chewed out if a guy got a hit on 0 and 2."

Unlike Harrah, Sundberg did not welcome the pressure at all. It upset him to the point, he said, where for most of that first year he had heart palpitations and feared that ultimately he might fall seriously ill.

"There was always so much pressure. I always felt like I had either high indigestion or heart palpitations. I never had it checked but it always scared me. I was always kind of quiet about it and then, I guess, after that first year, when I was used to it a little more, I didn't pant quite so much."

Sundberg understood all about winning and toughness; it was part of his own makeup, but it came with a personal cost. "The only reason I think I wound up handling the pressure as well as I did was because I was used to it at home. Pressure for winning and success. I was used to all that," Sundberg said. "I got known as being a tough kid because of the way I did handle it. But I never saw myself being that tough, I just coped with it."

Harrah and Sundberg saw the same things unfold on the team, but reacted differently to them.

Losing:

Toby Harrah: "Whoo, now that you bring up that subject, to me that is the biggest difference between him and any other manager—he was the worst loser I ever saw. Today, if you lose a game, twenty minutes later when you hit the shower you hear guys laughing and joking—and on the bus, laughing. With Billy, if you lost, don't think of eating, he'd wipe the training table. If you lost, you better not be laughing, you'd be in that shower and he'd be screaming and all over your case. Especially if you lost lousy. He used to say this to me—and he was the only manager I ever heard say that—'You don't win games, the other team loses them.' It's so true."

Jim Sundberg: "Oh how he hated losing. Several times coming in after games where we lost or didn't play well, guys would be eating and he'd see them eating, and boy, he'd go over and wipe the whole table off on the floor. Those who were still hungry went by picking pieces off the floor. Not many would want to eat after that, though."

Sundberg and Harrah both saw that Billy seemed to go through violent mood swings, and both stressed that Billy was as good at picking a player up as he was at knocking him down. Both men remember his generosity—the many times he picked up tabs for players, coaches, strangers. Both remember that there were instances when Billy seemed, even in the dugout, to be out of it.

"One of the things that Billy told me is that, whenever the count was 3 and 2 and I didn't know what to call, just to look over in the dugout and he would tell me," said Sundberg. "I swear it happened forty times during the season where it was 3 and 2, an important time of the game, and I looked over to him—and he was getting a drink of water."

Harrah remembered that "Billy was funny. He could be talking like you and I or down at the water cooler and you'd think he was completely unaware of what was going on and—boom—just like that a guy takes off or he's got a guy picked off on a pitchout nobody saw coming."

Billy's many and unpredictable sides made him like family to Harrah, "the way your dad is, you know—you say anything, do anything because you're part of the family and you're free enough to do that, the next day is a new day, the slate is wiped clean."

Sundberg, more distant than Harrah, thought of Billy as a "multipersonality." Not attached as "family," he gradually slipped out from under Billy's hold. The pressures and the unpredictability, rather than keying him up or putting him on edge, began to weary him and turn him off.

In his second season, the aphrodisiac of winning gone, Sundberg remembers the moment when he finally stood up to Billy. It was in a game against the Twins in Minnesota. Ferguson Jenkins was pitching, the bases were loaded, and the batter, Dan Ford, had an 0–2 count. Sundberg, with robotlike sureness, flashed the sign for a curve ball. Jenkins shook him off. Sundberg signaled for a slider—again, he was shaken off. Jenkins wanted the fastball—and that was that.

"So he comes right down the middle with it and the guy fouls it off. I nearly had a heart attack," Sundberg said. "Go through the same sequence again and this time the guy smokes the fastball into centerfield for two runs. I hear bats and helmets flying all around the dugout, and I could see him out of the corner of my eye, on the top step, blood vessels popping out, yelling and screaming. When the inning was over I just wanted to go back to the Minnesota dugout because I knew what was coming. Well, he gets all over me and for the first time, I yell back and say, 'I didn't throw the pitch, he did, why don't you go talk to him?' He kinda stood there. He was kinda surprised I talked to him that way. He sorta stepped back, like he was thinking for a second, and then he says, 'You're out of the game.' He tells the backup catcher, he's in."

This incident, it turns out, had far more than personal or even symbolic import on the team. Following the game, Bobby Brown, the Rangers president for baseball operations, who just happened to be present, turned up in the clubhouse. Billy—loudly and angrily—confronted Brown and demanded that Sundberg be immediately shipped to the minors. Sundberg says he left the locker room and went to the training room "because it was embarrassing," and there saw many other players who had sought refuge, wanting to get away from the scene in the other room.

The move demanded by Billy was turned down by Brown and, Sundberg remembers, "A couple of days after that, we're leaving Minnesota, heading for New York, we're on the plane and he starts telling me I'm the greatest catcher since Bill Dickey—like none of that ever happened." Sundberg was aware, as Harrah was, that Billy had this extraordinary ability to lift the same player he had put down, but that was no longer enough. As he gained more distance from him, Sundberg came to see Billy's hold on the team slipping. Seeing Billy on a day-to-day basis, on and off the field, he believed there was something more than moodiness and relentless energy that pushed him. In the way he dealt with others, there was, at times, something almost out of control about him. Billy had one celebrated fight within the team, aboard a team charter, when he began quarreling with the Rangers' road secretary, an elderly man named Bert Hawkins. Hawkins's wife had apparently organized a players' wives club, Billy didn't like the idea of it, told Hawkins so, and a quarrel followed. Billy later said Hawkins was drunk and said things that were out of line to him, while Hawkins and others had a different recollection. The upshot was that Billy suddenly slapped the old man across the face.

"Billy just wanted to control everything," Sundberg said. "He got into this fight with Bert Hawkins one night because Berty's wife had all the wives get together one time for lunch while the team was out on the road. Billy didn't want that, that's all. He'd probably had one too many and he just hit him."

But there were other "incidents."

"I saw him tear phones off the walls in the dugout because he didn't like the song that was being played between innings," Sundberg said. "It got crazy. He'd call upstairs about it and then he'd get mad and tear the phone off the wall."

Then there was a time when Billy came to believe that some of his coaches were betraying him, going to the front office behind his back, turning his team against him, possibly even tipping off other teams on how he was running games from the bench—to the point of giving his signals away.

"I really don't know how he got to this," Sundberg said, "but he reached a point where he decided that he wasn't going to give his coaches hand signals from the dugout. Instead, he consulted this electronics firm and he designed this system where he had his coaches all wired so he could speak to them while they were on the lines. There's this one great story playing Boston in Texas. See, he thought Boston was getting the signs he was giving Frank Lucchesi. So the electronics guy came out and wired up Lucchesi—got a mike for Billy and earplugs for Frank and all the other coaches. . . . Instead of hand signals, Billy's in the dugout with this little mike attached to his shirt which he can speak into. You know, he lowers his head and mumbles—looks like he's asleep to people across the way, but he's going, 'Hit and run, Frank, hit and run.' Or something like that.

"Okay, so now it's the last of the ninth, game's tied, one out, man on third base, Luis Tiant's pitching for the Red Sox. Frank looks into the dugout and sees Billy mumbling into his shirt but there's nothing coming over his earphones. Frank starts waving his hands, trying to get Billy's attention. Meanwhile Billy, it turns out, is calling for the suicide squeeze—except that the electronics system has gone dead. Merrill Combs is over at first—and we did have this backup system that, if you didn't get the sign from Frank, Merrill would have it. You know, if his feet were together that was one sign, if his hands were down at his side that was another, if he hit himself on the top of the head that meant he didn't get the sign and wanted it repeated. So you look over to first and Earl has his feet apart, his hands are down, and then he starts hitting himself on top of the head. Meanwhile Billy's in the dugout going crazy and he starts yelling 'Suicide squeeze! Suicide squeeze!' Well, Tiant just looks over at Frank, stares at him—'cause I guess Frank couldn't hear with the earphones in—and he yells at him as loud as he can, 'Hey, Frank, he wants you to squeeze!' "

Harrah and Sundberg both knew that Billy lost control of the team, that over time the accumulation of incidents wore people down and turned them off.

"What happens with Billy is that he's so high up and down, he can really be fire one day and then the day after, totally nice," Harrah said. "And with Billy, there were always these things not related to baseball. After a while it wears on the guys. Emotionally he can get you going back and forth where there's finally nothing left."

Both these players vividly remembered Billy's departure. They were both touched by it—and again, for different reasons. Sundberg perceived, beyond the sense of relief which he shared with most of his teammates, that Billy had paid a price in human terms for the rocket ride and crash:

"The day he got fired in Texas, he called me into the back room," Sundberg remembered, "and he was just crying his eyeballs out. I started feeling bad, which in a way was kinda funny because at that time I was not feeling a lot of compassion for him. Yet at that moment, suddenly all I could feel was compassion. He was really torn up.

It was like all I could feel in that moment was hurt because it obviously went so deep."

Toby Harrah did not recall Billy in tears, but there was something else:

"The day he got fired, he called me into his office and he gave me this picture of the Original Texas Ranger that had always been hanging in his office. I put it up at home and it's been hanging there ever since. The feelings we had for each were mutual, he could say anything he wanted to me, it didn't matter—kinda like my dad. Your dad can yell and scream but you still love him."

In the end, though, there was just too much resentment and weariness among too many players. Billy, said Ranger trainer Bill Ziegler, believed that he had been stabbed in the back by his coaches and by players who had gone to the front office with their complaints. Ziegler remembered him in his office at the end, surrounded by his coaches, weeping, really hurt. "It was a pitiful sight, seeing him sitting behind his desk [like that]."

The front office had been watching—and listening. Jim Sundberg did not know if players or coaches actually went to the front office with stories about Billy, but he did know that the team's owner, Brad Corbett, sought out others in the clubhouse for whatever information they had on a situation he saw as increasingly untenable. More than one source told the owner about the quarrel and fight with Hawkins; anyone could have told him that a charter flight with Billy Martin was, almost literally, a midair frontier saloon:

"Billy gave almost everyone total freedom," Randy Galloway recalled."He had the wildest charters I've ever been on in my life. They did things like tearing up airplanes, every flight was like a drunken party—you wouldn't have believed it. Well, I was sitting there drinking with him so I'll never pass judgment on that, but in the process there was so much turmoil, he wore down his welcome with everyone."

Other members of this flying Shangri-la were less open-minded and more openly resentful. One player who did not want to speak for the record acknowledged that he did answer questions about Billy from the front office. He recalled that Billy did abuse the charter privileges of the team and that, at least on one occasion, his bending of the rules aroused resentment among many of the players.

"It was a DC-10 flight," this player said, "where there were just enough first-class seats for the team, and Martin brought one of his girlfriends on and bumped one of the players to the back. That just used to go on—and it was something that players remembered and probably helped turn the team against him."

The press corps had a name for these extra passengers of Billy's. "We used to call them road-holders," Randy Galloway said, "because they'd hold up the charter—he'd be sitting up there in the front with them and, as wild as a lot of the players were, that kind of thing was part of the tearing-down process."

The tearing-down process went well beyond the team and beyond the obvious signs of Billy's temperament in the clubhouse, or the openness of his boozing and womanizing.

His life was falling apart. The home he had had for sixteen years, never solid to begin with, always subject to the vagaries and lures of the road, was turning out to be just another center that would not hold. Not all the adulation, all the boomtown doors that seemed to swing wide for him, could spare him yet another collapse. He did not make it as the Number One Cowboy in Texas. When he was fired there, however, he lost more than just another baseball job.

The week following his departure from the Rangers, Billy was in Colorado, fishing and hunting with friends. His wife, Gretchen, and young son, Billy Joe, were with him. Sometime in this week, he was told that his father-in-law had been trying to get in touch with him. When he returned this call, he was informed the Yankees were trying to locate him.

The back and forth of the job offer that ensued is another of those *Rashomon* stories, the details changing with the eye of the beholder and the mouth of the storyteller—but the deed remains the same. Billy, within days of his firing at Texas, accepted—at about the same money he had been making at Texas, $75,000—George Steinbrenner's offer to manage the New York Yankees.

When he went off to New York, though, Gretchen informed him that she would not be coming with him. Not then, not afterward. After sixteen years, her desire to be played or traded had been transformed into a more elemental desire for an unconditional release. Besides, she liked Texas; it was a good and solid place to bring up a child. When Billy left for the Bronx, his marriage, though a formal divorce would not come until years later, was over. Billy may have been returning to the home he'd been banished from by George Weiss nearly two decades earlier, but a real home—and family—was again beyond his grasp.

# CHAPTER 13

If Jim Northrup is to be believed, Billy had begun campaigning for the Yankee job as early as 1973, the year that George Steinbrenner bought the team from CBS. Steinbrenner and Gabe Paul, the Yankees' head of baseball operations, knew otherwise. From the moment Billy was fired in Texas, they began pursuing him. The decision to do so was obvious and agreed upon almost instantaneously, Paul remembered. He was dispatched, along with Yankee scout Birdie Tebbetts, to find Billy in Colorado where he had gone immediately after his firing.

Tebbetts met and sought to persuade Billy to take the Yankee job at a hotel in Denver. At the appropriate moment, Paul, hiding in an adjoining room, was brought in to add weight to the offer, which was ultimately accepted.

It was not automatic. The Yankees knew all about Billy and Billy knew enough about the team's new ownership so that questions were raised on both sides. The Yankees demanded that a series of "good-boy" clauses be written into the contract. "The thing was," Paul said, sounding like everyone who ever hired Billy, "we knew exactly what we were getting but we were sure we would be able to handle him." For his part, Billy needed the advice and support of his old friend Bob Short, a man in whom he still placed enormous trust, and of his soon-to-be-estranged wife, Gretchen, whose business acumen he trusted.

In a sense, though, the deciding factor was that he had been really campaigning for the Yankee job all his life—from the moment when, in a child's dream, he fused the idea of ultimate success in life with stardom for the New York Yankees.

Billy had been a star once, but a strange kind of star. He shouldn't have been one; his hands were too stiff, his legs too slow, his body too slight, his baseball skills, though street-sharpened and well-coached, never up to the gods of the pantheon. Joe DiMaggio once said, after Billy's plaque had been included among those of other Yankee immortals in Monument Park, "He doesn't deserve to be there as a player, but he does as a manager."

Billy knew that better than anyone. He knew what he could do, what he had done, and now, in New York, New York, what still might be done.

For the Yankees, the decision to bring in Billy was as commonsensical and as mundane as calling in a mechanic for the family car. The Yankees had been languishing on the field for years; so had their business. In recent years, for the first time since World War II, attendance had fallen below the million mark. Steinbrenner and his group had been able to buy the Yankees for a song. The hard part, anyone might have told them, would be turning it into grand opera or, at least, profitable soap opera. Hiring Billy Martin was an obvious step in that direction. As drama, it would succeed beyond any producer's wildest dreams.

Billy's entrance was in the best traditions of New York theater. He took over the team—in New York—on August 2, 1975. It was Old Timers' Day. The Yankees were playing at Shea Stadium then while Yankee Stadium was being remodeled. Shea was a shabby, sorrowful space to begin with and was doubly so for the descendants of Ruth, Gehrig, DiMaggio and Mantle, who now had to battle a bumpy field, cracked and peeling paint, grungy clubhouses, and airplanes regularly drowning out even the on-high voice of Bob Shepperd. They were reminded every day that they were only guests in the house of a far more popular team.

On this Old Timers' Day, the Yankees went all out. Championship banners going all the way back through the team's history decorated the place; the great ones, those who still were living, were all present. In the usual manner of these occasions, the immortals, in ascending order of stature, were introduced to the crowd. But the last introduction, at the insistence of the owner, was not Mickey Mantle, Joe DiMaggio (the perennial valedictory selection), or even the widow of the Babe; it was Billy—the Yankee past *and* the Yankee future. He was, to some degree, embarrassed by the accolade. But he was also thrilled. With this moment, he was able to create himself once again. The almost perfect instinct he had for following a moving spotlight led him, in this one glorious moment, to secure his future by claiming his past. He had found not a way but *the* way to come back to the most important home he had known:

"Waiting there, I was uptight, nervous. I was coming back so many years after the Yankees expelled me," he said. "It was eighteen years later, and here I was coming back as the leader. I thought back to Casey Stengel, and how he had given me my start in baseball, and here I was now in his shoes. I felt funny. I only wish it had been in Yankee Stadium instead of Shea Stadium . . .

"I was so light-headed it barely registered when I heard my name over the loudspeaker, and I ran out there and everyone was happy for me, and the applause was deafening, and in the stands I could hear some boos, which I could understand because Bill Virdon was well-liked, but I said to myself, 'They're booing right now, but before I'm through everyone will be cheering.' "

It is hard to keep in mind that Billy first and last was a professional baseball man, that this sort of Ghosts of the Yankee Past prose in which he frequently indulged, as much as it reflected deep emotion in him, also reflected hard professional ambition.

This team, in its present state, with its storied history and traditions, was perfect for a manager on the make. For an actor looking for a vehicle, the Yankees were *the* property—a little offbeat these days but, for anyone with a baseball mind, the best on the planet. While others—Ralph Houk, for instance, or Bill Virdon, or a few New York sportswriters who had become acquainted with George Steinbrenner—might have remained uncertain, Billy was not. As the song went, if you made it here, you made it anywhere.

There were problems. The Yankees were not about to give him control of personnel. The farm and scouting systems were off limits. He was just a manager, no more. He could not even name his own coaching staff. "We looked at the people he had around him," Gabe Paul said, "and we just didn't think it was wise or professional to choose coaches in the obviously personal way Billy did." That meant no Merrill Combs, no Art Fowler—or anyone else whose baseball skills could ever be confused with his financial needs or ability to hoist a few with the manager. Elston Howard was brought aboard; when Yogi Berra was fired as manager of the Mets, he was added to the staff—possibly at Billy's urging (Yankee brass today denies that), certainly with his consent. All of these compromises were acceptable in the end to Billy because it was the Yankees, not the Twins or Tigers or Rangers, he was about to lead.

But if the Yankees thought they had corralled Billy, they were as mistaken as all the others who ever thought they could handle him. Billy's strength and weakness was his ability to do just what he wanted—regardless of the consequences. Whether in a bar or a dugout, he did whatever he had to, and the devil take the hindmost. He improvised, he dreamed, he battled. He had the sort of foolhardy and sometimes admirable courage that enabled him, almost in the name of little guys everywhere, to tell any boss, anytime to take his job and shove it; he exceeded boundaries to a point where he could destroy his life—but also create it. George Steinbrenner may have thought he could control Billy when he hired him, but Billy, unlike the Yankees, was no song; he was a composer of songs, a singer of his own story, a baseball man beyond the power of George Steinbrenner's wallet or will.

Yankee history meant a lot to Billy, but in this latest incarnation of his it nearly possessed him. Casey Stengel was never far from his thoughts. If he was "Casey's Boy" as a player, as a manager in New York he was determined to be his true heir. There was deep and sincere emotion in that—and also good public relations sense.

There are, of course, innumerable media stories of Billy's allusions to the old man, to his professional and personal attachment—up to and including references he unabashedly made to Stengel's being a father figure to him. Everyone knew, for example, about his celebrated split with Stengel and the fact that seven years later, as though nothing had ever happened, their friendship resumed—because Billy had decided it was time.

But in all this, there is a moment—magical, obscure, quite specific—where Billy in a bizarrely symbolic way seemed to absorb the living spirit of Stengel into his own body. This more personal, more private reaching out to Stengel had nothing to do with public relations, and everything to do with the sort of standard Billy was setting for himself as he took over the Yankees. Billy, in this moment, actively sought to imbue himself with the spirit of his old manager.

This strange transfer of power took place at Casey Stengel's funeral at the end of the 1975 season. Stengel died just before the opening of the playoffs. His funeral was scheduled on a traveling day in the Oakland-Boston series, but Billy turned up early, the day before the funeral. He went to Stengel's house, Charlie Silvera remembered, and asked the caretaker if he could sleep there that night. He was given permission. He stayed the night—in Stengel's bed. The following day, the day of the funeral, he returned to Stengel's house again after the ceremonies in which he had been a pallbearer.

Silvera remembered a certain odd joyousness about the funeral itself—the preacher got everyone laughing by suggesting, "The Good Lord's getting an earful tonight." That joyousness turned to remembered warmth when the mourners were subsequently asked to make sure that they said a prayer for Stengel that night. Billy, Silvera, and a few friends took the suggestion to heart. "I said I'd pray for him," Silvera recalled, "and some of these guys said, 'Oh yeah, Charlie,' but Billy and I and his friend Babe Herman and Phil McDonald—there were two others who came along also—went back to Casey's house. We were there for hours. Billy showed me all kinds of things of Casey's—like this old sweatshirt of his that he used to wear under his uniform. Then we left—that is, everyone except Billy. He stayed on by himself, and I'm almost certain he spent the night there again. At the time, he told me it would bring him a little closer to Casey and that it was the proper thing to do," Silvera recalled.

In any event, when he went back to work, Billy was determined to take control of the Yankees just as Stengel had—by bringing them to the top, and right away. He measured this new team of his quickly. He had a professional idea of who the different players were, whom he'd be able to count on to play his way, and who would not. He saw that he had a basically veteran team, a team with holes that needed to be filled, but one that was tough enough, mature enough. Players like Thurman Munson, Graig Nettles, Sparky Lyle, Roy White, and Chris Chambliss had been around. They didn't need scaring, they didn't need babying. Getting them on his side quickly, of course, depended on his ability to convey to them that all he wanted from them was winning baseball. He also—his employers be damned—had a few other ideas about the way to secure loyalty and loosen things up.

Bill Kane, the Yankees road secretary then, remembers the day in 1975, shortly after Billy took control of the team, when he came to him and told him about what he wanted on team charters:

"Practically the first thing he told me was when I ordered liquor for the charter flights, to make sure it was Chivas," said the man affectionately known to successive generations of players as "Killer." "I told him, 'Billy they got a policy here of no beer or liquor on the plane.' He says, 'Who's got the policy?' I says, 'That's what they told me.' He says, 'This is a major league ballclub and I'm tellin' you these guys are allowed to drink. They have enough problems. You put the Chivas on the plane, whatever they want.' "

Billy's goal was to secure loyalty quickly and completely. Gabe Paul believes that Billy's genius was not as a strategist so much as a motivator, someone, he said, "who could get any player, whether he loved Billy or hated him, to play at their very best." Sparky Lyle, among others, called Billy "a player's manager, not necessarily because he was a good guy [which Lyle believed he was] but because he knew how to make players believe in themselves, to have the confidence that they were going to win."

Killer Kane was in the clubhouse at the beginning of the Yankees' pennant winning 1976 season, the season that Billy, many of his players and critics agreed, was his most trouble-free. Kane remembers a speech Billy gave to the troops. It was in Milwaukee and while by oratorical standards it fell somewhat short of Henry at Agincourt, it had something:

"He said, 'Listen, I want to tell you guys something. We're gonna win this thing. I don't know whether you guys know that, you're good players, so listen: If you don't think so, if you don't believe it, let me know so I can get you to one of the other teams we're gonna beat. You do just what I tell you and we're gonna win. That's a promise, so don't worry about it. I'll protect you all the way—just do what I tell you on the field. I don't care what time you come in at night or who the fuck you're with, when you come in the clubhouse just do what I tell you—you're gonna win.' "

The kicker, Kane said, was this: Many of the players, hardened professionals used to locker room speeches, merely shrugged. As Sparky Lyle said, "They could have named God manager at that point and it wouldn't have mattered because we knew whoever he was, he wasn't going to be there for long." But then in the second game of the season, Billy went out and did something that caught his players' attention: He went out and actually seemed to steal a game for them. It happened at game's end, the bottom of the ninth, with the Yanks leading by three runs. The Brewers loaded the bases and then Don Money hit a grand slam, ostensibly winning the game for Milwaukee.

"All of a sudden," Kane said, "Billy's out of the dugout going at the first base umpire. You know, sitting up in the press box, you can't figure out what's going on, but Billy's screaming at this guy—not long, just a second or two it seemed like—and then he goes down to the home plate umpire, the crew chief, I guess, and he yells at him—again for just a second or two. Then the two umps confer, with Billy right on their heels—and just like that the home run is called back! No one could believe it. The Brewers yelled their heads off but it didn't matter, the home run didn't count—and we won."

Later, on the plane, Billy recounted the blow-by-blow of his protest to Kane:

"He went to the first base umpire and he just asked him, 'Did you call time?' The ump said, 'Yeah, but . . .' and then Billy started screaming, 'There aren't any "buts," you don't need any "buts," that's enough.' And then he ran right down to the home plate umpire and said the first base umpire had called time and that he had to go check with him. The ump says, 'Yeah, I'll go check with him.' Billy says, 'Don't ask him about anything else, only if he called time.' Billy followed him down, listens to the guy say to the first base ump, 'Did you call time?' He says, 'Yeah, but . . . ,' and then Billy runs in and says, 'There's nothing more to talk about.' The umps looked at each other and they said, 'Yeah, he's right'—and they called the home run back and we won the game."

That incident, Kane said, early in the season though it was, was a turning point. Never mind that Dave Pagan, the Yankee pitcher at the time, at first thought Billy was running out of the dugout with the intention of assaulting him for surrendering a game-winning homer—Pagan actually turned from the mound and fled toward the outfield when he saw Billy coming. Billy had taken control of his team not by hectoring and browbeating anyone but by adding this extra dimension of himself when it counted most. When he talked about winning and standing up for his players, he backed up his words with actions.

Players on Billy's teams, particularly this team, often talk about him as though he was an extra player on the field, as though getting to the eighth or ninth inning in a tie or one run down meant that he would actually take over and find a way to win. Much of that had to do with Billy's extraordinary sense of the game.

Killer Kane remembers that Billy once told him he had the ability to see the entire field all at once, and this gave him a kind of advantage in running a game. Billy had discovered this when he was starting out—Kane was unsure whether Billy meant his first days as a coach in Minnesota or his first days with the Denver Bears—but what happened was that Billy had this "experience."

"It was like the first or second day he was down on the field and he had this sense that he could see everything. He was standing there and he realized there was nothing he couldn't see, he said everything was very clear to him. If this was done or that was done, you could win a game. Move this way, one thing happened; move that way another thing did. He said he just saw it all at once, all so clear."

At his best, at every step of the way, Billy was able to demonstrate this sense to his players. Whether it was knowing which opposing players to knock down, how to steal signs, what strategies to use in what situations, it was all part of what enabled players, even ones who didn't like him, to believe in him, in the mystique that lent power to his leadership.

So, too, did his willingness to battle for his team—to hound umpires, defend his players in the press, and stand up to the front office—including, most especially, George Steinbrenner. The players on that first Yankee team of Billy's all have their Steinbrenner stories. They are, for the most part, ribald, nasty, catty.

"The only thing George Steinbrenner knows more about than baseball," said Graig Nettles, the team's ninja wit, "is weight control."

Steinbrenner regularly and offensively assaulted his players in their own domain, giving them pep-talks, sending in tape-recorded messages to be played for them, hounding, harassing, trading, demoting them and, of course, firing managers and coaches.

Billy was harried and battered by Steinbrenner. Steinbrenner, unlike Calvin Griffith, did not ask for a daily four o'clock chat before he took his nap, but he often loudly took his case to the clubhouse and, by means of a red telephone on the dugout wall, to the playing field itself, phoning down messages, complaints, suggestions, and imprecations as games were in progress.

In his autobiography, Billy acknowledges the obvious: the owner's unceasing interference drove him crazy. But, in a curious way, it also cemented his early relationship with the team. The welts, brickbats, thunders, and stupidities that might otherwise have rained down on the players, came down on Billy instead. He took it for them, and enough of them appreciated him for it so that between the manager and at least a core of the team there was a bond approaching the sort of loyalty Billy craved.

"We won and we won early," Sparky Lyle said, "and that should have been the story—but it wasn't. That should have overshadowed all the other shit but it didn't. The guy upstairs just kept nitpicking all the time, but the players never felt the brunt of that because Billy kept it away from us. Who knows what he went through then—it became clearer later—but we knew about all those calls. We just didn't know what was said and all that stuff; Billy kept it away from us the best he could."

The Yankees won, and that was what counted—to the owner, to the manager, to the players. The rest was rock and roll. In a way, there was no magic to it. Though the Red Sox were heavily favored to win that year, dissension and a slow start all but doomed them within the first half of the season. After losing a big series to the Yankees in New York in May, Carl Yastrzemski seemed to speak for the rest of the league in making what almost sounded like a concession statement: "Billy Martin has had the ability to take mediocre teams and make them good; now he has taken a good team and made them great."

The '76 Yankees were a different team from the one Billy took over in August 1975. They had made a series of spectacular trades over that winter and during the season itself. Added to the roster were Mickey Rivers and Willie Randolph—speed, table setters; Oscar Gamble was acquired from the Indians—left-handed home run power; an up and down pitching staff saw the departure of Doc Medich, Pat Dobson, and Larry Gura (as well as Tippy Martinez), and the addition of Ed Figueroa, Dock Ellis, Ken Holtzman, Doyle Alexander, and Grant Jackson—enough pitching strength to carry the race. The Yankees may have surprised some of the experts and some opponents, but that was only because it was hard to tell what was coming. The Yankees were clearly the best team in the American League in 1976.

"We were just there at the right time. Sometimes there's a right time in history when the right people just get together—and that's basically what happened to us in '76," Chris Chambliss said. This elementary lesson in chemistry had a subtext for Chambliss. It said a lot about Billy, who Chambliss believed was the best manager he ever saw, but it also said a lot about the Yankees:

"I think everybody's favorite team was '76 because that was the first year we won together, and that was the first year we were in Yankee Stadium. Most people think we won because of all the free agents we signed," Chambliss said, "but actually that team was built on all those trades—and, of course, Thurman was in the organization. We just wound up with a bunch of players that could beat a team in a lot of different ways. We had strong pitching, which was a key, and then we had this tremendous versatility. We had speed with Mickey Rivers, Willie Randolph, and Roy White; we had power with Graig Nettles—actually he was our biggest power threat on that team, though we had Thurman and myself who were in the teens in home runs; we had great guys who could play off the bench. Of course, Lou [Piniella] was one of those guys, Oscar Gamble another. We had veterans all the way through the lineup; we had Willie who brought youth to us. And we had Billy."

Professionally, the year was so deceptively easy. The Yankees, playing through their one poor stretch, still led the American League East by nine games in early August. There was a brief flurry of speculation that month that George Steinbrenner, openly seen in the company of Dick Williams, a manager whose services he had previously coveted, was becoming impatient with Billy. It was not so—not yet. By September, the Yankees' lead was again in double figures and Billy was signed to a new two-year contract. The clubhouse, even with its mix of strong personalities, was happier than at any time in the Steinbrenner era. Graig Nettles, one pregame afternoon at the Stadium, complained that it was too dark. "Can't you get them to turn on the lights?" he groused to Billy. Billy barked up into the empty recesses of the Stadium, "Turn on the lights!" A moment or so later, the lights came on. Clearly, this was a manager with connections.

The Yankees won the East on a sullen September day in Detroit. Billy had kept his promise—but still had miles to go. The Yankees won the pennant in a dramatic five-game playoff series against the Royals, featuring a bottom of the ninth-inning home run by Chris Chambliss that touched off a near riot in Yankee Stadium. And even then the manager was not at rest.

Chambliss, by the time he reached second base on that historic trip around the bases, gradually realized he was about as secure as a tuft of tumbleweed in a tornado. The field was engulfed with surging, pounding fans. Chambliss remembers that "the only thing I could think of was keeping my hat on my head. People were trying to tear at it, but I held on to it." By the time he reached third base, the base itself was gone, the way to the plate clogged with screaming fans. Chambliss says he never reached home, that he simply ran wide away from the area, along the edge of the stands, and into the clubhouse. The manager, who saw everything all at once, somehow was aware of this, too. He gathered together a cordon of police and had Chambliss escorted back to the field so he could touch home plate, lest the winning blow be nullified.

But of course there was more to Billy's life than this almost storybook surface. His drinking and carousing, which had caused so much grief in the past, continued unabated.

Though he was celebrated as never before—he could not go down a New York street without people, cabdrivers, executives, streetcleaners shouting out to him—he was a lonely man. There were neither enough bars nor enough one-night stands to ever take the edge off this raw sense of aloneness, of unabating insecurity that assaulted him in everything he did. He had known for years that his marriage was not working, that his own life-style had made marriage and family life virtually impossible—yet, without Gretchen now, he was as bound as he was free. He could not accept his own responsibility for what had happened. He felt she had destroyed the marriage by not coming with him to New York, though clearly her deepest needs were a secure and stable life in a community where it was actually possible to raise a child.

He did not or would not see that. Instead, he suspected her of being interested in other men. Eventually, with separation and divorce looming, his pain, as blinding as when his marriage to Lois ended, drove him to prove that it was Gretchen, not himself, who was principally to blame for the failure. He was the one, finally, who filed for divorce. In the end, he had private detectives shadowing his wife to prove his suspicions that her infidelity was at the root of all their problems.

At this same time, Kelly Ann, his daughter by Lois, was arrested and jailed in Colombia for attempting to smuggle cocaine out of the country. The arrest occurred in the fall of 1975, her incarceration lasted two years, and all the while, on an almost daily basis, Billy was in torment as he did what he could to free her. His efforts were extensive, complicated, and for the longest while fruitless. Fear and uncertainty were there on a daily basis, even in the midst of his pennant-winning work. Often, the phone would sound in his office during pre- and postgame press conferences. Reporters, always on the alert for George, were never quite aware that it was Kelly he was talking to in whispered tones, his back averted.

Billy turned to a number of people for help. Because he was friendly with Frank Sinatra and because Sinatra had connections, he turned to him. A friend who was an executive with Chiquita Banana helped. Billy turned to his Michigan friend Bill Reedy, who, as a city council aide, was connected in Michigan politics; Gerald Ford, from Michigan, was President of the United States at the time and Reedy knew people who knew him.

"I knew a guy named Harry Levine—guy's dead now," Reedy said. "Harry owned Ewald Steel Company here in Michigan and he used to fly Ford around everywhere when he was state senator—before he was president. So I called Billy and said, 'Is it okay if I go to Harry Levine and ask Mr. Levine if he wouldn't ask the President to look into this?' He said 'Fine'—and so I did."

What followed then—though Reedy was not sure how it happened or whether Harry Levine was principally responsible—was that Kelly Ann, though not released from jail, was transferred to a women's facility run by nuns, where she stayed until her release. All the while, Billy was coming up with sums of money—for lawyers, for other third parties; in all he paid out around $40,000, and none of it really seemed to help. According to Kelly, the fact that Billy had money and was willing to pay may have only compounded the problem: the more money he paid, she said, the more there were people, principally in Colombia, willing to put off releasing her.

"My dad used to tell me in the beginning, 'Pack your bags, you're leaving tomorrow.' Tomorrow would come and I'd still be there and my dad was sick about it. I'd speak to him a week later and he'd say, 'Now it's all set, pack your bags.' But it didn't happen. I would tell him to hold on to his money, too, that it only made things worse, but he'd say, 'I want you home, I want you home.' I'd tell him, 'I know, I want to come home more than anything.' I was a nervous wreck down there; the Americans were worse than anybody because they wouldn't let up about how my being Billy Martin's daughter caused them all kinds of bad publicity—you know, I was likened to Patty Hearst, Charlie Manson, the whole thing."

The worry for Billy was made worse by the fact that he was not really close to his daughter. Beyond her incarceration, he was confronted with her life—which was troubled beyond his ability to help as a parent. Once freed, she confirmed his worst fears—that her arrest was no mistake.

"I said, 'Dad, I did something stupid and foolish because I wanted to make some extra money and I'm going to pay for that for the rest of my life, it's going to come back to haunt me—but you know what, I did it. I fucked up. I paid for it.' "

Billy, in turn, Kelly said, was angry—but not at her. "He said, 'I figured as much—I'd like to kill the SOBs who sent you down there.' I said, 'Dad, my arms aren't broken, they aren't ripped out of the socket. I've known those kinds of people all my life—all my life, I've been just like you—the tough people, that's the ones I like, 'cause I'm tough. That way people don't really know how soft we are.' "

Billy, she said, could not or would not understand this. Kelly wasn't talking about the people who set her up, she said, she was talking about herself, what she had done. She knew her father loved her, and she loved him—but between them there was no time and little understanding.

Billy had professional problems, too. When Casey Stengel took the Yankees to a pennant in his first year, he crowned the effort with a World Championship. The Yankees, under Billy, were swept in the World Series in four straight by the Cincinnati Reds. The weaknesses of the team, not apparent during the regular season, were exposed in the wake of what was, finally, a humiliating defeat. Changes, George Steinbrenner let everyone know, were going to be made. Immediately following the last game of the Series—the very next day, according to Ed Linn—Steinbrenner assembled his "baseball people," strangely excluding Billy—to determine what changes the team required.

The fundamental question was what free agents the Yankees were going to sign. The absence of Billy at the meeting signaled the most important aspect of the decision, at least to Billy: that it would be the front office and not he who would choose the players.

Steinbrenner, personally blaming Fred Stanley for the loss of the second game of the Series, and generally for poor play through the season, wanted a top shortstop. There were none in the free-agent draft, though they were able to pick up Bucky Dent from Chicago just before the start of the season. Billy let it be known that he wanted a right-handed power hitter, specifically Joe Rudi of the A's. Gabe Paul, who understood the men he was dealing with as well as the needs of the team, proposed Bobby Grich, the Orioles' power-hitting second baseman who had been an excellent minor-league shortstop. Behind Grich, second on the list of regulars the Yankees would pursue, was Reggie Jackson. Rudi was considered a year too old and not able to consistently put up Reggie's power numbers.

It is clear that Billy would not have chosen Reggie, that he didn't see him as fitting the team's basic need (right-handed power), and that his view of the man, till then, was largely the one afforded him through the cross hairs of their rivalry. But there is simply no evidence, despite numerous "insider" stories, that Billy didn't want Reggie. Billy wanted someone who could put the ball in the seats for the Yankees. When Bobby Grich signed with the Angels and the Yankees then signed Jackson, Billy, according to his own word and to that of Gabe Paul, was in accord. And, as both men stressed, he had no choice in the matter anyway.

What did bother Billy was the *way* Reggie came to the Yankees. He came as royalty, wined and dined by George Steinbrenner at all the top New York eateries. Steinbrenner's public courtship of Jackson, amply described in gossip pages as well as subsequent chronicles of the period, made clear that a new breed of player was upon the clubhouse and upon the game. In this first-ever open season for free agents, the game and the dugout were changed forever. Players would never again be the dependent, subservient entities they had been. Beginning in 1977, they were suddenly more like partners than employees. In one whisper of a fountain pen, they earned four and five times what managers did, and their direct ties in the organization were to the men who wooed them—people like George Steinbrenner.

But at this point, it was Billy's sense of isolation, his uneasy sense that what control he had was slipping away, even his sense of jealousy, that ate at him.

In his autobiography, he acknowledged, "The only thing I didn't like were the comments I read in the newspaper. . . . George was taking Reggie to the 21 Club for lunch all the time, and I was sitting across the river in my hotel room the entire winter and George hadn't taken me out to lunch even once. Reggie told a reporter, 'It's going to be great with the Yankees because George and I are going to get along real good, and that's very important.' I said to myself, You're going to find out George isn't the manager."

This picture of Billy in his hotel room "across the river" is easy to skip over. But it is more than a rhetorical flourish. Billy was in exile when he returned to New York, even though his baseball homecoming had been a supreme triumph. The incongruity of how completely he had captured public sentiment and how isolated he actually felt suggests the degree to which he did not fit Yankee pinstripes after all—at least those tailored for him by George Steinbrenner.

Bob Robertazzi, a New Jersey car dealer who became friendly with Billy, remembered him then. He accompanied him once to a dinner at the New York Athletic Club, a dinner also attended by Steinbrenner.

"Billy was at the end of the dais," Robertazzi recalled, "and he got all the play. After the dinner, there was a private party upstairs but there were all kinds of people lined up for him, the glee club, people from the audience. He was trying to make his way out, but they wouldn't let him go and he just stayed there signing autographs for everyone, saying hello and whatever. Steinbrenner wasn't exactly stumbling around, but he never got the play."

But out in Hasbrouck Heights his life seemed very different to Robertazzi. Billy's apartment was small and had a balcony with a little wooden fence around it where, during summer months, he kept pepper and tomato plants. He liked cooking—nearly always Italian dishes—and, it was clear, he didn't much like being alone. It was also clear he was alone a good deal of the time. He drank, Robertazzi remembered, not at home but in bars nearby, nondescript places. "It was usually after games, he'd come by—there was a place next door to my car dealership called Martha's Vineyard, and I think he just wanted to be with people, to have some company where he wouldn't be hassled. He'd have a drink and sometimes people would come up to him, a lot of times they'd just leave him alone. This wasn't a well-known hangout and so he could sit there and drink and talk about the car business, the baseball business—just shoot the bull with anyone, you know. There usually weren't a lot of people in there. So he'd sign a few autographs, have his drinks and say, 'I gotta go.' "

By the beginning of spring training in 1977, it was clear to many who followed the Yankees that whatever else lay ahead, the seas would be choppy and that Billy Martin, in the pilot house, would have an interesting time holding on to the wheel.

The spring camp was as chaotic as any Billy had ever been involved with. Contract complaints abounded, largely stemming from Reggie's whopping three-million-dollar deal. Thurman Munson, who had been promised by Steinbrenner that he would always be the highest-paid Yankee, discovered that he was not—and he didn't like it. Neither did Graig Nettles or Sparky Lyle or several other players. Then there was Reggie himself. Jackson knew why he had signed with the Yankees long before he ever made the fatal mistake of telling the world that he, not Thurman Munson, was the straw that stirred the drink. "The club was a great team. They needed one more thing—and I thought I was that extra thing they needed," Jackson said, "one extra dominant player. And I did know that I couldn't be that kind of dominant player I wanted to be without a team like that."

But this more sober self-analysis, delivered only recently, does not reflect the impact he had on the team at the time. He was, exactly as he now maintains, the missing piece of a puzzle, and the Yankees did provide exactly what he said they did (as did the City of New York). But the impact of Reggie Jackson—voluble, articulate, full of himself, sensitive (some would argue oversensitive) to his position in the game not only as a star but as a *black* star—made him a force beyond analysis. He was, like George Steinbrenner and Billy Martin, a colossal—and colossally insecure—universe on two feet. And alone among them, almost as if that was the secret way he had of actually lashing himself to accomplish what he wanted, he had this way of talking about himself that left him in a position where the only option he had was out of the starship he had just scuttled to fly on his own.

The major problem for Billy, for anyone employed by the Yankees then, was obviously George Steinbrenner, the owner whose idea of "hands-on" was a stranglehold. The usual problems any team had going into the spring—unsigned players, roster adjustments, getting players prepared for the season—were all made more difficult by Steinbrenner's determined efforts to remain up close and personal. He wanted to know why certain players were not in the lineup on given days, he insisted on games being won rather than used for work, he wanted discipline and fines and longer working hours, he demanded explanations at all times. In return, players walked out of camp, or they refused to run in the outfield, or they demanded to be traded, or, in the case of Mickey Rivers, personal and financial problems seemed to explode in public, right under the nose of the owner.

Billy was having a hard enough time simply trying to hold himself together. He was, according to any number of people in that camp, drinking more heavily. He was living in Boca Raton, sharing an apartment with Mickey Mantle, getting to and from the Yankee camp in Ft. Lauderdale by car and sometimes noticeably late. He often traveled to games by car rather than by team bus, another sharp bone in the throat of the owner, who wanted discernible leadership from his manager. Matters came to a head late that spring when the team lost an exhibition game to the Mets in St. Petersburg. Losing an exhibition game to the Mets, death itself to the owner, was in this instance compounded by his understanding that Billy had again arrived for the game solo, by car, rather than with the team. Steinbrenner charged into the Yankee clubhouse afterward. What followed occurred in the presence of several members of the media, and was later reported by Ed Linn in *Steinbrenner's Yankees:*

> "I want to talk to you right now!" he shouted at Billy. "You lied to me."
>
> Billy knew exactly what was coming. "I don't want to hear it, I don't want to hear that shit anymore."
>
> "You heard what I said! That thing is going to stop right now!"
>
> "You fat bastard, I don't give a shit what you say! I'm going to do it my way."

"You lied to me! You told me you were going to ride on the bus."

"Fuck you, I'm not riding on no fucking buses. Get the fuck out of here."

"Hey," Gabe Paul said, "hey, watch yourself, Billy. . . . Don't," he said, as he placed himself between them. "Billy, don't."

George was back near the wall, about ten feet away, staring at Billy incredulously. "What did you say?" he muttered, as if he couldn't bring himself to credit what he was hearing. "What did you say?"

"Billy," Gabe was saying, "don't talk to him like that."

"Then *you* can tell that fat bastard to go fuck himself. Hear me? He can go fuck himself!"

This time George heard him. "You don't talk to me like that, goddammit! You don't ever talk to me like that!"

"I'll talk to anybody like that," Billy said. He turned and went striding into the trainer's room, with George and Gabe right behind him. Everybody was ordered out. The door slammed shut. The screaming went on.

George was yelling that Billy had lied to him. And not only about the bus. He had promised to play the starting team all the way.

"Don't tell me how to manage my ball team you lying sonofabitch," Martin yelled back. "I'm the manager and I'll manage how I want to manage. It was an *exhibition* game. . . ."

They were on opposite sides of the trainer's table, shuffling back and forth, and as Billy was shouting that you didn't prepare for a 162-game baseball season the way you prepare for a 10-game football season, his fist went slamming into the big bucket of ice in which the pitchers soaked their elbows, the ice cubes and the water went splashing all over George, and George went into total rage. "I ought to fire you!" he screamed. He was wiping off his face, digging ice cubes out of his pockets.

"You want to fire me, fire me! But leave me the fuck alone."

George sent for Coach Yogi Berra and offered him Billy's job on the spot. "You're the manager," he said.

Billy, after a meeting with Steinbrenner and Gabe Paul, was back on the job the following day. This, it turned out, was not the march to the scaffold, just another spring training day—reminiscent of the one Billy had with Jim Campbell and Willie Horton years before. And, just as obviously, 1977 was not the New York Yankees' version of the *Pequod* but a World Championship year, the team's first since 1962, the only one Billy would experience as a manager.

But what insiders knew, the world—or at least a national television audience, watching a critical Yankee–Red Sox game in Fenway Park—learned by midseason: that Billy and the Yankees were in a death dance. The dance partner that day happened to be Reggie Jackson, who misplayed and then seemed to nonchalant a ball in right field and was immediately pulled from the game, precipitating a near-brawl between the manager and the star in the dugout.

Of course, the play and the situation had a background, principally Billy's long-smoldering resentment of the way George's free agent had set himself apart from everyone else on Billy's team.

On this particular June day in Boston, the Yankees were in the process of being buried by an avalanche of Red Sox home runs—five the previous day, five more in this game.

In the sixth inning, with the Red Sox already leading 7–4, and after the Yankees had scratched out a run in the top of the inning, Fred Lynn started another Sox rally with a single. The next hitter, slugger Jim Rice, dumped a soft hit to right, in front of and away from Jackson, who seemed to jog after the ball as Lynn cruised into third and Rice, stretching a single, safely reached second.

Billy, said one game story, then "brought his red neck to the mound" to replace his pitcher, Mike Torrez. At the same time, he sent Paul Blair into the game to replace Reggie, who was leaning against the outfield fence talking to pitchers in the Yankee bullpen when Blair approached and told him he was out of the game. Reggie, in total disbelief, humiliated at being shown up on national television, charged from the field and confronted Billy on the steps of the dugout. Billy—*take shit from no one*—was ready to fight him, and shouted right back in Reggie's face as NBC's cameras recorded every move, every bulging vein. The two had to be separated by coaches Elston Howard and Yogi Berra.

The images of that episode remain fresh fifteen years later, the impact as dramatic as they were that day. Sparky Lyle, from his vantage point in the bullpen, thought he knew exactly what happened:

"Reggie didn't feel he did anything wrong, he just butchered the ball—but from where we were looking, he didn't seem to have his eye on it—in other words it was that taboo thing, he wasn't paying attention. . . ."

Reggie, in the hours following the incident, told two reporters in an emotional interview in his hotel room that he had tried, that his troubles on the team went deeper than his relationship with Billy. Whatever Billy felt or did not feel about him, it was the team that did not like him, that had exiled him in his own clubhouse. The predominantly white team regarded him, he said, "as a nigger."

There was a meeting called by Gabe Paul between Billy and Reggie the next day to smooth things over. For a while, matters only worsened. Billy, according to Gabe Paul, "inadvertently used the word 'boy' in criticizing Reggie and Reggie really thought Billy was saying something else." There was, finally, a truce but no peace. Jackson refused to shake Billy's hand.

The aftermath went far beyond their quarrel. Anyone who picked up a newspaper in New York that summer as the Yankees struggled to stay in the race understood that Billy's job was in daily jeopardy. There were any number of exclusive stories that had the decision to fire him already made, the time and date of the specific announcement set. There were any number of not-so-*sotto voce* stories that had players complaining about Billy to the front office—in one notorious and almost ludicrous instance to Steinbrenner himself. This particular episode involved Thurman Munson and Lou Piniella visiting Steinbrenner, who had joined the team on a road trip, in the owner's hotel suite in Milwaukee. At the post-midnight meeting, the two players and Steinbrenner discussed what they all felt was the chaotic state of the clubhouse. There are differing versions of whether the players openly advocated firing Billy to the owner—who later said that they did—but in the midst of this, Billy, apparently on a full tank, was returning to his own room, heard loud voices from the owner's suite, and knocked on Steinbrenner's door. He eventually pushed his way into the room and discovered Piniella and Munson—so the story goes—hiding in the bathroom. In any case, Billy, super-sensitive to the fragility of the hold he had on his job, subsequently became the source for a number of firing stories that were published through that summer.

But the Yankees, trailing the Red Sox by five games well into August, won forty of their last fifty games. In addition, because Billy's problems were so public and because the public, in any contest between the team's battling, "blue-collar" manager and its blustering, blue-blazered owner, had an easier time choosing sides than they would at a staged professional wrestling match, there was no firing—just the victory that Steinbrenner, Reggie Jackson, and Billy each seemed to crave more than life itself.

The Yankees won one hundred games, taking the American League East by two and a half games over both the Red Sox and Orioles; then they won the pennant, taking the Royals in another dramatic five-game series, scoring three ninth-inning runs in the final game to do it; finally, majestically, they disposed of the Dodgers in the World Series, with Reggie Jackson's Oscar-winning three-home-run performance capping it all at the stadium. Afterward, Reggie and Billy embraced in the clubhouse.

Many, including those who followed the team closely, had a hard time believing what they saw. But each man, in that moment, profoundly understood and appreciated the other. Their embrace, theatrical though it may have been, was something real. For Reggie, the home runs were, he maintains to this day, "the most memorable thing in my career." But in that game, in that Series victory, he said that "Billy and I had established togetherness, unity." It came through victory, a World Championship that allowed each man to claim his place at center stage in the most magnificent of all theaters.

"The reason that game was the most important thing I had ever done in baseball," Reggie said, "was because there were so many circumstances involved—final game of the World Series; national television; Dodgers and Yankees, so it was a transcontinental series where every person was involved and there is no greater series than one that takes place from coast to coast. So I was fortunate with all that happening, with all those personalities in attendance—Howard Cosell was on the microphone, George Steinbrenner owned the team, Billy Martin was the manager—and all those things were that big because they were happening in New York."

For Billy, the moment, just as certainly, was not about friendship but about winning. At the very least, he still had his job. But at what should have been the summit of his career, the one World Championship he would claim as a manager, the joy and satisfaction he obviously felt were peculiarly diluted. He went to a victory party in Hasbrouck Heights after the game, and there, in the crush of guests including his wife and son who had come up for the series, the wild force of the season and of his life flying apart caught up with him. He quarreled publicly with Gretchen, finally taking his drink glass and smashing it to the floor. He fled from the party held to celebrate his greatest triumph, unable to get a handle on the deep and twisting emotions that kept him from fully claiming this moment for which he had been waiting so long.

"I drove to a little bar nearby all by myself," he wrote in his autobiography, "and I sat there and rested where no one could bother me."

# CHAPTER 14

It was as though the mark of Cain was upon him. He should have been in the strongest position of his professional career, but he was not. Winning a World Championship should have elevated him as nothing else—and in a sense, it had. Though he remained "on the other side of the river," he was recognized and toasted everywhere he went. The World Champion Yankees were his Yankees, as earlier teams had been Casey's or Joe McCarthy's or Miller Huggins's. And he had done it his way as those old great ones had done it theirs. He was a celebrity like no other. He did not hang out with George or the crowd at Elaine's that included George's friends Roy Cohn, Bill Fugazy, Barbara Walters. He was never into the celebrity scene in New York. When he "hung out" in New York, it was often at small bars and discos like D. L. Sutton's on York and 84th. One night when he went to Danny's Hideaway, a favorite spot from his playing days, photographers from one of the gossip pages were waiting for him. "It was the last time he went there," remembered Mickey Morabito, a friend, then a Yankee publicist.

"Billy always thought of himself as a cowboy from the Old West," said Bill Mayback, a New York hotel manager and longtime friend, "and, even in New York, he dressed that way with boots, jeans, jacket—the whole thing. I think he considered himself the underdog, the old-fashioned gunslinger who'd come into town and take on the big guy."

Commercial New York, Madison Avenue, picked up on it. To millions of New Yorkers, and then tens of millions across the country, this quintessential in-your-face baseball manager was transformed into the cowpoke nursing a drink who swore he was not the one who punched that dogie. In a series of vastly popular Lite Beer commercials for television, Billy's largely self-created character became as well known as any pop figure of his time.

Bob Giraldi, the maker of those commercials, which usually featured Rodney Dangerfield and a squadron of brawling rowdies, remembers Billy well. Billy, he said, really had none of the talents—acting skill, voice, camera sense—that a media star usually had. But, said Giraldi, "he acted the way he played ball—it wasn't fluid, it was pit-bull style, but it worked for him in both places.

"He was the workingman's hero, no question about it. He had this extraordinary hold on people because he bucked the boss, told the boss to go fuck himself. Billy did it his way and he also had the credentials. He was a fuckin' World Series hero, a Yankee. He rubbed shoulders with Whitey and Mickey, he belonged."

Billy was a catalyst in these commercials, too—a prankster, as he always had been, very much the life of the party both on and off the set. He was often the straw boss for Giraldi, corralling his beer-can chewing mates long enough to get them ready to work. Most interesting of all to Giraldi was the interplay between Billy and Rodney Dangerfield, *schlemiel* of the universe. There was in this relationship a confusion of creative and personal elements. In it, Giraldi thought he could see something of Billy's talent as a manager:

"Here they are, these sports heroes, all banding together, drinking together, waking up together, having a great time, coming to the set in a bus . . . and Rodney only comes to the set in his limousine, he won't come to hang around. And Rodney, in the commercials, wonders why nobody likes him, ya know. Billy would pick up on that and break his balls. I think Rodney was actually more petrified of Billy than he was of anybody. Billy was a genius, maybe that's why he was a good manager. But he was a genius at finding that vulnerability, that weakness of a person—that's what he obviously was able to do as a manager."

Giraldi remembers Billy's charm, his warmth, his street-toughness ("He's the guy I'd want before all of them next to me in a fight"), his undisguised drinking and womanizing ("All the guys were after Lee, the lady with Mickey Spillane. Billy was after her tits"). He was keenly aware of a side of him that Giraldi felt was purely self-destructive. From the time he met him, Giraldi had wanted to do a movie about him. Billy reminded him of Jake LaMotta in *Raging Bull*, he said.

It was this other side of Billy that seemed most troubling to George Steinbrenner. Steinbrenner initially hired Billy because he thought he could win. His decision was a business one. Though he may have had only a limited understanding of the man he was hiring, he had an astute sense of what he could do for his team. He also had a keen sense of how Billy would go over in New York. Billy's style *was* New York and Steinbrenner had counted on that to boost interest in the team. But nothing he had known prior to hiring Billy had prepared him for the raw shock of the man.

Billy frightened him. He frightened him professionally because his popularity itself had become a problem, and he frightened him personally because he believed, with Bob Giraldi and a growing number of New York writers who covered the team, that Billy's life was careening on a wildly unpredictable and self-destructive course. Gabe Paul confirms that Steinbrenner at this point was eager to have Billy enter some sort of alcohol rehabilitation. "Billy himself many times acknowledged the need," Paul said, though he was unsure anything ever came of it.

There was much talk then, and afterward, about the love/hate relationship between the two men, about Steinbrenner as another father figure, Billy as the perpetual kid and prodigal son. Though the feeling between them deepened over many years to include something like mutual admiration, the reality was that they did not have much of any sort of personal relationship. The two men were so different socially, economically, culturally, even temperamentally—volatile as they both were—that there was almost no chance that they could establish anything like closeness. And what points of contact they did have were so burdened with each man's suspicion of the other that a real relationship was nearly impossible. Gabe Paul, whatever other duties he had, was, in his own words, "liaison between George and Billy. George would talk to me, then I would talk to Billy and Billy and I would talk the way we talked."

What all of this added up to was a season in 1978 like no other.

The year of craziness began with another round of free agent signings—Goose Gossage (the game's dominant reliever who could all but guarantee a pennant, but meant instant trouble with 1977 Cy Young winner Sparky Lyle) and Rawley Eastwick (another reliever, traded only months later for Jay Johnstone)—and ended with the Yankees' miracle comeback against the Red Sox along with a second straight World Series triumph over the Dodgers. In between, all was chaos.

When Gabe Paul resigned in January of that year, his job was taken by Al Rosen. Rosen, friendly with Steinbrenner from Cleveland, was, like Paul, in charge of baseball operations and of shuttling messages from the owner to the manager. Rosen ultimately surrendered his job because, he said, "it was the only way I could keep George Steinbrenner as a friend." From the start, he had no illusions about what he was up against:

"I was there under difficult circumstances," he said later, "not because of Billy, but because the club had won the World Championship the year before, and that made it difficult. There was the Reggie story, the Munson thing, Lyle, Nettles, and all that stuff—it really was a hornet's nest."

His relationship with Billy, an antagonist from his playing days going back to the Pacific Coast League, was, he said, "decent enough," but was also marked by an absence of illusion. He knew what Billy was up against and he knew, too, what he described as "the Jekyll and Hyde nature" of Billy Martin. "Billy was perfectly delightful to be with except if he had a couple of drinks. The light could go on and off real fast."

Rosen remembered an episode from spring training that, in a way, marked out the turf for him. One evening, he was returning with his wife to the team hotel when he saw Billy in the roadway.

"Billy was standing there and he was raising hell. I told my wife that she better go on, Billy was obviously drunk. He was mad because the bartender shut him off at the bar," Rosen said, "he was going to go back and do this and that and the other thing. I said 'Billy, come on with me.' We went back in the bar and sat down. The bartender saw us and I told him to please serve us—and he did. So we're sitting there with our drinks and suddenly Billy notices these two guys at the next table. He leans over and tells me, 'Those two guys over there are talking about me.' He was on edge and ready to go, you could just see that, and then, just at that moment, this one guy that Billy had been eyeing said, 'Mr. Martin, I've been a fan of yours forever. I just can't believe I'm sitting in the same room with you. Would you mind signing this for me?' Well, Billy just turned completely from being ready to deck these two guys. The guys wound up at our table. I sat there for an hour with them while he was buying drinks for them. It was unbelievable. When you were with Billy you just never knew when you were going to have a problem."

Rosen recalls the sullen and frequently acrimonious nature of the contact between George and Billy. Steinbrenner's interference with the running of the team now not only included pep talks and phone calls to the dugout and clubhouse, but demands for meetings with the manager and coaches.

"Billy did not relate to the front office, he did not like the front office," Rosen said. "He resented the fact that he had to come up for meetings. George would say, 'Get the manager and the coaches up here after the game,' and boy, when Billy came up here he was really hopping. And I can understand that, why should you be called on the carpet because you did something on the field?"

As with 1977, only more so, the season seemed to unwind in reverse. The Red Sox again took charge of the division, as the Yankees, favored to win, struggled to stay abreast, but with injuries mounting they kept slipping further behind. And the further the Yankees slipped, the tenser the air between George and Billy—and Al Rosen.

In late May, when Thurman Munson removed himself from a game with a knee injury, Rosen, in the park at the time, made an immediate roster move, calling up a reserve catcher, Mike Heath, from the Yankee Double A farm team in West Haven. Billy was informed of the callup by writers immediately following the game. He was enraged. An argument with Rosen eventually erupted when the two men later met in the press room.

"It didn't seem earth-shattering to me," Rosen recalled. "I just wanted backup in case Munson couldn't catch. So I recalled Heath and because I didn't think it was a big deal and because I didn't want to bother him with it during the game, I waited till afterwards to tell him and then I couldn't call through because the line was continually busy. By then, the press had told him. I didn't see Billy until we were in the press room. He was sitting there with Art Fowler and somebody told me he was pretty upset. I went over to him and said, 'What's the problem?' Billy, like he could be, was really caustic—and I didn't take it from him when we were players and wasn't about to take it from him now, so we had a few words. I told him—if that happened to me, I'd say, 'Well, he probably did it and he'll let me know about it,' and then come and see me privately if he wanted to get something off his chest."

But things were falling apart, and quickly. Meetings with George included quarrels about where Reggie Jackson should be batting in the order—Billy had him hitting anywhere from second to seventh—and why Billy had given the finger to a fan at a game in Cleveland. The American League had a letter to that effect and they were investigating the charge. Billy also had the strong suspicion that his phone was being tapped. Steinbrenner had apparently cautioned him about a teenaged girl he had been seeing, and Billy concluded that the only way he could have known that was if he had been listening in on his private phone calls. Billy, aided by a batting practice pitcher on the team, Ray Negron, actually dismantled the phone in a fruitless search for the bug.

Then there was the uproar over Jim Beattie, a rookie pitcher on the team. The Yankees, in mid-June, had gone into Boston for what the media in both cities, as well as the Yankees' owner, were calling a crucial series. The teams split the first two games and then, in the third game, the Red Sox assaulted the Yanks' rookie pitcher, driving him to cover within three innings. The fiasco that followed was a highlight from George's Gong Show.

Beattie was ordered to the minor leagues by Steinbrenner, in attendance at Fenway Park, literally on the spot. While he was in the shower, "throwing strikes with a soapbar," he remembers, Cedric Tallis, on George's order, appeared in the clubhouse and pulled him from the shower.

"Supposedly, as I walked off the field, Steinbrenner was yelling at me from the stands, but I didn't hear him at all, didn't even know he was in the park," Beattie said. He was preoccupied with his performance and with the fact that fifty of his relatives and friends had come out to see him pitch. It was the first time that Beattie, a New England native, had pitched in Fenway Park.

"When I got down to the shower room," Beattie continued, "Cedric Tallis came down and pulled me from the shower and told me that I was being sent out. I was already ticked off about my performance, let alone being sent down . . . now I had to pack my bag and go out there and face my relatives, my fiancée, and tell them that I was going to Tacoma."

Beattie said that he understood it was George, not Billy, who was behind the move, and he was particularly resentful of the comments made by the owner to the effect that he lacked courage and had been a pampered Ivy Leaguer.

"He said I was an Ivy League kid that needed to be toughened up—this was pretty funny because I had gone to school on scholarship and never had the benefits everyone else did. I came from a working-class family and I fought and battled for everything I got."

The way Billy responded was the problem. Instead of backing up his employer or at least keeping quiet, he said, publicly, "Beattie didn't have his good stuff, but he has all the guts in the world." He knew the import of those words, as well. "I don't run scared," he added. "My mother didn't raise a quitter. I remember last year I was going to get fired here. I'll show you the ring I got fired with. It says World Champions."

Whether it was in response to Beattie's showing or to Billy's, Steinbrenner upped the ante by threatening to fire Art Fowler, Billy's pitching coach and aide-de-camp, who had been restored to the ranks toward the end of the previous season with the hope that he would provide needed companionship and comfort to the man in the dugout.

Everything that had happened till then was only a prelude to what followed. With the threat to fire Fowler, Billy made known his own intention to quit. He told his coaches that he would leave if Fowler went. There then followed a meeting in New York with Steinbrenner. In the meeting, Steinbrenner held out the promise that Fowler could stay but that Clyde King would become a second pitching coach and that further, it was expected that Billy, in accord with his contract and with past personal promises, would cease all criticism of the front office. Al Rosen recalled that Billy—prior to the meeting, during it, and afterward—"was very protective of Art." Afterward, for the first time in his tenure as Yankee skipper, he became noticeably quiet and withdrawn.

The next plot twist is somewhat harder to follow because it is once-removed and shrouded within the prerogatives of executive privilege. Lee MacPhail, then president of the American League, said he was aware that Billy's job was in serious jeopardy and also that Bob Lemon's job as manager of the White Sox was, too. MacPhail says he then interceded with Steinbrenner and Veeck, owner of the White Sox, to see if a managerial trade could be worked out:

"I knew that George would have fired Billy, I knew he was sort of anxious to get rid of him, and I knew that Lemon was on shaky ground with the White Sox. I liked both Lemon and Billy, so I thought I could save their jobs. I suggested they trade. I suggested it to Veeck and I suggested it to George. And Veeck was all for it. George took a wait-and-see attitude and then the Yankees went on a little bit of a winning streak and that's where it was left."

Except that that was not where the matter ended at all. What may have started with an almost half-humorous aside ended like the downward roll of an innocent pebble on a mountain slope.

MacPhail's suggestion was made sometime around the end of June or at the beginning of July, no one is quite sure. The Boston series at Fenway Park took place during the third week of June, the meeting with Steinbrenner in New York occurred on the twenty-sixth. All the while—and thereafter—New York papers were full of hints and suggestions, many of them from Steinbrenner, that Billy's job was on the line, that a firing could happen at any time.

At the All-Star break two weeks later, newspapers reported that Billy had been having health problems. The story, which involved the discovery of a spot on his liver, was leaked by Steinbrenner, Billy said. The medical aspect of the story was only the springboard for a larger, more elaborate firing story in which it was revealed that, because he was concerned with Billy's health, George had offered to let Billy resign with pay, to extend his contract for several years, and to employ him as a special consultant during which time George would help him open a camp for boys, something in which Billy had always expressed an interest.

According to Ed Linn, on the day following the All-Star break, Steinbrenner called Billy into his office, then went down to the Yankee clubhouse "to talk to the players for the first time all season." Following that day's game, Steinbrenner told a press conference what Billy and the players undoubtedly learned earlier—that henceforth, George would be taking a far more active role in running the team. In other words, he would be managing alongside his own manager whose power had, in essence, been reduced to that of a figurehead.

This vigorous twisting of the ratchet wheel, after years of gathering pressures—the humiliation it represented was simply incalculable. Whatever Steinbrenner's motives—even if cruelty was not among them—Billy could not have felt more stretched out. The media picked up on it. Because the situation was so grotesque and out of control, the drumbeat stories—including lurid photographs of the wasted and harried manager—now emphasized the state of Billy's mental health.

Maury Allen, a writer covering the team for the *New York Post*, had a midnight visit from Billy in the days before he was fired. Billy was obviously drunk, but Allen saw more than drunkenness.

"One night in Milwaukee, Billy Martin drank heavily with Art Fowler," Allen later wrote in his book *Damn Yankee*.

> Then Fowler had to leave to visit with some old friends. Martin was alone. He should never have been left alone. He was terribly depressed. He was drinking too much. He was not eating enough and was losing weight. He didn't know which way to turn. Over and over he considered quitting. He wondered if he could ever get a job in baseball again if he quit. He wandered back to his room at the Pfister Hotel. At 2 A.M. he knocked on the door of this writer's room. I jumped up, asked who it was, heard Billy's voice, and opened the door. "C'mere, I want to talk to you," he said.
>
> I followed him into his own room a couple of doors away. He was wavering with drink. "Why should I have to take all this shit?" he said. "I'm a Yankee. I've been a Yankee all my life. What's he [Steinbrenner] been? Rich. He's not a Yankee. I'm a Yankee. I don't have to take this. I can leave this team now. I'll live. I don't have to listen to this crap, take his phone calls, ruin my life and my health. What for? I'm a Yankee." A dozen message notes were on his nightstand.
>
> Then he burst into deep, excruciating, sobbing weeping, his entire body shaking, his arms flailing, his head in his chest, his hands squeezing his legs, his hair disheveled, his face sallow, and his skin pulled tight. "I'm a Yankee, I'm a Yankee," he repeated.

On July 17, thirteen games out of first, playing with lineups "influenced" if not dictated by George Steinbrenner, the Yankees played a game against the Kansas City Royals at the Stadium. The lineup that night included Reggie Jackson, who had been benched and moved up and down the order for weeks, DHing and batting cleanup. Jackson's position in the lineup was critical because, even though it was more than likely ordered by Steinbrenner, it was unsettling and even provocative to Reggie. He could not remember the last time he hit cleanup. When he played, as on this night, batting cleanup against Paul Splittorff, he was inserted mainly against left-handed pitching, a strategy that he concluded was designed to waste him, to humiliate him, to teach him a lesson.

The game went to extra innings tied 5–5. In the Yankee tenth, with Al Hrabosky, another lefty, pitching for the Royals, Thurman Munson led off the inning with a single to center. Jackson was the next batter, and as he stepped into the batter's box, he was carrying with him instructions from Billy to bunt. Then he picked up a sign to bunt from third-base coach Dick Howser. The fuse was lit.

Jackson took an inside pitch for a ball and then saw that the bunt sign was taken off. On the next pitch he squared to bunt anyway—

and missed. Dumbfounded, Howser called time and walked to the plate.

"He wants you to *hit,*" he said.

"I'm going to bunt," Jackson replied.

Blasting cap in place. Reggie, with Billy beside himself on the bench, fouled off two additional bunt attempts and was gone, an official strikeout victim. When he got back to the bench, he said, he was expecting Billy to confront him. Instead, he was met by coach Gene Michael, who told him that Billy wanted him to leave the bench. Jackson had prepared himself for a fight. He had removed his glasses and was waiting. But Billy never approached him, never said anything to him. He eventually went on to the clubhouse.

Billy, according to friends and his own word, was never angrier in his life. And he had all the reason in the world on his side. He was the manager and his leadership had openly been flouted. No team, no manager, could endure that kind of insubordination. Billy went wild long afterward, demolishing things in his office, but Nick Priori, the clubhouse man, said that what was most eerie following the game (lost by the Yankees, 7–5) was the silence of the locker room. Billy's rage included an immediate and direct demand that Jackson be suspended. He was—not for the season, as Billy wanted, but for five games, a slap on the wrist.

Billy might have expected that the press, as well as the owner, would back him to the hilt. But that was not the case. It was subsequently learned that Sparky Lyle, earlier in that same game, had refused to enter the game in middle relief and, without penalty, had showered, dressed, and left the ballpark. Jackson's suspension was further diluted by charges of favoritism.

Jackson for the longest time explained the bunt by denying what he did. In the immediate aftermath, he told the press that his only intention had been to "advance the runner." In his autobiography, written six years later, he recalled that when Billy told him before he went to the plate that he wanted him to bunt, his mind "went blank." In effect, he said, he snapped, and, without thought, without intent, allowed an accumulation of hurts and slights to take over.

Now, away from the playing field, the fires of that time banked, Jackson is considerably less vague about what he was up to:

"I was asked to bunt by Dick Howser," he said. "I was hitting cleanup and Billy and I were having a rift at the time. I was really upset that I had been asked to bunt. I felt like, 'Hey, if you're going to ask me to bunt, fuck it, I shouldn't be hitting cleanup—most of that time I was taken out of the lineup and only DHing against left-handed pitching. Which made no sense. So I figured, if you're going to do this, gonna make me bunt, it's stupid. Then they came back and said, 'Okay, you're going to hit away now.' I said. 'No.' They asked me to bunt, this is a chance for things to come to a head. That's why I bunted."

If it was Reggie's intention to bring the roof down, he succeeded beyond his wildest expectations. What he incited was not so much his conflict with Billy as Billy's with George Steinbrenner. It may not have been part of the game plan, but Jackson almost certainly knew that, aside from Fran Healy, a reserve catcher nicknamed "Henry Kissinger" by his teammates because he was perceived as Reggie's emissary to the rest of the team, the only real ally he had in the organization was George Steinbrenner. He counted on Steinbrenner to recognize that, in the new baseball equation post–free agency, players of his stature added up—perhaps to more than any manager.

With Jackson gone, the Yankees won all their games. When he returned, in Chicago, he reported not to his manager but to his locker, where he was met by an army of media. The crush of interest around Jackson, the fact that he did not deign to apologize or even speak to Billy, that he did not even take batting practice that night, had to sharpen all the razors of resentment and rage. Billy could barely conceal his anger in the comments he made to the press as he stood near the batting cage before the game.

Following the game and prior to the team's departure for Kansas City, Billy, still fuming over Jackson, sat drinking with Bill Veeck in the press room. Veeck, an old friend, told him the story about MacPhail's proposal for a managerial trade. It was the first Billy had heard of it and it was more than he could take. Only one person could have been behind this proposal, he believed, and it was neither Lee MacPhail nor Bill Veeck. It all made sense now to Billy—the light sentence meted out to Reggie, the weeks and months of torture.

When the Yankees reached the airport, they learned that their flight to Kansas City had been delayed. For the next couple of hours, Billy drank heavily in a lounge near the gate. Sometime in this period, he located Murray Chass of *The New York Times* and unleashed a torrent of abuse—for the record, he said—aimed at Jackson and George Steinbrenner. The diatribe, certain to make headlines and breathless reading back home, was overheard by at least two other reporters, including Henry Hecht of the *Post*, a writer clearly unfriendly to Billy who recently had been calling for the manager's firing and suggesting that Billy's principal strategy with Reggie had been to drive him crazy. The reporters then called in their stories to their papers. When the team's flight was finally announced, Chass and Hecht walked with Billy to the gate. Billy, obviously drunk, let loose another blast. Recalling a remark of Reggie's concerning the bunt episode, and thinking of Steinbrenner's guilty plea on charges of making and concealing illegal campaign contributions, he hit high E on his bugle of self-destruction: "One's a born liar and the other's convicted," he said.

When the plane got to Kansas City, Chass called Steinbrenner, informing him of what Billy said. He wanted a reaction. Steinbrenner, who had been through this too many times, wanted to know if Billy had been drinking. Chass said he did not know. When Hecht called after that, Steinbrenner asked him if Billy had really made the remarks. Hecht assured him that he had.

There was only one thing left to do: Billy was gone, there was just the matter of how and when. Steinbrenner understood perfectly the ramifications of getting rid of him, knew the abuse he personally would have to endure, understood that it might be bad for business, and realized, perhaps better than anyone, that drink, not clear thinking, was behind this. None of that mattered.

He dispatched Al Rosen to Kansas City. Rosen said he got a call from Steinbrenner that night, waking him. Steinbrenner told him what happened, ordered him to go to Kansas City "and straighten it out." Was it a firing call?

"Yeah, yeah. George couldn't stomach that [remark] and shouldn't have had to," he said. But Rosen knew that it was left to him, that the owner, like Henry II, asked for someone to rid him of a meddlesome priest. Rosen told George:

"Why don't you go out there? You're the one he called a liar."

"Get your ass out there!" Steinbrenner ordered.

There was no firing. Instead, there was a miserable, terrible, even pathetic leavetaking. Billy stood shaking before a hastily called hotel press conference, sunglasses unable to hide uncontrolled sobbing, and read a statement of resignation, one that cited reasons of health and the best interests of the ballclub. He never got to the end of it.

The statement was his own, in his own hand, says Mickey Morabito, who was in the hotel room with Billy when he wrote it. "He wrote it on hotel stationery in pencil," he recalled. Al Rosen had come to his room and, fighting with himself over what he had to do, was relieved when Billy told him that he was voluntarily leaving.

Phil Rizzuto, watching his old friend deliver his farewell, was shocked that no one tried to help Billy afterward, that he left the press conference and hotel by himself.

"He broke up and started crying at the press conference and nobody walked out with him," he said. "I went running after him. I was the only one who went after him. I thought he'd walk under a truck."

Billy, in his autobiography, underscored the idea that the resignation originated with him, that working for Steinbrenner had made him "a nervous wreck," and that he simply couldn't go on.

There was more to it than that, it turns out. As devastated as he surely was, as sincerely overwhelmed as he was in his farewell, the portrait of him as a basket case—brushstrokes supplied by himself—was a little off.

The night the team pulled into Kansas City, he was also on the phone. By the time he reached his hotel, Billy fully realized what his remarks to Chass and Hecht meant. He called his agent, Doug Newton, and his lawyer and advisor in New Orleans, Eddie Sapir, to tell them what happened. Sapir let Billy know that if he got fired "for cause"—and this might clearly constitute cause—then "the rest of the contract is null and void." There was a problem that both men recognized and which, Sapir said, he eventually solved.

"What we did is I got Billy sick. I had him resign before Al Rosen got off the airplane," Sapir said. "We said 'health reasons'—we said we felt it was better not only for Billy but for the team, the organization, the fans—so that when Al got there to hand him the pink slip, we had already officially resigned for health reasons. And doing it for health reasons, the paycheck kept coming and the contract stayed intact." Never mind that this strategy also happened to be in accord with the line Steinbrenner had been developing prior to the incident.

The most wondrous part of all was that even this sleight of hand was as nothing compared to the move Steinbrenner then concocted over the next twenty-four hours. Possibly feeling remorseful, certainly aware of the eruption of sympathy for Billy (with its exactly corresponding outcry of protest directed at him), and very possibly aware that a young Mets official had floated the possibility of yet another managerial swap for Billy, Steinbrenner decided that Billy would continue as manager of the Yankees—in 1980, a season and a half away. Because he had just hired Bob Lemon—with Al Rosen's strong backing—Billy could not return sooner. But that worked out just as well—Rosen's objections notwithstanding—because there was an old-timers' game two days hence at Yankee Stadium, a chance to undo, with one unbelievable theatrical gesture, everything that had just been done.

The intricate plotting that moved Billy from a Florida golf course, where he had gone to be with Mickey Mantle, to his flabbergasting reemergence from the Yankee dugout on old-timers' day might have done John le Carré—or at least the producers of Wrestlemania—proud. First, when the opposition old-timers were announced for the day, Al Rosen was among them in a Cleveland uniform. Steinbrenner had insisted on it. Rosen vehemently protested, but to no avail. When he stepped from the visitors' dugout, he was greeted by a huge and unmerciful cascade of jeering and booing. With the surprise announcement still to come, this was George Orwell's two minutes' hate for Yankee fans.

Billy and his agent, Doug Newton, had meanwhile been spirited into the stadium in absolute secrecy. "We were dressed in trenchcoats and hidden in a boiler room for hours until the very last minute so the secret wouldn't be tipped off," Newton recalled. And then there was the ultimate introduction, intoned by Bob Shepperd, that beginning in 1980 Bob Lemon would assume the duties of general manager and "managing the Yankees in the 1980 season, and hopefully for many seasons after that . . ."

He sprang from the dugout, in uniform, waving his cap over his head as he ran across the field to delirious cheering from above, and something approaching disbelief and shock on the ground. Steinbrenner, in the end, had staged the raising of Lazarus at little cost to himself.

If the film of Billy Martin's life could be stopped at any point to mark its climax, this would probably be the place: on the field of Yankee Stadium, a boisterous crowd roaring its approval of him, his enemies stunned, even his friends shocked. He had not conquered his demons, but he had survived them. His team—his once and future team—was still World Champion. There was much tragicomedy to come, but here, when Billy's Return was still a masterstroke, before it had become a seasonal cliché, it was a last hurrah presented to adoring multitudes as a last laugh.

In a real sense, the outer limits of Billy's stay with the Yankees had been reached. Billy could be brought back but, like Lazarus himself, there was no way he could be given a clean bill of health. The new contract to manage the Yankees in 1980 and for many years thereafter was, at this point, oral, not written, and surely depended on Billy's toeing the line. The tenuousness of his continuing affiliation with

Steinbrenner was highlighted over that winter when Billy was involved in yet another off-field brawl, this one involving a young reporter in Reno, Nevada.

Billy had gone to Reno with a Minnesota friend, Howard Wong, to do a favor for another Minnesota friend, Bill Musselman, then coach of a minor-league basketball team. While in Reno, Billy either knowingly or unknowingly consented to an interview with a local reporter named Ray Hagar, and got into a quarrel with him. Hagar may or may not have wound up shoving Billy's friend, Howard Wong, a diminutive and elderly man; either way, Hagar wound up on the receiving end of Billy's Sunday song.

When news of the fracas reached Steinbrenner, he let it be known that Billy would have to clear himself of all criminal *and* civil charges involved—out-of-court settlements not allowed—if he expected to return to manage the Yankees. The diligent and loyal Judge Sapir, working feverishly with attorneys for Hagar, managed to secure an arrangement where all charges were dropped in exchange for an apology from Billy—one he wasn't about to give. Sapir himself, with Billy sitting tight-lipped at his side, proffered the apology—for his client *and* Hagar! The matter (there was said to be a payoff by the Reno Big Horn basketball team) then went away.

Over that winter, however, the situation on the Yankees changed dramatically. First, the team, under Bob Lemon, was coming off its miracle run for the pennant and its second consecutive World Championship.

Then there was the situation with Lemon himself. During the off-season, his twenty-six-year-old son, Jerry, was killed in an auto accident. The father and son had been unusually close and the loss was devastating to Lemon. He was, by all accounts, simply not the same man when he returned the following spring.

Billy returned that spring, too. He took an apartment in nearby Boca Tica, nervous and still uncertain about his status. There were those who believed that Steinbrenner was already thinking of replacing Lemon, moving him up in the organization and away from the responsibility of field leadership. There was also the suspicion that Billy's presence in camp meant that he was politicking for the job right then rather than in 1980. The reality was that Steinbrenner was still unsure he wanted Billy around at all. The matter in Nevada was taking time to clear, and Steinbrenner was again busy leaking stories about Billy's off-field behavior, the latest incident involving reports of a drunken scuffle at a nearby nightspot (which proved to be innocuous). When—and if—he returned to the Yankees, when and if a contract was actually signed, it would be on his, Steinbrenner's, terms, and the terms clearly were going to require not just a reformed but an entirely new Billy Martin.

Had the Yankees picked up where they left off the season before, there is a strong chance that Billy would never have returned. But the Yankees were not the same team any more than Bob Lemon was the same man in the dugout. They finished a poor spring with a slow and somnolent start. Injuries changed the face of the squad. The pitching staff, even with addition of free agents Tommy John and Luis Tiant, was in tatters. Ed Figueroa, who had won twenty games the previous season, battled a career-ending arm injury through the '79 season, winning only four. Catfish Hunter, whose pitching down the stretch probably secured the '78 pennant, had also reached the end of the line. Ron Guidry, nursing a back injury, was not the same pitcher he had been the year before when he won twenty-five games and the Cy Young Award. Goose Gossage, early in the year, got into a clubhouse scuffle with Cliff Johnson and sustained a season-ending injury to the thumb of his pitching hand; there was no closer in baseball who could replace him. Mickey Rivers, in and out of the lineup, was beset with personal and financial problems that rendered him more than usually distracted; he was traded away by mid-season. Roy White, Graig Nettles, Thurman Munson, and Reggie Jackson were all a year older. The real miracle of '78, it increasingly appeared, was caused as much by the Red Sox injuries down the stretch as by Yankee strength.

Billy returned to the team in mid-June, in typical cloak, dagger, and headline fashion. He was first summoned to Columbus, Ohio, to meet with Steinbrenner. The meetings took up the better part of a weekend and involved three issues: One was Billy's willingness to take over. He was, and he wanted to do it immediately. Second was his willingness to cooperate with the front office, which clearly extended to staying out of trouble away from the field. Though the contract Billy eventually signed was a standard one, without "good-boy" clauses this time, Doug Newton, his agent, acknowledged that the boilerplate language about a manager doing nothing detrimental to the game or the team clearly was important to Steinbrenner. The third and narrowest stricture was simply to get along with Reggie Jackson.

The following Monday, June 18, Billy was spirited away from a Florida golf course and flown to New York where he was met on his arrival at LaGuardia by hordes of press. The next day, his first on the job, was full of expectation—mainly having to do with what kind of coming together there would be with Reggie Jackson. There was none: Jackson, injured at the time, came and left, avoiding the press and not speaking with Billy. When he did make a clubhouse appearance, it was with his agent, Matt Merola. Merola said he might have been there "only as a bag-schlepper or as a buffer for Reggie," but there were no fireworks, not even a meeting. The Peace of Columbus held—but, unfortunately for Billy and the Yankees, the team did no better under him than it had under Lemon.

On August 1, on a day off for the team, Thurman Munson died in a plane crash. In a real sense that was the end of the season for the Yankees. There could be no recovery from such an event. It went beyond the world of games. The tragedy left the team without even the will to continue. Billy heard the news while he was out fishing with his son and he went to pieces. His relationship with the surly, hard-nosed catcher, though usually warm, was complicated. The two men quarreled and nearly came to blows on a team charter once because Munson had been playing his stereo too loudly; Munson was also one of the players involved in that infamous post-midnight meeting with Steinbrenner in Milwaukee. Munson was his own power center on the team, as much a spiritual "heart and soul" of Yankee baseball as Billy. Billy admired and loved him for that—even as he may have been suspicious of it. He also loved Munson for the way he handled the press.

"Thurman was Dad's favorite," Billy Joe Martin said, "and the thing he probably loved most about him was that Thurman wouldn't talk to the press. He'd turn his back on 'em and just look into his locker or he'd look at 'em and say, 'Go to hell, get out of here. I'm not giving you leeches anything.' My dad used to just look at him and say, 'I wish I could do that.' "

With the team inert, barely able to complete the remaining weeks of the season, Steinbrenner's justification for bringing Billy back was fading. There was tranquility in the clubhouse, but it was not the kind Steinbrenner sought. Relations between Billy and Reggie, though not cordial, were better than at any time in their joint stay with the Yankees. But Reggie's relationship with Steinbrenner had soured and it was clear his playing days with the team were numbered.

Then there was Billy's relationship with the front office. For his part, he went nearly an extra mile to get along. Al Rosen, within a month of Billy's return, resigned. Gene Michael, close to Steinbrenner—close enough for Billy to regard him as a likely spy in the clubhouse—reported few problems with Billy. But occasionally it was hard to locate Billy. When he didn't want to be found on the road, he had a system; he bumped a trusted coach, usually Art Fowler, from his room and stayed there, receiving only those messages he chose to receive.

Steinbrenner was hardly impressed with the new Billy Martin. His nightlife was just as visible as ever. The relationship he was having with "a teenager," was, in fact, considerably more than that. The young woman, Heather Ervolino, eventually Billy's third wife, was sixteen and Billy had met her while she was literally hanging around the players gate at the Stadium. She lived in a housing project nearby and was an autograph hound—for her younger brother and his friends, for herself. She had long hair and was, said nearly everyone who eventually saw her with Billy, exceptionally pretty. Billy's "aunt," Lucille Sabatini, saw up close what Steinbrenner undoubtedly was discovering from his own vantage point:

"In New York, in '79, we went to this Yankee game and had seats in Billy's box. There were these two young girls sitting in front of us and they were really into the game, they were real Yankee fans," Sabatini remembered. "This one girl had to be about sixteen—it was Heather. I said, 'How do you come to know someone on the team?' and she said that she and her girlfriend used to stand outside the players entrance after . . . after every single game and they got to know the players. She said Billy had told them they were such great fans, he would let them sit in his box. So they went to the games on him. Well, *right*. Big dumb Dora's sitting back there saying, 'Oh, how nice.' Well, next thing I know, he's going to *marry* Heather. I learned that a year later in Oakland when I was sitting behind the dugout in the first row and Billy introduced me to this girl, Heather. I said to myself, Where have I seen her before? I said, Ahh, I know who it is, same girl who was sitting there in Yankee Stadium. She was seventeen now and she had hair down to here."

What Steinbrenner probably surmised was, whether because of the distractions of Billy's off-field life, the numbing loss of Munson, or the gradual effects of familiarity, Billy's magical ability to jump-start a team was no longer there. In '78, when he was fired, even players who supported him were wearied by life in the clubhouse. "There was just no peace of mind," Sparky Lyle remembered. "The team started going through the same things Billy did. You know, either leave him alone or get rid of him. . . . I mean, all of that was just affecting the atmosphere . . . I'm not gonna say any one person or the whole team—but there was always that air. You just hated it."

Billy did finish the year, and with a winning record. The team, which had been 34–30 when he took over, finished with a record of 89–71. But that meant fourth place and, in terms of movement in the standings, it actually represented a decline. The Yankees were eleven games out when he took over, thirteen and a half behind at season's end.

It is likely that Billy would have been retained in 1980—even if his status made him seem more like a condemned man waiting for a stay of execution than someone with a new vote of confidence. Steinbrenner, though, was spared having to make a decision.

In late October, only weeks after the season ended—and well before the winter meetings—Billy was involved in his now-famous run-in with a marshmallow salesman. The details of the dispute were highly troubling. Initially, Billy said the salesman's injuries were caused not by a fight but by a fall the man took as he followed Billy and a friend out of a hotel lounge. Another, more plausible version of a quarrel was given later: The guy had been relentless in pestering and then challenging Billy, and blows ultimately ensued. Steinbrenner, said Eddie Sapir, was particularly enraged by the accidental fall story. "He just felt betrayed when he heard it—but the thing was he hadn't spoken to us yet," Sapir said, always willing to include himself in his man's troubles. Five days after the event, Steinbrenner had completed his own investigation—by phone, he said—and he was satisfied that his worst fears about the new Billy Martin were confirmed.

"I didn't believe the story about the guy falling down for one second," Steinbrenner said. "Who would? I made a couple of phone calls to the hotel. I found out quickly what happened. Billy hit the guy. I was afraid for Billy. I had to get him away from people, away from bars, away from this kind of thing. I was worried some guy would pull a gun or a knife on him. I didn't want that for Billy or his family. There was one other thing that made up my mind quickly. When Billy hit this guy, he fell down inches away from one of those huge metal andirons. If the guy hits his head on that, he's dead. Wouldn't that be something, the manager of the Yankees on trial for murder?"

Fortunately for Billy, Steinbrenner never let him find out. Rather than having to face the music as Casey Stengel's heir, he now would be able to do it as just another out-of-work baseball manager—and one who had seemingly run out of options at that. There were, it seemed, no owners in the game willing to hire the new Billy Martin—or the old one—when he hit the unemployment line that winter.

# CHAPTER 15

The winter meetings came and went without Billy finding a job. In fact, not only was there no job, there was trouble. The umpteenth brawl of Billy Martin's career brought a response from the baseball commissioner's office. Billy was going to be investigated with a view to possibly barring or suspending him from the game. There was no doubt in Billy's mind that George was behind the move though he could not prove it, and he of course fought it.

Because there was neither real substance nor much appetite to prosecute, the matter was soon resolved, though testily rather than happily: Sapir and Billy assumed, on the basis of a meeting in New York they had with Sandy Haddad, the commissioner's chief investigator, that the matter had been resolved with no action taken or contemplated, just an unofficial and amorphous warning to stay out of trouble. In fact, subsequent correspondence indicated that as far as the commissioner's office was concerned, Billy, though not penalized, was on probation, officially compelled to remain on his best behavior so long as he was in baseball.

In a curious way, this heavy-handed and inept intrusion by the commissioner's office may have saved Billy. The commissioner at the time was Bowie Kuhn, despised by many owners and none more so than Charles O. Finley, owner of the Oakland A's. Finley, hearing of Billy's troubles, and suspecting that Kuhn was trying to bar him from the game, simply stepped in and offered Billy a job. Talks were begun with Billy's agents sometime in January 1980, and contracts were signed on February 21, only days before the scheduled opening of spring training.

On the face of it, the chance to manage Finley's A's was about as appealing as getting a sheriff's badge in a frontier town two hundred miles from the nearest law. (Of course, for Billy that would be immensely appealing.) Finley was in his last year in baseball. His one-man war against big salaries and free agency had left him tilting against baseball windmills—and his own team—for years. The once dominant A's of the early 1970s finished dead last the year before Billy was hired, losing 108 games. More than that, the organization was on life-support. Finley was his own general manager, the scouting and farm departments had been all but eliminated, and the office staff had been reduced to a single secretary who worked with limited phone privileges and without use of a copying machine. To many, Finley was a laughingstock, no longer a legitimate owner.

But beyond the opportunity to drop a banana peel at Bowie Kuhn's feet, Finley had shrewd and sound reasons for hiring Billy. Uppermost was his belief that, if anyone could quick-start interest in his team, it was Billy. Attendance the previous season had dropped to just over 306,000. There were games when there were hundreds, not thousands, in the stands. (A local columnist asked the following trivia question: "On April 17, an Oakland-Seattle game drew 653 people. Name them.") Any kind of winning would be sure to help there. Of course, there was also Billy's star appeal—no one else on the team had even a grain of it; and then, Finley knew, Oakland was Billy's home, so he would be playing to a hometown crowd, excited to have him back among them.

For Billy, the pay was no incentive. In fact, he was initially reluctant to work for the money Finley offered—an insulting $50,000 a year for two years—but when the pot was sweetened by Steinbrenner himself, willing to avoid a battle on Billy's last contract—was he or was he not fired for cause?—by paying the difference so that the A's contract matched the Yankees' ($125,000), the question of dollars simply vanished.

Billy, of course, was also worried about Finley, another infamously "involved" owner. But Finley was no George Steinbrenner and, in fact, was in the process of weaning himself from baseball entirely. The deal he had with Billy was simple. "Billy understood right from the start how things would work. I had only two conditions," Finley said. "One was that I had the final say in everything; the other was that I never wanted to talk to him when he was drinking. We got along just fine. He was great. I used to joke with him years later that I was the only owner he ever worked for who didn't fire him."

For a while, Billy never saw Finley—even when he wanted to. Finley was in Europe for a period and then conducted most of his business by phone from his office in Chicago. Billy actually wound up complaining about it—not to Finley but to friends. Bill Reedy remembers hearing it from Billy enough to have finally told him, "Listen, you were forever bitching about owner interference and now you're complaining about the owner *not* bothering you?" Billy, if he did not understand it going in, soon came to see that he really was taking his stand in Finley's mock-up of the Last Chance Saloon.

Actually, he did not need Charles O. Finley or anyone else to tell him about last chances. He began managing the A's against a consensus view that he was nearly unemployable, that drinking, brawling, and endless feuding with management finally outweighed any advantages he brought to the field. His last year with the Yankees had compounded that view; he had been unable to jump start the team he took over from Bob Lemon, the first time a Billy Martin team responded to his leadership with—nothing. So, in the most fundamental way, he knew that it was not only his good name but his professional career that was now on the line.

But, as Finley had reminded him, he was home. That was a decided plus. He was back among his own and away from the pressures and distractions of New York with its snarling and unforgiving press. His family was here, most of his childhood friends—a few with whom he had stayed in touch—were now within easy reach. In West Berkeley, all through the lower bay, his earlier problems had long been forgotten. He was a hero, someone who had gone out and been a Yankee, a famous one at that, and who all the while had never let anyone forget where he came from and why. Here, in this one place, whatever kind of team he had, he could at least experience to some degree his deep-seated desire to be famous and still be himself.

The fact that expectations were so low was also an advantage. When the A's assembled for spring training in that first year under Billy, there was youth and a pitching staff that had given up almost five runs a game the previous season. These A's were more like the first page of a ledger sheet than a major league roster.

To all of these young players, to the staff Billy had assembled under him, to the minor league coaches he brought in to learn the system, to the curious media accompanying the team, to anyone who would listen, Billy declared that the A's were not only going to do better in 1980, they were going to win. Of course, he had said this before—but he had never had to back it up with a team quite like this.

But just because he was dealing with young and inexperienced players rather than veterans, with a farm system that was as dead as an abandoned mine, he was able to put his stamp on the A's from the start, to shape the team to his own image. Billy, making his last stand, pulled out all the stops. In this one time and place, with his back to the wall, he was able to create himself as never before. Here he could be a kind of supreme genius. The inept A's, far from being his albatross, could be his wings. With one monumental creative effort, summoning all his experience, all the tricks of the trade acquired over a lifetime, he might now swoop down from the shadows of defeat and show the world who he really was.

To the greenhorns in that first camp, just the sight of Billy, with that Yankee past and the almost visible Yankee logo over his heart, brought an aura of greatness. Players were initially frightened of him, pitcher Mike Norris remembered.

"Very early in spring training, he had this team meeting to tell us what he wanted from us. I mean here he is, Billy Martin, everybody is scared shitless to begin with," said Norris, "and then after he tells us the do's and don'ts, like how we're supposed to dress, he looks at us with these hard eyes and says, 'I want you guys to know that I'm the type of manager who if you try to screw, I screw back harder.' Well, you could have heard a pin drop after he said that. When I saw the looks people had on their faces, I just started laughing. Billy glares at me. 'I want to see you after the meeting,' he says.

"So afterwards, I go into his office and he asks me why I was laughing, what was it he said that was so funny? I told him it wasn't anything he said, it was the way people took it—that they were scared shitless of him. Then he looks at me and says, 'You weren't scared?' I just laughed again. 'No,' I told him. So he sorta smiled and nodded and said, 'Okay.' "

Norris also remembered a lesson about losing that he picked up from Billy. Early in that first season, Billy elevated Norris from the depths of his staff. He called him in one day and told him he would henceforward be the ace, a designation, Norris said, "that gave me a tremendous boost of confidence." After winning an early game, Norris lost a close one in extra innings and on a team flight afterward, feeling in a playful mood, Norris removed a doily from the passenger seat in front of him.

"I cut out this mask, you know, like a Ku Klux Klan mask, and put it on and went up front—you know, just a joke—to see if I could scare Billy," he said. "The guys tried to stop me, to warn me, but I went up to the first-class section and went, like, 'Boo.' Well, Billy just totally lost it. He started screaming at me, 'Don't you ever fucking do that when you lose a game. When you win twenty games, then you can do it.' When I won my twentieth game, I did do it again—because I had never forgotten that. I cut out another mask, put it on, and scared him with it. He just busted out laughing."

From the start, Billy's goal was not to pull rank but to get his troops to play and see the game the way he did. He was after something. For the young players, it was new, it was different, it was exciting.

Playing baseball in Oakland then, Rickey Henderson said, was "more fun than at any other time" in his career. "When Billy Martin came in, he made the game more fun—he made all of us what we are today. . . . Because we had rookies and guys in their first year and stuff, everybody wanted to listen to what he had to say—he was more like a teacher than a manager. We didn't have great hitters or great players, we had scrap players. He taught us to manufacture that run without a hit. He taught us how to win."

Billy taught them relentlessly. He intimidated, coaxed, praised, lashed out. He wanted to impart experience but, above all, he was after a way of thinking—his way—a way that was always ready to take advantage of any situation, to improvise, rattle, unsettle, undo the opposition so that they would be forced into mistakes, into having to play defensively, back on their heels.

"He pushed hard, he was a little intimidating, but he kept you always on your toes," said Dave McKay, the second baseman. "He taught us how to manufacture runs. Every one of us became bunters. He'd want you to bunt the ball on a hit and run play, you know, guy takes off for second, you bunt towards third and then the guy doesn't stop at second, he keeps going, you've moved him from first to third on a bunt. We worked on almost everything, so that if you were ever asked to do it in a ballgame you knew you could."

Billy taught Henderson what he had taught Rod Carew: that stealing came first from the head and then the legs. Henderson in those days was never allowed to steal on his own. It was always off a direct sign from Billy. But that was a teaching tool, Rickey said.

"He taught me how to read a pitcher, to get as far away from the base as I could. He taught me how to go on a pitcher's windup, the point where he reaches the top of his stretch, before he comes set, tells you when you can go—people don't normally think of that, it's much too risky, but you can see it if you study them enough. Billy at first made me take the sign from him, but then he said, 'When you catch on to what I'm doing, then I'm going to turn it over to you and you'll have the green light.' That's what he did."

Billy had his players steal on odd places in the count—on 3 and 0, for example, where a steal would not only be unexpected but might seem almost foolhardy. "You draw a throw—say it's on ball four—you draw the throw and that throw very often will go into center field because the steal then isn't being looked for."

Billy taught them his old standbys, like the double steal of home, with the runner at first falling down to draw a throw. He taught the runner at first to make sure he fell near enough to the first baseman so that a tag would be instinctively applied—the tag itself forcing the first baseman to stretch out so that he would not be able to recover in time to make a throw home. He taught the suicide squeeze, and the shock value of stealing bases with two out.

He taught them odd things like the value of a safety squeeze when three runs or four runs had already scored in an inning and the likelihood of an even bigger inning was in the offing.

"He liked to finish off a rally with a squeeze," said Bob Didier, a minor league manager who was in that first camp to learn the system Billy wanted taught throughout the organization. "You'd have two or three runs, a guy hits a triple and is on third, there's only one out; a lot of teams—most teams—would say, let's get three more. Billy just wanted the one more. He'd get a four-run inning and he'd use that squeeze. I think it's one of the most intimidating plays in baseball when you bunt a ball ten to fifteen feet and score a run and the other team is crushed."

With a player like Rickey Henderson, Billy could do more with the running game than he ever had before. Henderson, running with a pitch, not only had the ability to unsettle defenses, he could always take the extra base. He had the speed and the aggressive instinct, for example, to score from second base on a routine ground out—something he did several times in those years.

What all of this added up to was that Billy's rag-tail army wound up believing in itself. As intimidating as Billy might have sometimes been, the players wound up convinced that what they were learning gave them an advantage others did not have.

Billy's staff mirrored the man. Clete Boyer, his third base coach, was, Billy said, "the best in the business because he perfectly anticipated me, he never tried to manage the game from the third base coach's box." Art Fowler not only kept 'em laughing, but more pointedly, he taught his young pitchers how to cut, scuff, moisten, and otherwise do funny things with baseballs. He was expert at it—and loyal. Billy had a little mound built near his trailer where Fowler worked out of the view of the media and other camp followers, showing his young pitchers every last nut and bolt in his burglar's bag.

More than anything, Billy fashioned a team—distinctive in style and able to compete. It was unlike other major league teams in that it was really a Swiss watch of delicate and specific cogs and wheels. "There was a guy on that team named Jeff Cox," recalled Syd Thrift, "who we had released two or three times when I was at Kansas City. I had him at the baseball academy. Billy actually hired this guy that first year at Oakland just because he could bunt. That was it. Jeff Cox was a bunter and Billy used him specifically when he wanted a squeeze. Billy had him pinch hit three times in one week and three times the guy squeezed a run home! Never saw anything like that in my life."

Neither had the American League. The A's did not win anything in 1980 but they astonished everyone. For the first couple of months they doggedly trailed Kansas City, heavily favored to win the pennant. At the end of May, the A's had a winning record (25–22) and trailed the division-leading Royals by a scant two and a half games.

The Royals put the race out of reach in June, but the A's revival had just begun. Trailing by twelve games, nine under .500 in fourth place, the A's won fifty-one of their next eighty-seven games, finishing the season in second place with an 83–79 record. Though still fourteen games off the pace, they had gained almost thirty games in the standings. And, in terms of business, the swing meant more than half a million additional paying customers. Billy, hands down, was named AL Manager of the Year and Charles O. Finley was impressed enough to sell the team, gratefully declining Billy's suggestion that he make a bonus payment to him for so obviously increasing the value of the franchise.

When Finley sold the A's at the end of that season, Billy's fortunes, unlike those that accompanied the sale of the Rangers after his initial season there, were dramatically improved. The Haas family, purchasers of the club, was not only wealthy but was totally committed to putting the A's back on the baseball map. And Billy, it turned out, was at the center of their plans. They, even more than others, were impressed by his genius. He was immediately given a new and generous contract—five years with an understanding (at least on Billy's side) that an additional five years might be added later; he was given full use of a magnificent home in the exclusive Blackhawk area north of the city—and, at the end of ten years, he would have the option to buy the house from the team at the original price they paid for it.

The new management, quick to acknowledge its own inexperience, relied heavily on Billy. A decision was made early in the new regime to have no general manager interposed between the ownership and the dugout. In effect, that turned the function of general manager over to Billy. He became the team's director of player development. In that first year, at any rate, the baseball future of the organization itself was placed entirely in Billy's hands.

Suddenly, there opened for him a realm of control and opportunity he had never known. He had a free hand now to do what he wanted, with the owners' money and confidence behind him. Not only did he have a decisive say in trades but in hiring as well. He was able to fill the farm system with coaches and managers of his choosing, to build a scouting staff, even to bring people into secondary administrative positions.

Billy became a one-man hiring agency, remembering many old friends, teammates, drinking pals, people he knew only casually but whose talents or needs he valued. Over that winter and all through the following season, Billy stocked the system. Steve Vucinitch, a friend and one of the A's clubhouse people, remembers accompanying Billy on some of these sentimental hiring forays:

"He had an open checkbook when the new owners took over, he could hire his own people," Vucinitch said. "So the scouting director, farm people, minor league managers, scouts—he was able to hire them all. What he really wanted to do was hire a lot of his old friends from the Oakland Oaks—just to be bird dog scouts, right in this area. They didn't have to pay them that much money, but they would have the card and it would be such a help to their self-esteem. When he and I would drive through the old neighborhoods in Berkeley, he'd go into his old haunts and see some of his old drinking buddies that he had played ball with. I remember one guy—can't remember his name, but we went into this bar and waited for him. Billy hadn't seen him in fifteen or twenty years and all he knew was that he hung out in this place. Guy comes in—he was driving a Pepsi truck—and Billy said, 'I'm going to do everything I can, I want you to be one of our scouts'—and you could just see the look of pride rise in this guy's face.

"He did that with one guy after another."

That next spring, Billy began his labors full of hope. He ran an oversized camp, bringing in minor leaguers from every level, coaches and managers from the entire system. By comparison, the large camp he had for the Rangers was as nothing; at the A's camp, Frank Ciensczyk, the equipment manager, remembered "there was even a guy out there with a uniform number in the hundreds on his back—never saw that before."

There is another story that Frank Ciensczyk tells of a side trip that Billy took to Tombstone then, when he felt free enough to enjoy the symbolism of such a diversion.

"We had two cars and we went to Tombstone. Billy wanted to see the O.K. Corral, he wanted to go to the bar where they all hung out," Ciensczyk said. "There was a local guy who ran the museum and he had the key to this place so it took awhile to find him when we got into town. I found the guy finally, and he came down and opened the place up for us about nine o'clock. Billy was like a little kid in a candy store, so excited. The guy showed us the rooms where the whores were, showed him the room the madam had—where Lillie Langtry would end up with a cattle baron. Then the next day we went to the corral where the shootout was. Billy said to Art Fowler, 'You be one of those guys and I'll be Wyatt Earp and let's have a gunfight.' "

The energy, the joie de vivre, with which Billy hurled himself at his expanded job, was infectious right down to the clubhouse. The players, with a year of success behind them, were by now believers and fierce partisans. The majority of them felt passionately about Billy—and played that way.

Roy Eisenhardt, the team's first president, acknowledged that he was "on a steep learning curve" when he took the job. He literally went to school under Billy Martin, he says, more so than any of the players. The time and effort Billy took with this former Berkeley law professor was both exciting and touching.

"I was the luckiest guy in the world," Eisenhardt said. "I had a tutorial in the game and Billy Martin was my tutor. It had to have been pretty hard to work for a lawyer who had never been in baseball, but he protected me from people who were out to take advantage of my naivete. When I told him I didn't understand something about the game, he'd sit me right next to him in the dugout and he'd show me. He did that all through our first spring training. He took pains to do it. He'd show me how the hit-and-run worked, how to watch the second baseman so that I could pick up his timing—because it was all a matter of timing, you could tell if someone was leaving his position early or not; he showed me how positioning worked, was a guy too close, too far from the bag? Did he bail by taking a throw on a steal in front of the bag or did he stand in? He taught me how to read situations in ways that I couldn't begin to imagine—and he did it all with a sense of charm and humor. He used to call up to the owner's box from the dugout during a game just to make a joke about something. He made my assimilation into the game a very good one and I'll never forget him for that."

Billy again reminded his players how important it was to get off to a good start. He had the players set their minds on sweeping the season's opening games, Dave McKay remembered.

"You learn to win by winning and we had won," McKay said. "Before the season, Billy said to us, 'Show you how good we are, we're gonna sweep these guys,' the California Angels—or whoever it was. See, Billy was never afraid to go out on a limb, that was what made him so good—and he gave that to us. I think when Billy made that remark about sweeping, that was the time that Bobby Grich came out with that line, 'That's what drinking does to your mind.' Billy didn't like that—and we went out and swept them. And then a couple of other teams, too, so that we were in first place that year right from the start."

Billy was not just inspirational and improvisational, he also had a calculated eye out for ways in which he could boost the team and organization. He was a tireless public speaker and luncheon guest. He had a keen sense of what he could do to build the sort of interest on the field that would carry over into profits. Winning, of course, was the key. But there were other things, too—like jousting with the California Angels. "The A's really didn't have a traditional rival when we got here," Mickey Morabito said. "Billy always felt they would fill that role, and he went out and promoted that—and very successfully. The Angels have become our big rivals and attendance now shows that."

Above all, Billy understood the value of the imagery he had created. Whatever personal benefit he derived from being the kind of leader and celebrity he was, the team benefited as well. The excitement, the aggressive daring, the genius of the old-style game that the A's presented, so clearly a reflection of the manager, sold the team better than anything. A local sportswriter coined the term "Billyball," and when the A's roared through April with a record 18–3 mark, carrying them to the top of the division, Billy's picture appeared on the cover of *Time* magazine and "Billyball" had become part of the national lexicon. The idea of bedeviling opponents by out-thinking and out-hustling them, by doing "all the little things," captured the imagination of the baseball world. Even battling with umpires seemed to have a certain kind of publicity value. When Billy was involved in a dirt-kicking—and -throwing—argument with Terry Cooney in a June game at Cleveland, footage and headlines followed. It was all part of the new Oakland A's. The fact that Billy was fined and suspended for a week by the American League really seemed beside the point. Billy had simply stood up to an umpire as he stood up everywhere else. Little guys—and some big ones—continued to applaud this little engine that could, even as the clouds of a major labor strike continued to gather over the season.

The strike surely marred this miracle. Nearly two months were cut from the season—two months in which there was time for steam to be released from the engine and strength from pitching arms. Mike Norris later said the long layoff period was an underlying cause of his subsequent injury problems. The A's, still effective, were not quite the team they were when they finally resumed play later in the summer.

Still, as first-half winners (by a game and a half over the Rangers), they qualified to play the second-half winners, Kansas City, for the Western Division title. They swept the heavily favored Royals with their patented combination of tough pitching and daring, improvisational offense. Mike Norris pitched a 4–0 shutout at Kansas City in the opener; Steve McCatty held the Royals off, 2–1, the following day, and then the series switched to Oakland, Rick Langford pitching a complete-game 4–1 victory for the title.

The AL East winners were the Yankees, and much was made of the collision that followed because Billy was going up against his old team. Billy publicly denied but privately acknowledged how much the series meant to him, and his anguish at losing—being swept—matched any he had known. But the reality, inescapable and overarching, was just what he had accomplished. With or without asterisks, he was clearly the Manager of the Year—for the second straight time. In the minds of many, he was the manager of the era. He had not only made good on his last chance, he had turned it into an El Dorado. By any standard, he should have been on top of the world, able to control his own destiny as never before.

However, that was not to be. Roy Eisenhardt, years later, said that Billy was the "greatest manager I ever saw from the first pitch to the last. It was the time from the last pitch to the first the next day that got him into trouble." His life away from the field was as rudderless and as subject to capsizing as ever.

All through Billy's years in Oakland, he had been trying to get back in touch with his roots. He spent time with his family, with old friends. Billy's mother, publicly proud of her son as he was of her, was a regular and conspicuous visitor at the ballpark. There was, though, a nagging question of money—how much Billy helped or did not help his family out. Frank Ciensczyk, who organized and handled personal expenses for Billy then, remembers that Billy "regularly wrote out checks for a thousand dollars to his mother," and that "he sent the whole family to Hawaii in '81 or '82, and picked up the tab for all of them, plane fare, hotel, all of it." Ciensczyk acknowledged, however, that conflict existed within the family over the level of Billy's financial support. Though he wouldn't give details, Ciensczyk said, "I don't think Billy deserved what he got from his family."

Lucille Sabatini remembered that Jenny got thousand-dollar checks from Billy, but also that they were delivered to her by third parties, not, apparently, by Billy himself. There were long periods of time when mother and son didn't see each other. Jenny, apparently, was never a guest in Billy's Blackhawk house in all the time he resided there.

There was a quarrel within the family at one point over Billy's apparent unwillingness or inability to find a job for his half-brother Tudo.

"Tudo came over to my house one day," Lucille Sabatini said, "and he was so mad at Billy—because Billy was managing Oakland and he felt that he should have given him some kind of job. And I said, 'Tudo, maybe he can't give you a job.' He said, 'He could make me a scout.' "

Billy, in this same period, grew closer to his father, with whom he had had virtually no relations over the years. Al Martin was ill with terminal cancer and Billy, when he found out about it, began making hospital visits to him.

"He went to the hospital to see him all the time," Frank said, "they actually grew very close then. Whatever happened between them, Billy wound up forgiving him everything." Kelly, Billy's daughter, did not remember closeness developing, but that there was indeed a visit. Her grandfather was delirious, "talking to the angels," holding on only so he could see his son one more time, asking that nothing be said to Billy about his mother's past as a hooker. Billy did see his father, Kelly said, in those final hours. Whatever was said then, or in the weeks and months previously, she was not privy to, but closeness, contact of any kind, meant that the whole gnawing uncertainty surrounding Billy's birth and early family life was once again part of his day-to-day thinking.

Then there was the issue of the woman—or women—he was seeing.

Heather Ervolino, the sixteen-year-old girl Billy had been going with, he brought to California, installing her—and then her family—in the house at Blackhawk. He eventually married her in a small, quiet ceremony in New Orleans in 1982. At the same time, he was openly seeing another woman, Jill Guiver, a twenty-five-year-old freelance photographer who sometimes worked for AP. Guiver met Billy on assignment at an Angels-A's game in 1980 when, she said, "Billy just walked up to me and said, 'I think I'm in love.' "

The triangle that subsequently developed was in the best traditions of *Captain's Paradise,* except that Billy didn't have an ocean separating him from his loves—both of whom were young enough to be his daughters—and he was no Alec Guinness caught in a droll celluloid fantasy.

The two women, though both extremely young, were radically different. Heather came from a family that had known hardship and poverty, Jill from a family that had money and connections in the sports world. Heather, according to many people who met her with Billy, was self-effacing, very much in love with Billy, and happy to remain in the background. "She dressed very properly, primly almost," said one friend, "because she knew Billy had a tendency to be jealous. She had few friends and kept to herself a lot. She had little interest in spending money, but then again Billy had her on a budget and wouldn't allow her to have credit cards." Friends who were closer to Billy had little impression of her. Tex Gernand, Billy's longtime chauffeur, remembered Heather's youth and not much more. Lucille Sabatini was struck by Heather's almost inert presence in the house at Blackhawk. Shortly before the arrival of guests for a fancy dinner party at the house one night, Mrs. Sabatini, helping in the kitchen, noticed that Heather was still in a housecoat.

"Heather, your company will be here pretty soon, don't you think you better get dressed?" Sabatini remembers asking. "Heather said, 'Oh, I've got plenty of time, I'm so nervous I don't know whether I'm coming or going.' I guess she was ashamed to meet these people or something, I don't know. I said to myself, when you're in the limelight like that and you're supposed to be entertaining, you just can't let things like that happen to yourself."

Jill Guiver, on the other hand, was a much more forceful woman. Young as she was, she had her own career, her own strong interests, and her own sense of what she wanted from her life—and, ultimately, from Billy Martin.

The two relationships deepened simultaneously. Billy lived with Heather in Blackhawk and, sometimes, with Jill in Newport Beach, outside Los Angeles. For a time, Billy managed to slip from residence to residence, from life to life, without attracting attention.

Vicki Figone, the daughter of a close friend of Billy's, who was herself Billy's—and Heather's—friend, sometimes met Billy at the airport when he returned from one of his stays with Jill. "He used to give me his car when he'd go out of town on so-called business trips and stuff. I can remember a couple of times picking him up at the Oakland airport," she said, "and him paying off the guy at the baggage area—$20, $40, $100, Billy was a big tipper—and he'd go to United and get maybe three baggage tags from New York, rip off the AirCal–Orange County tags from where he was with Jill and replace them with the United tags."

The cost of this deception, whatever it was in emotional and spiritual terms, was increasingly difficult financially. Not only did Billy maintain two households, each had its own costly complication. Heather's New York family, including her nearly paraplegic mother, a grandmother, and a young brother, came out to visit and, at Billy's suggestion, stayed on permanently in the house at Blackhawk.

Jill had an expensive passion for show horses. Increasingly, as she appeared in Billy's company on road trips, in and around hotels and airports, and on team flights (Jill said Billy's travel costs for her in one season were $50,000), the triangle became almost common knowledge—except, apparently, to Heather, who remained in Blackhawk, out of touch with Billy's everyday life.

And then there was Billy's drinking, which continued unabated—and in plain view. Ciensczyk, the clubhouse man, had a drink waiting on Billy's desk at the end of every home game. Vicki Figone, a kind of surrogate daughter, used to meet Billy frequently after games and drink with him and his coaches in lounges and restaurants near the ballpark. Figone believed Billy had gotten a bad rap as a drinker and brawler over the years, but she was also certain about his drinking habits.

"I saw Billy drunk so many times, I mean almost every night he was drunk when we left to go home. He was an alcoholic, completely," she said, "no question about it." But, she emphasized, "Billy handled his alcohol well. A lot of times you couldn't tell he was drunk. Usually, Billy was always in a better mood when he drank; if Billy would drink, I would say that he was more of a happy drunk. Unless something happened that would tee him off," she said, "then he would get moody."

Old friend Lee Walls, then a coach on the A's, also observed Billy's postgame drinking. "Listen, I know Billy," he said, "I tried to drive him home many nights to Blackhawk and the SOB wouldn't let me drive."

Though many of his friends remained unaware of it, Billy was deeply concerned about his health during his years with the A's. In the seventies, that "spot" that Steinbrenner leaked to the press had been discovered on his liver. The report of this to Billy, according to Dr. Harvey O'Phelan, the former Minnesota team doctor who was familiar with the case, was done "more to scare him off drinking as much as he was" than to alert him to an actual condition. It is unclear if Billy ever learned that this was a piece of medical sleight of hand. What is clear is that, sometime around 1980, Billy got news of a very different kind. Following treatment of some sort—what exactly and where remains uncertain—he became convinced that he had cancer.

In spring training that year, Steve Vucinitch remembered that Billy stopped drinking for a while. "He told the press that he needed to lose some weight, and here was this skinny, fragile person. And the truth was, it was bothering his stomach, and he needed to *gain* some weight. They wrote that he needed to lose weight."

Lucille Sabatini and her daughter, Carol Lazaro, were Billy's guests one night after an A's-Orioles game in Baltimore that year. Sabatini was visiting her daughter, a Maryland resident, and the women and Billy were driven by limousine to a crabfest at a local restaurant. During the course of the evening, Mrs. Sabatini said, Billy stayed close to her—and then told her something that alarmed and frightened her.

"All through that dinner, he sat with his arm around my neck," Mrs. Sabatini said. "He confided in me. He told me that night he was kinda sick. He said, 'I don't want you to say nothing to nobody, but I'm kind of . . . sick.' I told him he had to take better care of himself, but he had never been like that with me before so I asked him what he was sick with. 'Cancer,' he said. He told me that they had discovered cancer. And I didn't believe it. I told him, 'I don't think you're telling me the truth, Bill.' And he said, 'Well, it's the starting of it.' "

Steve Vucinitch remembered Billy telling him about cancer, too. But he was uncertain about the specifics.

"I was pretty sure that he had colon cancer," he said. "I didn't know anybody else knew about it, but I didn't think I was getting any privileged information on it, either. One year, when he wasn't managing here, I know he was having problems. I suggested that he see this one doctor, I said, 'Why don't you talk to him, you have all the confidence in the world in him.' Then I talked to that doctor, I said, 'Doc, talk to Billy, you're one of the people he trusts. Maybe you should talk to him and find out what's wrong.' And I thought—I didn't know if it had been officially diagnosed as colon cancer at the time, but I thought somewhere along the line he told me he had that, but it wasn't that bad."

Sometime in 1986, long after two well-publicized operations for hemorrhoids, Billy also told Secoro "Choke" Mejia, one of his old boyhood Berkeley friends, that he had cancer—and that it was colon cancer.

"Billy told me he had it for quite a few years," he said. "I was with him this one night about three, maybe four years ago. He was so thin, thin as a rail, and he looked so bad. I grabbed him and said, 'What's the matter with you, Billy, you're so skinny'—he didn't weigh over 130 pounds. He says, 'Oh, Choke, I've got it.' He told me he had it. I don't know how bad it was but I know he had it taken care of twice. He told me he had colon cancer."

Mejia was uncertain but believed he had been treated, at least once, at the Mayo Clinic in Minnesota.

Whether or not Billy actually had cancer—or only believed he did—is at present impossible to say. Jill Guiver Martin heatedly denied that her husband had any history of cancer. She promised but ultimately did not produce medical records that would have corroborated her contention. She did acknowledge Billy's problems with hemorrhoids but referred to them as minor and of no consequence.

Billy's closest friends—Bill Reedy and Mickey Mantle—as well as his longtime advisor and friend, Eddie Sapir, also—and just as emphatically—say that Billy never told them about having cancer, and that he would have if he had had it.

There seems to be no possibility of reconciling the different versions. Because not one but three different and unrelated sources remember Billy telling them that he had cancer, there is reason enough to believe that *he* believed he had it—at least for a time. The fact that he did not share that information with others like Bill Reedy or Mickey Mantle or even with his wife is similarly inconclusive. It is certainly plausible, if not provable, that he might have wanted to keep such information from anyone who might—even if only accidentally and unintentionally—reveal his secret within the circles of his profession.

There is another possibility: Billy's belief might well have been a tangential result of his chronic drinking. Ryne Duren, the ex-Yankee and recovering alcoholic, is just one of many professionals in alcohol rehabilitation who believes that fear of cancer, specifically, is common among drinkers.

"I wouldn't trust that Billy actually had cancer at all; the alcoholic mind is kind of funny," Duren said. "Let me give you a little insight. When I was going through that low time in my life, I didn't truly want to die and I couldn't take my life, I guess—though on some level I did want to die. I wanted to go out legitimate; a suicide would have been the coward's way, I suppose, so there's a kind of death wish—there's no doubt whatsoever in my mind about that. The death wish for me was, well, maybe I've got the big C and will die from it. I had tremendous pains going on in my abdomen and unconsciously—I never could bring myself to admit it directly—[I felt] if it's cancer, so be it, that's it, I die. I kept drinking right through it till I had such pain and was throwing up all the time that I went into the hospital, finally, and they took out my appendix. I've since seen that kind of mind-set again and again in my work with alcoholics."

Ultimately, all of the pressures Billy was dealing with—financial, marital, familial, medical—became silent partners to what he was doing on the field. The A's in 1982 were unable to repeat their triumph of the year before. The team got off to a miserable start and never recovered, finishing fourth with a 68–94 record, more like the dormant A's of '79 than the division-winning Billyball team of the year before.

The reasons for the skid were plain enough. One after another, beginning in spring training, the A's starting pitchers, the backbone of the team, went down with disabling arm injuries. Without great pitching, the A's in the field and at bat, except for the outfield of Rickey Henderson, Dwayne Murphy, and Tony Armas were a very ordinary group. And, as the pitching staff broke down, a willingness to blame Billy for it emerged. He had been the one who, putting winning ahead of players' careers, pushed these pitchers to record numbers of complete games, exposing them to injury. The charge probably carried more weight than substance. Though it was true A's pitchers led the league in complete games and innings pitched for two years, they were breaking-ball pitchers who normally got balls in play before going deep into the count. Their low pitch count per game (often in the 90–100 range) was better than average and a better barometer of their actual work load. The pitchers themselves never blamed their ills on overwork—or on Billy. Norris cited the strike; Matt Keough, a fall he took that caused a partial rotator-cuff tear during one game; Langford, an accumulation of innings early in his career. Still, the charge persisted. It became one more plank in an old scaffold. Billy was a cattle-rustler, he got things moving quickly but sooner or later managed to bring on a hanging party.

Billy, sooner rather than later, seemed to know that there might be a hangman's rope waiting at the end of 1982. He was unusually testy as early as spring training. Discovering that Art Fowler was absent or late for work one day, he fired him. He discovered Fowler, after kicking his door down, asleep in his room and on the spot told him he was finished. Typically, Billy re-hired him the next day, but the tone for the year was set.

There were incidents during the year, late arrivals at the ballpark, drunkenness aboard team flights. One of Billy's coaches, on one occasion, was so inebriated he walked through a plate glass window in an airport lounge. Another coach passed out with drink outside one of the team hotels. Then there was the front office.

No one—not Billy, not any of the A's executives—ever was willing to go on record with reports of dramatic flareups between them, because there were none. Instead, there was a continual, low-level, debilitating unpleasantness, compounded by the losing. Management at one point wanted to introduce computers to aid him in his work. Billy emphatically told the front office that he was not interested.

Then there was the question of Billy's propensity for hiring cronies and friends. While there was no problem in the beginning, there was when Roy Eisenhardt's old friend, Sandy Alderson, joined the organization at the end of 1981.

Alderson's job duties were initially administrative, but Billy was quick to suspect him, especially when it became clear that Alderson did have large authority within the area of baseball operations. Alderson made frequent trips to the different minor league teams in the system, the only A's executive to do that. He made the trips to learn, he said, because he, like Eisenhardt, had no background in baseball. But Billy was the team's director of player development—an official title.

Unlike Eisenhardt, Alderson did not go to school with Billy Martin. In fact, his view of the manager was considerably different from his friend's.

Alderson, from the start, was aware that the A's were still losing money, and was skeptical of the team's success on the field. "Billy might have understood winning a lot better than the rest of us," he said, "but a franchise is a franchise, just the term alone connotes something more substantial than a year-to-year proposition. Certainly in Oakland it was something we had to establish, because we were in very rocky financial shape in those days."

Alderson never questioned Billy's tactics or strategy, whom he played or didn't play. Instead, he looked around at the House That Billy Built and saw the patronage-seekers lined up at the doors. The payroll was fat with waste—long-term contracts to players, scouting and coaching jobs for too many people whose chief qualification seemed to be their closeness to Billy. Team costs were top-heavy with expense-account charges made by scouting and player development people who got A's charge cards from Billy. Minor league managers and coaches, most working for wages that would not sustain them through the winter months, had been given large bonuses by Billy. The manager and director of player development, Alderson concluded, was good for his friends but not always for the A's.

Billy's reaction to what he believed was interference and even hostility from the front office was all too predictable. He became suspicious even of those who were his friends and supporters. He suspected his old comrade-in-arms and drinking buddy Clete Boyer of spying on him for management. For almost a year following his dismissal from the A's, his conviction that Boyer had actually been politicking for his job remained firm. He refused to speak to him. He told Lee Walls, who went with him to the Yankees the next season, that he would fine him a thousand dollars if he so much as exchanged greetings with Boyer or coach Jackie Moore when the Yankees and A's met for the first time that year.

His problems with Roy Eisenhardt, the devoted executive who sat as a student at his feet, seemed even more self-inflicted. Over the course of the '82 season, he grew impatient with Eisenhardt, with his questioning, with his naivete, with his scrupulous fairness. Eisenhardt, at one point, became upset that Billy was managing a game by telephone after he had been ejected by the umpires. Billy laughed Eisenhardt's objections away.

Far more seriously, at one point Billy, trying to deal with cascading financial and tax problems, wanted to get an advance on his future salary. Because he had already been advanced money, and because a new advance would mean a contract commitment the A's at that point were not willing to make, Eisenhardt turned him down. Billy was furious.

That night the A's lost a tough game to the Brewers, 10–6. Any loss was liable to turn Billy's blood to bile. This one caused a septic system backup.

Entering the clubhouse from the field after leaving the dugout early, Billy proceeded to physically demolish his own office. The destruction was shocking and almost unbelievable. Furniture—chairs, sofa, desk—was savaged, personal objects were hurled and smashed, walls were battered; a large, heavy metal chart of the A's entire minor league system was ripped from its fastenings and thrown to the floor. When the fury subsided and the cleanup was completed the following day, the costs of the damage ranged anywhere from $10,000 and up. Billy's job with the A's, nearly everyone understood, was about to end.

Roy Eisenhardt and Sandy Alderson both deny that the office destruction played any real part in their ultimate decision to fire him weeks later at the end of the season. For Eisenhardt, the real issue was that a change had become necessary for both Billy and the team. They had wearied of each other, the cycle had run its course. Eisenhardt was personally pained because of his feelings for Billy, but he ultimately made the decision to fire him.

Alderson had a narrower and sharper view. He was overwhelmingly concerned for the organization, only secondarily for Billy. But just because he did have an almost philosophic commitment to structure and process, his view of Billy, seemingly incidental, was haunting:

"To me, there are two basic components to success, professional and personal," he said. "It is very possible for someone to be greatly accomplished in one area but not at all in the other. Something I read some time ago distinguishes between the pursuit of excellence and the pursuit of winning, and I guess I would say that the A's over a long period of time have been committed to excellence, and that has sometimes been inconsistent with winning. I'm not saying we have always erred on the side of excellence, but there has always been this commitment to process. We built a structure in which people could go about their work with a sense of security, knowing there's going to be a fairly consistent response to what they do, positive or negative. That's not quite the way Billy operated.

"If I can go back to those two components again—the professional and the personal—his success on the field wasn't matched by any sort of success in his ongoing personal relationships. When that happens, once the professional success disappears—which is going to be the case in any professional sport eventually—there won't be any underlying good will. There were any number of incidents beyond the office destruction that preceded his firing. The office destruction was not as important as the destruction of some of his relationships. I think his downfall was the destruction of his relationships."

Alderson also had a clear view of what it was Billy accomplished—and lost—when he left Oakland:

"Probably his most important contribution was that he re-established the A's as a power—as a baseball entity, I would say, more than a power. He was an incredible baseball entity himself—and that was something on which we were able to build. A number of us came into the game at that time and learned a great deal from him; any number of our players today, Mark McGwire, Jose Canseco, came into the organization while he was there, so I think he deserves a lot of credit for re-establishing the franchise and for doing something for others to build on."

Billy Joe Martin, Billy's son, had a simpler sense of what his father lost when he left Oakland. "He was happier there than I have ever seen him in his life," he said.

# CHAPTER 16

The last years of Billy's life were forever marked by the mocking and unsparing divisions of his hirings and firings. Billy III, Billy IV, Billy V, became tags for these divisions, and for the absurdity, inflated importance, and ultimate pathos they represented. Billy in these final years, said longtime Yankee beat writers Bill Madden and Moss Klein, "was not the same cunning, calculating, and combative manager he'd been in 1976–77. He had become a caricature of himself."

Whatever one makes of this last phase of Billy's life, its most significant aspect is that it was Billy's own choice, reflecting that oldest desire of all in Billy's makeup: to reach that place he had been striving for all his life, where once and for all he might stand unequivocally honored and accepted. He chose to return to the Yankees—to the waiting arms of George Steinbrenner—and that choice, it turns out, was a knowing and calculating one.

Billy was fired by the A's on October 20, 1982. He was hired by the Yankees on January 21, 1983. But the hiatus between those dates was illusory. Within days of his firing, talk was rampant in New York that he would be returning. By November, all of the metropolitan dailies carried stories that he was the next Yankee manager, awaiting only the formality of an official announcement. But the Yankee job was probably in the works before the A's fired him.

Tex Gernand, chauffeuring Billy on the East Coast then, remembered that Billy told him on the A's final 1982 visit to Baltimore that he would be coming to New York the next season. "It was the last game Oakland played in Baltimore that year," Gernand said. "Billy told me in the car that he was going to be the manager of the Yankees next year."

The last Oakland-Baltimore game in Baltimore in 1982 was on July 25—a month before the office trashing, almost three months before the firing.

Rickey Henderson, who had grown close to Billy, also remembered Billy telling him—prior to the office carnage—that he was going to manage the Yankees the following season.

"He told me about two or three weeks before he tore up his office. It was on the road and we were just messing around," he said. "I knew he was a diehard Yankee fan and we got to talking about the team going down, it was losing, going nowhere, and then he just told me. And he knew that if he was the manager of the Yankees he could turn it around."

In September, after the office trashing, the Yankees asked for permission to speak to Billy—the first clear indication that something was taking shape—though it now seems all but certain that this end game in Oakland was more elaborate than anyone knew at the time. The Yankees may or may not have tampered with Billy, Billy may or may not have been actively politicking for the Yankee job while he was still under contract to the A's, but clearly more than impulse was bringing about Billy's last days on the West Coast. When the change was made, it was anything but impulsive; Billy was headed for the place he had decided he most wanted to be.

Billy's friends, relatives, former teammates, and opponents all talk about his ongoing attachment to the Yankees. It never was and never could be a put-on. Because he was not the most talented Yankee, Billy was always fond of saying he was the proudest one. He said it early and late, through the last part of his life; the words have since been carved on his tombstone.

It's not hard to figure why the Yankees meant so much to him—or why they inspired in him this almost pathological desire to lead them when ordinary common sense should have made him run the other way. The Yankees were still the symbol, no matter what, of the baseball world, the standard which others hoped to outdo. Their name, their history—which George Steinbrenner cherished—clung to them despite George Steinbrenner. They were the most powerful, most prestigious, wealthiest sports franchise in the country. As they had been in the gray days of Ike, so they continued to be in the gaudier, greedier days of Reagan.

However, Billy was anything but a sentimentalist in negotiating his return. He knew the team well; its personnel had played both for him and against him. He knew he could bring them a World Championship, and knew in personal terms what that would mean for him. In recent seasons the team had slipped. They had lost in the playoffs in 1980, had dropped the split-season World Series of 1981, had lagged badly through several managers in 1982. They were a team exactly in need of his talents.

There was another, even more basic reason for his return: money. However lucrative his future might have seemed in Oakland, it could not compare with the promise of New York. He was hard-pressed; he was at least three years late in filing tax returns; two wives and a girlfriend had claims on him. Business investments had not worked out; he had to sell his share in a Western wear store he had in New York, and another he partly owned in Minnesota went belly-up. A racehorse he had purchased with a friend in California had not paid off. In addition, TV commercial offers were drying up; the freewheeling Miller Lite spots that had brought him fame and money in the seventies had stopped. It was a different age—one in which a battling cowpoke who didn't slug that dogie was no longer a comfortable fit.

The Yankee contract he worked out, however, was satisfying on many levels. Steinbrenner, because he knew better than anyone that his ship had developed a list, made ample provision for Billy this time. The contract was multi-year—with no good-boy clauses. There were even safeguards built in against owner impetuosity. Part of the contract was guaranteed at the highest level of pay, manager's pay; the remaining years were also guaranteed, but in other capacities: broadcaster, special assistant to the owner, scout. Judge Sapir, Billy's advisor, believed then and afterward that the contract not only showed Steinbrenner's good intentions but his good heart, his actual concern for Billy. "See, what the press never understood is that every time George fired Billy, he didn't fire him—he just moved him to another position. The contract allowed George to be George and at the same time it gave Billy security." There was also an attempt—acknowledged by Sapir—to make this contract so advantageous that Billy would not be tempted in the future to stray from the reservation. The contract was, at the time, unique—and Billy knew it.

But clearly it was not just money Billy was after. He was fifty-three now, and time and mortality ticked away in his body, were on his mind, were visible in the drawn and haunted look of his face. He had still not accomplished what he wanted. After all these years, after all the experience and accolades, he was still scuffling to make it, still Billy the Kid, still on the move, still unsure of how things might turn out.

What he wanted from himself, how he saw himself, was plainly visible on the wall of his office in Yankee Stadium. There was, most prominently, a framed uniform jersey and photographic montage of Casey Stengel. There were framed magazine covers, one from his days as an over-achieving Yankee player, another more recent one celebrating his days as a manager with the headline "The Yankees' Fiery Genius." There was a photo of Willie Nelson, a celebrity friend whose mother let him grow up to be a cowboy, and then there was a cherished letter from Ronald Reagan, a president whose unabashed patriotism and elemental sense of right and wrong were most in accord with his own.

Billy, above all, wanted to be a leader.

Leadership—the idea of it, the practice of it—fascinated him. It lay at the heart of how he wanted to be remembered as a manager. He had always been interested in leadership, from the time he was a gangking and sometime student of history in West Berkeley to the present. From the time World War II first fired his imagination, military figures and military campaigns fascinated him. As an adult, he maintained a continuing interest in military and Civil War history. He could spend hours with friends—Rex Barney's son-in-law in Maryland; Chris Cavanagh, the son of Detroit's mayor, in Michigan—disputing battlefield body counts, explaining strategies or his fondness for the Confederacy (rebels wanting to be free). His heroes were men like Douglas MacArthur, George S. Patton, Robert E. Lee, George A. Custer, Jeb Stuart—men whose extraordinary achievements came from an unorthodox fighting ability matched to passionate devotion to a flag and cause; unorthodox men, leaders all, who inspired their troops by a willingness to risk hopeless odds and dare the unexpected for the sake of a victory that might never come—whose own nature often earned them the scorn of superiors even as history elevated them to positions of honor and renown.

The Yankee yearbook for 1983 has a cartoon cover depicting Billy nose to nose with an umpire. Given the actual battles with umpires that soon were to occur, it is not unlikely that this notion of leadership—a turnstile clicker and certainly not foreign to Billy's style—was a public relations paste-on by George Steinbrenner. But Billy was yearning for much more.

Howard Cosell, an old friend, remembered introducing Billy to Col. Earl "Red" Blaik, the celebrated Army football coach, at a golf tournament shortly before Blaik died in 1989. Cosell had pointed Blaik out to Billy and recalled how Billy grew excited:

" 'I've got to meet that man, Howard, he's always been one of my heroes, he's one of the great leaders,' " Cosell remembers Billy saying. "DiMaggio was with us and he said that Blaik was not only one of the great sports leaders but of our country. So I took them over. I thought Martin was going to go out of his mind. Blaik says, 'I know about you, young man, you're a leader, you can lead young men.' And I tell you, I never saw Martin like that in my life. He had gotten praise and he said, 'Howard, did you hear what he said to me? Col. Blaik said I'm a leader of men.' "

The Yankees of 1983 offered Billy the army he did not have in Oakland. It is true they were not the championship Yankees of the late 1970s—gone were Thurman Munson and Reggie Jackson, as well as a number of other key players like Mickey Rivers, Chris Chambliss, Catfish Hunter, and Bucky Dent—but the team was solid enough. Dave Winfield, while no favorite of Steinbrenner's, was not only a superstar but a great all-around player. Don Baylor was tough, powerful, a presence in the clubhouse; Ken Griffey gave the team a bat, some speed, and championship experience in the outfield. The team was top-heavy in designated hitters—nothing new there—and somewhat thin in pitching—again, nothing new. There was veteran experience from one end of the dugout to the other, and players like Graig Nettles, Willie Randolph, Ron Guidry, Goose Gossage, and Lou Piniella whom Billy knew and, above all, could count on. This team did not require the manipulations of Billyball to win, they did not have to overachieve; all they had to do was stay clear of injury and play the way Billy wanted them to. The Yankees were a reasonable favorite to win everything in 1983.

It was all a pipe dream.

There was neither a championship nor a semblance of coherent leadership on this team. The same old Billy and George show began in the spring with the principal owner bidding his team good-bye and promising them that he would not see them again until the All-Star break—if everything was going well. Less than three weeks into the season, with the team struggling below .500, the vow of silence, like Esmeralda's monthly vow of chastity, was broken. The owner, alarmed at the team's slow start and concerned that Billy was not exerting the necessary "discipline" to keep things focused, appeared in Texas at the end of April to greet and meet his team. Preceding the owner's arrival, there were the usual blasts to the press about his willingness to have the "kids from Columbus" lose if his high-priced stars couldn't win, and also about what moves Billy should be making that he wasn't. It was all so predictable, so wearying. The owner presented the manager with statistics showing why Butch Wynegar rather than Rick Cerone should be the team's everyday catcher, he criticized other players, and then he made sure the press understood that he was worried about his manager's well-being—hadn't he, after all, been ejected from a game only days before when he kicked dirt all over umpire Drew Coble?

Steinbrenner's unspoken message was harder to take than those he voiced: Leadership came from above, not from below. The manager's responsibility was down on the field, to be the leader's surrogate in the dugout.

Leadership, from any side, was exactly what was impossible under the circumstances. The closed door meeting in which George singled out different players for criticism—which Billy, after George had left, told his players to forget—was soon leaked to the press. By the time the team returned to New York, Henry Hecht had written a column in the *Post* carrying what appeared to be a direct and accurate account of what had taken place in the supposedly sealed locker room.

Some of the regular reporters who covered the team then are convinced that the next turn of the wheel—Billy's frightening and stunning locker-room denunciation of Henry Hecht—was actually engineered by George. At least one writer remembered that the day before, at Billy's post-game briefing, the telephone on his desk rang and that Billy, in the course of the conversation that followed, used the phrases, "No, I hadn't read it. . . . Henry, huh? . . . I'll take care of it tomorrow, George."

Tomorrow turned out to be an infamous confrontation with Hecht, a longtime antagonist of Billy's (and someone known to have had good relations with George). Hecht was one of the reporters who was present for Billy's "One's a born liar" broadside, and his writing had always seemed to underscore what was menacing, unstable, out of control in the manager's off-field life. Billy was reasonably convinced that Hecht, if he could, would always go out of his way to get him fired. The account of Billy's tirade by Geoffrey Stokes matches that of nearly all other accounts that appeared at the time:

Because of a persistent drizzle, batting practice was cancelled before the Yankees' May 15 game with the White Sox, and the players were all hanging around their lockers. So when Martin, in undershirt and uniform pants, emerged from the trainer's room and began shouting, "Hey, everybody, we have a meeting right here," he had no trouble drawing a crowd. As the reporters present—including Hecht—prepared to leave, Martin said, "No, no, you guys don't have to leave." He looked directly at Hecht and said, "Particularly this little prick right here."

"We had a meeting down in Texas," he rasped. "It was supposed to be a private meeting, and I think it was. At least I haven't read anything true about it in the papers. But I did read, in a column by a guy who wasn't even there, about some things that were *supposed* to have happened. Now I didn't say don't ever talk to writers, but I'm saying right now: Don't talk to Henry Hecht."

"There he is," shouted Martin, pointing an accusing finger at Hecht, who stood as calmly as possible under the circumstances—perhaps ten feet away, "and if there ever was a fuckin' bastard, there he is. He's the worst fuckin' scrounge ever to come around this clubhouse. He doesn't care if he hurts you or gets you fired, he just wants to *use* you. He got me fired twice, and now he's trying to make it a third time. And if you talk to him, don't talk to me, 'cause I don't want to have anything to do with anyone who talks to this little prick."

"You're paranoid," said Hecht.

"I'm not paranoid. I don't have to be paranoid to see that you're a little prick. You're not welcome in my office. You can come into the clubhouse—I wouldn't ever take away a man's right to earn a living—but you're not welcome in my office," he repeated as he marched past Hecht and toward the sacrosanct retreat, finally muttering, "If that little bastard comes in here, I'll put him in the fuckin' whirlpool."

George Steinbrenner had no particular comment about what happened—strange, in light of Billy's wild behavior and of the universal and embarrassing coverage it received. There was no great effort either to immediately challenge or protest Billy's edict limiting a reporter's clubhouse privileges—which may or may not have reflected a general sense that Billy's feelings for Hecht were not entirely unjustified. In the overall scheme of things, this was just another day in the zoo, soon replaced by diversions in other cages. But what was not forgotten—and what cost Billy dearly—was the memory of this outburst. No one needed to take sides or to analyze anything. Billy's behavior was either so calculatedly mad or so compulsively driven that conclusions were inevitably drawn. In the press corps covering the Yankees then, there were writers who liked and admired Billy. But there were fewer than ever. The overwhelming number, especially the veterans who had been there before, who were used to turmoil and more in the erratic life and times of Billy Martin, knew nothing had changed and they had been around long enough to know that weariness and frayed nerves, more than excitement and winning, were going to be the team's daily bread. Whatever anyone thought of Henry Hecht, there was, among the people Billy—or any manager—needed most on his side in a duel with George Steinbrenner, an unspoken assumption that the manager was unbalanced.

If the owner was not disturbed by the outburst at Hecht, he was certainly soon engaged by other incidents that pointed up Billy's increasingly erratic and unreliable behavior. On May 24, just ten days later, Billy was in a brawl with a patron in an Anaheim bar. After losing five out of six games at the end of a home stand in early June, Steinbrenner ordered a mandatory workout for the team in Milwaukee; Billy countermanded the order, making the workout "voluntary." Steinbrenner, inevitably, found out.

Then, during that weekend, Billy was seen, by fifty thousand people in County Stadium and most of those in the press corps, carrying on a conversation, passing notes to and fro, with an attractive blonde—Jill—who was sitting in the front row next to the dugout—while the game was in progress.

Around this same time, during one of the team's home stands, Lee Walls, again coaching for Billy, remembers a particular dugout phone call from Steinbrenner.

"When I picked up the phone, this guy says he wants to talk to Billy. I knew who it was, but I asked anyway," Walls said. " 'It's George,' he says. I say, 'George who?' Well, he just screams, 'George *Steinbrenner*, let me talk to Billy!' Okay, I hand the phone to Billy, he listens for a few seconds and then you know what he does? He says, 'Fuck you, George,' and he just rips the sucker right out of the wall. Fifteen hundred dollars' damage at least."

By the time the Yankees had finished that Milwaukee-Cleveland road trip in mid-June, Steinbrenner, amidst flurries of media leaks and reports all concerning Billy's behavior, was ready to move. At a midnight meeting in Cleveland the day before the team returned to New York, a decision was taken not to fire Billy, but to fire Art Fowler. The decision was revealed the next day in New York and ultimately touched off a clubhouse explosion of far greater magnitude than the one involving Hecht.

This time, Billy's target was an innocent bystander—a woman reporter for *The New York Times*, Deborah Henschel, who was in the clubhouse taking a survey for the paper on player preferences for the All-Star game. Only a short time before, Fowler had been informed by Steinbrenner of his decision to let him go. He had passed Lee Walls in one of the hallways under the stands with a $30,000 check—his remaining salary—pasted to his forehead. Billy, highly distraught and possibly drunk, had also had his meeting with Steinbrenner and saw Henschel when he entered the clubhouse. His explanation for what followed was that he thought Henschel was someone's girlfriend, dressed with "a slit skirt up to here, like a professional [hooker]," and that she had no business in the locker room.

Henschel, seven years later, still remembered the sight of Martin suddenly coming toward her, fury on his face:

"I was standing there . . . and out came Billy Martin. I knew it had to be him because he looked really forceful and angry. I thought, Oh boy! . . . I tried to start to ingratiate myself. . . . What he said then, I don't remember very well, what he said afterwards I remember very well. . . . I left in order not to make him more angry. I left everything there. Notebook, pencils, ballots, everything. I sort of left with my hands up, like to tell him I wasn't going to attack. . . . There was such rage in his face. It's funny, one thing stands out in my mind more than any other is this visual picture I have of him, of his *eyes* going like pinwheels, they were just . . . whirling . . . just like coming from nowhere, cutting through the air."

The uproar that followed had mainly to do with reports that among the profanities Billy used in driving Henschel from the clubhouse were several suggesting that she perform oral sex on him. Henschel today says that Martin's suggestions were directed at the *Times* rather than her personally, but her sense of having been abused and humiliated was overwhelming. The *Times* subsequently would not allow Henschel to comment on anything that had happened because it had a policy of not having its reporters submit to questions concerning their work or sources. That refusal ultimately spared Billy.

Immediately following her banishment from the clubhouse, Henschel called her desk, the desk notified Steinbrenner of what had taken place, and Steinbrenner summoned Henschel to his office. Henschel reported the results of the conversation that followed in an internal memo to her editor at the paper:

"Mr. Steinbrenner apologized for the manner in which Mr. Martin spoke to me," she wrote. "He said there was no excuse for it and that he was awaiting Mr. Martin in his office for a word with him. He told me off the record, Mr. Martin was drunk at the time, and that he was 'mad' in the head and they frankly do not know what to do with him. He said this was the end of the line and they did not know what they were going to do. He was apologetic and embarrassed. After the fifteen-minute conversation . . . Steinbrenner asked Mr. Pat Foley to escort me downstairs and assign a guard to remain with me during the duration of my assignment in the Brewers' locker-room."

The main reason that Steinbrenner did not fire Billy then—as he clearly said he intended to, as he undoubtedly had positioned himself to in the days preceding—was because none of the eyewitnesses to the incident (there were about five, Henschel remembered) were willing or able to corroborate her description of the language Billy used. An in-house investigation as well as one conducted at Steinbrenner's behest by the American League were left with no choice but to clear Billy of serious wrongdoing. The owner was left with a rather lame "boys will be boys" explanation for what happened, declaring that young women, if they were to enter such sanctuaries as a locker room, had to expect such rough and tumble.

But that of course was not the end of it, just the postponing of the inevitable. In reality, the generous contract Steinbrenner had with Billy left him little maneuvering room. The grounds for firing Billy "for cause" were severely limited; "shifting" him in mid-season risked the wrath of the public—which weighed in at the phone switchboards and in the mail rooms of the *Times* and the Yankees following the Henschel incident. Last but not least, getting rid of him also jeopardized their chances of winning. And Steinbrenner, though he may have thought his man was "mad in the head," though he may, in fact, have feared him as a politician might a great but unstable general, still had a campaign to win. He would take care of Billy later.

The Yankees themselves helped out by capturing nine of their next twelve games. For his part, Billy retained the backing of much of his team. The veteran players, used to a regimen of fear, loathing, and low comedy, simply went about their business.

"It was the same as before," Graig Nettles said, "we all knew what our job was, Billy knew what his was—and we did it. He wanted to win just as badly as ever and so did we."

Dave Winfield, in his third season with the team but already weary of a running feud with Steinbrenner, liked and appreciated Billy, he said, "because at that point he just let me go out there and do my thing and he tried his damnedest to put himself between me and the man upstairs."

The Yankees continued to win. From mid-June, when they were 6½ games back, till the end of July when they tied for first (their high-water mark that year), they won 23 of 33 games. Anyone following the team then felt the pickup in momentum and pace.

That changed with the season's—and perhaps the era's—most curious game. On July 24, in a game against the Kansas City Royals, the Yankees carried a 4–3 lead into the ninth inning. The win would have been their ninth in ten games and they came within an out of getting it. With two out and no one on and Dale Murray pitching, U.L. Washington rolled a single through the left side. Billy immediately brought in Goose Gossage to close out the game against George Brett. Instead, Brett homered, giving the Royals the lead. But Billy, who had been told by Graig Nettles that Brett used excessive pine tar on his bat contrary to league rules, and who remembered a "pine tar" hit taken away from Thurman Munson years before, leaped out of the dugout and protested. He was fully prepared for the moment, the exact paragraphs and subdivisions of text in the rule book clear in his mind. His protest was upheld, the home run was called back, and the game that was lost was won again. Billy had stolen another one for his team.

Except that this one didn't stay stolen. An on-field explosion from Brett, who charged the umpires with murder in his eye, was followed by a careful measuring of the combustible elements by the league office. The rules, which Billy had believed were so clear-cut, were ambiguous to League President Lee MacPhail, ambiguous enough that he allowed common sense to prevail. He reversed the pine tar decision. The home run stood. The last outs of the game, with the Royals ahead 4–3, would have to be played.

All through the days that followed, the labyrinthian preoccupation with the rules and their consequences, the game and its ramifications, seemed to distract and weigh on the team. The pine tar game became a kind of sideshow, a continuing source of statements, pronouncements, excuses. The Yankees barely managed to play .500 ball over the next weeks, falling from a first-place tie to third place when the pine tar game was completed—and lost—on August 18.

The completion itself was a farce and a further distraction. Up to the last minute, the Yankees were in court trying to get an injunction to stop the game. On the day the injunction was denied, the game was resumed as scheduled hours later in a nearly deserted stadium. Billy put Ron Guidry in center field and Don Mattingly at second base. Before the first pitch was thrown, Billy ordered his pitcher to throw to first base so he could get a ruling on whether or not Brett had actually touched the bag after he hit his homer. Tim Welke, the first-base umpire, gave the safe sign, and Billy was immediately out of the dugout with yet another protest: How could any of the umpires on the field then make a ruling when they were not on the field for the original game?

Dave Phillips, umpiring at second base, remembers exactly what followed:

"Welke was working first base and he was just an alternate at the time, so when he flashed the safe sign, [Billy] came over to me," Phillips said. "He says, 'I know where you were, you were in Seattle, I know you weren't here, and I want you to know I'm gonna protest this game if you're calling Brett safe at first.'

" 'On what basis?' I said.

" 'On the basis that he missed first base when he hit the home run,' he said. 'There's no way you'd know if he missed it or not.'

"I said, 'Billy, I'll tell you what. Just for your information, I've got an affidavit in my pocket.' I pulled it out.

"He screams, 'Affi-WHAT?'

" 'Affidavit,' I told him and I showed it to him. 'What it says is that all four umpires who were here signed this thing stating that George Brett not only touched first, but he touched second, third, and home legally—and the runner before him touched his bases—and it's all signed.'

"He was really pissed off. He says, 'This is a goddamn joke we're playing this.'

"I says, 'I don't know anything about jokes, I'm just doing my job.' "

The game—and then the season—was lost. The Yankees, never able to regain their mid-summer edge, dropped three out of four games to the first-place Orioles in the beginning of September to fall seven games off the pace. They never made a move after that, and when the season ended, George quietly "shifted" Billy to a scouting and special assignments slot in the organization. The off-season and the team's listless play precluded any upsurge of protest. On December 16, George named Yogi Berra as the team's manager. Billy, the mad and unpredictable general, was finally out of the way—for the moment.

In reality, Billy needed the time away to get a handle on his life. His health, as Steinbrenner was fond of pointing out, was not the best. At the All-Star break, Billy had been operated on at the Mayo Clinic in Minnesota for rectal bleeding, hemorrhoids. On the day Steinbrenner announced that he was being replaced, he was in Minnesota undergoing his second operation.

His drinking, at least according to those who traveled with the team, continued unabated. And then, on top of everything, his double "marriage" was in danger of flying apart.

Sometime in the beginning of 1984, Jill Guiver says she learned, purely by chance—from a remark by "one of the baseball wives"—that Billy was actually married. Until then, she claims, she knew only that Billy had been involved in another relationship—he had told her that from the start, she said—and her expectation had been that, in time, he would terminate it.

The idea that he was married—and had been for two years—was too much for her, she said:

"This friend of mine, and a very, very close friend of Billy's . . . said, 'You know, this is getting to be a bit much and if I was you, I'd call his bluff.' And I did. [I talked with him on the phone] and . . . I said, 'I have heard this and I don't believe you'—and bam! And the events that happened in the next two weeks in 1984, I have never seen anyone become—physically ill is the wrong thing but Billy was just . . . I mean the phone bill in that two weeks was just incredible. I mean, I told him I was very hurt, I never wanted anything more to do with him, you know, you've ruined my life, I trusted him, you know, all the horrible things you say out of anger and just being deeply hurt. And I wanted out."

But she did not get out. Instead, she said, "Billy just kept calling and calling and going back and forth on airplanes, it was just, you know, crying and desperately telling me how much he loved me and needed me and didn't want to lose me. And so, basically, I said if that's what's going on, you better do something about it. And you better do it real quick. And I was very hard on him."

The signs of just how vehement this quarrel between them became can be found in local newspaper stories in the Los Angeles area in early April, when police were called to Jill's house and Billy was briefly placed under arrest.

But, for many of Billy's friends who were either friendly with

Heather or mistrustful of Jill, the story of this uproar is regarded with skepticism. According to Bill Reedy and others, the person who called the police to the house was Jill herself, not her neighbors as she continues to maintain. The idea that she did not know Billy was married seems ludicrous to them.

"Jill said she didn't know he was married?" Peggy Sapir, Eddie's wife, said. "That's a crock. She just does not want to be portrayed as a person who went out with a married man, so her way of doing that is to claim she didn't know. But he was going out with both of them. Heather had no idea about Jill. Jill, I'm certain, knew, because she makes it her business to know everything—his house, the phone numbers, everything—it was quite obvious even before they were married."

Peggy and Eddie Sapir were in attendance when Billy married Heather in New Orleans in the fall of 1982, and the ceremony, though a small one at a French Quarter hotel, was made openly and drew local friends, including famed jazz trumpeter Al Hirt.

Billy, however, apparently did try to conceal the marriage. The day after the wedding, he left Heather in New Orleans "on business," meeting Jill in New York. The 1983 Yankees media guide, which routinely lists the marital status of players and coaches, said nothing about Billy being married or single.

His sensitivity to the whole question of marriage was apparent when he was told that a *Daily News* reporter had written up a description of his Milwaukee dugout sideshow with Jill. Hearing about it, he exploded, screaming at the reporter who informed him of the article, loud enough for others in the clubhouse to hear, "He wrote *what?* How the hell could he write that? Doesn't he know I'm *married?* I'm married!" But that outburst, sure to be picked up and passed on, not only risked further disclosure of his infidelity but also risked Jill's discovering that he was married—if, as she says, it was something he was trying to conceal.

Whatever the truth was, it is unmistakable that Jill Guiver, beginning in 1984, was no longer content to be Billy Martin's other woman. Her answer to his marriage—recently discovered or otherwise—was to hit him with a palimony suit, or at least the threat of one.

The threatened palimony suit, never brought to action, may or may not have been what she meant when she said that she was "very hard" on Billy, but it appears that he did then take steps to mollify her anger and to preserve his relationship with her.

"He paid somewhere between two thousand and twenty-five hundred dollars a month, purchasing her a brand new BMW," said Paul Tabarry, one of the lawyers who represented Billy in the matter.

Though Heather herself has declined to say anything, friends of hers were specific about the kinds of pressure they say Jill put on her. Jill telephoned Heather frequently, they said, suggesting strongly that she should vacate the Blackhawk house she occupied with Billy, that she should remove herself from a marriage her husband clearly did not want. Both Peggy Sapir and Vicki Figone remember Heather telling them of phone calls from Jill that were even more disturbing.

"The really painful part of this was that Heather wanted to have a child and they never did," Peggy Sapir said. "She'd say to me, 'I don't understand it, I don't use any birth control, I want to have a baby, but I don't know why it doesn't happen and I can't get Billy to go to a doctor.' So one of the things Jill did towards the end was, she called Heather and told her, you know, that Billy is sterile. Jill is telling this to Heather. And Heather was so taken aback by it. . . . Heather said, 'I felt like such a dumb jerk, here is this woman telling me that my husband is—it was all I could do to say, 'Of course I know that.' "

Vicki Figone, familiar with the same details, also thought that Billy himself knew that he could no longer have children. "I heard it was an accident—or the result of an operation," she said.

Jill Guiver, far from acknowledging any of this, claims that she had gotten pregnant from Billy—"sometime in 1984 or 1985," she wasn't sure—and that she subsequently had an abortion.

It is hard to precisely define anyone's motives where there are only clues along an empty trail. Why was Billy caught in this kind of dilemma anyway? What was it about him that not only accepted but induced such impossible and painful traps? It is hard to imagine that he did not intend injury to Heather, if only on some subconscious level; it's also hard to see what he sought in his other "marriage," beyond its excitement, its passion, its obvious trouble.

The temptation with Billy Martin, because the pieces of his life seem always to explode and to bring on hurt—to himself and others—is to see him only through these melodramatic leaps and bounds.

For the most part, Billy, even in his most troubled periods, tried to live quietly, tried to have a life grounded in the basics he craved from the very start. He wanted a life that would answer to a very different part of him than the battler, the winner, the leader of men—and women.

He tried, as best he could, to keep up with his children. Billy Joe, a teenager now, was of special concern. He visited him when he could in Texas. Billy Joe played baseball, and his high school team was coached by a man who embarrassingly played up a connection to Billy Martin. "Our team suddenly got green and gold uniforms one year, with the A's letter on it," Billy Joe recalled. "When my dad came to see me play, he'd just want to keep things quiet because he always had a deal with my mom that he'd never push me in sports—and he didn't."

On the road, during the summers, Billy Joe began to visit his father. Friendship slowly grew between them. "My dad was never a disciplinarian with me. He had only one thing he made a special point to stress—he always wanted to know if I had been going to church. On Sundays, he'd get me up and we'd go to church before he went off to the ballpark."

Billy's daughter Kelly also saw her father only sporadically. But she says they spoke often about their families and family life.

"He truly loved his granddaughter, my daughter Evvie," Kelly said. "There was one time, I remember Evvie gave him a baseball to sign and he just signed, 'Billy Martin.' I told him that was very warm-hearted and he got all upset about that. He took the ball back and signed it, 'To Evvie, with love from Grandpa.' "

The dream for him, away from the back-page follies, was the same one he always had, more elusive, more tormenting to him as it slipped further from his grasp.

In retrospect, the strangest symbiosis of all in his life—but the one that made most sense in the absence of real attachments—remained the one with George Steinbrenner. Where divorce long ago should have taken place, there was a marriage continued beyond all reason and all credibility, with each party bound to the other out of habit or need or greed. Billy certainly needed the job, the money, the attachment to the Yankees—the one family he always returned to. And Steinbrenner needed the constant publicity fix that any move involving Billy brought him. And he further needed the legitimacy that Billy, as a link to the Yankees' years of glory, provided.

The Yankees, under the kinder, gentler regime of Yogi Berra, meandered through a desultory season in 1984, finishing third, seventeen games behind the Tigers, who put the season out of reach in the first month and a half when they won thirty-five of forty games. A look at the attendance figures for the Yankees in 1983 and 1984 should alone have been sufficient warning. When Billy Martin returned that first year, attendance shot up by a quarter of a million to

2,258,000. In his year away, half a million fans went with him. The following spring, when Steinbrenner declared that Berra would be his manager for the entire season upcoming, the death-watch was on—and Billy's name again surfaced. It took all of sixteen games for Berra to be fired and Billy to be named as his replacement.

This time, however, not only was there disbelief, there was derisive laughter from the press and anger within the team. Don Baylor, hearing the news of Billy's return, upended a trash basket in the locker room to underline his sentiments. A day or so following, the trash basket had been transformed by one mocking columnist into a full-sized dumpster.

# CHAPTER 17

Jeff Torborg, then in his seventh season as a Yankee coach and Yogi Berra's man in the dugout when Billy returned, remembered how impossible it had been in 1983. The atmosphere was poisoned for him the moment Steinbrenner fired Art Fowler. Torborg was asked to step in and assume Fowler's duties, which had from the beginning of spring training been shared with Sammy Ellis. Torborg knew and respected Billy's feelings for Fowler and questioned the move. The owner talked about his decision for a while, Torborg remembered, and then simply told him he was going ahead, because "he definitely was the boss." Torborg, along with Ellis, then visited Billy in his office; it was the same day that Billy had the run-in with Deborah Henschel.

"He was very upset," Torborg recalled. "He felt that we had somehow been a part of that happening, that we had somehow undermined Art and undermined him, and we tried to tell him that we hadn't—he was in a real state of emotional distress. He was in tears and he was really shook that Art was fired, and he was very resentful towards us."

Ellis's memories parallel Torborg's except that he had been close to Fowler for a while and, he thought, to Martin. The three men regularly drank together during spring training that year at a local watering hole, The Greenbriar. Torborg, a teetotaler, was never included.

"As soon as the workouts were over," Ellis said, "we'd sit around there. I never laughed so hard in my life. The two of them were great storytellers and they'd entertain the patrons in the place hour after hour. One joke after another. Billy would remind Art of a joke and Art would tell it. Hilarious stuff. Then we came to New York and everything still went along pretty good . . . the idea of me working with Art as a co-pitching coach was Billy's idea, not George's, so from the start that never seemed to be a problem. . . . In New York, we continued to go out all the time. I would always go with Art, Lee Walls, and Billy would always join us—unless Jill was in town. Then after Art got let go, Billy just became paranoid—he became miserable to be with. After a ballgame, he would just get obstinate and talk down to people—talk down to me, talk down to others. I went along with that for a while and then after a few weeks I decided, uh-uh, I don't need that and I stopped going out with him—and from that day forward he thought I was one of *them*, but I never was. I was trying to help this team win. That's all Jeff was trying to do, all Zimmer and Yogi were trying to do."

The disintegration of the coaching staff, not unfamiliar on teams of Billy's where he had to use outside help, was almost total. Billy wound up believing his coaches either were directly spying on him for Steinbrenner or else were incompetent. Don Zimmer, who quit immediately following the season, had all but disappeared in the last half of the season. Torborg and Ellis remained branded as company spies, and were deeply and openly resentful.

"Billy made this statement later in the year," Ellis remembered, "that if it weren't for the jobs we had, Jeff and I wouldn't be able to get a job in Egypt. That was his quote. So after that, I made up a new team—called them the Cairo Pharaohs and they played in the Nile Valley League. And Jeff and I had already contacted the pharaoh over there who was gonna give us the job. And the thing was, he had more money than Steinbrenner ever thought of having, and we were gonna give Gossage—who was threatening then to become a free agent—we were gonna give Goose so much money, because he was coming with us along with a whole bunch of other free agents. And all that got into the paper the next day where everyone could read it."

When Billy began his tenure in '85, meeting his team in Texas, it was with another inherited coaching staff, one that everyone knew he distrusted. Stick Michael, for Billy, was a certain Steinbrenner informant. His relations with Jeff Torborg were sour from the first day and grew worse. On a team flight from Toronto, Billy blamed Torborg for a mixup in ticket assignments that left him, after a long airport delay, sitting in coach rather than the first-class section of the plane. Billy, who had been drinking, began to berate Torborg aboard the flight.

"When he gets on the plane, I'm sitting there reading a book," said Torborg, "and he's screaming at me, 'I'm the manager of the team! I'm the manager of the team!' I looked at him and said, 'I knew that.' He said, 'When you get the tickets, you get the tickets for me, not the players!' Boy, he was in rare form. I guessed he was loaded, but with that I unbuckled my seatbelt and jumped up and told him I wasn't the traveling secretary and I wasn't going to be talked to that way. The screaming could be heard all over the plane. I told him what he could do with his job. I assumed at that point I was fired." But he was not.

There was to be yet another fight later in the season, just after the Yankees had dropped three of four crucial games to the Blue Jays at Yankee Stadium. The Yankees, with just twenty-four games left, had closed to within two games of the first-place Blue Jays before that series and the losses, hard to take under any circumstances, had been compounded by Steinbrenner's public denunciations of the team and of Dave Winfield, derisively branded as "Mr. May." The day following, the Yanks played a makeup game against the Cleveland Indians. They led 5–3 going into the ninth inning when the Indians rallied for six runs, all against an ineffective reliever, Brian Fisher, while Dave Righetti, the team's top reliever, remained in the bullpen. To everyone watching that game or covering the team, the explanation for what happened seemed clear enough: Billy Martin had totally lost it. Jeff Torborg—because Billy Martin had informed him at the outset—knew otherwise. Righetti was to remain in the bullpen because the front office told the manager that Righetti had recently been overworked and should not be used.

Billy, undoubtedly in a funk, went after Torborg about the kinds of pitches Fisher was throwing. Four of the first five batters the Indians sent up in that inning were left-handed—with the left-handed Righetti standing there in the bullpen—and Billy wanted to make sure that Fisher, a right-hander, mainly threw fastballs prior to two-strike situations. A rookie catcher, Juan Espino, had been sent in from the bullpen—presided over by Torborg—and when Brook Jacoby, a right-handed batter, got a hit off a slider, the bullpen phone rang. Torborg recalled:

"Billy called me and said, 'Did you tell Espino to call for a slider on Jacoby?' When he told me that Espino said that he called for a slider, I said that I did. He started screaming, 'When I bring Fisher into a game I want fastballs.' I said to him, 'Well, Fisher's already been in there for an inning and a half or two, you had him sitting there on the bench with you, why didn't you tell him yourself?' With that he hung up. I was so mad, I tried to throw the bullpen phone onto the field but it didn't work because the cord came flying back. Righetti was so upset, he threw a ball out of the stadium—it was just an awful scene. And then when we got back to the clubhouse, I knew he was really upset with me, so he walked back to the coaches' room and started to get on me and I picked up the bullpen bag with all the balls in it and threw it—not necessarily at him but close to him. I hit a wall. A clock broke. I was really out of control."

There were no fisticuffs, just more angry words that carried all over the clubhouse. Everyone overheard them, but no one seemed to be paying much attention because by then the tone for the season had been so well established.

This team and this season, more than any other, had driven Billy into himself. The control he sought to exert, the leadership he wanted so badly to establish, seemed to elude him at every point. Players liked and supported him—some of them. Willie Randolph, Ron Guidry, Dave Righetti, and Rickey Henderson were solidly behind him. There were supporters even among players who had their moments with him. A woefully ineffective Mike Pagliarulo was asked, against his will, to turn around and pinch-hit right-handed in one game; even so, he believed that Billy was someone who "wanted to take chances, he didn't care how anybody looked, he tried to take advantage of every situation. He wasn't afraid of anything or anybody. Here's a little teeny guy, 150 pounds or whatever, and he'd just as soon fight anybody—and that always carried over. He'd always be arguing for his players whether they were right or wrong."

But too many players felt otherwise, either were at arm's length or, like Don Baylor, Butch Wynegar, and Eddie Whitson, were as alienated from him as any of the coaches. Baylor believed Billy Martin kept a doghouse from which there was no escape and that he had been in it since spring training, 1983, when he turned back a blank sheet to Billy when asked to note the names of any pitchers he would prefer not to hit against. Wynegar had come to feel so pressured and tormented by Billy that he literally feared for his own sanity. And Whitson, hounded and tormented by New York fans, impatient with his inability to produce consistently after signing a hefty free-agent contract the year before, was another case entirely.

In that crucial September series at the stadium against the Blue Jays, Whitson was hammered in the final game, won by the Blue Jays,

9–5. By the time the team reached Baltimore several days—and several losses—later, Billy who seemed to reporters to be near a breaking point, announced that Whitson would not be taking his turn as a starter because he had a sore arm. The person most surprised by the news was apparently Whitson himself. Whatever devils had been snapping at his heels through his time in New York this time nipped him higher up. Whitson, considered by many teammates as slightly crazy to begin with, clearly was in no mood for Billy's company the second night the team was in Baltimore. Following the game that day, won by the Yankees, 5–2, Whitson and a group of friends were drinking in the bar of the Cross Keys hotel, where the Yankees were staying. Billy, in the company of Bill Monboquette, arrived at the bar sometime later and, according to reporter Moss Klein, had mentioned that a minor incident he had been involved in the night before at the same bar had been instigated by George Steinbrenner, who had set him up in order to have an excuse to fire him.

Sometime later, Billy and Whitson collided. The fight was lengthy and terrible, spilling out onto the sidewalk in front of the hotel, resuming, unbelievably, after both men had ostensibly retired to their rooms only to confront one another again in a third-floor corridor. The press accounts were lurid and confusing, reminding readers of Billy's long history of brawling and drinking. The explanation he gave—that he was assaulted by Whitson only after he had tried to break up a disturbance at the pitcher's table—was treated with skepticism and a weight of history against which any explanation would have seemed dubious. Because no reporter actually saw the first blows, the matter was left as one more entry on Billy Martin's fight card.

There was a witness, however, who basically corroborated Billy's story. Albert Millus, a lawyer from upstate New York visiting Baltimore for the games, who knew neither Whitson nor Martin, was sitting at a table next to Whitson before the fight broke out. In a sworn deposition given on October 3, twelve days after the incident, he claimed that he was Whitson's original target. Millus noted that Billy had been drinking with Yankee broadcaster Frank Messer but "did not appear to be intoxicated" and that sometime later, shortly after midnight, Dale Berra and his wife joined Martin and Messer at the bar. Billy and Dale carried on what appeared to be a lengthy conversation and then, Millus said, "The woman who I believe to be Mrs. Berra stopped by the table next to us and spoke to Mr. Whitson. She knelt or squatted on the floor and he turned his chair to speak to her. As a result, they carried on a conversation directly to my right and no more than two or three feet away from me. I believe they spoke for approximately five minutes, but I did not hear any of the conversation until the end of it.

"At the end of their conversation, I noticed that Mr. Whitson was becoming agitated. At that point, I began to look at him. He was looking in the direction of Mr. Martin, and said, in words or substance, 'Because he isn't playing me' or 'Because the SOB isn't playing me.' At this point I deduced that Mr. Whitson was a ballplayer, and that he was unhappy with the amount of playing time he was receiving. . . .

"When Mr. Whitson saw me looking at him, he focused his attention on me, and loudly demanded to know why I was eavesdropping on his conversation. I do not remember the words he used, but I believe it was something like, 'Who do you think you are to stick your nose into my business?' I told him in words or substance that I did not know who he was, and had no interest in his business. . . . I then told him in words or substance that he was misbehaving for a man making '$90,000 a year' (it was my mistaken belief that $90,000 was the minimum salary for major league ballplayers). We may have exchanged other words but I do not remember what they were.

"After I made the comment about the $90,000, Mr. Whitson grabbed me by the throat. I was really taken by surprise, and did not really have time to react before Mr. Martin interceded. After holding me by the throat for one or two seconds, Mr. Whitson released his grasp. I do not know whether he released it voluntarily, or whether someone pushed him back. In any event, I looked up and saw Billy Martin between us. I do not remember what Mr. Martin said to Mr. Whitson. However, Mr. Conrad [Millus's companion, Glen E. Conrad, U.S. magistrate for the Western District of Virginia] informs me that Martin said, in words or substance, 'Eddie, you're drunk, you don't need this.' At that point, I believe Mr. Martin and Mr. Whitson were squared off."

Millus, who ironically was from the town of Fenton, New York, where Billy three years later bought property, may or may not have been a Yankee fan and may or may not have been a Billy Martin fan (or a Dale Berra fan), but the details of his statement are precise: Billy interceded between Whitson and himself. Millus went on to say that neither Martin nor Whitson appeared drunk, but that Whitson was clearly enraged while Billy at first seemed amused by the incident.

What followed, out of Millus's view, was what was picked up and reported. On the sidewalk in front of the hotel, the men grappled with each other and rolled on the ground, with Whitson taking Martin's head and smashing it against the concrete. Dale Berra, at one point, punched Whitson in the mouth, bloodying his lip; Whitson leveled Billy with a series of well-placed karate kicks—to the rib area, to the arm, to the groin. When the fight finally was ended, Billy, though still having to be restrained, had been devastated. He had suffered a broken arm, fractured ribs, multiple contusions of the face and body. Still, when it was done, he returned to the bar and finished his drink before going off to the hospital. When he returned, he spent the rest of the night talking to Willie Horton, the "tranquillity coach" he had been allowed to bring in with him when he took over at the beginning of the season. In these pre-dawn hours, according to Horton, Billy's overriding concern, despite the obvious pain he was in, was to walk through his clubhouse the next day and take his regular place in the dugout. "It was a matter of pride to him," Horton said.

And that he did, his arm in a sling, his gait unsteady. Prior to the game, Billy summoned pitcher Bob Shirley into his office. Shirley had been repeatedly passed over in his time with Billy, but because he was close to Dave Righetti, a Billy favorite, he retained something like cordial relations with the manager.

"He called me in and he had only one thing on his mind," Shirley said. " 'Can you believe that guy kicked me?' he said, 'He kicked me like a girl.' "

The real surprise was that Whitson returned to the team days later—with security guards positioned in the dugout—and that the Yankees, counted out, got up off the floor with their manager and actually made one last run at the pennant. Counted out after the Toronto series in New York, they edged back to within two games of the Jays going into Toronto for the final weekend of the season. An opening game victory moved them to within a game of the top, but they were finally eliminated the day before the season finale. Somehow Billy, surpassing the best traditions of Stella Dallas and the Mummy's Return, had kept them in it till the last moment.

Of course, from the moment the bodies hit the deck outside the Cross Keys, Billy's fate was sealed—in fact, it had been sealed long before. Just as in 1983, the turmoil, the unpredictability, the upheavals surrounding Billy's stewardship had already made up Steinbrenner's mind. The Whitson fracas was merely the excuse Steinbrenner needed and he took it: one week after the season ended, he named Lou Piniella the team's next manager. There was a certain amount of ego-soothing involved. All parties agreed that Piniella had all along been an heir apparent and that Billy had been grooming him for the job. In fact, when Billy took over the team that year, Judge Sapir had said as much. But anyone who followed the team knew otherwise or, at a minimum, knew that heirs apparent, at least in Yankee land, were also ax-bearers for The Lord High Executioner.

The real story of this firing was that it was not the end. It was, it turned out, just one more chapter in the chronicles of the living dead. Two years down the pike, there was a Billy V in the offing and then, say many close to the scene, there was, even at the time of his death, the strong possibility of Billy VI.

There was a hard reality between these men, one that had long since entwined them beyond these paroxysms of hiring and firing. Billy, according to the unique terms of his contract, was not really fired but merely relocated to another position within the organization. And yet, of course, Billy could have gone elsewhere. He had that option; that was also a feature of his contract, that he would be free at any time to go elsewhere if that was what he wanted (or could afford).

He did not want to go elsewhere even though, according to Judge Sapir, he could have. There was an incredible offer on the table from the Indians in this period, and another from the White Sox. The Indians offer promised Billy not only a good multiyear deal but also a piece of the action: fifty cents on every ticket sold, Sapir said. "It was the most incredibly generous, most amazing offer—and we had to turn it down because Billy just did not want to go to Cleveland."

There is no hard explanation for why Billy turned down such a deal other than Sapir's explanation that "Billy did just not want to go to Cleveland." At his age, facing the uncertainty the Cleveland franchise represented, knowing that any contract he signed with them would have to be balanced against the possible disintegration of a weak organization—something he had already experienced in his managerial career—there was more, a good deal more than geography behind his refusal.

The White Sox were another matter. They offered him good money, comparable to what he was making with the Yankees or better, Sapir said. They had new ownership and a stable base of operations, but the money over the long haul simply could not match what was in that Yankee contract, the judge said; "as much as we wanted to, we just couldn't afford to."

The reasons why were stunningly, punishingly clear.

In 1985, with Billy's tax debts piling into the hundreds of thousands, the IRS began attaching his salary. For most of the year, he had been placed on an allowance—"more than a hundred dollars, maybe two hundred dollars a week," Jill said. He made more money in those days when the team was out on the road and he could claim a per diem expense. It was extremely discomfiting, and for someone well into his late middle years, frightening.

All of that made staying not an option to be considered but an absolute imperative.

Steinbrenner knew there were other offers out there. He may or may not have been contacted for permission to negotiate with Billy. But he also knew his man, knew his misfortunes certainly as well as he knew his heart. He did not want to see Billy go elsewhere. Billy rising up from the shades to lead a ghostly tribe of Indians—from George's own hometown—or Pale Hose or any other kind of otherworldly warriors would surely set fans off screaming for the owner's head or, worse, get them out of the Yankee Stadium habit entirely. This was a fear that would not go away. No matter what Steinbrenner thought of Billy's private life, no matter how certain he was that ruin, insubordination, and a lack of discipline would sooner or later catch up with any team he led, he was unwilling to see Billy's still-great talent matched against the odds with any other team. He still believed that somewhere, somehow this man could still bring the glory he had once brought to the Yankees. Billy was, for all his flaws, a real Yankee; he had that secret in his breast, like an unseen fire that had burned through all those years, all those different eras, a mysterious passion that evoked fear in opponents, loyalty in allies, and continuing and ferocious adulation in those who kept coming back to the ballpark, willing to pay higher and higher ticket prices. Steinbrenner could not help firing Billy, but he could no more let him go than he could choose to stop breathing. Whatever else he thought, Billy had done—and still did—more for business than any single baseball person he knew, with the possible exception of Reggie Jackson.

Steinbrenner, knowing his man's financial woes, made sure he kept him happy. He renegotiated the contract, adding a couple of additional years at manager's pay. There were strong hints—not confirmed—that he tore up a quarter-of-a-million-dollar loan that he made earlier to help Billy out. In addition, he extended himself to encourage, to soothe, to flatter Billy's shattered feelings as best he could.

Billy had long wanted to have his number retired. It had become a thing with him, something, Sapir said, "he just kept pushing and pushing me to get. There never would have been a Billy Martin Day on August 10, 1986, if Billy hadn't been so persevering. We went after this real hard, harder than anything. 'Remember now, we want his number retired.' First we talked about it on the surface, you know, as a seed we planted. But then Billy kept on me and on me about it and George said, 'No problem, no problem at all. Let's do it.' "

Billy Martin Day came off without a hitch—almost. Old friends and family were there at his side along with former teammates and current players, all of whom extolled Billy and let him know how well deserved his inclusion in the pantheon was. Billy's mother was there, in a wheelchair. His half-sisters, Pat Irvine and Joanie, were there. His daughter and son were there. Only Jill, Billy's fiancée now, did not make it to the field—the result, she was told, of an "oversight" by George; under specific orders by Billy, said several of his friends.

The day was followed by an evening gala at a New Jersey hotel, where speechmaking, food, drink, and celebration were abundant. Billy's mother sang "My Man" from the dais; Ken Kaiser, speaking for many umpires whom Billy knew, liked, and had befriended over the years—in stark contrast to the usual images of umpire baiting and battling associated with him—presented him with a preliminary gift (a more conventional one followed) of a large cat box full of sand for him to kick in. Through it all Billy was tearful, happy, grateful.

But this day, sentimental, commercial, and professional, was a highly symbolic one in yet another way. It marked a subtle shift in Billy's makeup, one in which he passed from being a peripatetic Yankee to being a permanent one, from Puck in pinstripes to *éminence grise*. His sights, always set on another season, another team, another campaign, were now subtly shifted to just this one team, this one town, this one late era of his life. The time had finally come upon him where he knew that he had to stop running, that he could no longer tell anyone, anytime, in the words of the song, what they could do with their job. It was not a matter of acquired maturity or newly discovered mellowness—though newer friends of his said he seemed considerably more at ease—so much as acknowledging, for the first time in his life, that there were limitations to what he could do. He was no longer young, and the many wars had tired him, at least to the point where he was psychically less inclined to do whatever he wanted regardless of the consequences.

With this day and this time away from the field, Billy's personal life began to take on an appearance of stability as well. His bizarre double life was finally being resolved. At the beginning of the 1985 season—

though she may not have known it till later—Billy separated from Heather. She had certainly learned this by season's end, when Eddie Sapir—who had, in 1982, made a phone call informing her that Billy was proposing to her—called her again to tell her that her husband was leaving her. Heather sued for divorce, stating that Billy "simply never came home from the 1985 season" as cause. Billy, for his part, according to Heather's friends, tried to pin the blame on her, accusing her of infidelity. It was ugly and nasty—but temporary. The settlement—worth about $20,000, or $10,000 less than had been originally talked about—came about, Jill said, because she had managed to put a pair of investigators, including her sister, on Heather. Their investigation, Jill said, turned up information that was seriously compromising (Heather by then was involved in a relationship with the man she eventually was to marry), and that ultimately helped lower Billy's settlement costs.

Jill was with Billy full-time now. They were "engaged," and there would be a marriage, a partnership in which Jill's ambitious plans for her future husband would be matched with his willing acquiescence in finally getting his feet on the ground and a roof over his head.

Billy's demeanor, his cooperativeness—if not his effectiveness—in the broadcast booth, and the obvious attempt he was making to get his life together, impressed George Steinbrenner. True, there were lapses. According to one former Yankee publicist, he occasionally called the press box "when he might have had one too many." One time, said this publicist, "he went on and on trying to make sure we barred Henry Hecht from the press box." But the occasions were few and far between, and more conspicuous was Billy's willingness to be seen in the company of the owner, sitting in his box at the stadium, coming forward to back him up on public statements he made concerning the state of the team and the abilities, or lack thereof, of the team's manager, Lou Piniella.

The progress of the team and its newly "groomed" manager was, of course, the bottom line. The Yankees, though they finished second, five and a half games behind the Red Sox, in 1986, were out of the race most of the way. Piniella increasingly became the target of Steinbrenner's all-too-public asides. Media favorites of Steinbrenner's—like Howard Cosell—took their cue, sharply criticizing Piniella's lack of experience. The next year was worse. The team, after making a run at the top through early August, faded badly, finishing fourth, nine games off the pace. Piniella was asked to step aside—to move up to the post of general manager, a position for which he lacked even a day's experience—while Billy, well-rested and ready to go, was moved back to the dugout.

If the acid bath of cynicism that daily washed over this team could have been briefly lowered, Billy V and Steinbrenner's motives for producing it might actually have been examined seriously. Steinbrenner obviously knew that Billy would likely run into trouble again, just as he knew that his drinking had not ceased. But he remained the best manager he had under contract, and, in all likelihood, the best manager in the game. The bottom line for Steinbrenner was winning. Winning was Fourth of July pride, it was box office, it was the Yankees—it was good business, no matter what anyone said. Plus, he now had insurance built into this relationship that he did not have before: Lou II.

Billy's desire in '88 came out of this new sense of himself as a permanent member, a kind of elder statesman even as he retained the braids and insignia of a battlefield general. He knew this team, had followed it, had described its doings from the broadcast booth and in private consultation with the owner—undermining, some said, Lou Piniella's ability to do his job. The fact that the Yankees had not been in a World Series since 1981 and had not won a World Championship since 1978 allowed his own sense of urgency to blend with the owner's. His own sense of leadership had changed, deepened. He was no longer "Casey's Boy," trying to outdo the old man. That clearly had become impossible; he would never match Stengel's record of World Championships and domination of the game. What had come to him in this last period, even where an instinct for survival should have kept him as far from the dugout as possible, was the feeling, now all but settled in his bone marrow, that the Yankee past, all that was great and good and exemplary in the team's long history, had been passed on to him: He was The Last Yankee.

# CHAPTER 18

The Yankees, according to most observers, were headed for the middle of the pack in 1988. Billy's presence at the head of the team, said the *Bill Mazeroski Baseball Annual,* had "a nice ring to it, eh George? Yeah, kind of like Abbott and Costello." The respected yearbook picked the Yankees to finish fifth in the AL East (where, in fact, they did finish). Cynical laughter and low expectations were the norm in most other pre-season analyses.

But the Yankees, during that early part of the season while Billy was at the helm, were the surprise of the league. They won nine of their first ten games, the best start in the team's history, responding to that unorthodox whip at the starting gate so favored by Billy throughout his career. At the end of April, the Yankees were 16–7, half a game out of first and very much on the minds of opponents. May began even more promisingly. Setting out on a tough seven-game road-trip to Chicago, Kansas City, and Texas, they won their first four games, leaving Kansas City for Texas two and a half games up in first place.

Then there was Lace.

A topless bar, half-smashed drinking companions, and a post-midnight brawl in which he was nearly killed were elements so much a part of the legend that long ago had become a caricature that no explanation seemed even necessary. The details of Lace remain as *Enquirer*-titillating as they were when they first appeared:

The Yankees lose a game to the Texas Rangers, 7–6. Billy has been tossed, has left the park in a funk. He is back at the hotel, the Arlington Hilton, still in a funk but now in a crowded lounge, hoping for solace, to drown his anger or his sorrow—and who is there, sitting at the bar with his hat slouched down over his eyes, but Mickey Mantle, the familiar, mischievous grin splitting his face from ear to ear, the invitation to "have a beer, pard," almost unnecessary, because fun was already on the agenda. He was staying at the hotel that night, Mantle said, staying there so he could accompany Billy on a golf outing the next day. A little more laughter there.

Then the crowds of autograph seekers got too heavy, the people gawking and pushing with their pens and baseballs, the people with stars and dollars in their eyes.

"I know a quiet little place. . . ."

"Let's get out of here, pard."

Lace.

Smoky lights, gyrating bodies, twisty music, lots of booze—a place not so quiet after all, but quiet enough to get a few down and to watch and talk—until Mantle, who, according to his friends, could be trouble when he had one too many, said he wanted to go, and so he did, with a couple of Yankee coaches, including Mike Ferraro who had been there for Billy, and Mantle's son who needed a lift home—they all were reported to have left except Billy, who wanted to stay for a while: for one of the dancers he was interested in, for another drink or two, to straighten things out for Mickey who had gotten into it with some ugly patrons, just to hang out for a while—many motives fit, none are yet known to be certain.

And then, sometime afterward, that trip to the bathroom ending with Billy's broken body in the alley way.

The page-three story proceeds through various lurid flashes of fascinating tidbits—Billy arriving later, by cab, because Ferraro, the designated driver, somehow never got back in time to pick Billy up; the lawnful of hotel patrons, unfortunately including George Steinbrenner, all of them rousted from bed by a false fire alarm but there in time to see Billy stagger in, a gory mess. And then the aftermath, the endgame of another certain firing:

The ever loyal Judge Sapir assigning a Dallas private eye named Bullock to round up more than the usual suspects, the report unfortunately revealing that the culprits who beat and victimized Billy, who was totally innocent in this situation, were all on the lam from the law—check forgers, ex-cons and worse who had moved on to

Vegas and points west and hence could not be interviewed; the owner vowing to one and all that he would not fire Billy over Lace because "the man had suffered enough"; the wife, Jill, hysterically waking a reporter in the hotel whose name sounded like that of the Yankee trainer, Monahan, wanting to find out what happened (a total lie, she said later). All of it fit the usual throwaway verses of the never-ending ballad of "Battling Billy, The Barroom Brawler."

The most prosaic and most important part of this story is that Billy had been left alone. He had been in too many fights, had too many notches in his six-gun, had created himself too long ago so that he was a legend wherever he went—the sort of legend that made any real friend look out for him, make sure that his back was covered when he hoisted a shot glass, or at least be aware that it had become something of a chore for Billy to spend a simple hour of peace in a public place.

"I will regret to my dying day that I wasn't with my dad that night," said Billy Joe, the son who had become friendly with the father, enough so that he had also become a kind of bodyguard for him whenever they were out together.

There were other reliable friends who knew how to read crowds and how to interpose their bodies between him and an eager gunslinger looking to make his mark. Tex Gernand, Bill Reedy, big Lee Walls, Willie Horton, all knew the trails and buttes leading to and from the bars and lounges. Tex, a former cop, six foot seven, who would not touch a drop while "on duty," who always waited nearby at a decent distance, has one and a dozen stories about the patron who pushes forward with love in his eye, a glass in his hand, babbling to Billy, "Billy Martin, man, I've loved you all my life, you're the greatest, I love you and I love the Yankees and most of all I'd love to kick the shit out of you."

The real story of Lace was that no one was there for Billy that night, and Billy was foolish enough, vain enough, drunk enough to forget—and to pay with his shattered body and his baseball life.

In the end, once he had healed, all that was really at stake was his baseball future. Billy believed then, according to one friend, that Lace had given Steinbrenner the wedge he was looking for. But he knew, before and after Lace, that there were the usual other reasons.

Even before spring training, Billy countermanded a Steinbrenner order for a winter running program for his players. George's troika solution of having Lou Piniella serve as general manager was a fiasco; continuing differences with Billy and Steinbrenner apparently became too much for the new man in the front office, who abruptly resigned on May 29. Steinbrenner was shaken and genuinely disturbed, believing he and the organization had suffered a serious blow. Steinbrenner wanted mightily to keep Piniella in the fold—as he did Billy.

A day later, Billy had his second and most serious run-in with umpires that season (earlier he had been fined $300 for a dirt-kicking episode). In a game against the A's in Oakland that the Yankees lost, 3–2, Billy disputed a call by umpire Rick Reed that Yankee second baseman Bobby Meacham had trapped not caught a line drive, permitting an Oakland hitter to reach first. Billy appealed the call to Dale Scott, the first base umpire, who then banished him for using profanities. Enraged, Billy kicked dirt, then scooped more dirt and flung it at the umpire's chest. The ejection from the game was followed by a league ruling fining him and suspending him for three games and then, worse, a statement from the Umpires Association protesting the lenient treatment Billy had received. Richie Phillips, head of the Association, warned everyone that the umpires were mad as hell and were not going to take it anymore. For Billy to remain in a game, Phillips said, "from now on he's going to have to behave like an altar boy, sitting there with his hands folded and his lips shut. Every time for the next couple of weeks that he comes out of the dugout, he'll be ejected." The umpires, he went on to say, would act as vigilantes, imposing their own justice when none was forthcoming from the American League.

When George Steinbrenner cited difficulties with umpires as a major reason for firing Billy—their rulings so long as Billy was in the dugout were an unfortunate penalty the team could not afford—it was generally assumed that this explanation was about as reliable as any of his other statements for the record. But Steinbrenner was indeed concerned, as any owner might have been if he was convinced that umpires, either consciously or unconsciously, would actually penalize his team for the man in the dugout. Steinbrenner, it is true, had long made a mockery of himself by protesting league officiating, whining to league officials, badgering them with endless reels of videotape and other "evidence" purporting to show that the Yankees were constantly victimized by poor umpiring. But this was different down on the field. For a while, Steinbrenner conveniently let it be known that he might support the idea of a lawsuit against the Umpires Association urged on Billy by advisors—but then he backed off. The matter was too serious, the stakes too great.

Steinbrenner ultimately cited "a combination of factors" in his decision to let Billy go, but it is fair to assume that, for once, he did have an umpire problem on his hands and that he could actually relieve it by firing Billy Martin.

What is most interesting, however, is that George went out of his way to convince Billy that he was again being relocated *only* because of the umps. That, clearly, was not the exclusive reason.

According to any number of Billy's friends, this firing hit him hardest. Bill Mayback, with whom Billy drank immediately afterward, remembers that he was "inconsolable, so down and depressed afterwards." "It was the worst, because he had the team right up there near first place, everything was going so well, and then, just like that, he's gone," said another friend.

Steinbrenner, of course, could read the standings as well as anyone, and whatever concern he might have had for Billy's sensitivities, he understood what kind of job he had done—and though he now had him out of sight, he most assuredly did not yet have him out of mind. Steinbrenner maintained later that the biggest mistake he made with Billy Martin was firing him that last time. Immediately afterward, he undertook to make sure Billy saw his firing in the most positive light possible.

In an internal memo, marked "confidential," which somehow found its way into the hands of one of Billy's lawyers, Steinbrenner told Yankee executives Bill Dowling and Bob Quinn that he was going to be meeting with Billy Martin the next afternoon to "discuss his future involvement with the Yankee organization, and to try to explain to him the reasons that I felt the change was necessary." The memo is dated June 28, five days after the firing, and mentions only the umpiring situation as a cause for the decision. "We really didn't have much choice," Steinbrenner told his associates. "You could tell from our players that they had lost confidence in their ability to get a fair deal when their manager couldn't even come out and take their part in a questionable play.

"I haven't told this to the press and I don't want it told to them," Steinbrenner added, "but I may or may not, depending on how I feel, indicate it to Billy. I probably will not. I will apprise you of the results of the meeting." Steinbrenner, of course, did inform Billy by releasing the memo to Judge Sapir.

The ultimate result of the meeting was that Billy remained in the Yankee organization and then, as the team began its slide through the second half, a new contract—underscoring the Yankees' lifetime commitment to him—was drawn.

The following spring, Billy appeared at the Yankee camp in Ft.

Lauderdale, once again looking tanned and healthy. George and Billy both told reporters that managing again was out of the question. Said George, "That's not what I have in mind for Billy. I don't think that's what Billy wants and I don't think it's what's best for Billy. The man is sixty years old. He wants to get into other areas."

Said Billy, "I won't manage anymore, I've had enough managing. Well, I've done it for the Yankees before when I said I wasn't going to, and then I said I would and came back when George asked me to come back. But I don't intend to come back anymore. You can quote me on that one. That's for sure. That's firm. That can't be changed."

Of course, no one took anything Billy or George said about the Yankee managerial situation seriously and, almost certainly, they did not themselves. In light of the Yankees' 1988 finish down in the standings after they had been near the top, Billy's abilities, if anything, loomed even larger.

Jack Clark, the unhappy slugger who was traded to the Padres over the winter, probably expressed a bit of the owner's own misgivings when he said publicly that the Yankees probably would have won in 1988 if Billy had stayed.

"We all knew our roles," Clark told Steve Serby of the *New York Post*, "and I still will always feel, if he would have been there, and I'll feel this for the rest of my career and the rest of my life, no matter what happened on or off the field, I felt there was no way we wouldn't have gone to the World Series and won."

George had opted for order, and it hadn't worked. The team, in the days of Lou II, had drifted. Players, Jack Clark insisted, became uncertain of their roles, of what was expected of them. After Piniella was fired, Steinbrenner had hoped Dallas Green would be the miraculous disciplinarian he was searching for. But almost from the start, the owner, as he had with every other manager, began undermining his new man. Promises about expanded authority to handle personnel matters were undercut when he hired Syd Thrift as a vice president in charge of baseball operations. The usual statements about sticking with his manager through the season stuck like snow in July when the team began to lose.

Billy, on the other hand, was given expanded duties as a special assistant and baseball troubleshooter for Steinbrenner, with an authority and commitment very different from that of an old baseball man on generous retainer. He had the trappings if not the authority of executive power. And, strangely, given who he was working for, he seemed serious about what he did, serious about the organization and his own role in it. He was not managing, true, but he was still very much the Last Yankee, the torch bearer for a tradition he and George both agreed was in urgent need of upgrade.

Billy scouted players and teams on special assignment. He made public appearances, spoke to organizations and groups on behalf of the Yankees. He was living like a country squire, tending his garden, fishing his pond, on 150 acres near Binghamton, New York. He was just a couple of hours' driving time from Albany, home of the Yankees' Eastern League farm team, and he was a phone call away from Yankee Stadium.

Buck Showalter, manager of the Albany Yankees then and one of the bright lights in the organization, remembered how sharp and how imposing Billy was in his new capacity as organizational elder statesman:

"Billy was asked to come in and evaluate the Albany club that year; he was living in Binghamton and he called me and wanted me to make up a short thing on each player so he could evaluate them," Showalter recalled. "I ended up writing a page on each one because the last thing you want to do is not be prepared when Billy Martin comes into town."

Showalter remembered that "Billy didn't have a book, he never really managed by the book—and he wanted us to learn how to work that way. The book went according to how you felt about a situation. You managed according to the ability of your players."

Showalter recalled that Billy's interests were sharply Yankee-specific. He was especially interested in players who had left-handed home run power, suited to the dimensions of the Stadium. He had a Yankee Stadium view of outfield speed—you needed it most in left field, not center, a departure from conventional thinking, but an intelligent one if you were looking to build the New York Yankees.

If George Steinbrenner was looking—and surely he was—he had to be pleased with what he saw. Billy was home more and drinking less—or so it appeared. His new wife was constantly busy with plans for him, having him work for charities and go to public functions that made him and the Yankees look good.

It was all so good—and so familiarly deceptive. As certain as the moon, when things seemed at their fullest in Billy's life they were actually beginning to wane. This last period was no exception.

Billy began 1988 by getting married. The ceremony, captured on an elaborately produced video, was Camelot, complete with lines of yellow Rolls-Royces, a chorus of Jill's friends, bridesmaids happily dubbed "Billy's Bimbos" for the occasion, and elegantly attired guests and servants. The posh Blackhawk country club, the fabulously upgraded home—$70,000 worth of improvements just for the wedding—were all part of the sort of scripted happiness that left the expectation of a future filled with success, money, love.

But it was not quite what it appeared. Some of the guests—members of Billy's family, his sisters, brothers, brothers-in-law—groused and cursed at having to spend money for tuxedos. A few of Billy's old drinking pals ran a pool out behind the tent on how long the marriage would last. Mickey Mantle, unsteady on his feet for most of the week, drank himself into oblivion and had to be carried away. Before he did, he toasted the bride and groom, telling them that he hoped "this one lasts longer than the others." A sister of Jill's, at the moment the couple was exchanging vows, vocally—and embarrassingly—protested.

One wedding gift, innocently and good-naturedly given, had a certain symbolic value: Bill Mayback presented the new bride and groom with a hotel door that had a couple of holes in it. The holes had been put there by Jill's foot: She had been in a raging quarrel with Billy a year or so before the marriage and had tried to kick down a door that was closed on her by Billy. They had fought in the past, and they fought at the time of the wedding: Jill wanted to clear her house of guests and get on with a honeymoon, but Billy wanted people to stay, stay and dance, stay and drink, stay overnight, and then stay longer than that.

Underneath this bliss of Camelot, with its cakes in the shape of ice castles, was fierce, roiling, unstable temperament—something old and blue for Billy, but something equally entwined in Jill's bouquet. The basics were there in this ceremony—basics of blood, fire, and very divided ambitions all at the same time.

Ellen Vonitch, "Auntie Ellen" as Billy and Jill called her, was one of very few old Oakland friends of Billy's family who were invited to the wedding and one of very few who knew intimate details of how the couple got along. She believed Billy loved Jill fiercely, passionately, beyond reason. For years, prior to the marriage, she had been a kind of go-between for the couple, running telephone messages between them when they were separated. She remembers "wearing out three or four telephones" from all the calls she took from Billy in the middle of the night. Where was Jill? he wanted to know; find her, find out how long it takes her to answer the phone. His jealousy was proof of his passion, she said. But, clearly, there was more: "He'd call me four, five in the morning, 'Where is she, where's Jill?' I said, 'You're ruining your whole life, you wanna know where she is, she's not there, you're mad.' Then she'd contact me, 'If Billy calls, you tell him where I am'—it was mostly at the horses. Every time he'd call me, he'd say, 'Don't lie to me.' I'd say, 'Billy, I'm not gonna lie to you, what's the matter with you? She's there, she's gonna call me back.' This went on for years. . . . I began to lose sleep. I even had to call the Yankee clubhouse when the game was on. He'd say, 'Call when you get ahold of her, call me after the game, no, call me right away.' And he'd give me the number and I'd get through to him in the dugout."

But Jill, as attractive and as dangerous as she was for Billy, was no bimbo. She had ideas for him, was as ambitious as he was, perhaps more so, and her ambitions spread far beyond the relatively simple boundaries of 162 games and a pennant. Jill was interested every bit as much as Billy was in creating him. Like George Steinbrenner, she was a producer, but where Steinbrenner's grand production was the Yankees, Jill's was Billy Martin only.

Jill, in essence, made herself Billy's business manager, agent, and PR director. She quite literally created "Martin Productions," a title she uses to this day.

Financially, she saw ruin around her—not just the IRS, but Billy doling out money to anyone who asked, supporting hordes of family members, friends, hangers-on, anyone who asked for a spare dime or a spare thousand. She saw bills and bank accounts spread out like a litter of confetti all over the landscape and, she said, she sought to consolidate his phantom empire, basically by putting it under her control. She moved Billy's commercial interests away from Judge Sapir and Paul Tabarry in New Orleans, and she increasingly became the person who said "no" to those who asked for money—including Billy's children—and "yes" to those promotional engagements she thought would build their joint bank account as well as the corporate image that was the new face, person, and character of Billy Martin.

She wanted to "clean up" his image by having him associate with the right people. She wanted him to have friends—friends with some standing—not just drinking buddies or old neighborhood hangers-on from Berkeley. She wanted him to do the right events, the right charities—charities for deaf kids, to feed the homeless, preserve the wild, help the Salvation Army. A week before he died, Jill booked him into Tampa to sing Christmas carols for kids with George Steinbrenner.

If she didn't have him brush up on his Shakespeare, she was a certainly willing Henry Higgins to his Eliza Doolittle. Jill booked Billy for appearances with symphony orchestras in New Orleans and Binghamton for "Billy the Kid" or "The Night Before Christmas."

"We did a lot of work in the last couple of years," she said, "on how to enunciate and talk properly." She remembered sitting backstage at a symphony performance where he was going to narrate "The Night Before Christmas" and getting him to mouth out the words that were on a prompter, "*Twaaas* the night before Christmas . . . remember, you're talking to kids."

Billy needed no prompting in giving himself publicly to kids; he had always done that, as he had to autograph seekers and to people who were openly friendly and admiring. He needed no one to tell him about charities; it had been a dream of his, long before he met Jill, to buy Casey Stengel's old house and convert it into a home for elderly former ballplayers. He had been interested for years in seeing that players who left the game before the big-money days got upgraded pension and benefit rights. He personally took care of players he knew who needed a thousand here or five thousand there. He had once been the prime mover in a huge benefit for Ken Boyer, then dying of cancer. An ex-Twins player regularly received money; an ex-Yankee player owed him—and never paid back—large sums.

But he was also sick of being broke, suspicious that he was being taken advantage of, weary of earning a lot only to lose more than he earned. He was tired of saying yes when he couldn't figure out a way of saying no other than by the convenience of forgetfulness. He wished he was tougher that way, wished he was able to rise up and say, enough. He clearly wanted to see his fortune grow in order to feel that, once and for all, he was past the spectre of financial insecurity he had come from and that, amazingly, still hovered in the form of ever-present debts and the ever-demanding IRS.

But he could no more be the "new" Billy Martin for Jill than for George Steinbrenner. His habits, tastes, and temperament were those of a lifetime. He continued to seek out and befriend partners in drink wherever he went. He was a bar hopper—in Binghamton as in Oakland or New York, in New Orleans or Detroit or wherever he was. He could no more break himself of this than he could the life of the road, with its seemingly endless lure of women and good times—everything that made a simple and enduring marriage, especially one to a person so much younger and so different in her tastes, virtually impossible.

According to nearly everyone who knew them, Billy and Jill fought after the wedding as they had before it. Depending on the friend, the import of those quarrels was significant and deadly or inconsequential and passing.

Bill and Carol Reedy, close to the couple before the accident that killed Billy, bitterly at odds with Jill since, both remember quarrels that were fierce and not just briefly passing. At a Madison Square Garden horse show, Carol—but not Bill Reedy—had been asked to join Billy and Jill. The fact that somehow Bill, Billy's friend, had not been invited sparked a frightening fight.

"Back at the hotel they [Billy and Jill Martin] had the biggest fight I've ever seen," Carol Reedy said. "He took the Nancy Reagan book she was reading and tore the covers off it. He took a new hat that she bought and he tore the box all to shreds and just sailed the hat across the room. . . . So I went into the bathroom and shut the door. They have a television in there. I was watching re-runs of The 'Honeymooners' in there . . . next morning, he was so apologetic—he had had a terrible day and he said some of the things that had happened, and he said he was sorry. As soon as he goes out the door, Jill says to me, 'The only reason he apologized is because he doesn't want you to go back and tell Bill what an asshole he is.' "

Billy's personality, said Bill Reedy, "would just grate on her nerves." He remembered a time the two couples had driven to the Hall of Fame at Cooperstown together. Jill had been behind the wheel and Billy was in the back. "You know, he put on this disguised voice, and he starts making a sound like a police fire siren. Suddenly, she jams on the brakes, pulls over, opens the door and gets out and starts screaming at him: 'You don't like the way I drive—you drive!' and we didn't move until he drove."

Reedy believed Jill was humorless—a fatal flaw in a relationship with a person who could be as obviously childish as Billy.

Jill herself recalled an outing she had with Mickey Mantle and his wife Merlyn. It was after an old-timers game, probably in 1987. Afterward, the foursome drove downtown for dinner, and then drove along the FDR Drive. Billy was behind the wheel, Mickey sitting next to him in front, the wives in the rear, she recalled. And then—boys will be boys—Billy and Mickey did their thing. Billy slipped down behind the wheel, and set the car going at a high rate of speed:

"The two of them were in the front seat going as fast as they could go—trying to make Merlyn and I mad at them, tease us. . . . Merlyn and I wanted to strangle them. . . . Billy would sink down low in the seat and lean to the left and then to the right—and we ended just laughing hysterically and thinking, 'God, we're going to get in an accident,' but they were just doing their little-boy stuff."

In this regime of quarrels and personality differences all built around a "new" Billy Martin, it was harder than ever for the old one to assert himself. His life looked more stable, but inwardly things were changing. Jill believed—and, she said, Billy came to see—that among the freeloaders who had been ruining him were his own children. His son, Billy Joe, had been bilking him for college tuition payments over seven years—all the while grappling with his studies, experimenting with drugs, running afoul of the law in an assault case; Kelly Ann, the daughter who had cost him so much during her jail stay in Colombia, now claimed she had cancer—something Jill said she had been able to show her husband was false. The children deserved to be and were, in Jill's words, "cut off."

Old friends and family likewise saw less of Billy as he took up his new life, burdened with new plans and expenses for converting the Binghamton home into a sumptuous horse ranch. In this same period, there was even a falling out with Mickey Mantle—one that Bill Reedy and ultimately Mantle himself correctly or incorrectly blamed on Jill. The circumstances of the split, to say the least, were strange.

Shortly after Billy was fired in 1988, he and Jill were temporarily offered residence, which they accepted, in a house belonging to an upstate businessman, Mike Klepfer. Klepfer had become friendly the year before with Mantle and Billy when they took part in a dinner celebrating the thirtieth year of the company Klepfer worked for. Over the course of time, Klepfer's friendship with Mickey and Billy, particularly with Mantle, expanded to include business associates and mutual friends.

In the meantime, Jill told Billy that Klepfer was something less than a reliable character. All the while he had been professing closeness to Mickey and Billy, she said, he had been making unwanted sexual advances toward different people associated with them—including Jill. At one point, Jill said, Klepfer, their host, had actually pursued her across a room, trying to force himself on her. When Billy heard this, recalled Jill, he "was so angry he wanted to kill Klepfer."

While Billy apparently made no subsequent effort to confront Klepfer, he did, according to Bill Reedy and others, warn Mantle about him. But Mantle, it seemed, distrusted Billy's—or rather Jill's—motives in telling him. Billy in turn resented Mantle for resenting him. From then on, these lifelong friends, their egos ruffled, backed away from one another, and saw each other less and less over the following months.

Klepfer, for his part, vehemently denies that he had anything to do with their quarrel. He particularly denied that he had ever made advances to Jill—or to anyone else in the Martin-Mantle entourage. In fact, he said, a great deal of the trouble, "came from the fact that my wife and I had to ask them [Billy and Jill] to leave our house." The Martins, he said, had originally been invited in for a couple of weeks—at Mantle's suggestion, as a favor—but then "they just stayed on and on, and they fought all the time. It got so bad that Billy at one point simply took off for three weeks—just disappeared. There was one day, finally, where they physically went after each other and she wound up having to go off to the hospital to get fitted for a neck brace." It was at that point, he said, that he and his wife "told the Martins they had to go and we then moved them, in one day, bag and baggage to the Comfort Inn."

Jill maintains that their withdrawal was neither sudden nor involuntary, that they in fact stayed on with the Klepfers for some time, moving to the Comfort Inn only in stages, as they were preparing to occupy their own newly purchased house. She did not say, however, why she or Billy elected to stay on with the Klepfers after his alleged advances—a curious decision given Billy's temper.

Whatever actually happened, the estrangement between Billy and Mickey lasted for almost a year, from the early fall of 1988 until August 1989—only months prior to Billy's death. For all that while, the two friends, who had been "closer than brothers" since their Yankee playing days, were barely on speaking terms, each caught in his own private world of betrayal, loss, and narrowing certainty.

They eventually were reunited by either Jill or Bill Reedy. Jill says the key was Mickey's eventually accepting a reduced fee for his participation in a Billy Martin Roast that she was promoting in Atlantic City. Reedy says that he simply worked on each of the two men, reminding them both of how long and how close their friendship had been, and that "they finally saw that."

It matters little whether Jill's desire for a kinder, gentler Billy was executive or emotional, wise or foolish; it simply did not work. The happiness that Jill's friends saw or were told about did not match the complex and ever-conflicted man she was married to.

Billy had been down this way before, many times. It was not a question for him of finding that one right woman, but of whether he could remain in a stable and loving relationship with any woman. From the first experiences he had growing up in a house where he was at war with his mother, with the ferocity and unpredictability of her temper, the deepest lesson of love he had learned was to take shit from no one. He had also learned at an early age that what went on in a marriage and what went on in bed were not necessarily the same. Billy, from the start, had always had this old-world notion that wives were for babies and serving their husbands, while girlfriends were there for the rest. And in the world in which he moved, this division of passions was routinely accepted. Womanizing, like drinking, was just a part of the game.

What made all this more than tawdry, more than just cruel to the women he was with, was that he wanted so much more. There was a part of him, also old world, as sure as God was in Heaven that knew that a man and woman were meant to preside over a large and productive family, where the furtherance of work and obedience were all part of this one design called happiness, this service to the Creator. Instead, there was this endless and irreversible division of longing for and war with women, passionate desire for their company, an almost helpless willingness to fight against them, to hurt them—as though in the act of love, the pots and pans were flying still, and the blessing of love was the curse that made every single day a fight for survival and victory.

Billy was no brutalizer; he was actually a softie, someone easily hurt even as he hurt others, someone who, never able to quite figure out who he was, would fight, would lash out because from the earliest age he had learned that fighting back was the way a person kept from being dominated: by a rival gang member, by an opponent on the field, by a boss, by a woman.

Two weeks before his fatal accident, Jenny died. She had been hospitalized for some time. Her death, though not unexpected, hit Billy full force, as though he had not been prepared for it. At the same time, according to Jill, he learned from Auntie Ellen that his mother and father had never been married. The news, Jill said, was devastating, confirming his deepest and worst fears. The truth—that there actually *was* a marriage—was never learned by Billy before his own death.

That weekend—Jenny died on a Sunday—Billy had a speaking engagement in Terre Haute, Indiana. He had decided to keep it, and to have Jill stay behind, because there seemed to be no imminent danger of his mother's death. The day following the speaking engagement, he planned to go on to California.

When he finished speaking that night at Indiana State University, he located a bar, Larry Bird's Boston Connection. While he was sitting at the bar, a commotion broke out behind him and a woman dropped a purse to the floor. A loaded gun she had in it discharged, and the bullet whistled inches over Billy's head and slammed into a mirror on the other side of the bar—unbelievably, at almost the exact hour of his mother's death in Oakland.

Billy, according to anyone who spoke to him then, was deeply, inconsolably grieved by news of Jenny's death. He was incapable of sorting out the mountain of emotion that was suddenly upon him—love and regret, mourning and rage. Whatever he felt for his mother, aside from that link of love to his own roots, was directed away, at others.

While he was in California, he confided in an old friend, Lewis Figone, whom he had not spoken to since—and because of—his marriage to Jill, that after Christmas he was going to come home. He was going to leave Binghamton, leave the unsatisfying life and marriage he was caught in.

Billy's daughter, Kelly, heard this, too. "He said he'd be back here [in California] on the twenty-seventh, that he wasn't going back, that he was going to get rid of her and sell the place and then come back home."

A week after Billy died, Mickey Mantle revealed to three different people—including a prominent sportswriter and a well-known ex-ballplayer—that Billy also told him that he wasn't going back to Binghamton.

"Their marriage was not made in heaven," Greer Johnson said. "Jill had told me that, too. She said herself, no matter what she may say now, that it was a bad marriage. Billy came into Mickey's restaurant one day not long before he died, and he had lunch with Mickey. They stayed in the back from eleven to seven. He didn't want to go back—he had to be talked into it."

In Oakland, at his mother's funeral, there was a further unraveling—not with Jill but with his own family. A quarrel developed when one of Billy's sisters accused him of not having done enough for his mother—or for the family—before Jenny's death. Billy went into a total rage, vowing that he never wanted to see these surviving members of his family again.

Ruben DeAlba, Billy's closest childhood friend, was at Jenny's funeral, too. Over the years, he had seen Billy occasionally, shy about stepping into a spotlight that belonged to Billy. Ruben's life had gone completely contrary to Billy's. He had had a year in pro ball but he gave it up to be married. He had remained married to the same woman all his life, and had a family and a home not far from where he grew up.

But he thought about his friend constantly, followed his career, felt for the troubles—and the triumphs—he had had in his life. DeAlba remembered meeting Billy that night after the funeral, and being alarmed when he embraced his friend:

"There was alcohol on his breath—there always had been when we met over the years—and I understood why, with the death of his mother, why there might be now," he said, "but when I put my arms around him, I was frightened. He was so frail. So old and frail. He was always small and wiry, but this was so different. I said to myself, You can't go through life this way—though I couldn't say that out loud. When I got home I prayed for him. I felt something and I didn't know what it was. I prayed for him every night after that. And then two weeks later, there was the accident."

A few days before Christmas, Billy invited Bill and Carol Reedy to join him and Jill at the farm, "because he wanted company," Bill Reedy said. Reedy, who had been Billy's closest friend for years, who had built his own career as a legislative assistant in Detroit as a kind of Mr. Fix-it for others, put aside his own family plans for the holiday and took off with Carol for Binghamton.

The days prior to the accident, Reedy remembers, were filled with quarreling between Jill and Billy. The day before Christmas, Reedy says that he and Billy left for town, ostensibly to do some errands, and spent the day drinking. At one point, when he learned that Jill was intending to buy them a Christmas present, Reedy called back to the farm and told his wife what he had learned, advising her to go and get the Martins a present.

The following day—Christmas day—Carol Reedy says that Jill called her into her office and gave her an exact account of that conversation from the previous day: "It was her way of reminding me that she taped every telephone conversation that came into that house, that whatever Billy was up to she probably knew about. It wasn't pleasant."

Christmas day passed into late afternoon and evening. Again, there was a trip into town for "errands"—an afternoon of drinking, away from the quarreling. The drinking—slow and steady, though not enough, Reedy insists, "for either of us to be anywhere near impaired"—filled the hours that otherwise might have been spent in celebration. Christmas day, Reedy recalled ironically, was never big in Billy's life. It was the anniversary of his mother and stepfather's marriage, it was the time Billy often stopped in at medical facilities for his annual checkup. No big deal then. No big deal now.

Billy got in behind the wheel of the pickup truck, says Reedy, the only eyewitness to what followed. They drove back along darkened and icy roads and, Reedy adds, they took an alternate road because Billy missed an earlier turnoff. The truck came along a road that ran along the top of a ridge above the entrance to the farmhouse, then made a left turn, going down toward the front gate. The truck, apparently on a patch of ice, slid out of control and lurched to the side, toward a drainage ditch.

Billy's last words were no "Rosebud," no last meaningful clue to a life—only the cry in warning, "Hang on! Look out!"

It was over instantly, although Reedy for some time afterward thought that he and his buddy had survived one more scrape together.

# CHAPTER 19

Billy was buried four days later at the Gate of Heaven Cemetery in Hawthorne, New York. The funeral service at St. Patrick's Cathedral was splendid, worthy of a head of state. Many dignitaries, including former president Richard Nixon and others from the worlds of politics, commerce, and the arts were present. The only jarring note came when a church official said from the pulpit that St. Patrick's was the last place one might expect to find Billy Martin. Friends and family were offended because they knew that Billy had been a regular churchgoer all his life, sincere in his faith till the end.

Outside the great cathedral, dense crowds waited—to catch a glimpse of all the famous faces, and to say their own farewell.

"If it were Donald Trump or George Steinbrenner, they'd never get people to turn out like this," noted one observer.

A longtime friend, Sister Irene Fugazy, remembers that the crowds lined the way through the city and beyond. The cortege got off the Major Deegan Expressway at Yankee Stadium and circled the ballpark one last time, and all the workers there came and stood outside as the cars passed. "At Yonkers, there were people on the highway," she said. "I'll never forget it. There was someone standing there with a sign: We Love You Billy."

He had a true Yankee sendoff. His casket was decked with the famous NY logo, and with Yankee greats past and present standing on that cold hillside not far from the graves of Babe Ruth and Jimmy

Cagney, the occasion was almost mystical. At one point, clouds suddenly covered the sun and it began to snow. Whitey Ford cracked a joke about Billy still managing to stir things up.

But there were other, very different kinds of clouds covering this occasion, clouds unseen by most of the mourners that day. In death, as in life, the pinnacle was only the place where troubles seemed to gather for Billy Martin.

Some members of Billy's family bitterly resented his being buried in New York rather than in California, next to his mother. They blamed this on Steinbrenner Productions—and on Jill, who they were sure had contravened Billy's own wishes. Was it true? Never, said Jill, who maintained that her husband had told her as recently as the previous week, returning from Jenny's funeral, that he wanted to be buried in New York. George just happened to take care of all the rest. On the other hand, Tex Gernand believed that anyone close to Billy would have known otherwise. "Let's just say that Billy Martin hated cold weather more than anything in the world, okay? You can draw your own conclusions," he said.

But the wrangling over where to bury him was nothing compared to the question of how he actually died. All through the week of mourning, there was a far more disturbing controversy: Who was actually driving the vehicle in which Billy was killed? Newspaper and media reports immediately following the crash all identified Billy as the passenger, Reedy as the driver of the Ford pickup. There was nothing skewed or controversial in the reporting; Reedy himself was the principal source of information. He told rescue workers, police officials, anyone on the scene who asked, that he had been behind the wheel.

The trouble began sometime later when Reedy learned that Billy had died in the crash. Reedy had assumed that he had only been injured and, knowing what the consequences might be—loss of that looming Yankee managerial job, and of other commercial opportunities—Reedy says he took the rap. He was a loyal friend and had made a career out of doing small and important favors for people—including Billy. For example: During Billy's last spring training, Reedy later testified, Carol and Art Fowler's wife, Ruth, had come down to visit in Ft. Lauderdale. One evening, Billy had Reedy send the women—Carol and Ruth and Jill—back to their rooms so the men could go out and drink. Billy, Fowler, Clete Boyer, and Reedy then went on to a couple of watering holes, and a fight broke out in one of them when the boyfriend of a girl Billy was dancing with accosted him. The combatants were separated and the following morning, Reedy said, he got a call from Art Fowler asking him if he would say he (Reedy) was the one who did the punching—in case anyone, like the police or the news media, asked. He volunteered without hesitation then, he said—and had done exactly that this time. Only in this case, Billy was dead. The crash occurred at approximately 5:45 P.M. By eleven o'clock, he had changed his story.

The events of that evening were the subject of a minor criminal trial held in the town of Port Crane, and a major civil proceeding, yet to be held: a multi-million dollar wrongful death suit brought by Jill Martin against Reedy, the Ford Leasing Company (provider of the truck) and the town of Fenton (responsible for the building and maintenance of the road where the accident occurred).

The criminal proceeding was held in September 1990, and stretched out into almost two weeks. Batteries of expert witnesses—crash reconstructionists, pathologists, doctors—dueled each other to the accompaniment of daily headlines and media coverage usually reserved for celebrated murder trials. Jill Martin, flanked by friends and her own team of lawyers, sat in the front row of the small courthouse—"within handshaking distance of the jury box," one observer noted—daubing her eyes at different points of testimony, holding impromptu press conferences outside the court building, and on one occasion inviting a reporter back to her home for a more intimate picture of the life she had had—and lost—with her husband. "I've never seen a simple drunk driving case like this in my life," said Keith George, a local reporter who covered the proceedings for the Binghamton *Press and Sun-Bulletin*. It took a jury of eight men and women barely forty-five minutes to convict Reedy of driving with a blood alcohol level of 0.1 percent or more—a misdemeanor that carried a $350 fine and a six-month suspension of license in New York State. (He was acquitted on a second count of actually driving while impaired.) More serious charges, originally filed, had been dropped—held out, first, as part of a proposed plea bargain that was rejected by Reedy, then dropped unilaterally by the state. The guilty verdict, however, seemingly answered the question of who was driving—crucial to establishing a foundation for Jill's wrongful death action, and important beyond that in satisfying elementary questions of culpability.

In fact, the process that led to the conviction raised more questions than it answered. Billy, in death, was as embroiled in controversy as he ever had been in life.

* * *

The most obvious explanation for any lingering "controversy" would be that Reedy, in changing his story, was simply lying to save his hide, thereby keeping things stirred up. But much more was involved.

On the surface, Reedy's revised account complicated matters but did not deter authorities from their job. Their initial assumption that they had an open-and-shut case was gone, so they went about the routines of police work: trying to compile and gather enough facts and witnesses—evidence—to corroborate or disprove what Reedy had led them to believe in the first place, that he was the driver of the 1989 Ford pickup truck that skidded out of control on Christmas night.

The evidence presented at trial did seem to implicate Reedy. Witnesses swore that the position of the bodies in the cab in the moments following the crash was consistent with his being the driver: He was found in the middle of the cab reaching up and to the left, hanging on to the steering wheel, while Billy was slumped against a door on the passenger side. Reedy's injuries—including broken ribs and a circular pattern of lacerations on his forehead that matched an impact shattering of the windshield on the driver's side—were similarly consistent with his being the driver.

In addition, there was supporting fabric and hair analysis. The impact area on the driver's side of the windshield was found to have hairs imbedded in it. The hairs, on microscopic analysis, were consistent (though not an exact match) with Reedy's.

Anyone sitting in a jury box in that close, crowded courtroom could have accepted the state's case. But the decision, and the processes that led to it, did little for the name of small-town justice but much more to reflect the common notion that fairness under law is subject to the prerogatives of the rich and powerful. Reedy's conviction was, by any standard, a travesty.

The first and most obvious question raised in the handling of the case was the actual cause of death. The fatal injury was officially listed as a fractured neck, but an autopsy (routinely mandated in such cases) that would have far more certainly established the cause was never performed. Neither were X rays taken. Instead, the determination was made by an examining hospital physician from a simple visual inspection of the body. The physician's finding was passed on to a nurse and then to a hospital spokesman and then to the media. The coroner, Melvin D. Jones, required by law to make an official determination of the cause of death, picked up the news by telephone (he spoke to the nurse, he said) and by television, and then made his official finding—never once having viewed Billy's body. Jones subsequently testified that he intended to order an autopsy, but before he could he received two phone calls: one from Jill, another from a man identifying himself as a lawyer for George Steinbrenner. Jones said he was told that Jill was Jewish (she is half-Jewish and, by her own account, that part is something of a joke to her; in any case, her concern for Jewish religious law did not extend to a concern for immediate burial, as Billy's body subsequently lay in state for almost a week before traditional Catholic services were performed at St. Patrick's Cathedral), and that "under no circumstances could I draw blood or do an autopsy on Billy Martin." Another Broome County coroner, Patrick Ruddy, on duty the following day, said that because Jones had gone off on vacation and could not be reached, he did not want to countermand Jones's decision unilaterally, and so he declined to order an autopsy as well. The body was then released and taken out of the county—to New York City—the following day, December 26, at around noon.

The fact that the body was removed from the county created problems, said the D.A.'s office months later. Broome County district attorney Gerald Mollen asserted that had he known initially that the coroners passed on an autopsy he would have sought one himself, but that he didn't learn about the coroner's decision until the body was released the next day. Subsequently, with the body out of county, getting a court order would have been too complicated, he said, and "in light of the family's obvious objections" he did not want to pursue the matter more vigorously.

While Reedy's attorney, Jon Blechman, stressed the importance of an autopsy to the defense, no witnesses were called who might have explained that the absence of an autopsy marked a significant departure from the norm.

The D.A.'s explanations, it turns out, were highly debatable. At the time of the trial, he told reporters that he did not have the authority to overrule the coroners without a court order. The statement was never challenged, in or out of court, but the strong likelihood is that he possessed sufficient authority to order an autopsy even after the body was removed from his immediate jurisdiction. A district attorney's power to order autopsies in New York State does not wait upon coroners, nor does it stop at county lines. New York district attorneys are generally able to employ what amount to pre-signed court orders from a presiding grand-jury judge. They routinely act upon these orders merely by filling in the necessary blanks. The question of jurisdiction is only mildly complicated when the autopsy order involves a body out of county but still within the state. "So long as the case remains within the boundaries of New York State, the D.A. really has no trouble at all ordering an autopsy," said Jim Brown, a former assistant district attorney who worked in the Manhattan D.A.'s office for many years. "If the case had remained in county, all the district attorney needed to do was sign a piece of paper on his own—it would have been that simple. Once he was dealing with another county, still within the state, he would routinely have gone to the judge supervising the grand jury and gotten his okay—and that would have been pro forma, too." In other words, the district attorney's decision to forgo an autopsy may not have had that much to do with the coroners or with any difficulties in securing court orders—and the jury never learned any of that.

What the district attorney was up against was, at a minimum, a prospect of endless legal wrangling and difficulty that might be brought to bear by powerful and influential people. That threat, apparently, was enough to compromise normal procedures.

From the start, the district attorney was well aware—as was the coroner—that someone representing the "Steinbrenner Organization" had interceded on Jill Martin's behalf to block an autopsy. During the week that Billy's body was lying in state, there were negotiations among the D.A.'s office, the Martin estate, and unofficial representatives of George Steinbrenner concerning the matter of an autopsy. One of the principals in these negotiations, according to Dr. Michael Baden, a medical examiner who subsequently became involved in the case, was Howard Rubenstein, a close friend of Steinbrenner's and a known mover and shaker in New York politics.

Why would Steinbrenner interject himself so forcefully as an interested party in what was almost certainly developing as a criminal matter? The reasons are open to conjecture, yet not impossible to surmise. Apart from whatever feelings of compassion George had for a grieving widow, there were funeral arrangements to make for a bona fide Yankee hero. Steinbrenner was willing to pay for the works, from the moment Billy's body left Broome County until he was set to rest amidst state pageantry alongside Babe Ruth—and, clearly, the image of a drunk driver did not fit the sort of send-off he had in mind. The likelihood of insurance money—lots of it—should also not be cast aside as a motive; it is common practice among baseball owners to carry life insurance policies on big-contract employees. Billy was clearly such an employee and Steinbrenner, according to Judge Sapir, regularly carried policies on Billy. If Billy had been the driver rather than the passenger in this crash, depending on the exclusions attached to the policy, it is possible that no money would have been paid, which, apart from any revenue loss in itself, would have meant that any additional payouts from George to the Martin estate, by contractual obligation or otherwise, may not have been covered. (The Yankees have neither confirmed nor denied the existence of any continuing contract obligations, but an attorney for Jill Martin, Robert Pearl, did acknowledge that "the Yankees did not financially abandon the Martin family" afterward.)

Whatever Steinbrenner's interest was in helping Jill block an autopsy, Broome County prosecutors clearly felt the heat. At the very least, said D.A. Mollen, "we weren't eager to go in and seize Martin's body out of St. Patrick's Cathedral if our concerns could be addressed in other ways."

The D.A.'s concerns, at that point, were to make sure the prosecution had enough evidence, independent of an autopsy, to convict Reedy. "I had to make a decision," Mollen said, "whether the autopsy was so critical that I should initiate that kind of litigation or whether a limited examination, consented to by the family, would suffice. Mrs. Martin had just lost her husband; she was seriously opposed to the autopsy. We had what we thought was overwhelming evidence that he was not the driver of the car." With the matter of the autopsy thus compromised away, the prosecution, by the D.A.'s own words, now rested on other evidence.

But this other evidence, it turned out, was far from overwhelming and presented some real problems. Several crucial developments occurred on the night of the accident that the prosecutors had to be worried about.

At Wilson Memorial Hospital where Billy was taken immediately after the crash, efforts were made to resuscitate him. In the course of those efforts, doctors noticed a distension in the stomach area, possibly indicating internal injuries. The doctor in charge, Walid Hammoud, performed a peritoneal lavage, a test specifically designed to ascertain the presence of intra-abdominal injury. Hammoud's emergency-room report contains these words: "A peritoneal lavage was done and this was mildly positive and became strongly positive soon after." In other words, a stomach tap was done, causing a huge discharge of blood, indicating massive intra-abdominal injury—the kind possibly associated with steering-wheel injury.

Another immediate problem was establishing what lawyers call a secure "chain of custody." This legal term has to do with making sure that any physical evidence used in a criminal proceeding is never compromised between the time it is taken into custody and the time it is used in court. The principal physical evidence, doubly important in the absence of an autopsy, was the truck itself. The state had towed it away that night, but the truck was delivered not to a police pound but to a local establishment called John's Body Shop. For twenty-four hours the truck remained unattended in a junkyard next to the shop. Anyone, at any time in that period, had access to the vehicle. When the truck was finally pulled indoors and placed under police guard, any usable evidence—in any legal sense—had been hopelessly compromised. And, indeed, physical tampering did occur. The driver's side windshield—crucial to the prosecution's case in court—was missing. The owner of the shop and his son had taken it, according to an investigator for the defense, hoping to keep it or sell it as a souvenir. At that point, the state, far from having an open and shut case, literally did not have a hair to comb. What it did have was an unenviable choice: drop the case, or convict Reedy with the evidence it had. It went ahead. In addition, for whatever reason, Reedy's local defense attorney chose to play the game by the prosecution's rules, never challenging the admissability of any of the state's evidence subsequently presented at trial.

At this juncture—and in the days following, leading up to Billy's funeral and burial—the D.A.'s office, under duress and most likely understaffed, was faced with a profound dilemma: either order an immediate autopsy, whatever the consequences, or risk losing any case it had against Bill Reedy. It sought and found a compromise: It did not order an autopsy; instead, it entered into an agreement, worked out by Steinbrenner's unofficial representatives, with Jill Martin. The agreement called for a third-party inspection of Billy's body—but no autopsy, no invasive procedures of any kind—to try to establish the cause of death and the likely identity of the driver.

Enter Dr. Michael Baden.

Baden was the compromise worked out between the state and Jill Martin. He has an illustrious, even slightly infamous background: He became prominent in a number of celebrity murder cases, including the Dr. X curare-poisoning case in New Jersey, the long, drawn-out Von Bulow case, and, more recently, the homicide case involving Marlon Brando's son, Christopher, in California. Baden, a former New York City medical examiner, worked regularly on contract with the New York State police and had standing enough to inspect Billy

Martin's body and make a report that would be legally and medically credible.

But Baden's position, from the start, was without the authority or even the independence necessary to determine much of anything. He was called into the case, he said, by the Martin family—not the State of New York. "The first contact I had," he said, "was from Howard Rubenstein, who was involved, I believe, with the family and with the Yankees." He was acceptable—but not accountable—to the state. And when he arrived on the scene, at the Frank Campbell funeral home in New York City, he had yet to prove that he was going to be acceptable to Jill, who remained terrified that some move still would be made for an autopsy or, worse, a later exhumation of her husband's body. In her conversations with Broome County officials, she said, she had "been as pleasant and as ladylike as possible; the old Jackie O had to come out completely" as she warded off their efforts to get an autopsy. When Baden arrived she was, by her own word, "gone," absolutely determined to let no one touch Billy's body—even someone who now was actually in her employ.

Baden, a highly skilled pathologist and an equally skilled handler of the media, conducted an admittedly limited examination. He acknowledged that an autopsy would have been preferable and that he indeed initially sought to find space in the New York City area to do an autopsy—either under the auspices of the city medical examiner or under those of a medical examiner in Nassau County—but was turned down. He advised all parties concerned, he said, that an autopsy would be preferable but was told "the family lawyers did not wish an autopsy."

Baden then made a physical examination of the body in the funeral home. He removed hair follicles, took photographs, observed the body.

This examination and Baden's subsequent explanation of it suggest that his role in the affair had far more to do with public relations than forensic analysis. Whatever report he ultimately submitted—not available as a public record—he seemed to have little doubt about what had happened: "I felt it was important for me to look at the body, because by law physicians have to look at the body," he said in a later interview. "When I examined the body, there were bruises on the right side of the face, nose, arm, elbow, and legs, which are typical for passenger impact in this type of an accident. There were no injuries on the left side."

Baden corroborated without absolutely confirming the likely cause of death as a broken neck. In addition, he later reviewed Reedy's medical records and concluded that his injuries, while "not having all of the driver impact marks," were nevertheless "consistent with his being the driver."

There were two obvious problems with Baden's conclusions. The first was that they were the result of so limited an examination that they would have never stood the test of court scrutiny (in fact, by mutual consent, he was permitted to testify only to his taking of photographs, not to any findings). The second was that later interview statements he gave concerning his examination were not exactly accurate. Baden's photographs of the body were inconsistent with a later assertion given in an interview that "there were no injuries to the left side." His photos show, in addition to the right-side injuries, a blackened area between the elbow and the wrist (identified by the state's forensic pathologist as most probably a bruise though conceivably representing "something smeared on") as well as injuries to the left leg and heel. The facial injuries—including a severe gash across the bridge of the nose—were center as well as right.

In the same interview Baden also said there was no evidence of abdominal injury on the body "when I examined [it] externally." However, he chose not to comment on the obvious sign that an abdominal tap had been done, though his own photographs show an incision just below the navel—the likely mark of a peritoneal lavage. Reedy's defense, possibly not wanting to inadvertently allow Baden's conclusions to enter his testimony, did not ask him any questions concerning signs of abdominal injury.

Baden's representation of his own findings was more in line with his being a spokesman rather than a disinterested investigator. In that role, his presence at the side of Jill Martin and the prosecution lent the case against Reedy at least an appearance of necessary expertise, important to the prosecution. While his conclusions were not presented at trial, Baden nonetheless played an important and highly unusual role in shaping the prosecution's case, as we shall see.

During the following summer, after consultations that almost certainly began in the days after the crash, Jill Martin filed her wrongful-death suit. There was no dollar figure to it because the amount was, in the words of her attorney, Robert Pearl, "beyond calculation; this will be one of the biggest wrongful-death cases ever." The suit, however, clearly depended on two critical points: first, that Billy was the passenger, not the driver of the vehicle; second, that he was in the kind of shape that would have, in any actuarial sense, projected nineteen or more useful years of life ahead for him (in dollar terms, setting his income at around a million dollars a year, that meant around twenty million dollars). Physical problems like alcoholism or cancer would be devastating to the suit, as would a legal finding that Billy was the driver of the truck.

These circumstances would certainly give Jill Martin strong reason to do anything she could to block an autopsy. An autopsy, even if it did not conclusively establish who was driving, would have inevitably turned up any unwanted medical information: the condition of internal organs (like the liver), the presence of disease, anything that might have severely reduced if not absolutely eliminated the dollar amount of the suit.

The interests of the state and the estate in prosecuting Reedy, both for very different reasons, were thus joined. In the months following the crash, right through the trial itself, there was not, according to Robert Pearl, cooperation per se so much as "prodding," which involved, in Pearl's words, almost "daily contact" with the district attorney in charge of the case. As Pearl explained it, the team he had assembled—including Dr. Baden, crash reconstructionists, and other investigative specialists—was in a position to provide the state with what it might not have had: the kind of expert advice and assistance necessary to convict Reedy. The state, in the words of D.A. Mollen, was willing to involve Jill's people as "we would any expert witnesses who would be able to help in presenting a case."

But the state, possibly fearing the precariousness of its position, actually sought to avoid a trial—which would have been fine with Jill and her attorneys. Reedy, during the early summer, was offered a deal: In exchange for a guilty plea, charges would be reduced from Driving While Intoxicated (with the ever-present threat that they could be upgraded to one of several manslaughter counts) to Driving While Impaired, a misdemeanor carrying easily manageable consequences of a small fine ($350) and a limited driver's license suspension in New York State (completely inconsequential, as Reedy was a resident of Michigan). Reedy, however, turned down the deal. He wanted his day in court, he said, believing he would be able to clear himself. "Because I wasn't the driver," he said.

As the state continued to marshal its evidence and witnesses, the pattern of "prodding" or cooperation between Jill's team and the prosecutors continued. Shortly before the trial opened, Pearl learned that the state's chief medical witness, Onondaga County medical examiner Eric Mitchell, had taken the position that while he could speak to the cause of death (even though he too had never seen Billy's body), he had made no finding as to who was driving. Pearl, with an obvious go-ahead from the prosecution, had a crash reconstructionist he had hired invite Dr. Mitchell to a meeting with the reconstructionist and others including Assistant D.A. Kevin Guyette, a third-year attorney whose inexperience troubled Pearl but who nevertheless was scheduled to try the case for the state. The physical evidence—the truck—was made available. This meeting, which the defense says it may or may not have known about in advance, determined the outcome of the trial—at least according to Robert Pearl. Though he asserts he himself was not present, Pearl was emphatic about what happened.

"[On the] Friday before the trial, Baden, Mitchell, and my accident reconstructionist met and examined all the physical evidence," Pearl said, "examined the truck, the two forensic pathologists sat in the truck, we enacted the motions of the bodies, photographs were taken, and Mitchell said at the end of this that there was not a shred of doubt that Reedy was driving. His testimony won the case."

While it is not unusual for families of victims to meet with and even to assist the prosecution, the extent of the reliance by the prosecutor on people with an interest in the outcome of this case raises legal and ethical questions. While there are those who view this type of unofficial involvement in a prosecution as proper, at least one expert is not so comfortable. "Within the framework of criminal justice, and firmly embedded in New York state law, is the notion that even the appearance of prosecutorial impropriety is as intolerable as impropriety itself," says Andrew Sears, a former New York prosecutor, currently a panel member of the Departmental Disciplinary Committee of the Supreme Court, Appellate Division, New York City, and an expert in legal ethics.

In Sears's opinion, the defense should have been notified, prior to or when formal charges against Reedy were filed, that key physical evidence was being turned over to persons with clearly biased interests in the outcome of the case. Additionally, the prosecutor should have informed the defense of possibly exculpatory information. The Friday meeting with Jill's team, during which Dr. Mitchell radically altered his view from no opinion to a firm conclusion that Reedy was the driver "could certainly be used as exculpatory data," said Sears. The information emerged only in Mitchell's testimony; under such circumstances, Sears noted, "defense counsel is obviously deprived of fair opportunity to explore such information and to incorporate it into a defense. The state at all times," he emphasized, "must be interested in serving objective truth, and if it ever aligns itself or appears to align itself with an interested group with an axe to grind, it forfeits that position."

When the matter of this Friday meeting came up at the trial, the defense, in cross-examining Dr. Mitchell, questioned the presence of Jill or Pearl at the meeting. But there the matter was left. The impropriety of the meeting itself was never pushed nor was it ever explained to the jury that the involved crash-reconstructionist, Stu Bennet, working out of a garage in Pennsylvania where the truck was now domiciled, was actually in the employ of the Martin estate.

Neither Pearl, nor Stu Bennet, nor Jill Martin were ever called as witnesses by either the prosecution or the defense. No line of questioning from either side fully explored the importance (or lack of importance) or changes to the vehicle—like the disposition of the steering wheel or other evidence within the cab of the truck, even the windshield—perhaps because that would have opened the entire question of chain of custody to more scrutiny, a possible liability to *both* sides. The steering wheel, bent from impact and perhaps containing important traces of hair and blood, had been removed and impounded from the start, with the prosecution's consent, by the defense; likewise, articles within the cab—a glove, part of a mirror—were also turned over to the defense without prior examination by the state. Billy Martin's clothing, potentially important in any fabric analysis, had similarly been turned over to the family—to Jill and her team—without prior analysis.

With the handling of evidence so uniformly slipshod, there was little room for the defense (or the prosecution) to mount any serious challenges to admissability. The most damaging piece of evidence against Reedy—the driver's-side windshield showing an impact area with embedded hair said to be consistent with Reedy's—was open to several challenges but not, as it turned out, to the fundamental one of admissability. Two key prosecution witnesses, the police investigator who first impounded and packaged the windshield and the state crime lab scientist who later examined it, testified to the strong likelihood that between the time the windshield was first packaged and the time it was opened at the lab so that hairs (later identified as consistent with Reedy's) could be removed for shipment to the FBI, the packaging had been changed. If the original packaging was disturbed, did that mean the windshield, with its evidence so vital to the prosecution, had been removed and possibly tampered with? Or, more likely, was the change an innocuous one? The on-going trial never provided a clear answer.

Similarly, a hair sample taken from Reedy while he was in the hospital in Syracuse, and later used for comparative purposes against the windshield analysis, was mistakenly labeled on a release form as property taken from the deceased, Billy Martin. This mixup was casually alluded to in court but without any sharp insistence that it might or might not have caused a mixup in the subsequent hair-analysis tests done by the FBI.

There was a further mixup with yet another potentially important hair sample. The day following the crash, after he had summoned police investigators to John's Body Shop, defense investigator William Fisher said he found a hair on the driver's-side visor of the truck. The hair, Fisher said, was placed in a folded piece of paper, in the presence of authorities, and pinned to the visor before the visor itself was removed and impounded in a police locker. The note—minus the hair—was opened at the trial. There was never an accounting offered for or serious challenge to the disposition of the missing strand of hair.

The prosecution, for its part, never challenged the admissability of certain exculpatory evidence introduced into the trial by the defense—principally a driver's glove said to belong to Billy. The glove and other evidence had been kept, almost from the time of the crash, in an evidence locker in the offices of the defense investigator.

With admissability never an issue, the trial turned on the particulars of the evidence and testimony as presented. Reedy's defense lawyer had little trouble discrediting the testimony of the police officer who administered a sobriety test, who meant to show that Reedy was too impaired by drink to properly operate a motor vehicle. Because Reedy was bedridden, the only test the officer could give him was an alphabet test and, said the officer into a tape recorder he had running at the time of the test, "he could say it [the alphabet] better than I could."

The defense had a harder time with the state's chief medical witness, the Onondaga County medical examiner, Dr. Mitchell. Unable to shake Mitchell's now determined conclusion that Billy had been the passenger, Blechman brought up the question of the peritoneal lavage, the abdominal tap that strongly suggested the presence of intra-abdominal injury. Dr. Mitchell acknowledged that the test was normally done to determine the presence of internal injuries otherwise masked to the naked eye. He insisted, though, that the massive discharge of blood in Billy's case might have come from the testing needle accidentally nicking a vein or an artery, a mishap Mitchell claimed was a common occurrence in administering the test. The defense wrested from Mitchell the assertion that an autopsy would have cleared up any confusion and that internal injuries, the kind resulting from steering-wheel trauma, are, in fact, often masked.

But, apparently convinced that such admissions from Mitchell were enough, Blechman chose not to call a pathologist of his own who might have further explained to a jury that the chances of generating the kind of discharge of blood that occurred here by striking a vein or an artery during an abdominal tap were slight, if not nonexistent. The main artery in that area is, according to most expert opinion, too deep in the body to be easily reached by the testing needle; additionally, if Billy at that point was dead, discharge of blood in any large amount from any vein or artery would be wholly implausible.

Left with the evidence at hand, the defense labored with the few clues it had that Billy was actually behind the wheel. A boot print faintly (and inconclusively) burned into the brake at the point of impact seemed to match a boot of Billy's, not one worn by Reedy. An impression of the car radio—toward the passenger side of the vehicle—was found on Reedy's jacket (again, the marking, as well as its meaning, was not sufficiently clear). A single—and compelling—bit of evidence was ignored by the jury: that left-handed glove found in the cab of the truck. Across the fingers on the palm side of the glove was a clear impression of the steering wheel with its peculiar pattern of stitching. The mark was almost certainly branded there by the force of the impact. One of Reedy's injuries was a severe laceration of the left pinky, requiring multiple stitches. If, in fact, this glove represented the hand on the wheel at the time of the crash, Reedy was not the driver: The glove was intact, and there were neither tears nor blood stains on it. The only other person in the cab with Reedy at the time of the crash was Billy Martin. (The prosecution, never challenging the admissability of the glove, contended only that Billy might have reached over to grab the wheel—at best a dubious proposition. To make so firm an imprint on the glove—in effect, to brand the pattern into it—simple physics would require the force of a person's body pressing against the glove and wheel on impact; a hand reaching across from the passenger side would be thrown off the wheel rather than pressed against it.)

None of this settles the matter by any means. The limited amount of evidence that can be relied on seems to point to Reedy. The position of the bodies in the cab immediately following the crash suggests that Billy was probably the passenger. The first witness on the scene saw Reedy, a large man, hanging on to the steering wheel from a position in the middle of the cab. Only afterward did this witness notice Billy, behind Reedy, slumped against the passenger door "as though he was asleep." Simple logic placed one man to the left—the driver's side—of the other. Reedy would therefore have been the driver. And according to many crash experts, the transposition of bodies in an accident is highly unlikely. The defense's explanation that the truck, as it skidded off the road and proceeded in the ditch into the stone abutment, was tilted rightward at a severe angle—forty-five degrees or more—so that when the vehicle came to a stop, the passenger door had almost become the floor in a topsy-turvy room. If Reedy was the passenger on impact and had been hurled forward, he could have been wedged under the passenger-side dashboard, his right leg splayed out to the side (the position his leg would have been in if he had been the passenger, pressing his leg out for support as the truck tilted to the side in the seconds before the crash). Billy, rebounding from the steering wheel, could have fallen into the space vacated by Reedy, or at least might have slipped down there in Reedy's attempts to extricate himself. There were minutes between the crash impact and the time the first witnesses arrived on the scene. The space behind Reedy on the front seat, according to the defense, would have been clear as a chute, and the tilt of the cab would have made it possible for Billy to literally fall down—and against the passenger door. Balanced against that, however, was Reedy's size and the narrowness of the cab space—made narrower by the fact that the front end of the vehicle was pushed in on impact by almost two full feet. The likelihood of bodies flip-flopping under those circumstances was not very great. In addition, according to at least one independent forensic pathologist, Bennett Derby, a man widely renowned in his field who has testified in countless numbers of motor vehicle fatality cases, Reedy's injuries to the rib and chest area (he had two fractured left ribs and tenderness to the touch in the area of the sternum) indicated that he was the driver.

But such evidence, speculative or otherwise, was never the issue. The trial was. The jury found Reedy guilty, but the manner of the judicial proceeding—carelessness or worse in the handling of key evidence, the highly questionable though unofficial partnership between the prosecution and Jill's "team,"—and above all, the absence of an autopsy with its possibility of providing definitive answers to the most difficult questions raised at trial, undermined the integrity of any verdict in the case. The presumption of innocence in our system (at least in theory) is preserved until reasonable doubt is eradicated in a truly fair and impartial hearing. The possible motives of the different parties beyond the courtroom—the Martin estate with its wrongful death suit; George Steinbrenner, with possible obligations to the Martin estate; the state, looking to cover itself; even the defense, not wanting to make waves—all hung over the prosecution of this case, leaving to the world an unburied ghost. Billy Martin was finally unable to create himself, but after his death he was subject to those who would recast him. Thus, a recent press release sent out by a public relations firm purporting to represent Jill Martin could contain this item concerning Billy's Death: "Christmas night 1989 Billy Martin played and read 'The Night Before Christmas' to 2,000 homeless children in an overpacked theater. Billy Martin was killed by a drunk driver on his way home from that event."

# AFTERWORD

That alcohol would be involved in Billy's death seems almost inevitable. Booze had been associated with his career ever since his playing days with the Yankees. Depending on the friend or relative talking, he either used alcohol socially and acceptably or was plagued by it, an alcoholic unable to avoid the trouble it brought him.

Alcoholism is a specific disease. Any expert in the field stresses that it is both a physiological and psychological affliction. The physical part comes from addiction, from a reaction to alcohol in the body that is allergic, setting off a tissue craving that can only be satisfied with more drinking, sooner or later. Because of the addictive character of the drink, because it so often is done long term, there is further specific physical damage up to and including high incidences of cancer and liver disease as well as certain necrotic changes in the brain and arterial systems of the body, all of which have fairly predictable behavioral consequences including aggressiveness, self-pity, paranoia, and unpredictability. It is common for alcoholics to be unable to hold on to jobs or families. Their lives inevitably become centered around their drinking—and, usually, the pattern of denial they use so that they can continue drinking.

Because an alcoholic cannot help drinking, shame is a key component in his or her makeup. Avoidance of that sense of shame can also become a bedrock part of his behavior, so that the outside world will see only a tough guy or someone constantly "on," a charmer, everyone's friend. The other, dark side of all that light is filled with unpredictable moods, remorse, and anger—directed outwardly or at oneself. The pattern, obviously, is close to Billy's.

It is also possible for an alcoholic to maintain a life, to function in the world and to function well. Winston Churchill, Beethoven, Babe Ruth, and others did what they did without rehab or apparent regret. It is also possible to drink regularly and to imbibe large amounts—and to *not* be an alcoholic. The difference is physiological. A big drinker can stop; an alcoholic—unless there is therapeutic intervention, self-accepted—cannot.

It matters little whether Billy was technically an alcoholic. He drank without letup, with varying degrees of intensity, throughout his adult life. Alcohol was clearly implicated in one scrape after another in which he was involved. It was a regular part of his working, day to day, and familial life; it was—if George Steinbrenner and Gabe Paul are to be believed—something from which he understood he needed therapeutic relief. Even if that was never the case, as Jill Martin and others maintain, that lack of therapy was hardly a blessing. "I knew Billy Martin for twenty years and he never stopped drinking," Bill Reedy said.

But he functioned, like many other professional baseball men who were also heavy drinkers, and he functioned well—well enough to rise to the top of his profession and stay there for a long time.

It is hard to ignore the possible effect alcohol had on his ability to manage. Drinking in all likelihood shortened his playing career, but its effect on him as a manager is less clear. One professional rehabilitation counselor noted that a chronic drinker is a person who is often necessarily in a mind-altered state, to the point where physical space, everyday reality, becomes unreliable and demands spur-of-the-moment improvisation to deal with. If that is so, it matched Billy's volatility and unpredictability—his genius—perfectly, enabling him, like Cat Mantou or any number of Louis L'Amour heroes, to better work his craft with a slug or two warming his veins.

Alcohol certainly had an effect on his relationship with various owners. Only Charlie Finley seemed to have a solution other than firing for Billy's drinking.

In and out of the clubhouse, on flights, at team hotels, with the media, sometimes with players, the drinking also clearly had a negative effect. The number of times that Billy ran into costly trouble with writers, players, coaches, with his own temperament, were just too many for anyone to forget or excuse the fact that he was a constant drinker. It cost him—and dearly.

His style with the media, particularly, cost him. He could be flattering, friendly, communicative—he would often play favorites—but then he would whip, cajole, intimidate, bully, and, in the case of someone like Henry Hecht, discharge the sort of venom that was ultimately turned against him, particularly in New York, where in the end he was regularly portrayed as a pathetic figure.

This last picture of him was grossly inaccurate. Billy Martin was the best manager of his era, possibly of many eras, but because of who he was, because distraction seemed to accompany every step he took, it was hard to see just what he accomplished.

A manager's job is to win. Billy won. In sixteen big-league seasons, there were only two seasons when teams of his had losing records: 1975 in Texas and 1982 in Oakland. His overall winning record of 1258–1018, .552, compares favorably with every manager of his time and many in the past. Earl Weaver and Sparky Anderson have higher winning percentages; Whitey Herzog, Tony LaRussa, Tommy Lasorda do not. Past managers—Casey Stengel, Charley Dressen, Leo Durocher—have lower winning percentages. Billy's winning percentage, given the number of years and games he managed, most closely parallels that of Miller Huggins, who had a .555 winning percentage over seventeen seasons.

But winning percentage alone, of course, is a misleading barometer. Good managers have bad teams and vice versa. Casey Stengel was a genius with the Yankees, a dud with the Boston Braves and the New York Mets. Joe McCarthy, the all-time percentage leader among managers, was blessed with powerhouse teams through twenty-four seasons, while Connie Mack spent fifty-three managerial seasons generally looking up from the basement floor.

In 1988, the Elias Sports Bureau, after years of tinkering, came up with a statistical model for measuring the effectiveness of managers. It was based on winning, but balanced by measuring the kinds of teams each manager led. It allowed for losing without penalty even as it suggested a certain penalty for winning with good teams. The intriguing model worked up by the Elias calculators had built into it a projection of *expected* wins for a team in any season, and then against that projection it placed the team's actual record. The number of actual wins in excess of the team's expected number of wins was the number of wins the bureau assigned to the manager. The model for a team's expected record was based on its performance in the years immediately preceding, on developing trends within a team—that is, a team that had lost heavily at the outset of the period but had begun to win more consistently later on was given a higher level of expected wins than a team with an equal past record without any such developing winning trend. On the managerial side, a minimum of one thousand games was necessary for a meaningful measurement—fewer games than that gave excessive weight to accidents of the season, injuries, the sudden flowering young players not anticipated in the model.

The bureau measured the managerial careers of all managers in the game at the time and then added in all other managers with records totaling more than a thousand games going back to 1903. In other words, all significant managers were included. The leader was Billy Martin. The Elias people, trying to figure out why George Steinbrenner opted for Billy V in 1988, said that it had nothing to do with the owner losing his marbles. "No one suggested what we feel was the best reason of all for bringing Billy back for a fifth term as Yankee skipper," the Elias analyst wrote. The real reason was: *"Billy Martin happens to be the best manager in the history of major-league baseball"* [italics theirs].

By the analysts' measurements, Billy accounted for 7.45 more wins than expected every year he was in the dugout. His closest rival, Billy Southworth, was more than one full win below him (6.38). Earl Weaver, who almost always had powerful teams to work with, registered 4.27, Sparky Anderson 5.27, John McGraw 4.52, Leo Durocher 2.51. Casey Stengel, on the other hand, wound up with a losing ratio when he was with bad teams (−4.9 wins) and a winning one during his Yankee years (4.0). Billy's winning ratio was big when he had good teams (5.0), and off the charts when he had teams expected to lose (12.6).

There are obvious qualifications to this model, chief among them the weight necessarily afforded to turnaround teams. Billy managed three teams that were expected to do very poorly but did spectacularly well—the turnaround value, the quick-fix effect, was therefore unusually strong. But is it so wrong to attribute those turnarounds to Billy? And the interesting feature was that even in those other years, after the quick fix, Billy still—except for two seasons—had a higher-than-expected win ratio.

There are other numbers buried in this workup that are intriguing as well. Teams that Billy took over increased their stolen base output by 39 percent, and their run production by an average of 93 runs per season. But these figures are balanced by others and do not begin to register the impact Billy had in the dugout.

The bureau notes that there were 44 percent more complete games from pitchers on Billy's teams. That mainly reflects his first two years in Oakland when he had no bullpen, but also raises the question of just how well Billy handled a pitching staff.

The argument over whether Billy ruined that brace of young pitchers in Oakland obscured the more significant fact that he was really his own pitching coach. For all the years he had Art Fowler with him, there was no question who ran pitchers in and out of games, who called different pitches in different situations. What Billy wanted from his pitchers was relatively simple: He wanted outs, and he wanted wins. Pitchers on Billy's staffs were trained by Fowler how to throw the spitter, and they were called on to throw the pitch, especially in two-strike situations. Dave Righetti recalls laughingly that whenever a two-strike hit was given up and a pitcher came back to the dugout, he invariably talked his way out of a confrontation with Billy by saying that he threw a spitter. Because he relied mainly on himself and because his knowledge of pitching was narrowed not by instinct but, strangely, by set notions of what he wanted, he was undoubtedly limited. He was, with pitchers as with other players, an inspirer; he could rouse a pitcher like Mike Norris—or Ron Guidry—not by what he taught him about the art of pitching but by somehow getting inside him, reminding him of what heart he already possessed. Another sort of young pitcher—like Jim Beattie or Ken Clay, or a veteran like Ken Holtzman—was, despite talent, seemingly beyond Billy's reach.

Billy was a divider as well as a conqueror. Any team he managed had loyalists and enemies. He had players willing "to go to war" for him, and others who hated him for the doghouse he confined them to. He didn't seem to care, reiterating throughout his career that a team would always have "eight players who loved you, eight players who hated you—and the manager's job was to keep the others away from the guys who hated you."

There was more to it than that. The divisions on a team, particularly as baseball and society itself changed, became more complex, more difficult to contend with. Big money often meant that players were higher salaried than the manager; multi-year contracts, high-powered agents, and unionism all made it harder for a manager of the old school like Billy to be the kind of absolute boss he wanted to be in the dugout.

His limited education, combined with his absolutist view of almost everything, needlessly complicated things for him. He was no racist, but several black players like Reggie Jackson, Don Baylor, and Elliott Maddox, all extremely intelligent men, thought he was. He neither explained himself to them nor ever cared to. He wanted to win, period. If others thought he was misusing those players, even when winning was supposedly the only criterion, that was their problem not his. Other black players—Rod Carew, Rickey Henderson, Willie Randolph, Dave Winfield, even Willie Horton, with whom he had warred—knew differently. "I would play Hitler, Mussolini, and Tojo on my team if I thought it would help me win," he once explained. There was nothing pretty about it, but he meant it.

Billy ultimately cannot be confined to numbers or even his own words, which too often raised rather than calmed suspicions about him. He was an injustice collector. People did things to Billy Martin; he was nearly always blameless. He never started a fight in his life, he said—he just never backed down from one; he liked drinking, but drinking was never a problem; he was never fired nor divorced for cause in his life. This victim's face to the world when the world suspected him of being a victimizer robbed him of a manager's greatest asset: his ability to make real allies of the media. He had them for a while wherever he went, but he lost them eventually. The arts of laughter, bantering, time-killing—used to mastery by Casey Stengel, Sparky Anderson, Earl Weaver—were used only fitfully and unpredictably by Billy. He collected enemies along with the injustices.

Still, with all his flaws, with all his obvious shortcomings, he roused the game. He brought people out. Every place he went, attendance was sure to increase. He put fans—or fannies, as George Steinbrenner put it—in the seats as no other manager could. He was the only manager in memory who himself became a reason to see a game.

Any number of players said that Billy was like a tenth man on the field, an active and often decisive factor in the outcome of games. Willie Randolph said that "you always knew if you got to the eighth or ninth inning and you were tied or one run down, Billy would find a way to win." Graig Nettles said it another way: "You always knew that when the game was on the line, Billy would never do anything to lose it. That gives a team an extra edge of confidence you won't see in a box score but that is always there."

We have probably passed into an age where winning at all costs is a subliminal rather than an acceptable feature of our lives. Whether we are better or worse for that, it remains harder than ever to be quite as front-and-center about it as Billy was through his career. Billy, no matter the age, was old-fashioned not new-fangled: spikes-in-flesh, horsehide-and-fist-in-the-mouth old-fashioned, the way it was when he was young and full of dreams.

Billy dreamed of success all his life. And because he was a boy and man of baseball, he dreamed of the New York Yankees, of the glitter and fame they represented. There is an image, a fleeting glimpse of Billy, sailing down a road in his gold stretch limo with its floorboard lighting, its bar with five different liquor spigots, its inside video and phones, its license plate with his name boldly plastered on it, the ensemble a moving marquee to his own accomplishments and to the gaudiness of the age, that seems to symbolize who he was in the game. "Going down a highway," said Tex, his chauffeur, "we would just surprise the shit out of everybody."

His game was surprise. His life was, too. "He lived in the moment; you had the feeling nothing was real for him that was five minutes old or that was five minutes ahead," one friend said. He seemed to have an infinite number of sides, so that his life seemed mysterious while all his troubles seemed predictable. He was a showman and a misanthrope, a charmer and a scoundrel, a truth-teller and a deceiver, a man of faith and of infinite suspicion. He was warm-hearted and generous and coldly cruel. He was born in poverty and he rose to the top, challenging his bosses, taking millions of working people along for the ride. He was who he was and he never accepted responsibility for any of it.

He wanted to win, that was all. And for the time he was in the game, everyone knew it. And he won.

We will not see his like again.

# INDEX